KT-152-284

Language, Culture, and Teaching

Critical Perspectives, Second Edition

CITY COLLEGE
NORWICH

Distinguished multiculturalist Sonia Nieto speaks directly to current and teachers in this thoughtful integration of a selection of her key writings with cr. pedagogical features. Offering information, insights, and motivation to teach student of diverse cultural, racial, and linguistic backgrounds, the text is intended for upper undergraduate- and graduate-level students and professional development courses.

Examples are included throughout to illustrate real-life dilemmas about diversity that teachers face in their own classrooms; ideas about how language, culture, and teaching are linked; and ways to engage with these ideas through reflection and collaborative inquiry. Each chapter includes Critical Questions, Activities for Your Classroom, Community-Based Activities and Advocacy, and Supplementary Resources for Further Reflection and Study.

Language, Culture, and Teaching, Second Edition:

- explores how language and culture are connected to teaching and learning in educational settings
- examines the sociocultural and sociopolitical contexts of language and culture to understand how these contexts may affect student learning and achievement
- analyzes the implications of linguistic and cultural diversity for classroom practices, school reform, and educational equity
- encourages practicing and preservice teachers to reflect critically on their class-room practices, as well as on larger institutional policies related to linguistic and cultural diversity based on the above understandings
- motivates teachers to understand their ethical and political responsibilities to work, together with their students, colleagues, and families, for a more socially just classroom, school, and society

About the Second Edition: Over half of the chapters are new to this edition, bringing it up-to-date in terms of recent educational policy issues and demographic changes in our society.

Sonia Nieto is Professor Emerita of Language, Literacy, and Culture, School of Education, University of Massachusetts Amherst.

233 182

Language, Culture, and Teaching
Sonia Nieto, Series Editor

Visit **www.routledge.com/education** for additional information on titles in the Language, Culture, and Teaching series.

Language, Culture, and Teaching

Critical Perspectives, Second Edition

Sonia Nieto

University of Massachusetts, Amherst

Routledge
Taylor & Francis Group

NEW YORK AND LONDON

NORWICH CITY COLLEGE

Stock No.	233 182		
Class	370. 117	NIE	
Cat.	SSA	Proc	3wL

First published 2010
by Routledge
270 Madison Ave, New York, NY 10016

Simultaneously published in the UK
by Routledge
2 Park Square, Milton Park, Abingdon, Oxon OX14 4RN

Routledge is an imprint of the Taylor & Francis Group, an informa business

© 2010 Taylor & Francis

Typeset in Minion by
RefineCatch Limited, Bungay, Suffolk
Printed and bound in the United States of America on acid-free paper by
Edwards Brothers, Inc.

All rights reserved. No part of this book may be reprinted or reproduced
or utilized in any form or by any electronic, mechanical or other means,
now known or hereafter invented, including photocopying and recording,
or in any information storage or retrieval system, without permission in
writing from the publishers.

Trademark Notice: Product or corporate names may be trademarks or
registered trademarks, and are used only for identification and explanation
without intent to infringe.

Library of Congress Cataloging in Publication Data
Nieto, Sonia.
   Language, culture, and teaching : critical perspectives for a new century /
Sonia Nieto. – 2nd ed.
      p. cm. – (Language, culture, and teaching)
   Includes bibliographical references and index.
   1. Multicultural education – United States. 2. Minorities – Education –
United States. I. Title.
   LC1099.3.N543 2009
   370.117 – dc22
   2009010311

ISBN 10: 0–415–99968–5 (hbk)
ISBN 10: 0–415–99974–X (pbk)
ISBN 10: 0–203–87228–2 (ebk)

ISBN 13: 978–0–415–99968–7 (hbk)
ISBN 13: 978–0–415–99974–8 (pbk)
ISBN 13: 978–0–203–87228–4 (ebk)

This book is dedicated to all those teachers who teach critically and with respect and love for their students, and with determination and hope for a more socially just future.

Contents

Acknowledgments

We are grateful to the following publishers for permitting previously published journal articles and book chapters to be reprinted in this book.

Introduction
Nieto, S. (2000). Language, literacy, and culture: Intersections and implication. In Timothy Shanahan & Flora Rodríguez-Brown (Eds.), *49th Yearbook of the National Reading Conference* (pp. 41–60). Chicago: National Reading Conference. Reprinted with the permission of the National Reading Conference and Sonia Nieto.

Chapter 2
Nieto, Sonia (2006). Stances on multilingual and multicultural education: The limitations of labels, *Language Arts*, Volume 84, Number 2, November 2006, p. 171. Copyright 2006 by the National Council of Teachers of English. Used with permission.

Chapter 3
Nieto, S. & Bode, P. (2008). Understanding the sociopolitical context of multicultural education. In *Affirming Diversity: The Sociopolitical Context of Multicultural Education*, 5e. Published by Allyn & Bacon, Boston. Copyright 2008 by Pearson Education. Reprinted by permission of the publisher.

Chapter 4
Nieto, S. & Bode, P. (2008). Multicultural education and school reform. In *Affirming diversity: The sociopolitical context of multicultural education*. Boston, MA: Allyn & Bacon. Copyright 2008 by Pearson Publishers. Reprinted by permission of the publisher.

Chapter 5
Nieto, S. (2005). Public education in the twentieth century and beyond: High hopes, broken promises, and an uncertain future. *Harvard Educational Review*, 75 (1), 57–78. Used with permission.

Chapter 6
Nieto, Sonia (2001). We speak in many tongues: Linguistic diversity and multi-cultural education (revised and updated). From Diaz, Carlos F. *Multicultural Education For The 21st Century*. Published by Allyn and Bacon, Boston, MA. Copyright © 2001 by Pearson Education. Reprinted by permission of the publisher.

Chapter 7
From Sonia Nieto, *The Light in Their Eyes: Creating Multicultural Learning Communities*, New York: Teachers College Press. Copyright © 1999 by Teachers College Press, Columbia University. All rights reserved. Reprinted by permission of the publisher.

Chapter 8
Nieto, Sonia (1994). Lessons from students on creating a chance to dream. *Harvard Educational Review, 64* (4), 392–426. Used with permission.

Chapter 9
Raible, John & Nieto, Sonia (2003). Beyond categories: The complex identities of adolescents. In Michael Sadowski (Ed.), *Adolescents at School: Perspectives on Youth, Identity, and Education* (pp. 145–161). Cambridge, MA: Harvard Education Press. Used with permission.

Chapter 10
Nieto, Sonia (2003). Profoundly multicultural questions. *Educational Leadership, 60* (4), 6–10.

Chapter 11
This is a slightly revised version of the following article: Nieto, S. (2006). Solidarity, courage, and heart: Learning from a new generation of teachers. *Intercultural Education, 17* (5), 457–473. Used with permission. The Journal's web site can be found at http://www.informaworld.com.

Chapter 13
Nieto, Sonia (2008). Nice is not enough: Defining caring for students of color. In Mica Pollock (Editor), *Everyday Antiracism: Getting Real About Race in School* (p. 31). New York: New Press.

Chapter 14
Nieto, S. (1999). What does it mean to affirm diversity in our nation's schools? *The School Administrator, 56* (5), 32–34. Reprinted with permission from the May 1999 issue of *The School Administrator* magazine.

Preface

Ten years have passed since the first edition of *Language, Culture, and Teaching* was published, and they have been momentous years both nationally and globally. Because of events such as 9/11 and the invasion of Iraq, as well as global immigration and the dramatic demographic changes in our own society during the past decade, the issues addressed in this book remain significant for today's classrooms. Whether you teach in a large urban public school system, a small rural schoolhouse, or an affluent private academy in the suburbs, you will face students who are more diverse than ever in terms of race, language background, ethnicity, culture, and other differences. The United States today is enormously different from what it was just a generation ago. For example, in 1970, at the height of the public school enrollment of the "baby boom" generation, White students accounted for 79 percent of total enrollment, followed by 14 percent African American, 6 percent Hispanic, and 1 percent Asian and Pacific Islander and other races. The situation is vastly different now: Currently, about 60 percent of students in U.S. public schools are White, 18 percent Hispanic, 16 percent African American, and 4 percent Asian and other races. The Census Bureau's population projections indicate that the student population will continue to diversify in the coming years. In addition, the number of students who are foreign born or have foreign-born parents is growing rapidly. More than 49 million students, or 31 percent of those enrolled in U.S. elementary and secondary schools, are foreign-born or have at least one parent who was foreign-born (Shin, 2005). This situation has major implications for teaching and learning, and for whether or not teachers feel sufficiently prepared to meet the challenges of diversity.

Because of these changing demographics and dramatic global realities, including massive relocations of populations due to war, famine, and other natural and human catastrophes, language and culture are increasingly vital concerns in contemporary classrooms across the United States. Yet few educators besides specialists in bilingual education, ESL, or urban education feel adequately prepared through their course work and other pre-practicum experiences to teach students who embody social and cultural differences. As a result, many educators are at a loss as to what to do when faced with students whose race, ethnicity, social class, and language differ from their own. They are equally unprepared to understand—or to deal effectively with—the significant achievement gaps that arise from unequal and inequitable learning conditions. For many teachers, their first practicum or teaching experience represents their introduction to a broader diversity than they have ever experienced before. This is true for all teachers—not just White teachers—because our society is still characterized by communities that are largely segregated by race, ethnicity, and social class.

In spite of these realities, many textbooks designed for current and future teachers devote little attention to issues of difference, and even less to critical perspectives in teaching. In looking over the variety of textbooks available for current and future teachers, I found many to be little more than dry and boring treatments of so-called "best practices" or thoughtless techniques that leave teachers' creativity and analysis on the sidelines. Thus the motivation behind this textbook is to provide a different model, one that engages you as an active learner and that builds on your creativity. It is addressed primarily to you, current and future teachers in our nation's schools, and in it I hope you will find the information, insights, and motivation to teach students of diverse backgrounds.

Throughout this book I have attempted to present examples of: real-life dilemmas about diversity that you will face in your own classrooms; ideas about how language, culture, and teaching are linked; and ways to engage with these ideas through reflection and collaborative inquiry. There are no easy answers, no pre-packaged programs that can fix the uncertainties that teachers encounter every day. However, there are more thoughtful ways to address these problems than those which are currently presented in many textbooks; there are ways that honor both teachers' professionalism and students' abilities and social and cultural realities. Specifically, the goals of this book are to:

- explore how language and culture are connected to teaching and learning in educational settings;
- examine the sociocultural and sociopolitical contexts of language and culture to understand how these contexts may affect student learning and achievement;
- analyze the implications of linguistic and cultural diversity for classroom practices, school reform, and educational equity;
- encourage practicing and preservice teachers to reflect critically on their classroom practices, as well as on larger institutional policies related to linguistic and cultural diversity based on the above understandings;
- motivate teachers to understand their ethical and political responsibilities to work, together with their students, colleagues, and families, for a more socially just classroom, school, and society.

About the Second Edition

Language, Culture, and Teaching is a compilation of previously published journal articles and book chapters, most of which I have written over the past decade. Although the goals and basic framework of this second edition remain the same as those of the first edition, more than half of the chapters are new to this edition. Given the vast changes in our schools and society in the past decade, I thought it was important to attend to some of these changes in this edition. For example, newer and more nuanced understandings of identity led me to include a number of chapters that address this topic in more contemporary ways (for example, see Chapters 2 and 9). I have also added two chapters (3 and 4) that discuss the current focus on rigid accountability processes, and specifically No Child Left Behind (NCLB), topics that are now at the top of most educators' agendas but were just looming on the horizon a decade ago.

Overview

The book is organized in four parts, and each begins with a brief description of the themes considered in that section of the text. Following the chapters are critical questions, ideas for classroom and community activities, and suggested resources for further reflection and study. Critical Questions are based on the ideas presented in the chapter and they ask you to build on the knowledge you have learned by analyzing the concepts further. Activities for Your Classroom are suggestions for applying what you have learned by engaging in a deeper analysis of the concepts. Often, it is suggested that you work with colleagues in developing curriculum or other classroom-based projects. Community-Based Activities and Advocacy are projects outside of your particular classroom setting, and they may take place in the school or the school district, in the city or town in which you teach, or even at the state or national level. Supplementary Resources for Further Reflection and Study end each chapter with a list and brief description of resources that will be helpful as you continue to reflect on and study the issues addressed in the chapter.

The Introduction consists of a preliminary chapter, "Language, Literacy, and Culture: Intersections and Implications." This chapter provides an overall background for the text by describing how language and culture are manifested in twenty-first century schools and society. It also suggests some implications for teaching and learning.

Part I: Setting the Groundwork consists of six chapters that set the conceptual framework for links among language, culture, and teaching. Chapter 1 concerns the age-old question of the purpose of schools, a consequential question all teachers should be asking themselves as they enter the profession. Chapter 2, "The Limitations of Labels," is a brief piece that repudiates the all-too-common practice, based on deficit views of students, to use labels to describe children. Chapter 3, co-authored with Patty Bode, proposes a sociopolitical definition of multicultural education and introduces you to major concepts and significant literature in the field, including an analysis of NCLB. Chapter 4, also co-authored with Patty Bode, provides a comprehensive definition of multicultural education that takes it far beyond superficial approaches that focus only on holidays and heroes. Chapter 5 presents an overview of public education in the twentieth century through three focal movements for social justice—desegregation, multicultural education, and bilingual education—and it discusses the future of these and other movements for equity in education. The final chapter in this section (Chapter 6), "We Speak in Many Tongues," expands the conventional framework of multicultural education by incorporating language and language differences as central to diversity.

Young people of all backgrounds struggle with issues of identity and belonging, and for those who are culturally marginalized, the stress is even greater. Questions of identity are related to learning because it is through their identities as competent learners that students can succeed academically. Hence, matters of identity are central to an appreciation of linguistic and cultural diversity. Part II: Identity and Belonging focuses on identity—social, cultural, racial, and linguistic—and how it influences students, teaching, and learning. Chapter 7 introduces you to a wide-ranging definition that rejects simplistic understandings of culture that focus primarily on superficial trappings. Chapter 8, first published some 15 years ago yet still relevant today, centers on the views of a diverse group of young people about schooling, identity, and success. Part II ends with Chapter 9, which I wrote with John Raible on the complex identities of adolescents, including understanding identity as complex, heterogeneous, and hybrid.

The chapters in Part III: Becoming Critical Teachers concern the kind of information teachers need about diversity in order to be effective with a wide range of students. The two chapters in this section focus on what it takes to become critical teachers of such students. Chapter 10 is a short piece that encourages teachers to look beyond the superficial treatments of diversity and to instead ask "profoundly multicultural questions," that is, questions that are at the heart of social justice, access, and equity. Chapter 11 gives concrete examples of teachers who work with students of diverse backgrounds with "solidarity, courage, and heart," suggesting the lessons that all teachers can learn from them.

The final part of the text, Part IV: Praxis in the Classroom, is a critical analysis of multicultural education in practice. Chapter 12, "Affirmation, Solidarity, and Critique: Moving Beyond Tolerance in Multicultural Education," describes five concrete scenarios that illustrate different levels of support for multicultural education and suggests specific practices for classroom instruction. Because many teachers have had little personal or professional experience with diversity, they are often unaware of how to critically address questions of race, identity, and achievement. Chapter 13 provides specific suggestions for "going beyond niceness" in teaching students of color. The final chapter (Chapter 14), "What Does it Mean to Affirm Diversity in Our Nation's Schools?," is a short piece that proposes a number of guidelines for affirming diversity. It also serves to recapitulate many of the points addressed throughout the book.

Final Thoughts

Educational inequality is repugnant in a society that has pledged to provide an equal education for all students regardless of rank or circumstance. Yet educational inequality is commonplace in schools all over our country. It continues to be the case that far too many students are shortchanged because educational policies and practices favor students from backgrounds that are more privileged in social class, race, language, or other differences. At the same time, schools remain grossly unequal in terms of the resources they are given, and it is undeni-

ably true that students' zip codes have more to do with the quality of the education they receive than most of us would care to admit. In addition, students'
linguistic and cultural differences are often dismissed or ignored by teachers who
have been trained to be "color-blind" and refuse to see differences. The chapters
in this book ask you not only to *see* differences but also to critically affirm and use
them in your teaching.

These realities make it apparent that educational change needs to take place in
a number of domains, including at the ideological, societal, and national levels.
In the meantime, students who differ culturally and linguistically from the mainstream are particularly vulnerable in a society that has deemed differences to be
deficiencies and poverty to be a moral transgression. But change can begin at any
level, and the chapters in this book are based on the assumption that teachers can
and, in fact, *must* make a difference in the lives of the children they teach.
Teachers alone cannot do it all, of course, because institutional barriers to student
learning—including macro-level impediments such as lack of access to higher
education for parents and guardians, substandard housing, lack of appropriate
health care, inadequate employment opportunities, and lack of access to quality
child-care—are enormous. Nevertheless, when teachers work together with other
educators and concerned citizens, they can do a great deal to change not only
their own practices but also help schools and districts change their policies to
become more equitable for all students. When district-wide policies as well as
classroom practices change to promote the learning of all students and when our
society, teachers, and schools view students' differences in a more hopeful and
critical way, the result can be that more students will soar to the heights that they
are capable of reaching and deserve.

We are living in a new century. This century different from any other in many
ways, not the least of which is the tremendous cultural and linguistic diversity
evident in our schools. Yet the ways in which new teachers are prepared to face
these differences, and the books used to help them, have not changed enough.
New times deserve new textbooks that respect the professionalism of teachers and
other educators, honor the identities of students and their families, and validate
the nation's claim to educate all students of all backgrounds. That is the premise
of this book.

Acknowledgments

Finally, a word of thanks to friends and colleagues who had a hand in this book.
When I originally wrote the journal articles and book chapters reprinted in this
text, many of them helped me think more clearly and carefully about my ideas.
These friends and colleagues are too numerous to mention here, but I acknowledged them in the original works. For this edition, I want to specifically thank
Patty Bode, my co-author for Chapters 3 and 4, and John Raible, my co-author
for Chapter 9, for allowing me to include them in the book. Their insights have
contributed greatly to my thinking. I also want to reiterate that my work has been
enormously enriched by the wise counsel of the numerous colleagues, students,
and young people I have worked with over the years. Finally, I want to express my

gratitude and profound respect for Naomi Silverman, Senior Acquisitions Editor at Routledge and friend of many years. Many years ago when we first met, Naomi helped me think differently and creatively about textbooks for teachers, and I feel blessed to still be working with her on this and other projects.

Reference

Shin, H. B. (2005). School enrollment: Social and economic characteristics of students— October 2003. *Current Population Reports*. Washington, DC: U.S. Census Bureau.

Introduction

Language, Literacy, and Culture: Intersections and Implications

It has only been in the past several years that scholars have begun to connect the issues of language, literacy, and culture in any substantive way. Prior to this time, they were considered to exist largely separate from one another. As a result, educators usually thought about culture, for example, as distinct from language and from reading and writing except in the most superficial of ways; or as English as a Second Language (ESL) divorced from the influence of native culture on learning; or as the contentious debate about phonics and whole language as somehow separate from students' identities. These dichotomies have largely disappeared in the past 20 years. It is now evident that language, literacy, and culture are linked in numerous ways and that all teachers—whether they teach preschool art or high school math—need to become knowledgeable in how they affect students' schooling.

Even more crucial to our purposes in this textbook, until recently, critical perspectives were almost entirely missing from treatments of reading, writing, language acquisition and use, and an in-depth understanding of race, culture, and ethnicity. If broached at all, differences were "celebrated," typically in shallow ways such as diversity dinners and the commemoration of a select few African American and other heroes and through "ethnic" holiday fairs. But discussions of stratification and inequality were largely absent until recently in most teacher education courses. Despite their invisibility, questions about equity and social justice are at the core of education. As such, education is always a political undertaking.

The fact that education is not a neutral endeavor scares many people because it challenges cherished notions that education is based solely on equality and fair play. Power and privilege, and how they are implicated in language, culture, and learning, also typically have been invisible in school discourse. This situation is changing as the connections among language, literacy, and culture are becoming more firmly established, and as inequality and the lack of access to an equal education faced by many students is becoming more evident.

In this chapter, I describe the links among language, literacy, and culture beginning with my own story and concluding with some central tenets of sociocultural theory: agency, experience, identity/hybridity, context, and community. As you read this chapter, think about how your own understanding of language, literacy, and culture has shifted over the years, and how you have changed your ideas about teaching as a result.

Introduction: Language, Literacy, and Culture: Intersections and Implications[*]

Given my background and early life experiences, I should not be here today talking with you about literacy and learning. According to the traditional educational literature, my home and family situation could not prepare me adequately for academic success. My mother did not graduate from high school, and my father never made it past fourth grade. They came to the United States as immigrants from Puerto Rico and they quietly took their place in the lower paid and lower status of society. In my family, we never had bedtime stories, much less books. At home, we didn't have a permanent place to study, nor did we have a desk with sufficient light and adequate ventilation, as teachers suggested. We didn't have many toys and I never got the piano lessons I wanted desperately from the age of five. As a family, we didn't go to museums or other places that would give us the cultural capital (Bourdieu, 1986) it was thought we needed to succeed in school. We spoke Spanish at home, even though teachers pleaded with my parents to stop doing so. And when we learned English, my sister and I spoke a nonstandard, urban Black and Puerto Rican version of English: we said *ain't* instead of *isn't* and *mines* instead of *mine,* and no matter how often our teachers corrected us, we persisted in saying these things. In a word, because of our social class, ethnicity, native language, and discourse practices, we were the epitome of what are now described as "children at risk," young people who were described when we were coming up as "disadvantaged," "culturally deprived," and even "problem" students.

I was fortunate that I had a family that, although unable to help me with homework, would make sure that it got done; a family who used "Education, Sonia, education!" as a mantra. But they kept right on speaking Spanish (even when my sister and I switched to English), they still didn't buy books for our home, and they never read us bedtime stories. My parents, just like all parents, were brimming with skills and talents: They were becoming bilingual; they told us many stories, riddles, tongue-twisters, and jokes; when my father, 20 years after coming to this country, bought a *bodega,* a small Caribbean grocery store, I was awed by the sight of him adding up a column of figures in seconds, without a calculator or even a pencil. My mother embroidered beautiful and intricate patterns on handkerchiefs, blouses, and tablecloths, a trade practiced by many poor women in Puerto Rico to stock the shelves of Lord and Taylor's and Saks' Fifth Avenue in New York. These skills, however, were never called on by my teachers; my parents were thought of as culturally deprived and disadvantaged, another segment of the urban poor with no discernible competencies.

Sometime in my early adolescence, we bought a small house in a lower middle-class neighborhood and I was able to attend a good junior high and an excellent high school. I didn't particularly like that high school—it was too competitive and impersonal and I felt invisible there—but in retrospect I realize that my sister and I got the education we needed to prepare us for college, a dream beyond the wildest imagination of my parents, most of my cousins, and the friends from our previous neighborhood. My new address made a profound difference in the education that I was able to get. I eventually dropped the *ain't* and the *mines*, and I hid the fact that I spoke Spanish.

I begin with my own story, not because I believe that autobiography is sacrosanct, or that it holds the answer to all educational problems. My story is not unique and I don't want to single myself out as an exception, in the way that Richard Rodriguez (1982) ended up doing, intentionally or not, in his painful autobiography *Hunger of Memory*. I use my story because it underscores the fact that young people of all backgrounds can learn and that they need not be compelled, as Rodriguez was, to abandon their family and home language in the process for the benefits of an education and a higher status in society. In many ways, I am like any of the millions of young people in our classrooms and schools who come to school eager (although perhaps not, in the current jargon, "ready") to learn, but who end up as the waste products of an educational system that does not understand the gifts they bring to their education. They are the reason that I speak with you today about language, literacy, and culture, and the implications that new ways of thinking about them have for these children.

Language, literacy, and culture have not always been linked, either conceptually or programmatically. But this is changing, as numerous schools and colleges of education around the country are beginning to reflect a growing awareness of their intersections, and of the promise they hold for rethinking teaching and learning. My own reconceptualized program at the University of Massachusetts, now called Language, Literacy, and Culture, mirrors this trend.[1] I believe the tendency to link these issues is giving us a richer picture of learning, especially for students whose identities—particularly those related to language, race, ethnicity, and immigrant status—have traditionally had a low status in our society. One result of this reconceptualization is that more education programs are reflecting and promoting a sociocultural perspective in language and literacy, that is, a perspective firmly rooted in an anthropological understanding of culture; a view of learning as socially constructed and mutually negotiated; an understanding of how students from diverse segments of society—due to differential access, and cultural and linguistic differences—experience schooling; and a commitment to social justice. I know that multiple and conflicting ideas exist about these theoretical perspectives, but I believe some basic tenets of sociocultural theory can serve as a platform for discussion. I explore a number of these tenets, illustrating them with examples from my research and using the stories and experiences of young people in U.S. schools.

The language of sociocultural theory includes terms such as *discourse, hegemony, power, social practice, identity, hybridity*, and even the very word *literacy*. Today, these terms have become commonplace, but if we were to do a review of the literature of some 20 years ago or less, we would probably be hard pressed to find them, at least as currently used. What does this mean? How has our awareness and internalization of these terms and everything they imply changed how we look at teaching and learning? Let's look at literacy itself. It is generally accepted that certain family and home conditions promote literacy, including an abundant supply of books and other reading material, consistent conversations between adults and children about the books they read, and other such conditions (Snow, Barnes, Chandler, Goodman, & Hemphill, 1991). I have no doubt that this is true in many cases, and I made certain that my husband and I did these things with our own children. I am sure we made their lives easier as a result. But what of the children for whom these conditions are not present, but who nevertheless grow up literate (Taylor & Dorsey-Gaines, 1988)? Should children be doomed to educational failure because their parents did not live in the right neighborhood, were not privileged enough to be formally educated, or did not take their children to museums or plays? Should they be disqualified from learning because they did not have books at home?

Tenets of Sociocultural Theory

I began with my story to situate myself not just personally, but socially and politically, a primary premise of sociocultural theory. Given traditional theories, the only way to understand my educational success was to use traditional metaphors: I had "pulled myself up by my bootstraps;" I had "melted;" I had joined the "mainstream." But I want to suggest that these traditional metaphors are as unsatisfactory as they are incomplete because they place individuals at the center, isolated from the social, cultural, historical, and political context in which they live. Traditional theories explain my experience, and those of others who do not fit the conventional pattern, as springing primarily if not solely from our personal psychological processes. Sociocultural theory, on the other hand, gives us different lenses with which to view learning, and different metaphors for describing it. This is significant because how one views learning leads to dramatically different curricular decisions, pedagogical approaches, expectations of learning, relationships among students, teachers and families, and indeed, educational outcomes.

Sociocultural and sociopolitical perspectives are first and foremost based on the assumption that social relationships and political realities are at the heart of teaching and learning. That is, learning emerges from the social, cultural, and political spaces in which it takes place, and through the interactions and relationships that occur between learners and teachers. In what follows, I propose five interrelated concepts that undergird sociocultural and sociopolitical perspectives. These concepts are the basis of my own work, and they help me make sense of my experience and the experiences of countless youngsters that challenge traditional deficit views of learning. The concepts are also highly consistent with a critical multicultural perspective, that is, one that is broader than superficial additions to content or "holidays and heroes" approaches.

I focus on five concepts: *agency/co-constructed learning; experience; identity/ hybridity; context/situatedness/positionality;* and *community.* Needless to say, each of these words holds many meanings, but I use them here to locate some fundamental principles of sociocultural and sociopolitical theory. In addition, the terms are both deeply connected and overlapping. I separate them here for matters of convenience, not because I see them as fundamentally independent concepts.

Agency/Co-constructed Learning

In many classrooms and schools, learning continues to be thought of as transmission rather than as *agency*, or mutual discovery by students and teachers. At the crudest level, learning is thought to be the reproduction of socially sanctioned knowledge, or what Michael Apple (1991) has called "official knowledge." These are the dominant attitudes and behaviors that society deems basic to functioning. The most extreme manifestation of this theory of learning is what Paulo Freire (1970) called "banking education," that is, the simple depositing of knowledge into students who are thought to be empty receptacles. In an elegant rejection of the banking concept of education, Freire instead defined the act of study as constructed by active agents. According to Freire (1985), "To study is not to consume ideas, but to create and re-create them" (p. 4).

Although learning as the reproduction of socially sanctioned knowledge is repudiated by teachers and theorists alike, it continues to exist in many schools and classrooms. It is the very foundation of such ideas as "teacher-proof curriculum," the need to "cover the material" in a given subject, and the endless lists of skills and competencies "that every student should know" (Hirsch, 1987). This contradiction was evident even near the beginning of the 20th century when John Dewey (1916) asked:

> Why is it, in spite of the fact that teaching by pouring in, learning by a passive absorption, are universally condemned, that they are still so entrenched in practice? That education is not an affair of "telling" and being told but an active and constructive process, is a principle almost as generally violated in practice as conceded in theory.
>
> (p. 38)

Why does this continue to happen? One reason is probably the doubt among the public that teachers and students have the ability to construct meaningful and important knowledge. Likewise, in low-income schools with students from diverse cultural and linguistic backgrounds, very little agency exists on the part of either students or teachers. In such schools, teachers learn that their primary responsibility is to "teach the basics" because students are thought to have neither the innate ability nor the experiential background of more privileged students. In the case of students for whom English is a second language, the assumption that they must master English before they can think and reason may prevail.

Let me share some examples of agency, or lack of it, from the words of students of diverse backgrounds who a number of colleagues[2] and I interviewed for my first book (Nieto, 1992, 2000). We found that students' views largely echoed those of educational researchers who have found that teaching methods in most class-rooms, especially those in secondary schools and even more so in secondary schools attended by poor students of all backgrounds, vary little from traditional "chalk and talk" methods; that textbooks are the dominant teaching materials used; that routine and rote learning are generally favored over creativity and critical thinking; and that teacher-centered transmission models still prevail (Cummins, 1994; Goodlad, 1984). Students in my study (Nieto, 2000) had more to say about pedagogy than about anything else, and they were especially critical of teachers who provided only passive learning environments for students. Linda Howard, who was just graduating as the valedictorian of her class in an urban high school, is a case in point. Although now at the top of her class, Linda had failed seventh and eighth grade twice, for a variety of reasons, both academic and medical. She had this to say about pedagogy:

> Because I know there were plenty of classes where I lost complete interest. But those were all because the teachers just, "Open the books to this page." They never made up problems out of their head. Everything came out of the book. You didn't ask questions. If you asked them questions, then the answer was "in the book." And if you asked the question and the answer *wasn't* in the book, then you shouldn't have asked that question!
>
> (pp. 55–56)

Rich Miller, a young man who planned to attend pharmacy school after gradu-ation, described a "normal teacher" as one who "gets up, gives you a lecture, or there's teachers that just pass out the work, you do the work, pass it in, get a grade, good-bye!" (p. 66).

The students were especially critical of teachers who relied on textbooks and blackboards. Avi Abramson, a young man who had attended Jewish day schools and was now in a public high school, had some difficulty adjusting to the differ-ences in pedagogy. He believed that some teachers did better because they taught from the point of view of the students: "They don't just come out and say, 'All right, do this, blah, blah, blah.' . . . They're not so *one-tone voice*" (p. 116). Yolanda Piedra, a Mexican student, said that her English teacher "just does the things and sits down" (p. 221). Another student mentioned that some teachers "just teach the stuff. 'Here,' write a couple of things on the board, 'see, that's how you do it. Go ahead, page 25' " (p. 166).

These students didn't just criticize, however; they also gave examples of teachers who promoted their active learning. Hoang Vinh, in his junior year of high school, spoke with feeling about teachers who allowed him to speak Vietnamese with other students in class. He also loved working in groups, con-trary to conventional wisdom about Asian students' preference for individual work (demonstrating the dangers of generalizing about fixed cultural traits). Vinh particularly appreciated the teacher who asked students to discuss import-ant issues, rather than focus only on learning what he called "the word's *meaning*" (p. 143) by writing and memorizing lists of words. Students also offered thought-ful suggestions to teachers to make their classrooms more engaging places. One student recommended that teachers involve more students actively: "More like making the whole class be involved, not making only the two smartest people up here do the whole work for the whole class" (p. 125).

Teaching becomes much more complex when learning is based on the idea that all students have the ability to think and reason. Sociocultural and sociopolitical theories emphasize that learning is not simply a question of transmitting knowledge, but rather of working with students so that they can reflect, theorize, and create knowledge. Given this theory of agency, "banking education" (Freire, 1970) makes little sense. Instead, the focus on reflective questions invites students to consider different options, to question taken-for-granted truths, and to become more critical thinkers.

Experience

That learning needs to build on experience is a taken-for-granted maxim, based on the idea that it is an innately human endeavor accessible to all people. But somehow this principle is often ignored when it comes to young people who have not had the *kinds* of experiences that are thought to prepare them for academic success, particularly those students who have not been raised within "the culture of power" (Delpit, 1988), or who have not explicitly learned the rules of the game for academic success. The experiences of these students—usually young people of culturally and linguistically diverse backgrounds and those raised in poverty—tend to be quite different from the experiences of more economically and socially advantaged students, and these differences become evident when they go to school.

Pierre Bourdieu (1986) described how different forms of cultural capital help maintain economic privilege, even if these forms of capital are not themselves strictly related to economy. Cultural capital is evident in such intangibles as values, tastes, and behaviors and through cultural identities such as language, dialect, and ethnicity. Some signs of cultural capital have more social worth, although not necessarily more intrinsic worth, than others. If this is true, then youngsters from some communities are placed at a disadvantage relative to their peers simply because of their experiences and identities. Understanding this reality means that power relations are a fundamental, although largely unspoken, aspect of school life.

We also need to consider the impact of teachers' attitudes concerning the cultural capital that their students *do* bring to school, and teachers' subsequent behaviors relative to this cultural capital. Sociocultural theories help to foreground these concerns. For example, a 1971 article by Annie Stein cited a New York City study in which kindergarten teachers were asked to list in order of their importance the things a child should learn in order to prepare for first grade. In schools with large Puerto Rican and Black student populations, socialization goals were predominant, but in mostly White schools, educational goals were invariably first. "In fact," according to Stein, "in a list of six or seven goals, several teachers in the minority-group kindergartners forgot to mention any educational goals at all" (p. 167). This is an insidious kind of tracking, where educational ends for some students were sacrificed for social aims. The effects of this early tracking were already evident in kindergarten.

All children come to school as thinkers and learners, aptitudes usually recognized as important building blocks for further learning. But there seems to be a curious refusal on the part of many educators to accept as valid the *kinds* of knowledge and experiences with which some students come to school. For instance, speaking languages other than English, especially those languages with low status, is often thought of by teachers as a potential detriment rather than a benefit to learning. Likewise, although traveling to Europe to ski is generally considered culturally enriching, the same is not true of traveling to North Carolina, Haiti, or the Dominican Republic to visit relatives. The reason that these kinds of experiences are evaluated differently by teachers, and in fact in the general society, has more to do with their cultural capital than with their educational potential or intrinsic worth.

The reluctance or inability to accept and build on students' experiences is poignantly described by Mary Ginley, a teacher in Massachusetts who taught in a small city with a large Puerto Rican student population. A gifted teacher, Mary also knew that "being nice is not enough," an idea she elaborated on in a journal she kept for a class she took with me:

> Every child needs to feel welcome, to feel comfortable. School is a foreign land to most kids (where else in the world would you spend time circling answers and filling in the blanks?), but the more distant a child's culture and language are from the culture and language of school, the more at risk that child is. A warm, friendly, helpful teacher is nice but it isn't enough. We have plenty of warm friendly teachers who tell the kids nicely to forget their Spanish and ask mommy and daddy to speak to them in English at home; who give them easier tasks so they won't feel badly when the work becomes difficult; who never learn about what life is like at home or what they eat or what music they like or what stories they have been told or what their history is. Instead, we smile and give them a hug and tell them to eat our food and listen to our stories and dance to our music. We teach them to read with our words and wonder why it's so hard for them. We ask them to sit quietly and we'll tell them what's important and what they must know to "get ready for the next grade." And we never ask them who they are and where they want to go.
>
> (Nieto, 1999, pp. 85–86)

A case in point is Hoang Vinh, the Vietnamese student I mentioned previously. Vinh was literate in Vietnamese and he made certain that his younger siblings spoke it exclusively at home and they all wrote to their parents in Vietnam weekly. He was a good student, but he was also struggling to learn English, something that his teachers didn't always understand. He described how some teachers described his native language as "funny," and even laughed at it. But as he explained, "[To keep reading and writing Vietnamese] is very important . . . So, I like to learn English, but I like to learn my language too" (Nieto, 2000, p. 178).

Even more fundamental for Vinh was that teachers try to understand their students' experiences and culture. He explained: "[My teachers] understand some things, just not all Vietnamese culture. Like they just understand some things *outside* . . . But they cannot understand something inside our hearts" (p. 178). Vinh's words are a good reminder that when students' skills and knowledge are dismissed as inappropriate for the school setting, schools lose a golden opportunity to build on their students' lives in the service of their learning.

Identity/Hybridity

How students benefit from schooling or not is influenced by many things including the particular individual personalities of students and the values of the cultural context in which they have been raised. Traditional theories, however, privilege individual differences above all other circumstances. As a result, it is primarily through tests and other measures of students' individual abilities that their intelligence is determined. Socio-cultural theory goes beyond this limited perspective to include other issues such as students' cultural identities. But culture should not be thought of in this context as unproblematic. Mary Kalantzis, Bill Cope, and Diana Slade (1989) remind us that

> we are not simply bearers of cultures, languages, and histories, with a duty to reproduce them. We are the products of linguistic-cultural circumstances, actors with a capacity to resynthesize what we have been socialized into and to solve new and emerging problems of existence. We are not duty-bound to conserve ancestral characteristics which are not structurally useful. We are both socially determined and creators of human futures.
>
> (p. 18)

Culture is complex and intricate; it cannot be reduced to holidays, foods, or dances, although these are of course elements of culture. Everyone has a culture because all people participate in the world through social and political relationships informed by history as well as by race, ethnicity, language, social class, sexual orientation, gender, and other circumstances related to identity and experience.

If culture is thought of in a sentimental way then it becomes little more than a yearning for a past that never existed, or an idealized, sanitized version of what exists in reality. The result may be an unadulterated, essentialized "culture on a pedestal" that bears little resemblance to the messy and contradictory culture of real life. The problem of viewing some aspects of culture as indispensable attributes that must be shared by all people within a particular group springs from a romanticized and uncritical understanding of culture.

Let me share an example of this with you: Last year, I received an e-mail message with the subject heading "You Know You're Puerto Rican When . . ." The message was meant to be humorous, and it included a long list of experiences and characteristics that presumably describe what it means to be Puerto Rican in the

United States (e.g., being chased by your mother with a *chancleta*, or slipper in hand; always having a dinner that consists of rice and beans and some kind of meat; having a grandmother who thinks Vick's Vapor Rub is the miracle cure for everything). I laughed at many of these things (and I shared a good number of these experiences when I was growing up in New York City), but it was also sobering to read the list because it felt like a litmus test for *puertorriqueñidad* (Puerto Ricanness). If you could prove that you had these particular experiences, you could claim to be authentic; otherwise, you could not. By putting them to paper, the author was making it clear that these experiences defined the very essence of being Puerto Rican.

Reading the list made me reflect on my own daughters, born and raised in the United States by highly educated middle-class parents. My daughters would likely not pass the Puerto Rican litmus test: Their dinner was just as likely to consist of take-out Chinese or pizza as of rice and beans; they barely knew what Vick's Vapor Rub was; and I don't remember ever chasing them with *chancleta* in hand. But both of them identify as Puerto Rican, and they speak Spanish to varying degrees and enjoy rice and beans as much as the next Puerto Rican. But they also eat salmon and frog's legs and pizza and Thai food. The e-mail message I received made it seem as if there was only one way to be Puerto Rican. The result of this kind of thinking is that we are left with just two alternatives: either complete adherence to one definition of identity, or total and unequivocal assimilation. We are, in the words of Anthony Appiah (1994), replacing "one kind of tyranny with another" (p. 163).

My daughters' identities are complicated. They live in a highly diverse society in terms of race, ethnicity, social class, and other differences, and they enjoy the privileges they have received as a result of their parents' social-class position in society. The point of this story is to emphasize that culture does not exist in a vacuum but rather is situated in particular historical, social, political, and economic conditions, another major tenet of sociocultural theory. That is, culture needs to be understood as dynamic; multifaceted; embedded in context; influenced by social, economic, and political factors; created and socially constructed; learned; and dialectical (Nieto, 1999). Steven Arvizu's (1994) wonderful description of culture as a *verb* rather than a *noun* captures the essence of culture beautifully. That is, culture is dynamic, active, changing, always on the move. Even within their native contexts, cultures are always changing as a result of political, social, and other modifications in the immediate environment. When people with different backgrounds come in contact with one another, such change is to be expected even more.

Let me once again use the example of Linda Howard, one of the young women we interviewed for *Affirming Diversity* (2000). As I mentioned, Linda was a talented young woman who was graduating as valedictorian of her class. But the issue of identity was a complicated one for her. Being biracial, she identified as "Black American and White American," and she said:

> I don't always fit in—unless I'm in a mixed group . . . because if I'm in a group of people who are all one race, then they seem to look at me as

being the *other* race . . . whereas if I'm in a group full of [racially mixed] people, my race doesn't seem to matter to everybody else . . . Then I don't feel like I'm standing out . . . It's hard. I look at history and I feel really bad for what some of my ancestors did to some of my other ancestors. Unless you're mixed, you don't know what it's like to be mixed.

(pp. 51–52)

The tension of Linda's identity was not simply a personal problem, however. It was evident throughout her schooling, and especially when she reached secondary school. She found that teachers jumped to conclusions about her identity, assuming she was Latina or even Chinese, and identifying her as such on forms without even asking her.

Linda won a scholarship to a highly regarded university. When discussing her future, she exclaimed proudly, "I've got it all laid out. I've got a 4 year scholarship to one of the best schools in New England. All I've gotta do is go there and make the grade." Linda's future seemed hopeful, overflowing with possibilities, but she didn't quite "make the grade." When Paula Elliott, who interviewed Linda the first time, spoke with her again 10 years later, she found out that Linda dropped out of college after just a few months, and she never returned. Over dinner, Linda described her experience at the university in this way: "I felt like a pea on a big pile of rice." Using a sociocultural lens, we can see that identity is not simply a personal issue, but that it is deeply embedded in institutional life. Had there been a way to validate her hybridity, perhaps Linda might have graduated. She certainly had the intellectual training and resources; what she didn't have was the support for her identity to ease the way.

In some ways, we can think of culture as having both surface and deep structure, to borrow a concept from linguistics (Chomsky, 1965). For instance, in the interviews of students of diverse backgrounds that I mentioned previously (Nieto, 2000), we were initially surprised by the seeming homogeneity of the youth culture they manifested. Regardless of racial, ethnic, linguistic background, or time in the United States—but usually intimately connected to a shared urban culture and social class—the youths often expressed strikingly similar tastes in music, food, clothes, television viewing habits, and so on. When I probed more deeply, however, I also found evidence of deeply held values from their ethnic heritage. For instance, Marisol, a Puerto Rican high school student, loved hip hop and rap music, pizza, and lasagna. She never mentioned Puerto Rican food, and Puerto Rican music to her was just the "old-fashioned" and boring music her parents listened to. But in her everyday interactions with parents and siblings, and in the answers she gave to my interview questions, she reflected deep aspects of Puerto Rican culture such as respect for elders, a profound kinship with and devotion to family, and a desire to uphold important traditions such as staying with family rather than going out with friends on important holidays. Just as there is no such thing as a "pure race," there is likewise no "pure culture." That is, cultures influence one another, and even minority cultures and those with less status have an impact on majority cultures, sometimes in dramatic ways.

Power is deeply implicated in notions of culture and language (Fairclough, 1989). Indeed, what are often presented as cultural and linguistic differences are above all differences in power. Put another way, cultural conflict is sometimes little more than political conflict. Let me give you another example concerning the link between culture and context based on an experience I had that took me by surprise even as a young adult. As you probably know, rice is a primary Puerto Rican staple. There is a saying in Spanish that demonstrates how common it is: "*Puertorriqueños somos como el arroz blanco: estamos por todas partes*" (Puerto Ricans are like white rice: we are everywhere), an adage that says as much about rice as it does about the diaspora of the Puerto Rican people, almost half of whom live outside the island. As a rule, Puerto Ricans eat short-grained rice, but I have always preferred long-grained rice. Some Puerto Ricans have made me feel practically like a cultural traitor when I admitted it. I remember my surprise when a fellow academic, a renowned Puerto Rican historian, explained the real reason behind the preference for short-grained rice. This preference did not grow out of the blue, nor does any particular quality of the rice make it innately better. On the contrary, the predilection for short-grained rice was influenced by the historical context of Puerto Ricans as a colonized people.

It seems that, near the beginning of the 20th century when Puerto Rico was first taken over by the United States as spoils of the Spanish-American War, there was a surplus of short-grained rice in the United States. Colonies have frequently been the destination for unwanted or surplus goods from the metropolis, so Puerto Rico became the dumping ground for short-grained rice, which had lower status than long-grained rice in the United States. After this, of course, the preference for short-grained rice became part of the culture. As is true of all cultural values, however, this particular taste was influenced by history, economics, and power. This example was a good lesson to me that culture is not something inherent, but often arbitrary and negotiated.

Hybridity complicates the idea of cultural identity. It means that culture is always heterogeneous and complex; it also implies that assimilation or cultural preservation are not the only alternatives. Ariel Dorfman's (1998) autobiography *Heading South, Looking North: A Bilingual Journey* eloquently describes the turmoil he experienced as a child in developing his identity, first in New York City and later in Chile: "I instinctively chose to refuse the multiple, complex, in-between person I would someday become, this man who is shared by two equal languages and who has come to believe that to tolerate differences and indeed embody them personally and collectively might be our only salvation as a species" (p. 42). As an adult, he reflected on the demand to be "culturally pure" that he experienced in the United States as a graduate student:

> Sitting at my typewriter in Berkeley, California, that day, precariously balanced between Spanish and English, for the first time perhaps fully aware of how extraordinarily bicultural I was, I did not have the maturity —or the emotional or ideological space, probably not even the vocabulary —to answer that I was a hybrid, part Yankee, part Chilean, a pinch of Jew,

a mestizo in search of a center, I was unable to look directly in the face the divergent mystery of who I was, the abyss of being bilingual and bi-national, at a time when everything demanded that we be unequivocal and immaculate.

(p. 22)

The idea of hybridity, and of culture as implicated with power and privilege, complicates culturally responsive pedagogy. Rather than simply an incorporation of the cultural practices of students' families in the curriculum, or a replication of stereotypical ideas about "learning styles," culturally responsive pedagogy in the broadest sense is a political project that is, according to Gloria Ladson-Billings (1994) about "questioning (and preparing students to question) the structural inequality, the racism, and the injustice that exist in society" (p. 128). Culturally responsive pedagogy is not simply about instilling pride in one's identity or boost-ing self-esteem. It is also about context and positionality, to which I now turn.

Context/Situatedness/Positionality

When culture is thought of as if it were context-free, we fragment people's lives, in the words of Frederick Erickson (1990), "as we freeze them outside time, outside a world of struggle in concrete history" (p. 34). Context is also about *situatedness* and *positionality*, reminding us that culture is not simply the rituals, foods, and holidays of specific groups of people, but also the social markers that differentiate that group from others. It is once again the recognition that ques-tions of power are at the very heart of learning. This view of culture also implies that differences in ethnicity, language, social class, and gender need not, in and of themselves, be barriers to learning. Instead, it is how these differences are viewed in society that can make the difference in whether and to what extent young people learn.

Judith Solsken's (1993) definition of *literacy* as the "negotiation of one's orien-tation toward written language and thus one's position within multiple relations of power and status" (p. 6) brings up a number of questions that have tradition-ally been neglected in discussions of reading and writing, questions such as: How do students learn to use language in a way that both acknowledges the context in which they find themselves, and challenges the rules of that context? How do young people learn to negotiate the chasm that exists between their home lan-guages and cultures and those of school? Let me share with you another example from Linda Howard. What helped Linda go from a struggling student in junior high to valedictorian of her class several years later? There are probably many answers to this question, but one ingredient that made a tremendous difference was Mr. Benson, her favorite teacher in high school. He too was biracial, and Linda talked about some of the things she had learned from Mr. Benson about positionality and context:

I've enjoyed all my English teachers at Jefferson. But Mr. Benson, my English Honors teacher, he just threw me for a whirl! 'Cause Mr. Benson, he says, I can go into Harvard and converse with those people, and I can go out in the street and rap with y'all. It's that type of thing, I love it. I try and be like that myself. I have my street talk. I get out in the street and I say "ain't" this and "ain't" that and "your momma" or "wha's up?" But I get somewhere where I know the people aren't familiar with that language or aren't accepting that language, and I will talk properly. . . . I walk into a place and I listen to how people are talking, and it just automatically comes to me.

(Nieto, 2000, p. 56)

Linda's statement is an example of the tremendous intelligence needed by young people whose Discourses (Gee, 1990) are not endorsed by schools, and who need to negotiate these differences on their own. Linda's words are also a graphic illustration of James Baldwin's (1997) characterization of language as "a political instrument, means, and proof of power" (p. 16). In the case of African American discourse, Baldwin suggested—as Linda learned through her own experience—"It is not the Black child's language that is in question, it is not his language that is despised: It is his experience" (p. 16). As David Corson (1993) reminds us, ". . . education can routinely repress, dominate, and disempower language users whose practices differ from the norms that it establishes" (p. 7).

What does this mean for teachers? Situations such as Linda Howard's suggest that, in the words of Sharon Nelson-Barber and Elise Trumbull Estrin (1995), "We are faced with essential epistemological questions such as, what counts as important knowledge or knowing?" (p. 178). These questions are at the core of sociocultural theory, and they are neither neutral nor innocent. They are rarely addressed openly in school, although they should be. As Ira Shor (1992) said, "A curriculum that avoids questioning school and society is not, as is commonly supposed, politically neutral. It cuts off the students' development as critical thinkers about their world" (p. 12).

Sociocultural and sociopolitical perspectives have been especially consequential because they have shattered the perception that teaching and learning are neutral processes uncontaminated by the idiosyncrasies of particular contexts. Whether and to what extent teachers realize the influence social and political context have on learning can alter how they perceive their students and, consequently, what and how they teach them. A good example of positionality is the status of bilingual education. Bilingualism is only viewed as a problem and a deficit in a context where speakers of a particular language are held in low esteem or seen as a threat to national unity. This is the case of bilingual education in the United States, and especially for children who speak Spanish. That is, there is nothing inherently negative about the project of becoming bilingual (many wealthy parents pay dearly for the privilege), but rather it is the identities of the students, and the status of the language variety they speak, that make bilingual education problematic. This was clearly explained by Lizette Román, a bilingual teacher whose journal entry for one of my classes reads as follows:

Unfortunately, most bilingual programs exist because they are mandated by law, not because they are perceived as a necessity by many school systems. The main problem that we bilingual teachers face every day is the misconception that mainstream teachers, principals, and even entire school systems have about bilingual education. . . . As a consequence, in many school districts bilingual education is doubly disadvantaged, first because it is seen as remedial and, second, because little attention is paid to it. Many mainstream teachers and administrators see bilingual education as a remediation program and do not validate what bilingual teachers do in their classrooms even when what they are teaching is part of the same curriculum. . . . The majority think that there must be something wrong with these children who cannot perform well in English. As soon as the children transfer out of the bilingual program, these teachers believe that *this* is the moment when the learning of these children starts. The perception of the majority distorts the importance and the purpose of bilingual education. It extends to bilingual children and their parents. Bilingual children and their parents sense that their language places them in a program where they are perceived to be inferior to the rest of the children. What isolates children in the bilingual program is not the way the program is conducted, but the perceptions the majority has about people who speak a language different from the mainstream.

(Nieto, 1999, pp. 87–88)

Lizette's reflections suggest that if teachers believe that intelligence and learning are somehow divorced from context, then they will conclude that the political and economic realities of their students' lives—including their school environments—have nothing to do with learning. In short, teachers can delude themselves by believing that they and the schools in which they work inhabit an "ideology-free zone" in which dominant attitudes and values play no role in learning. When students are asked to give up their identities for an elusive goal that they may never reach because of the negative context in which they learn, students may be quite correct in rejecting the trade.

Community

How we define and describe *community* is of central significance in sociocultural theory. Lev Vygotsky's (1978) research in the first decades of the 20th century was a catalyst for the viewpoint that learning is above all a social practice. Vygotsky suggested that development and learning are firmly rooted in—and influenced by—society and culture. Accepting this idea means that it is no longer possible to separate learning from the context in which it takes place, nor from an understanding of how culture and society influence and are influenced by learning.

Vygotsky and others who have advanced the sociocultural foundation of cognition (Cole & Griffin, 1983; Scribner & Cole, 1981) have provided us with a framework for understanding how schools can either encourage or discourage the development of learning communities. Because schools organize themselves in specific ways, they are more or less comfortable and inviting for students of particular backgrounds. Most schools closely reflect the traditional image of the intelligent, academically prepared young person, and consequently, these are the young people who tend to feel most comfortable in school settings. But institutional environments are never neutral; they are always based on particular views of human development, of what is worth knowing, and of what it means to be educated. When young people enter schools, they are entering institutions that have already made some fundamental decisions about such matters, and in the process, some of these children may be left out through no fault of their own. The ability to create community, so important in sociocultural theory, is lost.

Maria Botelho, a former doctoral student of mine and an early childhood teacher and librarian, remembers very clearly what it was like to begin school as a young immigrant student in Cambridge, Massachusetts. After viewing a short video on bilingual education in one of my classes, she felt almost as if she had stepped back in time. The video highlights a number of students, one of them Carla, a young Portuguese student in a bilingual class in Cambridge. Maria reflected on her reactions to the video in the journal she kept for my class:

> I viewed the video "Quality Bilingual Education" twice. I wept both times. The Portuguese-speaking girl, Carla, attended kindergarten in a school that is less than a block from where my parents live in Cambridge; it was too close to home, so to speak. Like Carla, I entered the Cambridge Public Schools speaking only Portuguese. Unlike Carla, I was placed in a mainstream first-grade class. I still remember my teacher bringing over a piece of paper with some writing on it (a worksheet) and crayons. I fell asleep. There I learned quietly about her world, and my world was left with my coat, outside the classroom door.
>
> (Nieto, 1999, p. 110)

Sociocultural theories are a radical departure from conventional viewpoints that posit learning as largely unaffected by context. Traditional viewpoints often consider that children such as Maria who do not speak English have low intelligence. As a result, such children are automatically barred from entering a community of learners. A Vygotskian perspective provides a more hopeful framework for thinking about learning because if learning can be influenced by social mediation, then conditions can be created in schools that can help most students learn. These conditions can result in what Carmen Mercado (1998) described as the "fashioning of new texts—texts of our collective voices" (p. 92) that emerge as a result of organizing a learning environment in which literacy is for sharing and reflecting. Particularly significant in this regard is the idea of the *zone of proximal development* or ZPD (Vygotsky, 1978). But the ZPD is not simply an *individual* space, but a *social* one. Thus, according to Henry Trueba (1989), if we accept Vygotsky's theory of ZPD, then failure to learn cannot be defined as *individual* failure but rather as *systemic* failure, that is, as the failure of the social system to provide the learner with an opportunity for successful social interactions.

In order to change academic failure to success, appropriate social and instructional interventions need to occur. For teachers, this means that they need to first acknowledge students' differences and then act as a bridge between their students' differences and the culture of the dominant society. The metaphor of a bridge is an appropriate one for teachers who want to be effective with students of diverse backgrounds. This is a lesson I learned from Diane Sweet, a former student who had been an engineer until she fell in love with teaching ESL at the plant where she worked and decided to become a teacher. Diane was well aware of the benefits of bridges, and she applied the metaphor to teaching: A bridge provides access to a different shore without closing off the possibility of returning home; a bridge is built on solid ground but soars toward the heavens; a bridge connects two places that might otherwise never be able to meet. The best thing about bridges is that they do not need to be burned once they are used; on the contrary, they become more valuable with use because they help visitors from both sides become adjusted to different contexts. This is, however, a far cry from how diverse languages and cultures tend to be viewed in schools: the conventional wisdom is that, if native languages and cultures are used at all, it should be only until one learns the *important* language and culture, and then they should be discarded or burned. It is definitely a one-way street with no turning back.

The metaphor of the bridge suggests a different stance: You can have two homes, and the bridge can help you cross the difficult and conflict-laden spaces between them. Teachers who take seriously their responsibility for working with students of diverse backgrounds become bridges, or what Estéban Diaz and his colleagues (1992) called *sociocultural mediators*. That is, they accept and validate the cultural symbols used by all their students, not just by those from majority backgrounds. In sociocultural theory, learning and achievement are not merely cognitive processes, but complex issues that need to be understood in the development of community.

Three of my colleagues provide a hopeful example of using students' experiences and identities as a basis for creating community. Jo-Anne Wilson Keenan, a teacher researcher, working with Judith Solsken and Jerri Willett, professors at the University of Massachusetts, developed a collaborative action research project in a school in Springfield, Massachusetts, with a very diverse student body. The project—based on the premise that parents and other family members of children from widely diverse backgrounds have a lot to offer schools to enhance their children's learning—was distinct from others in which parents are simply invited to speak about their culture and to share food. Instead, their research focused on demonstrating how parents, through visits that highlight their daily lives, talents, and skills, can promote student learning by transforming the curriculum. But engaging in this kind of project is not always easy. The researchers pointed out that collaborating with families "requires that we confront our own fears of difference and open our classrooms to discussions of topics that may raise tensions among the values of different individuals, groups, and institutions" (p. 64). Through inspiring stories based on indepth analysis of the families' visits, Wilson Keenan, Solsken, and Willett (1999) described how they attempted to build reciprocal relationships with parents. They concluded:

> Both the extent and the quality of participation by the parents belies the common perception that low-income and minority parents are unable or unwilling to collaborate with the school. Even more important, our study documents the wide range of knowledge, skills, and teaching capabilities that parents are already sharing with their children at home and that are available to enrich the education of their own and other children in school.
>
> (p. 64)

The important work of Luis Moll, Norma Gonzalez, and their colleagues (1997) is another well-known example of research that builds on family knowledge.

Conclusion

No theory can provide all the answers to the persistent problems of education because these problems are not just about teaching and learning, but about a society's ideology. But sociocultural theories give us different insights into these problems. Although we need to accept the inconclusiveness of what we know, we also need to find new and more empowering ways of addressing these concerns. Maxine Greene (1994), in a discussion of postmodernism, poststructuralism, feminism, literary criticism, and other sociocultural theories, discussed both the possibilities and the limits they have. She wrote: "The point is to open a number of fresh perspectives on epistemology in its connection with educational research" (p. 426). But she added, "no universalized or totalized viewing, even of a revised sort . . ." (p. 426) is possible.

Nevertheless, despite this inconclusiveness, we know enough to know that teachers need to respect students' identities and they need to learn about their students if they are to be effective with them. This means understanding the students we teach, and building relationships with them. Ron Morris, a young man attending an alternative school in Boston, described the disappointing relationships he had with teachers before attending the alternative school where he now found himself, a school that finally allowed him to have the relationships he craved. He said:

> When a teacher becomes a teacher, she acts like a teacher instead of a person. She takes her title as now she's mechanical, somebody just running it. Teachers shouldn't deal with students like we're machines. You're a person. I'm a person. We come to school and we all act like people.
>
> (Nieto, 2000, p. 265)

Ron reminds us that we do not have all the answers, and indeed, that some of the answers we have are clearly wrong. Ray McDermott (1977), in an early ethnography, described this fact beautifully: "We are all embedded in our own procedures, which make us both very smart in one situation and blind and stupid in the next" (p. 202). More recently, Herbert Kohl (1995) suggested that students' failure to learn is not always caused by a lack of intelligence, motivation, or self-esteem. On the contrary, he maintained that "to agree to learn from a stranger who does not respect your integrity causes a major loss of self" (p. 6), or what Carol Locust (1988) called "wounding the spirit" (p. 315).

Much has been written in the past few years about teachers' reluctance to broach issues of difference, both among themselves and with their students (Fine, 1992; Jervis, 1996; McIntyre, 1997; Sleeter, 1994; Solomon, 1995; Tatum, 1997). This is especially true of racism, which is most often addressed in schools as if it were a personality problem. But prejudice and discrimination are not just personality traits or psychological phenomena; they are also manifestations of economic, political, and social power. The institutional definition of racism is not always easy for teachers to accept because it goes against deeply held theories of equality and justice in our nation. Bias as an institutional system implies that some people and groups benefit and others lose. Whites, whether they want to or not, benefit in a racist society; males benefit in a sexist society. Discrimination always helps somebody—those with the most power—which explains why racism, sexism, and other forms of discrimination continue to exist. Having a different language to speak about differences in privilege and power is the first step in acquiring the courage to make changes.

Finally, sociocultural and sociopolitical concepts give us a way to confront what Henry Giroux (1992) called our nation's "retreat from democracy" (p. 4). Paulo Freire (1998), writing a series of letters to teachers, focused on this problem:

> When inexperienced middle-class teachers take teaching positions in peripheral areas of the city, class-specific tastes, values, language, discourse, syntax, semantics, everything about the students may seem contradictory to the point of being shocking and frightening. It is necessary, however, that teachers understand that the students' syntax; their manners, tastes, and ways of addressing teachers and colleagues; and the rules governing their fighting and playing among themselves are all part of their *cultural identity*, which never lacks an element of class. All that has to be accepted. Only as learners recognize themselves democratically and see that their right to say "I be" is respected will they become able to learn the dominant grammatical reasons why they should say "I am."
>
> (p. 49)

All students are individuals as well as members of particular groups whose identities are either disdained or respected in society. When we understand this, then my own story and those of countless others, can be understood not simply as someone "pulling herself up by her bootstraps," or "melting," or joining "the mainstream," but as a story that the concepts I've spoken about today—*agency/co-constructed learning; experience; identity/hybridity; context/situatedness/positionality*; and *community*—can begin to explain. When language, literacy, and culture are approached in these ways, we have a more hopeful way of addressing teaching and learning for all students.

Notes

* This material is based on a keynote address given at the National Reading Conference in December, 2000.
1 I wish to acknowledge my colleagues in the Language, Literacy, and Culture Doctoral Research Area, School of Education at the University of Massachusetts, Amherst: Jerri Willett, Judith Solsken, Masha Rudman, Catherine Luna, and Theresa Austin. Working with them to conceptualize and develop our program over the past 3 years has had a profound influence on my thinking about these issues.
2 I am very grateful to those who assisted me with the interviews and gave me suggestions for crafting the case studies: Paula Elliott, Haydée Font, Maya Gillingham, Beatriz McConnie Zapater, Mac Lee Morante, Carol Shea, Diane Sweet, and Carlie Tartakov.

References

Appiah, A. (1994). Identity, authenticity, survival: Multicultural societies and social reproduction. In A. Gutmann (Ed.), *Multiculturalism* (pp. 149–163). Princeton, NJ: Princeton University.

Apple, M. W. (1993). The politics of official knowledge: Does a national curriculum make sense? *Teachers College Record, 95*(2), 222–241.

Arvizu, S. F. (1994). Building bridges for the future: Anthropological contributions to diversity and classroom practice. In R. A. DeVillar, C. J. Faltis, & J. P. Cummins (Eds.), *Cultural diversity in schools: From rhetoric to reality* (pp. 75–97). Albany: State University of New York Press.

Baldwin, J. (1997). If Black English isn't a language, then tell me, what is? *Rethinking Schools, 12*(1), 16.

Bourdieu, P. (1986). The forms of capital. In Richardson, J. G. (Ed.), *Handbook of theory and research for the sociology of education* (pp. 241–248). Westport, CT: Greenwood Press.

Chomsky, N. (1965). *Aspects of the theory of syntax.* Cambridge, MA: MIT. Cole, M. & Griffin, P. (1983). A socio-historical approach to re-mediation. *The Quarterly Newsletter of the Laboratory of Comparative Human Cognition, 5*(4), 69–74.

Corson, D. (1993). *Language, minority education and gender: Linking social justice and power.* Clevedon, UK: Multilingual Matters.

Cummins, J. (1994). Knowledge, power, and identity in teaching English as a second language. In F. Genesee (Ed.), *Educating second language children: The whole child, the whole curriculum, the whole community* (pp. 33–58). Cambridge, UK: Cambridge University Press.

Delpit, L. (1988). The silenced dialogue: Power and pedagogy in educating other people's children. *Harvard Educational Review, 58,* 280–298.

Dewey, J. (1916). *Democracy and education.* New York: The Free Press.

Diaz, E., Flores, B., Cousin, P. T., & Soo Hoo, S. (1992, April). Teacher as sociocultural mediator. Paper presented at the annual meeting of the American Educational Research Association, San Francisco, CA.

Dorfman, A. (1998). *Heading south, looking north: A bilingual journey.* New York: Penguin.

Erickson, F. (1990). Culture, politics, and educational practice. *Educational Foundations, 4*(2), 21–45.

Fairclough, N. (1989). *Language and power.* New York: Longman.

Fine, M. (1991). *Framing dropouts: Notes on the politics of an urban high school.* Albany, NY: SUNY.

Freire, P. (1970). *Pedagogy of the oppressed.* New York: Seabury.

Freire, P. (1985). *The politics of education: Culture, power, and liberation.* New York: Bergin & Garvey.

Freire, P. (1998). *Teachers as cultural workers: Letters to those who dare teach.* Boulder, CO: Westview.

Gee, J. P. (1990). *Social linguistics and literacies: Ideologies in discourse.* Bristol, PA: Falmer.

Giroux, H. (1992). Educational leadership and the crisis of democratic government. *Educational Researcher, 21*(4), 4–11.

Goodlad, J. I. (1984). *A place called school.* New York: McGraw-Hill.

Greene, M. (1994). Epistemology and educational research: The influence of recent approaches to knowledge. In L. Darling-Hammond (Ed.), *Review of research in education* (Vol. 20; pp. 423–464). Washington, DC: American Educational Research Association.

Hirsch, E. D. (1987). *Cultural literacy: What every American needs to know.* Boston: Houghton Mifflin.

Jervis, K. (1996). "How come there are no brothers on that list?": Hearing the hard questions all children ask. *Harvard Educational Review, 66,* 546–576.

Kalantzis, M., Cope, B., & Slade, D. (1989). *Minority languages.* London: The Falmer Press.

Kohl, H. (1994). *"I won't learn from you" and other thoughts on creative maladjustment.* New York: The New Press.

Ladson-Billings, G. (1994). *The dreamkeepers: Successful teachers of African American children.* San Francisco: Jossey-Bass.

Locust, C. (1988). Wounding the spirit: Discrimination and traditional American Indian belief systems. *Harvard Educational Review, 3,* 315–330.

Mercado, C. I. (1998). When young people from marginalized communities enter the world of ethnographic research: Scribing, planning, reflecting, and sharing. In A. Egan-Robertson & D. Bloome (Eds.), *Students as researchers of culture and language in their own communities* (pp. 69–92). Cresskill, NJ: Hampton.

McDermott, R. P. (1977). Social relations as contexts for learning in school. *Harvard Educational Review, 47,* 198–213.

McIntyre, A. (1997). Constructing an image of a white teacher. *Teachers College Press, 98*(4), 653–681.

Moll, L., & Gonzalez, N. (1997). Teachers as social scientists: Learning about culture from household research. In P. M. Hall (Ed.), *Race, ethnicity, and multiculturalism* (Vol. 1; pp. 89–114). New York: Garland.

Nelson-Barber, S., & Estrin, E. T. (1995). Bringing Native American perspectives to mathematics and science teaching. *Theory into Practice, 34*(3), 174–185.

Nieto, S. (1999). *The light in their eyes: Creating multicultural learning communities.* New York: Teachers College Press.

Nieto, S. (2000). *Affirming diversity: The sociopolitical context of multicultural education* (3rd ed.). New York: Longman.

Perry, T., & Delpit, L. (Eds.). (1998). *The real ebonics debate: Power, language, and the education of African-American children.* Boston: Beacon Press & Rethinking Schools.

Rodriguez, R. (1982). *Hunger of memory: The education of Richard Rodriguez.* Boston: David R. Godine.

Scribner, S., & Cole, M. (1981). *The psychology of literacy.* Cambridge, MA: Harvard University.

Shor, I. (1992). *Empowering education: Critical teaching for social change.* Chicago: University of Chicago.

Sleeter, C. E. (1994). White racism. *Multicultural Education, 1*(4), 5–8, 39.

Snow, C. E., Barnes, W. S., Chandler, J., Goodman, I. F., & Hemphill, L. (1991). *Unfulfilled expectations: Home and school influences on literacy.* Cambridge, MA: Harvard University.

Solomon, R. P. (1995). Beyond prescriptive pedagogy: Teacher inservice education for cultural diversity. *Journal of Teacher Education, 46*(4), 251–258.

Solsken, J. W. (1993). *Literacy, gender, and work in families and in school.* Norwood, NJ: Ablex.

Stein, A. (1971). Strategies for failure. *Harvard Educational Review, 41,* 133–179.

Taylor, D., & Dorsey-Gaines, C. (1988). *Growing up literate: Learning from inner-city families.* Portsmouth, NH: Heinemann.

Tatum, B. D. (1997). *"Why are all the Black kids sitting together in the cafeteria?" and other conversations about race.* New York: HarperCollins.

Trueba, H. T. (1989). *Raising silent voices: Educating the linguistic minorities for the 21st century.* Cambridge, MA: Newbury House.

Vygotsky, L. S. (1978). *Thought and language.* Cambridge, MA: MIT Press.

Wilson Keenan, J., Solsken, J., & Willett, J. (1999). "Only boys can jump high": Reconstructing gender relations in a first/second grade classroom. In B. Kamler (Ed.), *Constructing gender and difference: Critical research perspectives on early childhood* (pp. 33–70). Cresskill, NJ: Hampton Press.

Critical Questions

1   How have language, literacy, and culture affected your life and your experiences as a student and teacher? Write another introduction to this chapter by beginning with your own story. How is it different from mine? What implications might there be for teaching and learning? Would they be different?

2   How do you think that language, literacy, and culture affect your students' lives? What if you wrote the beginning of the chapter from the perspective of one of your students? What might you learn about them in the process?

3   Have you usually accepted the traditional metaphors I mention in the chapter ("pulling yourself up by your bootstraps"; "melting"; "joining the mainstream")? Can you think of other metaphors that might be more appropriate to describe the situations of the students you teach?

4   Look back on the examples I've used when describing the five tenets of sociocultural and sociopolitical theory. As you can see, they all proceed from my own experience. What examples might you use to illustrate these concepts from your experience, from the experiences of your students? What is the danger of using just one's own reality to reach conclusions about teaching and learning?

5   Give some illustrations of *hybrid culture* from your experience as a teacher of students of diverse backgrounds. (My assumption in asking this question is that *all* teachers work with students of diverse backgrounds because diversity encompasses many things, including race/ethnicity, gender, social class, native language, sexual orientation, family configuration, and so on.)

Activities for Your Classroom

1   For a serious semester-long project, develop a classroom-based curriculum that includes in a central way the major tenets of sociocultural and

sociopolitical theory as described in the chapter. Include the topic, goals, grade level/subject matter, several activities, resources, and evaluation. Clearly explain how each of the tenets is included in the curriculum.

2   Work with a colleague or group of colleagues (in this course or in your school). Think about ways to address students' experiences and backgrounds in your classroom. Be specific, referring to actual materials, family and community resources, and classroom projects.

Community-Based Activities and Advocacy

Are language, literacy, and culture significant issues in the community in which you teach? To find out, engage your students in research about their cultural and literacy practices. Depending on their age, experience, and grade level, you can ask them to:

> interview family members about their language use; do a survey of community language resources by finding out how many languages are used in everyday interactions; visit a community preschool to see how literacy is promoted; and do a study of the community's policies concerning language and culture (e.g., Is there an "English-Only" policy in place? Are cultural festivals encouraged? Does the public library promote multicultural literature? Literature in languages other than English? etc.).

Supplementary Resources for Further Reflection and Study

Appiah, A. (1994). Multicultural societies and social reproduction. In Amy Gutmann (Ed.), *Multiculturalism* (pp. 149–163). Princeton, NJ: Princeton University Press.

The author highlights some major problems with multiculturalism, including a focus on large categories such as gender, race, ethnicity, that are far removed from the individual.

Egan-Robertson, A. & Bloome, D. (1998). *Students as researchers of culture and language in their own communities.* Cresskill, NJ: Hampton Press.

In this edited text, various educators write compelling accounts of how students' research of language and culture in their communities has empowered them not only in terms of their literacy, but also in terms of their understanding of the world. This is an excellent resource for teachers who want to do similar research with their students.

Nieto, S. (1999). *The light in their eyes: Creating multicultural learning communities.* New York: Teachers College Press.

Using excerpts from journals kept in graduate courses, this text explores how teachers' reflections on course content, reading, and activities provide the framework for a deeper understanding of the effect of culture and language on students' education.

Reyes, M. (1992). Challenging venerable assumptions: Literacy instruction for linguistically different students. *Harvard Educational Review, 62*(4), 427–446.

In this thought-provoking article, Reyes challenges widely accepted progressive notions about teaching students of limited English proficiency and she critiques current implementations of process instruction that may have the tendency to ignore culturally and linguistically supportive adaptations for these students.

Part I

Setting the Groundwork

As you saw in the introductory chapter, a number of foundational elements are crucial to understanding the links among language, literacy, and culture. These include the learners' status and experience, the complex nature of identity, the community as a necessary part of learning, and the context in which education takes place. Consequently, a sociocultural understanding of education means learning to look at literacy and other schooling matters in a broader way than has traditionally been the case.

The chapters that follow build on the theme of the interconnectedness of learning. Each chapter defines in more detail some of the basic elements generally alluded to in the previous chapter. In Chapter 1, I reflect on the purpose of schools in this era of rigid accountability. I consider questions such as: What are the values and attitudes that should be at the heart of a public education? What are the implications of defining these values and attitudes? What is the link between public education and democracy?

Chapter 2 is a very brief piece I was originally asked to write for a segment on "Stances on Multilingual and Multicultural Education" for the journal *Language Arts*. Thinking about the use of labels to define students—a practice that is all too common in many schools—I challenged readers to reject labels and focus instead on the students themselves. Chapters 3 and 4 are from *Affirming Diversity*, a text widely used in teacher education courses around the country and beyond. For the fifth edition of *Affirming Diversity*, I asked my colleague and friend Patty Bode to join me as co-author. In Chapter 3, she and I define the sociopolitical context of multicultural education, and in Chapter 4, we offer a comprehensive definition of multicultural education that connects it with school reform and social justice.

To commemorate the seventy-fifth anniversary of the *Harvard Educational Review*, the editors asked me to write an article reflecting on public education during those years. In Chapter 5, I suggest that the major educational agenda of the twentieth century was the expansion of rights and opportunities for a broader range of students. Specifically, I explore three movements that helped define this ideal: desegregation, multicultural education, and bilingual education. Finally, Chapter 6 develops this idea further by placing language diversity squarely within the broader framework of multicultural education, with implications for school and classroom policy and practice.

1 What is the Purpose of Schools?

Reflections on Education in an Age of Functionalism

Since the early 1980s, the U.S. educational system has been focused on issues of accountability like never before. The essay that follows suggests that we may have lost our way in terms of how we define education. Instead of emphasizing rubrics and test scores, this essay considers not only *what* is taught, but *how*, *under what conditions*, and, in the end, *why* we teach at all. In doing so, the essay asks readers to think about the very purpose of schools in a democratic society, a purpose that must be based on social justice if we are to fulfill our promise of equal and quality education for all students, regardless of station or rank. Five implications for teaching with a social justice perspective are described.

Writing about the purpose of schools at a time when accountability, standardization, and privatization are the common discourse seems almost a frill, a throwback to an old-fashioned and romantic time when public education was a topic dominated by talk of democracy and equality. It brings us back to when people spoke of education as serving the common good, and when schools were defined as "the great equalizer" (Mann, 1868). Even though schools never did realize that ideal, it was at least an ideal worth believing in.

Who talks about such things anymore? The conventional talk these days is much more functional, even mean-spirited: It is about adequate yearly progress (*ayp*) and ubiquitous high-stakes tests for children; about multiplying the roadblocks for those wishing to teach; about vouchers and charter schools; and about de-regulating the teaching profession and eliminating schools and colleges of education. Public education, in essence, has been hijacked by a corporate, market-driven agenda, and many of us who disagree with this agenda are left to wonder what happened to the nobler goals of education.

What should the purpose of schools be in the current climate? Let me set the framework for what follows by quoting from the words of an educator who said far more eloquently than I what must be the basic educational goal of a democracy:

> The education that I propose includes all that is proper for all men and it
> is one which all . . . who are born into this world should share . . .
>
> Our first wish is that all . . . be educated fully into full humanity, not
> any one individual, not a few, not even many, but all . . . together and
> singly, young and old, rich and poor, of high and lowly birth, men and
> women—in a world whose fate it is to be born human beings, so that at
> least the whole of the human race become educated men of all ages, all
> conditions, both sexes and all nations.
>
> (Comenius, 1968)

These words are remarkable because they were written not by Horace Mann or
John Dewey (although they certainly could have been), but by John Amos
Comenius in *The Great Didactic,* first published in 1657. I begin with them for
two reasons. First, they make clear that the goal of an equitable and high quality
education for all students is neither a modern invention nor a strictly American
one. It has been a cherished ideal (and an elusive reality) for many generations
in many societies, our own included. Second, I do not wish to be thought of
as a naïve, "pie-in-the-sky" optimist with no understanding of the reality of
our schools today, characterized as they are by racism, other manifestations
of inequality, violence, bureaucracy, and apathy. These conditions are as clear to
me as they are to anyone else. But I want to place myself squarely in the company
of those who, in spite of these conditions, envision a world in which education
can be exciting, empowering, and safe.

In considering the purpose of schools, we need to begin with the vision we
have for our youth and society in this new millennium. What should we teach?
Why? What knowledge, skills, attitudes, and aptitudes do students need to
develop? But before we say what we want students to know and become, we need
to first ask ourselves what we think they are capable of knowing and becoming. As
we attempt to answer the age-old curriculum question of "What knowledge is of
most worth?", we need to also ask Paulo Freire's (1970) fundamental question
about whose interests we are serving through the curriculum we select. As we
determine what schools are for, we also need to ask what role we think young
people should have in improving, and not simply replicating, our society.

The vision that I am proposing is predicated not on a list of facts that will
somehow miraculously transform youngsters into literate and intelligent beings,
but on a broader conception of learning. Lists of "cultural literacy" items (Hirsch,
1987) notwithstanding, we know too well that there is no magic curriculum that
will make young people truly educated (Provenzo, 2005). There are only what
Deborah Meier has called "habits of mind" (Meier, 1995) that we can try to
promote. These habits of mind can help young people become critical thinkers in
the true sense of the word: to understand that knowledge is never neutral but
always reflects a particular point of view; to learn where and how to get information and how best to use it; to practice reflection and critique; and to discover
how to create and transform knowledge for the betterment and benefit of others.
Conversely, in the United States, historically, and even recently, we have witnessed
many examples of capable and talented individuals engaging in morally

repugnant actions: using unwitting African American inmates as guinea pigs for syphilis experiments near the beginning of the twentieth century; subjecting unsuspecting victims to plutonium from the 1940s to the 1970s; robbing people of their hard-earned savings through massive fraud; and too many others to name. These are chilling reminders that one can be technically and scientifically brilliant but ethically bankrupt. Therefore, simply assuring that all students graduate from high school with high levels of scientific or mathematical literacy, for example, is not enough.

If I had to come up with a list of suggestions for the kind of content that students should be taught, I would probably include broad-based literacy, the advanced sciences, a heavy dose of the arts, the full range of mathematics, technology, and vocational skills for all students (not just those going on to a trade), intensive health and physical education, practical skills for living in an advanced technological society and safeguarding our environment, and at least a second language for all students. I would also urge that these be taught with a multicultural perspective that is more reflective of our reality than the current largely monocultural curriculum. I would want to assure that assessment processes are intimately connected to real and consequential knowledge, not to minutiae or biased procedures that further discourage and punish the most educationally disadvantaged youth and penalize the most creative teachers by reducing them to test givers.

But focusing on content alone is a losing proposition because knowledge is always changing, always in flux. What should *not* change are the kinds of attitudes and values about learning at the heart of the purpose of public education. To the extent that we consider the question of curriculum content without an equally rigorous exploration of the context of education—that is, the organizational structures and practices and policies that can either enhance or limit educational achievement—it will be an incomplete and ultimately frustrating exercise. For example, without tackling the central but far more difficult and sensitive issues of stratification and inequity in funding, educational organization, and educators' perceptions of and interactions with students and communities, we are missing a crucial opportunity to rethink not only *what* we teach and learn, but *under what conditions*, and *how* and *why* we do so.

We need to consider questions such as whether our schools are currently organized based on a Darwinian idea of the survival of the fittest. Do they have rigid ability grouping that dooms some students while overly benefiting others, often for their entire academic lives? How do schools organize learning, and are these organizational decisions based on the assumption that all learning can take place in 50-minute time blocks? Is the funding that schools receive commensurate with the needs of students? Do students' race and social class too often predict the quality of the education they receive? Do disciplinary policies unfairly favor some students over others? Are tests accurate indicators of learning, or do they sometimes serve simply as convenient barriers to higher education and enhanced life options? Are some students considered to have exceptional gene pools and others to be culturally deprived? Are poverty and speaking a native language other than English thought to be insurmountable obstacles to high levels of learning?

I have taught students and teachers for many years, and in that time I have given a great deal of thought to what schools should be about. I have come to the conclusion that no program, set of guidelines, instructional strategies, curriculum, or even educational philosophy is worthwhile unless it takes into account two primary goals:

- to provide all students of all backgrounds the opportunity to learn through an equitable and high quality education;
- to help students become critical and productive members of our democratic society.

In the remainder of this essay, I address five specific implications that derive from these goals.

In order to provide all students with an equal and high quality education, we need to begin with the belief that all students are capable and worthy of learning to high levels of achievement.

Many young people cope on a daily basis with complex and pressing institutionalized barriers to an excellent education and a good quality of life. These include poverty, violence, racism, abuse, families in stress, and lack of health care and proper housing, among others. In addition, increasing numbers of young people live in female-headed households, have limited proficiency in English, and arrive at the schoolhouse door without basic academic skills. It is the responsibility of schools to teach them all because in our society schools have historically been charged with providing an equal education to *all* students, not just to those who happen to be middle-class and English-speaking, and who live with two parents. In the current mean-spirited discourse surrounding public education, the conditions in which poor students come to school often become a rationale for not having high expectations of them. In too many cases, rather than provide those students who most need it with a rigorous and exciting curriculum, they are instead tested yearly to see how well they have learned the conventions of test taking and the basic structure of the five-paragraph essay. These may be necessary skills for them to learn, but they are certainly not enough.

What often stands in the way of learning are the attitudes concerning what children living in difficult conditions are capable of doing: If they do not speak English, it's as if they do not speak at all; if they live in poverty, they are treated as if their minds are also impoverished; and the darker their skin, the lower their intelligence is thought to be. Numerous research studies, on the other hand, have reaffirmed that what teachers know and do, and what they believe their students are capable of learning, make a difference (Haberman, 1995; National Commission on Teaching and America's Future, 1996; Darling-Hammond & Falk, 1997). The unavoidable conclusion is that before we attempt to fix the curriculum content or the instructional strategies in our schools, we must first fix our society's expectations of students, particularly those who differ from the majority in terms of race, language, and culture, and those who live in poverty.

In order to expand their horizons, the education of young people must begin where they are, using their knowledge, experiences, cultures, and languages as the basis for their learning.

This implication is directly related to the first because it begins with the assumption that youngsters, particularly those who come from economically disadvantaged families, are not simply deficient. All children bring a set of talents to the educational enterprise, and these need to be accepted as a basis for further learning. For instance, instead of viewing students for whom English is a second language as "non-English speakers," why not consider them fluent speakers of another language? We can say the same about cultural and experiential differences, which have often been considered a deprivation rather than a resource that can be affirmed in the school. An alternative approach is to accept student differences as valid and valuable, and build on them. In fact, a number of studies have demonstrated that students who are encouraged to retain close ties to their ethnic cultures while adapting to mainstream U.S. culture are not only more academically successful but also more emotionally secure (for a review of these studies, see Portes & Rumbaut, 2006).

Starting with their experiences, however, does not mean that we stop there. It is the responsibility of public schools to broaden everybody's horizons because students of all backgrounds need to understand a range of perspectives, not only their own limited experiences. This leads to the next implication.

Students need to be prepared with the skills and attitudes necessary to live, work, and interact with others in an increasingly diverse, complex, and interdependent world.

Reading, writing, mathematics, and technological literacy need to be accompanied by *multicultural literacy* if young people are to learn how to live and work in a world characterized by ever-increasing diversity and global interconnectedness. Given the society young people will enter when they leave school, we do them a great disservice if we continue to prepare them for a monocultural, monolingual world that never existed in the first place and is more difficult every day to reconcile with reality.

Multicultural literacy is not about what critics have called "ethnic cheerleading." In fact, one could make the case that ethnic cheerleading is precisely what our monocultural curriculum has always been, since it has perpetuated the myth that one rather homogeneous group of people has made all the difference in our country and the world. I am also not referring to a superficial "Holidays and Heroes" (Lee et al., 1998) multiculturalism that focuses only on Chinese New Year or Chanukah. What I am suggesting is that all curricula, from science to English and from kindergarten through college, need to be more reflective and respectful of the diversity in which we live, and also need to more directly confront the racism and other institutional barriers that have gotten in the way of true equality. Giving young people an incomplete picture of reality results in some of them believing they are superior because their people have been the major movers and shakers, while others believe themselves inferior because they have learned that their people have done nothing of significance. Neither of these perceptions is accurate. Continuing to present a biased curriculum will perpetuate these perceptions even further.

Another essential skill that students need is how to work collaboratively. Schools need to develop a climate in which collaborative work is expected and rewarded. This skill is necessary for the workplace of the twenty-first century, but even more for simply living in a world that is shrinking every day. Many public schools have yet to realize these changes; they are still largely based on a philosophy of individualism and competition and, as a result, they provide unrealistic preparation for the future that young people will be facing.

Students need to be provided with an apprenticeship in democracy *if they are to become critical and productive citizens.*

We pride ourselves on living in a democracy, yet in school young people are given few experiences to prepare for it. Policies and practices such as rigid ability grouping, inequitable testing, sterile curriculum, and unimaginative pedagogical strategies contradict this goal. In many schools, we find democratic practices only in textbooks, and these are usually confined to idealistic discussions of the American Revolution. Most students have little opportunity to practice day-to-day democracy with all its messiness and conflicts. Even student involvement in senates and councils often becomes no more than popularity contests where students have little power over the quality of school life. In the curriculum itself, scant attention is paid to the undemocratic, exclusionary, and even ugly side of our history that is just as much a part of our collective heritage as is the democratic, inclusive, and noble side. As a result, not only is the process of democracy missing, but so too is the critical content of democracy that would expose young people to its contradictory dimensions. If schools are to provide students with an apprenticeship for the possibility of participation in democracy, both the process and the content are needed.

Relationships among teachers and their students are the most important ingredient in successful schools.

A great deal of research has concluded that relationships and caring are at the heart of teaching and learning (Noddings, 1992; Cummins, 2000; Nieto, 2003; Valenzuela, 1999). Such studies have consistently found that a significant factor that prevents students from dropping out is an adult in the school who knows and cares for them (Thiessen & Cook-Sather, 2008; for other examples, see case studies and snapshots in Nieto & Bode, 2008). Those who care about children— and schools and teachers should be at the forefront of this group—need to base every educational decision on one simple question: Is it good for the children?

In these times it is hard to keep social justice front and center on our educational agenda. But I suggest that rather than simply celebrating democracy with flag-waving and other manifestations of patriotic fervor, as those with a more conservative agenda might propose, we need to re-commit ourselves to the goals of democracy. We can best do this by teaching our students well.

Teaching our children well means teaching them the basics: how to read, write, and do math; how to use the computer and play instruments and create art; how to appreciate poetry and how to approach history; and, yes, even how to do well on tests (as long as this does not become our sole or overarching focus, as it has in far too many school systems). Teaching our children well means teaching them not only the glorious and heroic parts of U.S. history, but the complicated, unfair and disturbing parts of it as well. If we do not do this, how will they ever learn? Unless we do this, we end up with young people who get to college—those fortunate enough to even get there—uninformed of their history: shocked at the internment of U.S. citizens of Japanese ancestry during World War II; distraught at the realities of chattel slavery; incensed at the lynchings they never heard about, and the fact that they were carried out not only against Americans of African descent, also against those of Italian and Jewish descent; stunned when they first hear of U.S. imperialism; taken aback when they learn that Puerto Rico, in terms of its rights and privileges, is little more than a colony of the United States; troubled when they learn of the ravages of racism in our history, and the fact that *it still exists*. All of this is news to many of them. To address these omissions, the schools' curriculum needs to become more inclusive.

But teaching our children well also means affirming and honoring who they are, and believing that they are capable of doing great things. It means teaching them to become moral human beings, to care for others, the environment, and the earth, to be generous, to think beyond their own limited self-interests, and to become involved in civic life. It means teaching them to serve their communities and be generous with their time, energy, and resources. It means teaching them that living in a democracy is both hard work and a privilege that can be easily squandered. In the final analysis, it means discarding the functional view of education with a more visionary and utopian one. This, I believe, is the true purpose of schools.

References

Comenius, J. A. (1968). *The great didactic*, quoted in *The learning society*. New York: Mentor.

Cummins, J. (2000). *Language, power, and pedagogy: Bilingual children in the crossfire*. Clevedon, England: Multilingual Matters.

Darling-Hammond, L. & Falk, B. (1997). Using standards and assessments to support student learning. *Phi Delta Kappan, 79* (3), 190–199.

Freire, P. (1970). *Pedagogy of the oppressed*. New York: Seabury Press.

Haberman, M. (1995). Selecting "star" teachers for children and youth in urban poverty. *Phi Delta Kappan, 76* (10), 777–781.

Hirsch, E. D. (1987). *Cultural literacy: What every American needs to know*. Boston: Houghton Mifflin.

Lee, E., Menkart, D., Okazawa-Rey, M. (1998). *Beyond heroes and holidays: A practical guide to K-12 anti-racist, multicultural education and staff development*. Washington, DC: Teaching for Change.

Mann, H. (1968). Twelfth annual report to the Massachusetts State Board of Education, 1848. In M. Mann (Ed.), *Life and works of Horace Mann* (v. 3, p. 669). Boston: Walker, Fuller.

Meier, D. (1995). *The power of their ideas: Lessons from a small school in Harlem*. Boston: Beacon Press.

National Commission on Teaching and America's Future (1996). *What matters most: Teaching for America's future*. New York: Author.

Nieto, S. (2003). *What keeps teachers going?* New York: Teachers College Press.

Nieto, S. & Bode, P. (2008). *Affirming diversity: The sociopolitical context of multicultural education*. Boston: Allyn & Bacon.

Noddings, N. (1992). *The challenge to care in schools: An alternative approach to education*. New York: Teachers College Press.

Portes, A. & Rumbaut, R. G. (2006). *Immigrant America: A portrait*, 3rd ed. Berkeley: University of California Press.

Provenzo, E. F., Jr. (2005). *Critical literacy: What every American ought to know*. Boulder, CO: Paradigm Press.

Thiessen, D. & Cook-Sather, A. (2007). *International handbook of student experience in elementary and secondary school*. Dordrecht, The Netherlands: Springer.

Valenzuela, A. (1999). *Subtractive schooling: U.S.-Mexican youth and the politics of caring*. New York: State University of New York Press.

Critical Questions

1   Horace Mann, the first Commissioner of Education in Massachusetts in the mid-nineteenth century, was the first to articulate that the "common school" (what we now refer to as public schools) could be "the great equalizer." In the United States, this was a time of dramatically increasing immigration and diversity, as well as great social strife and inequality. Do you believe it would have been possible for schools to be the great equalizer then? What about now? Why or why not? What are some of the contextual differences between then and now?

2   Write down your definition of the purpose of schools. Did your ideas change after reading this chapter?

3   In small groups, discuss each of your definitions from Question 2. Do they differ? If so, how? Try to come up with a definition of the purpose of schools with which you can all agree.

4   What would a school that exemplified this definition of the purpose of schooling look like? How would it differ from the school(s) in which you currently work? What ideas from this vision can you take back to your current school(s)? How easy or difficult might it be to put these ideas into practice?

5   Attend a meeting of your local school board. List the topics that they spend time on. Are they related to any of the issues brought up in this essay? How might these agendas be changed?

Activity for Your Classroom

Engage your students in a conversation about their ideal school. What would it look like? Why? How would it differ from the way it is now? Ask students to prioritize what they would want to see in their ideal classroom and then, working in groups, ask them to think of ways to make some of the changes they envision. This can become a long-term project with significant implications for changing your classroom and even some of the policies and practices in the school and beyond. Some helpful resources for you and the students might be:

Ayers, W., Ladson-Billings, G., Michie, G., & Noguera, P. A. (Eds.). (2008). *City kids, city schools: More reports from the front row*. New York: The New Press.

Hoose, P. (1993). *It's our world, too! Stories of young people who are making a difference.* Boston: Little, Brown, and Company.

Shultz, J. & Cook-Sather, A. (2001). *In our own words: Students' perspectives on school.* Lanham, MD: Rowman & Littlefield Publishers, Inc.

Community-Based Activity and Advocacy

Develop a survey to use with residents in your community concerning the purpose of public schools. You may want to do this activity with a colleague or group of colleagues. Share the results with your school community.

Supplementary Resources for Further Reflection and Study

Coulter, D. L., Wiens, J. R., & Fenstemacher, G. D. (Eds.). (2008). *Why do we educate? Renewing the conversation,* 107th Yearbook of the National Society for the Study of Education, v. 1. Malden, MA: Blackwell Publishing.

An anthology of articles by numerous well-known educators of various ideological stripes, this volume asks readers to consider the fundamental reasons for public education in democratic societies. In doing so, they shine a spotlight on issues as diverse as education for global citizenship, the role of the arts and sciences in education, and the need for imagination in creating more equitable schools.

Forum for Education and Democracy (2008, April). *Democracy at risk: The need for a new federal policy in education.* Washington, DC: Author.

The Forum for Education and Democracy is an education think tank whose goal is to promote the renewal of the nation's commitment to strong public schools. Included among their members are leading educators, administrators, and policymakers across the country. In this report, they review the scant progress that has been made since *A Nation at Risk* was first published in 1983, and they challenge the nation to pay off the "education debts" by funding high-quality education for all students, investing in a new "Marshall Plan" for teachers and school leaders, supporting consistent educational research and innovation, and engaging and educating local communities about the significance of public education.

Meier, D. & Wood, G. (2004). *Many children left behind: How the No Child Left Behind Act is damaging our children and our schools.* Boston: Beacon Press.

Deborah Meier and George Wood, seasoned and highly respected educators of public schools, take on the NCLB law and maintain that the effects of the law are hurting, rather than helping, the children who most need support in our nation's schools. They also present evidence concerning the continuing inequality of opportunity for students living in poverty.

Nieto, S. (2005). *Why we teach.* New York: Teachers College Press.

This collection of 21 essays by teachers of all grade levels and subject areas who work with students of diverse backgrounds explores their motivations for teaching and the hopes and values that keep them in the classroom.

2   The Limitations of Labels

How do labels limit our understanding and sensitivity? In the brief piece below, I reflect on how labels are frequently used as a shortcut to define people. In the process, they also limit how we perceive people.

It was my first year of teaching. I was a 6th-, 7th-, and 8th-grade teacher of reading, Spanish, and French in Ocean-Hill/Brownsville in Brooklyn, a community of African Americans and Puerto Ricans that had seen more than its fair share of educational neglect. I was the first Puerto Rican teacher in the school in anyone's memory. I was also the "NE" teacher, so named because I taught the "NE" (non-English) students. Although I was perfectly fluent in English (and in Spanish), and I had a newly minted master's degree in literature, I was labeled right along with my students, and people didn't expect much from either of us. I often think of the beginning of my teaching career because it reminds me of the damaging effect of labels on all people, children or adults. But children are not "NE," or "ELLs," or "SPED," or "at risk," or "the bilinguals," or "AFDC," or "culturally deprived," or any other label that may be in vogue at the moment. They are children, and they each embody both wonderful individuality and the cultural imprint of their families and communities. They come to us with language, ideas, experiences, and other resources that can be used in the service of their education. Being multicultural means accepting and welcoming these differences—linguistic, cultural, racial, experiential, and others—and leaving the labels behind.

Critical Questions

1   Think about the labels you may unconsciously use on a daily basis in relation to both education and to life in general. What are they? What connotations do they embody? If the connotations are negative, what suitable alternatives are available? Come up with a list of suggestions.

2   In the brief piece above, I suggest that "being multicultural means accepting and welcoming" differences. How might you do this in your classroom? Come up with some specific examples.

Activity for Your Classroom

Ask students to bring in a "cultural bag" with concrete objects that describe their identities. These can include photographs, mementos, cards, gifts, and other artifacts that are important to them, and they can reflect not only ethnic and racial backgrounds but also family traditions, hobbies, and other interests. It is helpful for you to model what you mean, especially if you teach young children, by bringing in your own cultural bag. Asking for the help and participation of families is also a good idea. You may want to invite families to the classroom on the day that students bring in their cultural bags. On the assigned day, ask each student to show and describe the contents of their bag. I have seen this activity work for classrooms from early elementary through graduate school, but you will have to make accommodations for differences in your students' experiences and knowledge.

Community-Based Activity and Advocacy

Along with a number of your colleagues, come up with a list of suitable terms for negative labels currently used in your school. (For example, rather than "crack babies," which places the onus on the child, what about "babies born addicted to crack?") Even if the terms are not negative, they may be exclusionary. For instance, the terms "parents" and "mother and father" may unintentionally exclude grandparents or other relatives raising children, as well as foster families and gay- and lesbian-headed families. Ask your principal to eliminate the negative terms from the common discourse of the school by revising school forms and instead use the terms you suggest.

Supplementary Resources for Further Reflection and Study

Stances on multilingual and multicultural education. *Language Arts, 84* (2), 171.
  A series of brief commentaries (including the one you have just read) concerning various viewpoints on linguistic and cultural diversity in the classroom.

Herbst, P. H. (1997). *The color of words.* Yarmouth, ME: Intercultural Press.
  A useful dictionary on the evolution of ethnic and racial terms and the biases they contain.

Nieto, S. & Bode, P. (2008). *Affirming diversity: The sociopolitical context of multicultural education,* 5th ed. Boston: Allyn & Bacon.
  Chapter 2 ("About Terminology") presents a thorough discussion on making choices about what terms to use to describe people.

3 Understanding Multicultural Education in a Sociopolitical Context

(with Patty Bode)

Nothing occurs in a vacuum, unfettered by its context. This is especially true of education, which is always influenced by the social, political, historic, and economic context in which it takes place. In this chapter, my co-author Patty Bode and I define "the sociopolitical context of multicultural education" by considering some of the key assumptions underlying multicultural education. For example, although multicultural education began as a result of the Civil Rights Movement with a primary focus on equal education for African American students, it has grown to encompass a broader range of issues including gender, language, social class, ability, and sexual orientation, among others.

In this chapter, we also address such matters as school-level policies and practices, and how they influence the quality of education that students receive. We define key terms in education such as "equal educational opportunity," "social justice," and "achievement gap." These terms are ubiquitous in education but rarely defined in any depth. Finally, we present a demographic portrait of students in U.S. schools to underscore the need for education that affirms the realities and identities of all our students.

Decisions made about education are often viewed as if they were politically neutral. Yet, as we hope to make clear in this chapter and throughout the text, such decisions are never politically neutral. Rather, they are tied to the social, political, and economic structures that frame and define our society. The *sociopolitical context* of society includes laws, regulations, policies, practices, traditions, and ideologies.

To put it another way, multicultural education, or any kind of education for that matter, cannot be understood in a vacuum. Yet in many schools, multicultural education is approached as if it is divorced from the policies and practices of schools and from the structures and ideologies of society. This kind of thinking results in a singular focus on cultural artifacts, such as food and dress, or on ethnic celebrations. It can become "fairyland" multicultural education, disassociated from the lives of teachers, students, and communities. This is multicultural education *without* a sociopolitical context. Here, however, we are interested in how the sociopolitical context of the United States, and indeed of our global society, shapes schools and therefore also shapes the experiences of the children and adults who inhabit schools.

Assumptions Underlying This Chapter

It is important that we begin by clarifying a number of assumptions underlying the concepts described in this chapter.

Identity, Difference, Power, and Privilege Are All Connected

Race, ethnicity, social class, language use, gender, sexual orientation, religion, ability, and other social and human differences are a major aspect of the sociopolitical context that we will address in this book—that is, one's identity frames (although it does not necessarily *determine*) how one experiences the world. Identities always carry some baggage; they are perceived in particular ways by a society and by individuals within that society. An accent, for instance, may invoke positive or negative images, depending on one's social class, race, country of origin, and variety of language. As a consequence, in the context of U.S. society, someone who is French and speaks with a Parisian accent, for example, is generally viewed more positively than someone from Senegal who also speaks French.

At the same time, multicultural education does not simply involve the affirmation of language and culture. Multicultural education confronts not only issues of difference but also issues of power and privilege in society. This means challenging racism and other biases as well as the inequitable structures, policies, and practices of schools and, ultimately, of society itself. Affirming language and culture can help students become successful and well-adjusted learners, but unless language and cultural issues are viewed critically through the lens of equity and social justice, they are unlikely to have a lasting impact in promoting real change.

Educational failure is an issue too complex and knotty to be "fixed" by any single program or approach. Viewing multicultural education per se as "the answer" to school failure is simplistic because other important social and educational issues that affect the lives of students are thereby ignored. Multicultural education does not exist in a vacuum but must be understood in its larger personal, social, historical, and political context. However, if it is broadly conceptualized and implemented, multicultural education can have a substantive, positive impact on the education of most students. To be effective, multicultural education needs to move beyond diversity as a passing fad. It needs to take into account our history of immigration as well as the social, political, and economic inequality and exclusion that have characterized our past and present, particularly our educational history. These issues are too often ignored in superficial approaches to multicultural education.

Multicultural Education Is Inclusive of Many Differences

Another key issue in multicultural education is the groups that are included. Our framework and approach to multicultural education are broadly inclusive: They are based on the belief that multicultural education is for *everyone* regardless of ethnicity, race, language, social class, religion, gender, sexual orientation, ability, or other differences. One book, however, cannot possibly give all of these topics the central importance they deserve. We use race, ethnicity, and language as the major lenses to view and understand multicultural education. While we address other differences in one way or another, we give special emphasis to these. Both multicultural and bilingual education were direct outgrowths of the Civil Rights Movement, and they developed in response to racism, ethnocentrism, and language discrimination in education. These inequities continue to exist, especially for American Indian, Latino, and African American youngsters, and they are central to this book's perspective and approach.

Nevertheless, we believe that multicultural education includes everyone, and we have made an attempt in this text to be inclusive of many differences. Having a broad definition of multicultural education raises another dilemma. One reason that multicultural education is such a challenging topic for some educators is that they have a hard time facing and discussing racism. For example, whenever we bring up racism with a group of predominantly White teachers, we find that too often they want to move on immediately to, say, sexism or classism without spending much time on racism. Sexism and classism are certainly worthy of study and attention—in fact, they must be part of a multicultural agenda—but the discomfort of many White teachers to talk about racism is very evident. Racism is an excruciatingly difficult issue for many people. Given our nation's history of exclusion and discrimination, this is not surprising, but it is only through a thorough exploration of discrimination based on race that we can understand the genesis as well as the rationale for a more inclusive framework for multicultural education that includes language, social class, sexual orientation, gender, ethnicity, religion, and other differences.

Teachers Are Not the Villains

Another belief that informs our perspective and approach is that teachers cannot be singled out as the villains responsible for students' failure. Although some teachers bear responsibility for having low expectations because they are racist and elitist in their interactions with students and parents and thus provide educational environments that discourage many students from learning, most do not do this consciously. Most teachers are sincerely concerned about their students and want very much to provide them with the best education possible. Nonetheless, because of their own limited experiences and education, they may know very little about the students they teach. As a result, their beliefs about students of diverse backgrounds may be based on spurious assumptions and stereotypes. These things are true of all teachers, not just White teachers. In fact, a teacher's being from a non-White ethnic group or background does not guarantee that he or she will be effective with students of diverse backgrounds or even with students of his or her own background. Furthermore, teachers are often at the mercy of decisions made by others far removed from the classroom; they generally have little involvement in developing the policies and practices of their schools and frequently do not even question them.

Teachers also are the products of educational systems that have a history of racism, exclusion, and debilitating pedagogy. As a consequence, their practices may reflect their experiences, and they may unwittingly perpetuate policies and approaches that are harmful to many of their students. We cannot separate schools from the communities they serve or from the context of society in general. Oppressive forces that limit opportunities in the schools reflect such forces in the society at large. Our purpose is not to point a finger, but to provide a forum for reflection and discussion so that teachers take responsibility for their own actions, challenge the actions of schools and society that affect their students' education, and help bring about positive change.

Quality Public Education Is a Cause Worth Fighting For

Another of our key assumptions is that public education is worth defending and fighting for. In spite of all its shortcomings, and although it has never lived up to its potential, public education remains a noble ideal because it is one of the few institutions that at least articulates the common good, if not always achieves it. Public education remains the last and best hope for many young people for a better life. Yet, during an era characterized by rigid standardization and restructuring, the public schools have often been a target of scorn and disrespect in the press and among politicians. In spite of this, the public still believes in the promise of public education. A study published by the Public Education Network and *Education Week* reported that Americans are at least five times more likely to cite public schools (rather than places of worship, hospitals, or libraries) as the most important institutions in their communities. Moreover, more than 90 percent of the people polled maintained that a quality public education is every child's birthright, and the great majority claimed that education is their greatest priority.[1] Given this unambiguous and overwhelming support for public education, it is clear that public schools can provide all children with a good education and it is within the ability of teachers, administrators, and the public at large to ensure that they do so.

Defining the Sociopolitical Context of Multicultural Education

Now that we have explained some of our assumptions, we want to define what we mean by the *sociopolitical context of education*. As you will see in the remainder of this chapter, understanding this term is crucial to a critical view of multicultural education. A significant aspect of the sociopolitical context concerns the unexamined ideologies and myths that shape commonly accepted ideas and values in a society. The chapter provides a number of examples of how unexamined ideologies and myths contribute to the sociopolitical context.

Myths About Immigration and Difference

Because immigration is one of today's most contentious issues, it offers a particularly vivid example of the sociopolitical context. Immigration is no longer a romantic phenomenon of the past: Current headlines and other media reports scream about "illegal aliens," about electric fences along the U.S.–Mexico border, and about the self-appointed vigilante Minutemen adamant on guarding our borders, albeit illegally. The United States is not just a nation of past immigrants, often romantically portrayed, but also a nation of new immigrants who daily disembark on our shores, cross our borders, or fly into our metropolitan areas. For the most part, new immigrants, particularly those from Latin America, Asia, and Africa, are neither warmly welcomed nor given easy access to the resources in the United States. While we define ourselves as "a nation of immigrants," there is waning support for new immigrants.

Myths about U.S. immigration die hard. Even the widely accepted fact that immigrants came to North America and never returned to their countries of origin is not entirely true. According to Irving Howe, one-third of European immigrants who came to the United States between 1908 and 1924 eventually made their way back home, thus shattering a popular myth.[2] In addition, and in spite of conventional wisdom to the contrary, most European immigrants did *not* succeed academically. In his research, Richard Rothstein found that during the immigration period from 1880 to 1915, few Americans succeeded in school, least of all immigrants; immigrants of all backgrounds did poorly. Instead, it was the children and grandchildren of European immigrants who fared well in school, but the myth that first-generation immigrants "made it," at least in terms of academics, is firmly established in the public psyche. Because schools have traditionally perceived their role as that of an assimilating agent, the isolation, rejection, and failure that have frequently accompanied immigration have simply been left at the schoolhouse door.

U.S. history is also steeped in slavery and conquest. Millions of descendants of Africans, American Indians, Mexicans, Puerto Ricans, and others colonized within and beyond U.S. borders have experienced political and economic oppression and, in schools, disparagement of their native cultures and languages. But the history of racism and exploitation experienced by so many of our people, including their children, is rarely taught. Instead, conventional curricula and pedagogy have been based on the myth of a painless and smooth assimilation of immigrants.

Immigration and colonization experiences are a significant point of departure for our journey into multicultural education. This journey needs to begin with teachers, who themselves are frequently unaware of or uncomfortable with their own ethnicity. By reconnecting with their own backgrounds and with the suffering as well as the triumphs of their families, teachers can lay the groundwork for students to reclaim their histories and voices. This book invites you to begin the journey.

Educational Structures

The ideologies underlying educational structures exemplify how the sociopolitical context is operational at the school level. Schools' and the larger society's assumptions about people form a belief system that helps create and perpetuate structures that reproduce those assumptions. For example, if we believe that intelligence is primarily inherited, we will design schools that support this belief. On the other hand, if we believe that intelligence is largely created by particular social and economic conditions, our schools will look quite different. Likewise, if we believe that some cultures are inherently superior to others, our schools will replicate the cultural values that are assumed to be superior while dismissing others.

At a personal level, we take in the ideologies and beliefs in our society and we act on them *whether we actively believe them or not.* In the case of the ideology of racism, for example, Beverly Daniel Tatum has aptly described it as "smog in the air."

> Sometimes it is so thick it is visible, other times it is less apparent, but always, day in and day out, we are breathing it in. None of us would introduce ourselves as "smog-breathers" (and most of us don't want to be described as prejudiced), but if we live in a smoggy place, how can we avoid breathing the air?[3]

The "smog" is part of the sociopolitical context in which we live and in which schools exist. This context includes not only racism but also other biases based on human and social differences, including social class, language, sexual orientation, gender, and other factors. Pretending that the smog doesn't exist, or that it doesn't influence us, is to negate reality. A good example can be found in school funding: In their yearly report on funding of public schools, the Education Trust has consistently shown that low-income students and students of color are badly shortchanged by most states, proving once again that race and social class still matter a great deal in our nation. In their 2005 report, the Trust found that in the United States, as a whole, we spend $900 a year *less* on each student in public school districts with the largest number of poor students.[4] In another investigation, the *Christian Science Monitor* found that the difference in annual spending between the wealthiest and the poorest school districts has grown to a staggering $19,361 per student.[5] Surely, no one can pretend that this difference does not matter.

School-Level Policies and Practices

School funding is generally a state- and district-level issue. How does the sociopolitical context affect policies and practices at the school level? Let's take a very concrete example: Schools that enforce an "English-only" policy are, willingly or not, sending students a message about the status and importance of languages other than English. In some of these schools, students are forbidden to speak their native language not only in classrooms, but even in halls, the cafeteria, and the playground. To students who speak a language other than English, the message is clear: Your language is not welcome here; it is less important than English. While the policy may have been well intentioned and created out of a sincere effort to help students learn English, the result is deprecation of students' identities, intentional or not. In some instances, these kinds of policies are not innocent at all, but instead reflect a xenophobic reaction to hearing languages other than English in our midst. In either case, the result is negative and an example of how ideologies help create structures that benefit some students over others.

Another obvious example is the curriculum: If the content of school knowledge excludes the history, art, culture, and ways of knowing of entire groups of people, these groups themselves are dismissed as having little significance in creating history, art, culture, and so on. The sociopolitical context also undergirds other school policies and practices, including pedagogy, ability grouping, testing, parent outreach, disciplinary policies, and the hiring of teachers and other school personnel.

To correct the educational short-changing of diverse student populations, the curriculum and pedagogy must be changed in individual classrooms. But on a broader level, changes must go beyond the classroom: Schools' policies and practices and the societal ideologies that support them must also be confronted and transformed. That is, we need to create not only *affirming classrooms* but also an *affirming society* in which racism, sexism, social class discrimination, heterosexism, and other biases are no longer acceptable. This is a tall order, but if multicultural education is to make a real difference, working to change society to be more socially equitable and just must go hand-in-hand with changes in curricula and classroom practices.

Goals of Multicultural Education

Depending on one's conceptualization of multicultural education, different goals may be emphasized. In this book, we want to make clear from the outset how we define the goals of multicultural education. The major premise of this book is the following: *No educational philosophy or program is worthwhile unless it focuses on three primary concerns*:

- Tackling inequality and promoting access to an equal education.
- Raising the achievement of all students and providing them with an equitable and high-quality education.
- Giving students an apprenticeship in the opportunity to become critical and productive members of a democratic society.

We believe that multicultural education must *confront inequality and stratification in schools and in society.* Helping students get along, teaching them to feel better about themselves, and "sensitizing" them to one another are worthy goals of good educational practice, including multicultural education. But if multicultural education does not tackle the far more thorny questions of stratification and inequity, and if viewed in isolation from the reality of students' lives, these goals can turn into superficial strategies that only scratch the surface of educational failure. Simply wanting our students to get along with and be respectful of one another makes little difference in the options they will have as a result of their schooling. Students' lives are inexorably affected by economic, social, and political conditions in schools and society—that is, by the sociopolitical context in which they live and learn—and this means that we need to consider these conditions in our conceptualization and implementation of multicultural education.

Learning is an equally central goal of multicultural education. Unless learning is at the very core of a multicultural perspective, having "feel-good" assemblies or self-concept-building classroom activities will do nothing to create equitable school environments for students. Considering the vastly unequal learning outcomes among students of different backgrounds (see the subsequent discussion of the "achievement gap" in this chapter), it is absolutely essential that learning be placed at the center of multicultural education. Otherwise, too many young people will continue to face harrowing life choices because they are not receiving a high-quality, rigorous education.

Learning to take tests or getting into a good university cannot be the be-all and end-all of an excellent education. A third and equally crucial goal of multicultural education is to *promote democracy by preparing students to contribute to the general well-being of society, not only to their own self-interests.* Multicultural educator Will Kymlicka has expressed this sentiment in the following way: "We need to continually remind ourselves that multiculturalism is not just about expanding individual horizons, or increasing personal intercultural skills, but is part of a larger project of justice and equality."[6]

Defining Key Terms in Multicultural Education

We now turn to some central definitions that help explain our approach.

Equal Education and Equitable Education: What's the Difference?

Two terms often associated with multicultural education are *equality* and *equity*, which are sometimes erroneously used interchangeably. Both equal education and educational equity are fundamental to multicultural education, yet they are quite different. As educator Enid Lee has explained, "Equity is the process; equality is the result."[7] That is, *equal education* may mean simply providing the same resources and opportunities for all students. While this alone would afford a better education for a wider range of students than is currently the case, it is not enough. Achieving educational equality involves providing an *equitable education. Equity* goes beyond equality: It means that all students must be given the *real possibility of an equality of outcomes.* A high-quality education is impossible without a focus on equity. Robert Moses, who began the highly successful Algebra Project, which promotes high-level math courses for Urban Black and Latino middle school and high school students, has gone so far as to suggest that quality education for all students is a civil rights issue.[8]

Social Justice

Frequently invoked but rarely defined, *social justice* is another term associated with an equitable education. In this book, we define it as *a philosophy, an approach, and actions that embody treating all people with fairness, respect, dignity, and generosity*. On a societal scale, this means affording each person the real—not simply a stated or codified—opportunity to achieve their potential by giving them access to the goods, services, and social and cultural capital of a society, while also affirming the culture and talents of each individual and the group or groups with which they identify.

In terms of education, in particular, social justice is not just about "being nice" to students, or about giving them a pat on the back. Social justice in education includes four components. First, it challenges, confronts, and disrupts misconceptions, untruths, and stereotypes that lead to structural inequality and discrimination based on race, social class, gender, and other social and human differences. This means that teachers with a social justice perspective consciously include topics that focus on inequality in the curriculum, and they encourage their students to work for equality and fairness both in and out of the classroom.

Second, a social justice perspective means providing all students with the resources necessary to learn to their full potential. This includes *material resources* such as books, curriculum, financial support, and so on. Equally vital are *emotional resources* such as a belief in all students' ability and worth; care for them as individuals and learners; high expectations and rigorous demands of them; and the necessary social and cultural capital to negotiate the world. These are not just responsibilities of individual teachers and schools, however. Beyond the classroom level, achieving social justice requires reforming school policies and practices so that all students are provided an equal chance to learn. This entails critically evaluating policies such as high-stakes testing, tracking, student retention, segregation, and parent and family outreach, among others.

Social justice in education is not just about *giving* students resources, however. A third component of a social justice perspective is *drawing on* the talents and strengths that students bring to their education. This requires a rejection of the deficit perspective that has characterized much of the education of marginalized students, to a shift that views all students—not just those from privileged backgrounds—as having resources that can be a foundation for their learning. These resources include their languages, cultures, and experiences.

A fourth essential component of social justice is creating a learning environment that promotes critical thinking and supports agency for social change. Creating such environments can provide students with an apprenticeship in democracy, a vital part of preparing them for the future. Much more will be said throughout the text about how to go about creating such a learning environment.

The "Achievement Gap"

Another term that needs defining is *achievement gap*. This term has evolved over the past couple of decades to describe the circumstances in which some students, primarily those from racially, culturally, and linguistically marginalized and poor families, achieve less than other students. Although research has largely focused on Black and White students, the "achievement gap" is also evident among students of other ethnic and racial backgrounds.[9]

There is no denying that the "achievement gap" is real: In 2006, *Quality Counts*, the tenth annual report on the results of standards-based education, examined scores on the National Assessment of Educational Progress (NAEP) from 1992 through 2005. The report concluded that although student achievement in general had improved, the gap between African American and Hispanic students compared to White students remains very large. Specifically, the gap is the equivalent of two grade levels or more, almost what it was in 1992. For example, while 41 percent of Whites are reading at grade level, only 15 percent of Hispanics and 13 percent of African Americans are at grade level. The gap worsens through the years: Black and Hispanic 12th graders perform at the same level in reading and math as White eighth graders.[10] The gap is not only deplorable but is also an indictment of our public education system.

However, in spite of the fact that the "achievement gap" is a reality, sometimes this term is a misnomer because it places undue responsibility on students alone. As a result, we believe that what has become known as the *achievement gap* can also appropriately be called the *resource gap* or the *expectations gap* because student achievement does not come out of the blue but is influenced by many other factors—that is, student achievement is related directly to the conditions and contexts in which students learn. For instance, because some schools are well endowed in terms of materials and resources, the students in these schools have multiple means to help them learn. On the other hand, schools that serve students living in poverty, which tend to have fewer resources, provide fewer opportunities for robust student learning.

Of course, material resources alone are not the answer to the problem of achievement. The expectations that teachers and schools have of students are also important, and these unfortunately are sometimes related to students' racial and social class backgrounds. Educator Mano Singham has cited research that concludes that the impact of teacher expectations is *three times greater* for Black and Latino students than for White students.[11] This too is part of the sociopolitical context of the "achievement gap."

The problem with the term "achievement gap" is that it suggests that students alone are responsible for their learning, as if school and societal conditions and contexts did not exist. The result is that the problem is defined as a "minority" problem rather than as a problem of unequal schooling. For all these reasons, we use the term *achievement gap* with caution and always in quotation marks.

At the same time, the research on the "achievement gap" cannot be ignored, because it has uncovered salient differences in the learning outcomes for students of various backgrounds. According to Joseph D'Amico, the two major causes of the "achievement gap" are *sociocultural and school-related factors*. Sociocultural factors include poverty, ethnicity, low level of parental education, weak family-support systems, and students' reactions to discrimination and stereotyping.[12] One school-related factor is low expectations, particularly in schools that serve students who are both economically disadvantaged and from ethnic and racial minority backgrounds. A common response among educators and the public has been to focus on the first set of factors (that is, on sociocultural "problems" and "deficits") more than on school-related factors. Turning this thinking around would be a better policy because educators can do little to change the life circumstances of students but can do a great deal to change the context of schools.

For example, according to D'Amico, some schools *are* successful with students of color, students living in poverty, and students who live in difficult circumstances. What makes the difference? Schools that have narrowed the "achievement gap" are characterized by well-trained and motivated teachers who are teaching in their subject area; a curriculum that is culturally sensitive, challenging, and consistent with high academic standards; and a school culture that reflects a focus on high academic achievement among all students.[13]

Addressing school-related issues alone, however, will not completely do away with the "achievement gap" because poverty plays a large part in the differential learning of students. Recently, this argument has been made convincingly by several noted scholars, including Jean Anyon, who cites a wealth of research and other data to come to the following chilling conclusion:

> Thus, in my view, low-achieving urban schools are not primarily a consequence of failed educational policy, or urban family dynamics, as mainstream analysts and public policies typically imply. Failing public schools in cities are, rather, a logical consequence of the U.S. macroeconomy— and the federal and regional policies and practices that support it.[14]

Likewise, in a comprehensively researched article on the effects of poverty on learning and achievement, David Berliner makes the argument that poverty *alone* places severe limits on what can be accomplished through educational reform efforts, especially those associated with the No Child Left Behind legislation.[15] His conclusion is that the most powerful policy for improving our nation's school achievement would be a reduction in family and youth poverty.

The suggestion that poverty and other social ills negatively affect learning is unsettling and a reminder that schools alone cannot tackle the inequality and stratification that exist in society. Richard Rothstein, an economist who has studied this issue extensively, has suggested that school reform efforts alone will not turn things around. He advocates three approaches that must be pursued if progress is to be made in narrowing the "achievement gap": promoting school improvement efforts that raise the quality of instruction; giving more attention to out-of-school hours by implementing early childhood, after-school, and summer programs; and implementing policies that would provide appropriate health services and stable housing and narrow the growing income inequalities in our society. He contends that only by implementing all these measures would poor children be better prepared for school.[16]

Although it is true that the "achievement gap" is strongly related to poverty, race and ethnicity are also prominent issues to consider in understanding the gap. Joseph D'Amico found that the gap may be even greater among students of color with *high* socioeconomic status. In addition, he found that although the "achievement gap" between Black and White students was reduced by about half between 1970 and 1988, there has been a marked reversal of this trend since 1988.[17]

Perhaps the most dramatic example of the "achievement gap" can be found in high school dropout rates. Researcher Gary Orfield has cited a few hundred high schools in the nation—all overwhelmingly "minority," low income, and located in urban centers—where the dropout rate has reached catastrophic proportions. He calls these high schools "dropout factories." According to Orfield, the dropout rate of African American and Latino students is a civil rights crisis because it affects these communities disproportionately. Moreover, less money per student is spent in these "dropout factory" schools than in schools in other areas—sometimes a difference of over $2,000 less per student.[18] The fact that these schools are, for the most part, located in poor communities that serve African American and Latino students, that they employ more inexperienced teachers than in wealthier districts, and that less money is spent in them, cannot be dismissed as coincidence.[19] This is also part of the sociopolitical context of education.

Deficit Theories and Their Stubborn Durability

Why schools fail to meet their mission to provide all students with an equitable and high-quality education has been the subject of educational research for some time. As the "achievement gap" grows, theories about cultural deprivation and genetic inferiority are once again being used to explain differences in intelligence and achievement, and the implications of these deficit theories continue to influence educational policies and practices. Deficit theories assume that some children, because of genetic, cultural or experiential differences, are inferior to other children—that is, that they have deficits that must be overcome if they are to learn. One problem with such hypotheses is that they place complete responsibility for children's failure on their homes and families, effectively absolving schools and society from responsibility. Whether the focus is on the individual or the community, the result remains largely the same: blaming the victims of poor schooling rather than looking in a more systematic way at the role played by the schools in which they learn (or fail to learn) and by the society at large. All these factors need to be explored together.

Another problem with deficit theories is their focus on conditions that are outside the control of most teachers, schools, and students. Deficit theories foster despair because they suggest that students' problems are predetermined and thus there is no hope for changing the circumstances that produced them in the first place. Teachers and schools alone cannot alleviate the poverty and other oppressive conditions in which students may live. It is far more realistic and promising to tackle the problems that teachers and schools *can* do something about by providing educational environments that encourage all students to learn. This is why school policies and practices and teachers' attitudes and behaviors, rather than the supposed shortcomings of students, are the basis for the kinds of transformations suggested in this book.

U.S. Schools and Society: A Demographic Mosaic

In order to understand the sociopolitical context of multicultural education, we need to know something about the changes in the United States in the recent past, and how these changes have transformed our schools. In what follows, we provide a mosaic of the rich diversity of the population in the nation as well as in our public schools as a framework for understanding this context. We focus on population statistics, immigration, language diversity, and other differences that characterize U.S. schools and society in this decade, the first of the 21st century.

We begin with an overview of the U.S. population in terms of race and ethnicity. As we see in Table 3.1, in 2004 the population of the United States numbered over 293 million. This was the most complete official data available as this book went to press. The overall population has increased steadily since then. (For instance, on October 12, 2006, a press release from the U.S. Census Bureau reported that the nation's population would reach 300,000,000 on October 17.[20]) Nevertheless, we use this table because the Census Bureau had not yet published a more complete list documenting the growth of all the subgroups reported in Table 3.1.

Of the total population, the largest "minority" group is Hispanic/Latino (over 41 million residents), followed by Blacks or African Americans (37.5 million)(see Fig 3.1). Growth among different segments of the population has not, however, been proportionate: According to the U.S. Census Bureau, from 2000 to 2004, the number of Whites increased by 3.5 percent and the African American population increased by 5 percent. By far, the largest increases were in the Latino population, which had grown by 17 percent, and the Asian population, which had grown by 16.4 percent.

Even more dramatic than current population statistics are projections for the coming years: The U.S. Census Bureau estimates that from 2000 to 2050, the total population will have grown from 282.1 million to 419.9 million. Again, however, the growth will not be even: The White population is expected to grow to 210.3 million, an increase of 7 percent, although it is expected to *decrease* in the decade from 2040–2050. Whites are thus expected to comprise only 50.1 percent of the total U.S. population by 2050, compared with 69.4 percent in 2000. The African American population is expected to grow to 61.4 million, increasing from 12.7 percent to 14.6 percent of the total population. In contrast, the Latino population is expected to grow to 102.6 million, or 24.4 percent of the total U.S. population, nearly doubling its current percentage of 12.6. Asians are also expected to increase substantially in number, from 10.7 million to 33.4 million, an increase from 3.8 percent to 8 percent of the total U.S. population.

In addition, legal immigration has grown enormously in the past three decades, as is evident in Table 3.2. As we can see in this table, legal immigration hit a peak in 1991 in terms of numbers (although not in terms of percentage of total population, which peaked at the beginning of the 20th century), reaching more than 1.8 million. By 2004, it had fallen to 946,000, still a sizable number.

Another noteworthy indication of the growing diversity in the United States is the current number of foreign-born or first-generation U.S. residents, which in

Number (1,000)

Characteristic	2000² (April 1)	2001	2002	2003	2004	Percent change 2000 to 2004
Both Sexes						
Total	281,425	285,102	287,941	290,789	293,655	4.3
One race	277,527	281,048	283,761	286,481	289,217	4.2
White	228,107	230,506	232,348	234,199	236,058	3.5
Black or African American	35,705	36,249	36,667	37,082	37,502	5.0
American Indian and Alaska Native	2,664	2,711	2,749	2,787	2,825	6.0
Asian	10,589	11,107	11,512	11,919	12,326	16.4
Native Hawaiian and Other Pacific Islanders	463	475	485	495	506	9.3
Two or more races	3,898	4,054	4,180	4,308	4,439	13.9
Race alone or in combination:³						
White	231,436	233,978	235,935	237,901	239,880	3.6
Black or African American	37,105	37,744	38,238	38,732	39,232	5.7
American Indian and Alaska Native	4,225	4,280	4,323	4,366	4,409	4.4
Asian	12,007	12,586	13,041	13,498	13,957	16.2
Native Hawaiian and Other Pacific Islanders	907	927	944	960	976	7.7
Not Hispanic or Latino	246,118	248,042	249,464	250,887	252,333	2.5
One race	242,712	244,506	245,824	247,141	248,478	2.4
White	195,577	196,320	196,822	197,325	197,841	1.2
Black or African American	34,314	34,813	35,196	35,577	35,964	4.8
American Indian and Alaska Native	2,097	2,130	2,155	2,181	2,207	5.2
Asian	10,357	10,867	11,267	11,667	12,068	16.5
Native Hawaiian and Other Pacific Islanders	367	376	383	391	398	8.5
Two or more races	3,406	3,536	3,641	3,747	3,855	13.2
Race alone or in combination:³						
White	198,477	199,338	199,935	200,534	201,148	1.3
Black or African American	35,499	36,078	36,526	36,972	37,426	5.4

(*Continued Overleaf*)

Table 3.1 Continued

Number (1,000)

Characteristic	2000[2] (April 1)	2001	2002	2003	2004	Percent change 2000 to 2004
Both Sexes						
American Indian and Alaska Native	3,456	3,491	3,518	3,546	3,574	3.4
Asian	11,632	12,196	12,639	13,083	13,530	16.3
Native Hawaiian and Other Pacific Islanders	752	767	779	791	803	6.8
Hispanic or Latino	35,306	37,060	38,477	39,902	41,322	17.0
One race	34,815	36,543	37,937	39,340	40,739	17.0
White	32,530	34,186	35,526	36,873	38,217	17.5
Black or African American	1,391	1,436	1,470	1,505	1,539	10.6
American Indian and Alaska Native	566	582	594	606	618	9.1
Asian	232	240	246	252	258	10.9
Native Hawaiian and Other Pacific Islanders	95	99	102	105	107	12.6
Two or more races	491	518	539	561	583	18.7
Race alone or in combination:[3]						
White	32,959	34,641	36,000	37,368	38,732	17.5
Black or African American	1,606	1,666	1,713	1,760	1,806	12.5
American Indian and Alaska Native	770	789	805	820	835	8.6
Asian	375	390	402	414	427	13.8
Native Hawaiian and Other Pacific Islanders	155	160	165	169	174	12.0
Male						
Total	138,056	140,013	141,519	143,024	144,537	4.7
One race	136,146	138,023	139,465	140,906	142,352	4.6
White	112,478	113,798	114,810	115,820	116,832	3.9
Black or African American	16,972	17,246	17,455	17,662	17,873	5.3
American Indian and Alaska Native	1,333	1,357	1,376	1,396	1,415	6.2
Asian	5,128	5,380	5,578	5,776	5,975	16.5
Native Hawaiian and Other Pacific Islanders	235	242	247	252	257	9.4

Two or more races	1,910	1,990	2,054	2,119	2,185	14.4
Race alone or in combination:[3]						
White	114,116	115,508	116,578	117,647	118,720	4.0
Black or African American	17,644	17,966	18,214	18,461	18,713	6.1
American Indian and Alaska Native	2,088	2,116	2,138	2,160	2,182	4.5
Asian	5,834	6,118	6,341	6,565	6,789	16.4
Native Hawaiian and Other Pacific Islanders	456	466	475	483	491	7.7
Not Hispanic or Latino	119,894	120,919	121,675	122,428	123,190	2.7
Hispanic or Latino	18,162	19,094	19,844	20,597	21,347	17.5
Female						
Total	143,368	145,089	146,422	147,765	149,118	4.0
One race	141,381	143,025	144,296	145,576	146,865	3.9
White	115,628	116,708	117,538	118,379	119,225	3.1
Black or African American	18,733	19,003	19,212	19,420	19,630	4.8
American Indian and Alaska Native	1,331	1,354	1,372	1,391	1,410	5.9
Asian	5,461	5,727	5,935	6,143	6,352	16.3
Native Hawaiian and Other Pacific Islanders	227	233	238	243	248	9.2
Two or more races	1,987	2,064	2,126	2,189	2,253	13.4
Race alone or in combination:[3]						
White	117,321	118,470	119,357	120,254	121,160	3.3
Black or African American	19,461	19,778	20,024	20,271	20,520	5.4
American Indian and Alaska Native	2,137	2,164	2,185	2,206	2,227	4.2
Asian	6,173	6,468	6,701	6,933	7,168	16.1
Native Hawaiian and Other Pacific Islanders	451	461	469	477	485	7.6
Not Hispanic or Latino	126,224	127,123	127,789	128,460	129,143	2.3
Hispanic or Latino	17,144	17,967	18,633	19,305	19,975	16.5

Source: U.S. Census Bureau, "Annual Estimates of the Population by Sex, Race and Hispanic or Latino Origin for the United States: April 1, 2000 to July 1, 2004 (NC-EST2004-03)"; published 9 June 2005; www.census.gov/popest/national/asrh/NC-EST2004-srh.html

Notes
1 281,425 represents 281,425,000. As of July, except as noted. Data shown are modified race counts; see text, this section.
2 See footnote 3. Table 11.
3 In combination with one or more other races. The sum of the five race groups adds to more than the total population because individuals may report more than one race.

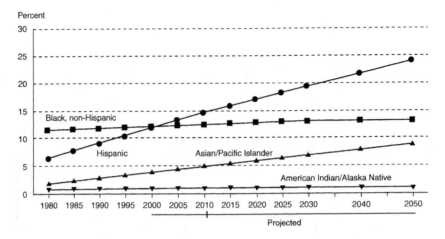

Figure 3.1 Percent of the Resident U.S. Population, by Minority Race/Ethnicity: Selected Years 1980 to 2000 and Projections to 2050.

Source: U.S. Department of Commerce, Census Bureau, *Statistical Abstract of the United States: 2000*, based on Population Estimates Program and Population Projections Program.

Table 3.2 Immigration: 1901 to 2004[1]

Period	Number	Rate[2]	Year	Number	Rate[2]
1901 to 1910	8,795	10.4	1990	1,536	6.1
1911 to 1920	5,736	5.7	1991	1,827	7.2
1921 to 1930	4,107	3.5	1992	974	3.8
			1993	904	3.5
1931 to 1940	528	0.4	1994	804	3.1
1941 to 1950	1,035	0.7	1995	720	2.7
1951 to 1960	2,515	1.5	1996	916	3.4
			1997	798	2.9
1961 to 1970	3,322	1.7	1998	654	2.4
1971 to 1980	4,493	2.1	1999	647	2.3
1981 to 1990	7,338	3.1	2000	850	3.0
			2001	1,064	3.7
1991 to 2000	9,095	3.4	2002	1,064	3.7
2001 to 2004	3,780	3.3	2003	706	2.4
			2004	946	3.2

Source: U.S. Department of Homeland Security, Office of Immigration Statistics, *2004 Yearbook of Immigration Statistics*. See also http://uscis.gov/graphics/shared/statistics/yearbook/index.htm.

Notes
1 In thousands, except rate (8,795 represents 8,795,000). For fiscal years ending in year shown; see text, Section 8. For definition of immigrants, see text of this section. Data represent immigrants admitted. Rates based on Census Bureau estimates as of July 1 for resident population through 1929 and for total population thereafter (excluding Alaska and Hawaii prior to 1959).
2 Annual rate per 1,000 U.S. population. Rate computed by dividing sum of annual immigration totals by sum of annual U.S. population totals for same number of years.

the year 2000 reached the highest level in U.S. history—56 million, or triple the number in 1970. And unlike previous immigrants, who were primarily from Europe, more than half of the new immigrants are from Latin America, and 25 percent from Asia.[21]

The growth in immigration has been accompanied by an increase in linguistic diversity. Currently, 18 percent of the total U.S. population speak a language other than English at home. Spanish is the language spoken by half of these, although there are also many other languages spoken in U.S. homes.

The impact of the growing cultural, racial, national origin, and linguistic diversity is clearly visible in our nation's public schools in several ways. First, the sheer number of students in U.S. public schools is growing. In 2003, 49.5 million students were enrolled in public elementary and secondary schools in the United States, an increase of more than 2 million since 2001.[22] Second, the nature of the student population is quite different from what it was just a few decades ago. In 1970, at the height of the public school enrollment of the "baby boom" generation, White students comprised 79 percent of total enrollment, followed by African Americans at 14 percent, Hispanics at 6 percent, and Asians, Pacific Islanders, and other ethnic groups at 1 percent. These statistics have vastly changed: In 2003, 60 percent of students in U.S. public schools were White, 18 percent were Hispanic, 16 percent were African American, and 4 percent were Asian and other races. The Census Bureau's population projections indicate that the student population will continue to diversify in the coming years. Third, our public schools' growing diversity is clearly evidenced by the number of students who are foreign born or have foreign-born parents. As of 2003, over 49 million students, or 31 percent of those enrolled in U.S. elementary and secondary schools, were foreign born or had at least one parent who was foreign born.

At the same time that diversity in schools around the country is growing, racial and ethnic segregation has been on the rise. That is, students in U.S. schools are now more likely to be segregated from students of other races and backgrounds than at any time in the recent past. Indeed, according to Gary Orfield, much of the progress made in integrating the nation's schools during previous decades was eradicated by the end of the 1990s. For Blacks, the 1990s witnessed the largest backward movement toward segregation since the *Brown v. Board of Education* Supreme Court decision, and the trend is continuing. For Latinos, the situation has been equally dramatic: Latinos are now the most segregated of all ethnic groups in terms of race, ethnicity, and poverty.[23] Despite this trend, there is growing evidence that schools with diverse student populations are good for students of all backgrounds.[24]

In addition, many young people live in poverty. Race and ethnicity have a strong link to poverty. The percentage of all people in the United States living below the poverty level is currently 12.4. However, while only about 8.3 percent of Whites live in poverty, nearly 25 percent of African Americans and Native Americans and 22 percent of Hispanics live in poverty.[25] In terms of the school-aged population, 40 percent of all U.S. children live in low-income families, and 18 percent live in poor families, which translates into the sobering reality that *almost half of all children in the United States live in some degree of poverty.* Even more disturbing, although the number of children living in poverty had declined from 1990–2000, it has been rising steadily since then.[26]

At the same time that the number of students of color, those who speak languages other than English and those who live in poverty has increased, the nation's teachers have become more monolithic, monocultural, and monolingual. For example, as of 2003, nearly 90 percent of public school teachers were White, 6 percent were African American, and fewer than 5 percent were of other racial/ethnic backgrounds.[27]

One implication of the tremendous diversity previously described is that all teachers, regardless of their own identities and experiences, need to be prepared to effectively teach students of all backgrounds. One way to do so is to learn about the social, cultural, and political circumstances of real students in real schools.

Multicultural Education, Backlash, and No Child Left Behind

Since its beginnings in the 1970s, multicultural education has been criticized for many reasons. While some of the criticisms have been warranted and have, in fact, helped the field develop more solidly, many of the arguments against multicultural education have been deeply ideological. That is, multicultural education has come under fire precisely because it has challenged the status quo, encouraged the emergence of previously silenced and marginalized voices, and championed the transformation of curriculum and the use of alternative pedagogies.

Eroding the Traditional Educational Canon

One argument against multicultural education is that it can easily slide into a separatist monoculturalism that pits Europeans and European Americans against people of other backgrounds, creating a divisive "us versus them" mentality. This argument assumes that no "us versus them" mentality currently exists and that there already is unity among all people in our country—both clearly erroneous assumptions. There are tremendous divisions among people in the United States, and glossing over these differences will not make them go away. On the contrary, supporters of multicultural education assume that a curriculum that is more multicultural is also more complicated and truthful and will, in the long run, help develop citizens who think critically, expansively, and creatively.

In terms of its impact on schooling, opponents have been especially nervous about how a multicultural perspective might translate into curriculum changes. Those who fear that the traditional educational canon is being eroded have vociferously criticized it because, they claim, a multicultural curriculum will do away with our "common culture." The ramifications of this stance can be seen in efforts to do away with specific courses at high schools and universities and, in the aftermath of September 11, 2001, in claims that it is now more important than ever to focus on a rigidly defined version of American history.

In countering this argument, we need to remember that the history of other groups of people in the United States is not foreign; it is *American history*. Our history was never exclusively a European saga of immigration and assimilation, although that is, of course, an important part of the American story. But our collective consciousness began with—and continues to be influenced by— Indigenous Americans as well as by those who were forcibly brought from Africa into slavery. No one in our nation has been untouched by African American, Native American, Mexican American, and Asian American histories and cultures (among many other groups, including women, European American immigrants, and working class people). The influence of these groups can be seen in our history, popular culture, civic engagement, and arts.

The trajectory of U.S. history has been characterized largely by the quest for equality, and this is no more evident than in the case of those who have been most marginalized by our society. The words *freedom*, *liberty*, and *equality* would have much less power today were it not for the protracted struggles against the abolition of slavery and for universal suffrage and civil rights, some of which continue today. Although these words were originally meant to apply to only land-owning White males early in our history, they came to be meaningful for others because of campaigns to extend these ideals to all people. Whether or not we acknowledge it in our history books, our culture and history have been shaped by the fusion of many people of different backgrounds.

The "Back to Basics" Argument

The backlash against multicultural education has also been evident in claims that a focus on diversity is a diversion from the "basics." This has especially been the case since the educational reform movement that began in 1983 after the publication of *A Nation at Risk*.[30] One vivid example of the back-to-basics argument is E. D. Hirsch's 1987 book *Cultural Literacy: What Every American Needs to Know*, which includes a list of several thousand terms and concepts that the author considers essential for every educated person to know or, at least, to recognize and be familiar with.[31] Many critics have charged that both the book and the list are provincial and Eurocentric, with little attention given to the arts, history, or culture of those from groups other than the so-called mainstream. Since publication of Hirsch's book, several hundred schools around the nation have been structured and organized according to the "cultural literacy" model promoted by Hirsch, further promulgating a notion of cultural literacy that flies in the face of the rapidly changing demographics—not to mention the rich multicultural history—of our nation. There are also numerous spin-off publications, sold at supermarkets, that focus on different grade levels, making Hirsch's cultural literacy model and ideas a virtual cottage industry that is hard to ignore.

While many of us might welcome a generally agreed-upon definition of the educated person, this is a complex issue that cannot be solved by a prescribed list, or even a prescribed curriculum. In a recent book, Eugene Provenzo challenged Hirsch's views by publishing his own book, *Critical Literacy: What Every American Ought to Know*, a critique of both Hirsch and the simplistic ideas behind the cultural literacy model that he promotes.[32]

NCLB and the Challenge of Working Within the Standards

The most recent iteration of the back-to-basics argument has occurred since the passage of the No Child Left Behind (NCLB) law in 2001, particularly because along with higher standards, the law requires that each state have an annual testing program of children in reading and math.[33]

NCLB is a response to several issues plaguing our educational system. First, NCLB needs to be understood as a response to the deplorable history of educational inequality in our nation. Educational inequality has been a fact of life for many children in our schools, but especially for students of color and poor children. Parents, educators, and other defenders of public education have long advocated for addressing this inequality. It is not surprising, then, that many advocates of equal education initially supported NCLB and that it remains popular with some.

At the same time, conspicuous among the most ardent supporters of NCLB are those who support privatization of schools, including vouchers, charter schools, and so forth. Thus, the goals of various groups promoting NCLB are not the same and, in some cases, may be contradictory. In the years since NCLB was first passed, it has lost favor with a great many people for many reasons, including its single-minded focus on tests as the primary criterion for viewing academic progress, as well as the dismal results this focus has produced so far.

Teaching to the Test and High Standards

As a result of the law, there has been immense pressure on teachers and administrators to "teach to the test" and to devote a lion's share of the school day to reading and mathematics. The effects have been mixed. While test scores are rising in some districts, one recent comprehensive survey found that the law's pressure on teachers has led to increased stress on the job and a negative effect on staff morale. The same survey found that 71 percent of surveyed school districts reported having reduced instructional time in at least one other subject to make time for reading and mathematics.[34] The arts, social studies, and even science have been reduced or eliminated in some schools. Recess and physical education have also been curtailed in many schools. And although multicultural education is not a subject area, it too has been one of the casualties of this pressure. One reason is that, as a consequence of NCLB, the testing frenzy has had a chilling effect on schools' and teachers' autonomy to develop and implement curricula, and this includes multicultural curricula.

Most state standards do not preclude the possibility of including multiple perspectives in the curriculum. In fact, there is no contradiction between high standards and multicultural education. Quite the opposite is the case: Since its very beginning one of the major arguments in support of multicultural education has been that some students—particularly students of color and poor students of all backgrounds–have been the victims of an inferior education, often based on their race/ethnicity, social class, first langauge, and other differences. Multicultural education, through a rich curriculum and rigorous demands, was seen as an antidote to this situation. Nonetheless, the pressure that teachers and administrators are under to meet "adequate yearly progress" (AYP), as defined by standardized tests, has resulted in little support for the arts and even for such subjects as social studies and science, much less for innovation and creativity in curriculum and instruction.

Effects of NCLB

There has been a great deal of criticism of NCLB and its negative effects, particularly on students living in poverty, those whom the law was purportedly intended to help. For instance, *The Boston Globe* reported in 2005 that the Massachusetts high school dropout rate had experienced the largest increase in 14 years and that the class graduating in 2007 was expected to have a dropout rate of 31 percent. Hispanics and other immigrants have been the most severely affected. The high dropout rate included thousands of students who failed the state's high-stakes exam, the Massachusetts Comprehensive Assessment System (MCAS).[35] Rather than helping such students, the MCAS has clearly had an adverse effect.

FairTest, a national advocacy group that promotes fair and open testing, has been especially critical of NCLB. It maintains, for instance, that NCLB is based on two false assumptions: one, that boosting standardized test scores should be the primary goal of schools; and two, that schools can be best improved by threatening teachers and administrators with severe penalties. In its analysis of the law, FairTest concludes that NCLB has failed to address the underlying problems of school achievement, namely, family poverty and inadequate school funding.[36] In addition, because test scores have been rising in some states, there is increasing criticism that tests are becoming easier rather than that achievement is improving.[37] FairTest has also reported on two research studies that found striking evidence that exit exams actually decrease high school completion rates, increase GED test-taking, and exacerbate inequalities in educational attainment.[38]

The Civil Rights Project, formerly at Harvard University, has also been critical of NCLB. In a 2006 report, the author of one study, Jaekyung Lee, compared findings of the National Assessment of Education Progress (NAEP) to state assessment results and concluded that although students were showing improvement in state exams in both math and reading, they were not showing similar gains on the NAEP, the only independent national test that randomly samples students across the country.[39] Lee concluded that state-administered tests tend to significantly inflate proficiency levels and deflate racial and social achievement gaps in the state. That is, the higher the stakes of state assessments, the greater the discrepancies between NAEP and state results. These discrepancies are especially significant for students living in poverty and for Black and Latino students.

There are also ethical concerns associated with the NCLB law. In 2006, the National Council of Churches Committee on Public Education and Literacy took a strong stand against NCLB. Its statement, titled "Ten Moral Concerns in the Implementation of the No Child Left Behind Act," affirms:

> Now several years into No Child Left Behind's implementation, it is becoming clear that the law is leaving behind more children than it is saving. The children being abandoned are our nation's most vulnerable children–children of color and poor children in America's big cities and remote rural areas–the very children the law claims it will rescue.[40]

The statement concludes with an indictment of the testing policies that have resulted in leaving so many children behind:

> We people of faith do not view our children as products to be tested and managed but instead as unique human beings to be nurtured and educated. We call on our political leaders to invest in developing the capacity of all schools. Our nation should be judged by the way we care for our children.[41]

NCLB has also had devastating effects on teachers' sense of professionalism. Many teachers are now reluctant to engage in interesting projects with their students, or even to collaborate with peers because of criticisms they are likely to receive from administrators, who are also under tremendous pressure to keep their schools out of the headlines for failing to meet AYP. The result in many schools around the country is that teachers are expected to follow a rigidly prescribed curriculum, particularly in reading and math, with little room for innovation or collaboration. What are teachers to do?

Teacher's Responsibilities Within NCLB

In terms of teachers' responsibilities, we must once again consider the socio-political context of education. Curriculum and pedagogy, along with other school policies and practices, are as much *political* issues as they are educational issues. The same is true of standards. Every curriculum decision also says something about the values, expectations, hopes, and dreams that a teacher has for his or her students. If this is the case, it becomes the responsibility of teachers to help define the curriculum and not simply to be automatons who implement a rigidly prescribed curriculum.

In a recent book about this topic, Christine Sleeter suggests that there is a difference between a *standards-driven* and a *standards-conscious* curriculum. A standards-driven curriculum, according to her, begins with the standards and draws the "big ideas" from them for further design and implementation. A standards-conscious curriculum, on the other hand, uses the standards as a tool rather than as either the starting point or the underlying ideology for the development of big ideas. In her book, *Un-Standardizing Curriculum: Multicultural Teaching in the Standards-Based Classroom*, Sleeter provides powerful vignettes of teachers who face the same pressures to "teach to the test" as all teachers. In spite of this pressure, rather than following the standards uncritically, these teachers developed standards-based curricula that are both creative and critical.[42] Another example of using the standards in inventive ways is

Mary Cowhey's *Black Ants and Buddhists: Thinking Critically and Teaching Differently in the Primary Grades.*[43] A first- and second-grade teacher, Cowhey uses the standards to develop curriculum that is inspiring, demanding, and multicultural.

These books, and a growing number of others, are challenging the notion that standards will necessarily lead to standardization. They provide vivid examples of how powerful learning and imagination can be promoted even within a testing and accountability context that tends to leave little room for these things.

The Complex Nature of Schooling and the Role of Teachers

We believe that multicultural education has tremendous promise and a great deal to offer public schools in the 21st century. However, we do not see it as a panacea, nor should you. As we hope we have made clear in this chapter, our schools reflect the sociopolitical context in which we live. This context is unfair to many young people and their families and the situations in which they live and go to school, but teachers and other educators do not simply have to go along with this reality. We believe that one of our primary roles as educators is to interrupt the cycle of inequality and oppression. Developing a multicultural approach can help, but it cannot eliminate the inequities in our schools. No program, philosophy, or approach can do this. It will take courage, creativity, hard work, and on-going collaboration with like-minded educators and others to change things. We can begin the process by teaching well and with heart and soul, by asking questions, and by seeking social justice in our schools.

Notes

1 Public Education Network and Education Week, *Action for All: The Public's Responsibility for Public Education* (Washington, DC: Author, 2001).
2 Irving Howe, *World of Our Fathers* (New York: Simon & Schuster, 1983).
3 Beverly Daniel Tatum, *"Why Are All the Black Kids Sitting Together in the Cafeteria?" and Other Conversations About Race* (New York: HarperCollins, 1997): 6.
4 The Education Trust, *The Funding Gap 2005* (Washington, DC: Author, 2005).
5 Nam Y. Huh, "Does Money Transform Schools?" *The Christian Science Monitor*, August 9, 2005. Available at: www.csmonitor.com/2005/0809/p01.S03–ussc.html
6 Will Kymlicka, "Foreword." In *Diversity and Citizenship in Education: Global Perspectives*, edited by James A. Banks (San Francisco: Jossey-Bass, 2004): xiii–xviii.
7 Enid Lee, "Equity and Equality." From a keynote speech at the annual Connecticut National Association for Multicultural Education (NAME) Conference, October 2004.
8 Robert P. Moses, "Quality Education is a Civil Rights Issue." In *Minority Achievement*, edited by David T. Gordon (Cambridge, MA: Harvard Education Letter Focus Series 7, 2002): 26–27.
9 Edmund W. Gordon, "Bridging the Minority Achievement Gap." *Principal* (May 2000): 20–23.
10 Quality Counts at 10: A Decade of Standards-Based Education, 2006. Available at: www.edweek.org/ew/articles/2006/01/05/17overview.h25.html

11 Mano Singham, "The Achievement Gap: Myths and Realities." *Phi Delta Kappan* 84, no. 8 (April 2003): 586–591.

12 Joseph J. D'Amico, "A Closer Look at the Minority Achievement Gap." *ERS Spectrum* (Spring 2001): 4–10.

13 Ibid.

14 Jean Anyon, *Radical Possibilities: Public Policy, Urban Education, and a New Social Movement* (New York: Routledge, 2005): 2.

15 David C. Berliner, "Our Impoverished View of Educational Reform." *Teachers College Record.* Available at: www.tcrecord.org/content.asp?contentID+12106

16 Richard Rothstein, *Class and Schools: Using Social, Economic, and Educational Reform to Close the Black-White Achievement Gap* (New York: Teachers College Press, and Washington, DC: Economic Policy Institute, 2004).

17 D'Amico, "A Closer Look at the Minority Achievement Gap."

18 Gary Orfield, "Losing Our Future: Minority Youth Left Out." In *Dropouts in America: Confronting the Graduate Rate Crisis*, edited by Gary Orfield (Cambridge, MA: Harvard Education Press, 2004): p. 1–11, 9.

19 Pamela M. Prah, "Schools With Poor, Minority Students Get Less State Funds." Available at: www.stateline.org

20 "Nation's Population to Reach 300,000,000 on Oct. 17." *U.S. Census Bureau News*, October 12, 2006. Washington, DC: Author, Public Information Office.

21 U.S. Census Bureau, *Profile of the Foreign-Born Population in the United States: 2000* (Washington, DC: U.S. Department of Commerce, 2002).

22 All the data cited in this paragraph are from the following U.S. Census Bureau publication: Hyon B. Shin, "School Enrollment: Social and Economic Characteristics of Students—October 2003." In *Current Population Reports* (Washington, DC: U.S. Census Bureau, 2005).

23 Gary Orfield, *Schools More Separate: Consequences of a Decade of Resegregation* (Cambridge, MA: The Civil Rights Project, Harvard University, 2001).

24 Eileen Gale Kugler, *Debunking the Middle-Class Myth: Why Diverse Schools are Good for All Kids* (Lanham, MD: Scarecrow Press, 2002).

25 U.S. Census Bureau, "Income, Poverty, and Health Insurance Coverage in the United States." In *Current Population Survey, 2003 to 2005 Annual Social and Economic Supplements* (Washington, DC: Author, 2005).

26 National Center for Children in Poverty, *Basic Facts About Low-Income Children: Birth to Age 18.* Available at: www.NCCP.org

27 National Collaborative on Diversity in the Teaching Force, *Assessment of Diversity in America's Teaching Force: A Call to Action* (Washington, DC: Author, October 2004).

28 Sharan B. Merriam, *Case Study Research in Education: A Qualitative Approach* (San Francisco: Jossey-Bass, 1998): 27.

29 Michelle Fine, *Framing Dropouts: Notes on the Politics of an Urban High School* (Albany: State University of New York Press, 1991).

30 National Commission on Excellence in Education, *A Nation at Risk: The Imperative for Education Reform* (Washington, DC: U.S. Government Printing Office, 1983).

31 E. D. Hirsch, *Cultural Literacy: What Every American Needs to Know* (Boston: Houghton Mifflin, 1987).

32 Eugene F. Provenzo; Jr., *Critical Literacy: What Every American Ought to Know* (Boulder, CO: Paradigm, 2005).

33 No Child Left Behind Act of 2001, Public Law 107–110.

34 Center on Education Policy, *From the Capital to the Classroom: Year 4 of the No Child Left Behind Act* (Washington, DC: Author, 2006).

35 Maria Sacchetti and Tracy Jan, "High School Dropout Rate Reaches Highest in 14 Years." *The Boston Globe*, October 22, 2005. Available at: www.boston.com/news/local/massachusetts/articles/2005/10/22/high_school_dropout_rates_reaches_highest_in_14-years?/mode+PF

36 Monty Neill, Lisa Guisbond, and Bob Schaeffer (with James Madison and Life Legeros), *Failing Our Children: How "No Child Left Behind" Undermines Quality and Equity in Education* (Cambridge, MA: The National Center for Fair and Open Testing, 2004). See also Deborah Meier, Alfie Kohn, Linda Darling-Hammond, Theodore R. Sizer, George Wood, et al., *Many Children Left Behind: How The No Child Left Behind Act Is Damaging Our Children and Our Schools* (Boston: Beacon Press, 2004).

37 Michael Winerip, "One Secret to Better Test Scores: Make State Reading Tests Easier." *The New York Times*, October 5, 2005. Available at: www.nytimes.com/2005/10/05/education/05education.html

38 "Exit Exams Decrease Graduation Rates," *Fair Test Examiner*, August 2006. Available at: www.fairtest.org

39 Jaekyung Lee, *Tracking Achievement Gaps and Assessing the Impact of NCLB on the Gaps: An In-Depth Look into National and State Reading and Math Outcome Trends* (Cambridge, MA: The Civil Rights Project, 2006).

40 National Council of Churches, "Ten Moral Concerns in the Implementation of the No Child Left Behind Act: A Statement of the National Council of Churches Committee on Public Education and Literacy, 2006." Available at: www.ncccusa.org

41 Ibid.

42 Christine E. Sleeter, *Un-Standardizing Curriculum: Multicultural Teaching in the Standards-Based Class-room* (New York: Teachers College Press, 2005).

43 Mary Cowhey, *Black Ants and Buddhists: Thinking Critically and Teaching Differently in the Primary Grades* (Portland, ME: Stenhouse, 2006).

Critical Questions

1 Think about the school in which you work or student teach. What particular sociopolitical conditions affect your school? Be specific, including such issues as funding, student demographics, poverty, or other matters. For example, is there a large immigrant population in your school? If so, how are U.S. immigration policies felt in the school? Is your school in an economically devastated area? If so, what is the unemployment profile in the community? Does it have an impact in the school? Conversely, do you teach in an economically privileged community? If so, how is that privilege manifested in your school?

2 Before reading this chapter, had you thought about *power* as having a role in education? Reflect on this issue and write about how you do or do not believe power is implicated in the decisions you make about your classroom, the curriculum you teach, the pedagogical decisions you make, and so on.

3 Explain how the "smog in the air" described by Beverly Daniel Tatum influences your perceptions of particular children or groups of people. What can you do to challenge those perceptions?

4 What impact has NCLB had in your school? Have teachers challenged it in any way? Share your thoughts with your classmates.

Activity for Your Classroom

Think about your particular subject area and develop a lesson or unit in which you frame the topic in as inclusive a way as possible. For instance, how might a lesson on tropical rain forests include issues of race, gender, social class, and other differences? What about a physics lesson on magnets? What about a poetry lesson?

Community-Based Activity and Advocacy

Create a demographic portrait of your classroom, school, and community. Include the number of people in each, their cultural, racial, and linguistic backgrounds, the number of immigrants and their countries of origin, the services available in the school and community, and so on. You might also include such data as the number of school suspensions by race, gender, and ethnicity, the number and percentage of dropouts by race, gender, and ethnicity, and so forth. What surprises you about your findings? What are the implications of your research? What services are needed but not available? What can you do with your findings? Make your research public by including your findings in a school or community newsletter.

Supplementary Resources for Further Reflection and Study

Christensen, L. & Karp, S. (2003). *Rethinking school reform.* Milwaukee, WI: Rethinking Schools.

Drawing on some of the best writing from the quarterly journal *Rethinking Schools,* this collection offers a primer on a broad range of pressing issues in school reform, including school vouchers and funding, multiculturalism, standards and testing, teacher unions, bilingual education, and federal education policy.

Nieto, S. & Bode, P. (2008). *Affirming diversity: The sociopolitical context of multicultural education,* 5th ed. Boston: Allyn & Bacon.

Using education research and case studies of students of diverse backgrounds, this book defines the field of multicultural education through an analysis of the sociopolitical context of education and society. It includes a discussion of personal, social, and institutional factors that influence learning and achievement, and suggests strategies at the classroom and school level and beyond to promote positive change.

No Child Left Behind, Public Law 107–110.

The law that has largely determined education policy in the United States since 2001, NCLB uses adequate yearly progress (*AYP*) through scores on standardized tests as the major criterion and stipulates the consequences for schools that do not reach yearly goals. In addition, it defines "highly qualified teachers" based on undergraduate and graduate programs, teacher test scores, and other criteria, and describes what families can do if their children's schools do not pass muster.

Rothstein, R. (2004). *Class and schools: Using social, economic, and educational reform to close the Black–White achievement gap.* New York: Teachers College Press, and Washington, DC: Economic Policy Institute.

This book is a powerful reminder that schools alone cannot solve the problem of the achievement gap. It suggests that other structural and institutional changes need to take place in order to close the gap. Roth provides an insightful analysis of both the possibilities and the limits of education reform.

Tatum, B. D. (1997). *"Why are all the Black kids sitting together in the cafeteria?" and other conversations about race.* New York: HarperCollins.

In this eminently readable book, Professor Tatum, now President of Spelman College in Atlanta, Georgia, presents the theory of racial and cultural identity and challenges the notion that it is only Black kids who "sit together in the cafeteria."

4　Multicultural Education and School Reform

(with Patty Bode)

Although the idea of multicultural education has been a mainstay in educational circles for more than two decades (and in academic circles for much longer), it has not been widely understood or systematically put into practice. In many schools, to have multicultural education means to set aside a particular time of year for special units or assembly programs about specific people or topics and/or to support extracurricular activities that center on ethnic diversity.

The following piece is a chapter from the fifth edition of the book *Affirming Diversity: The Sociopolitical Context of Multicultural Education*. My co-author, Patty Bode, and I provide an in-depth definition that challenges the conventional wisdom that multicultural education is simply a "feel-good" additive to the curriculum or a program to boost self-esteem for "minority" students. Instead, we frame multicultural education within a context of social justice and critical pedagogy that encompasses anti-racist and basic education for all students of all backgrounds. Throughout the chapter, we give examples of how this definition goes beyond the "heroes and holidays" approach to diversity, with various implications for our nation's schools.

"We don't need multicultural education here; most of our students are White."
"I don't see color. All my students are the same to me."
"We shouldn't talk about racism in school because it has nothing to do with learning. Besides, it'll just make the kids feel bad."
"Let's not focus on negative things. Can't we all just get along?"

In discussing multicultural education with teachers and other educators over many years, we have heard all these comments and other similar remarks. Statements such as these reflect a profound misconception of multicultural education.

When multicultural education is mentioned, many people first think of lessons in human relations and sensitivity training, units about ethnic holidays, education in inner-city schools, or food festivals. If multicultural education is limited to these issues, the potential for substantive change in schools is severely diminished. Moreover, those who called for an end to multicultural education after September 11, 2001, missed the boat. Rather than eliminating it, we believe that 9/11 underscored the need to emphasize multicultural education more than ever. In fact, we believe that nothing is more divisive than a monocultural education, because such an education excludes so many people and perspectives from schools' curricula and pedagogy.

When broadly conceptualized, multicultural education can lead to more understanding and empathy. It can also help to address the four areas of potential conflict and inequity—namely, racism and discrimination, structural conditions in schools that may limit learning, the impact of culture on learning, and language diversity. However, it is necessary to stress that multicultural education is not a panacea for all educational ills. Because schools are part of our communities, they reflect the stratification and social inequities of the larger society. As long as this is the case, no school program alone, no matter how broadly conceptualized, can change things completely without addressing inequalities in the larger society. It will not cure underachievement, eliminate boring and irrelevant curriculum, or stop vandalism. It will not automatically motivate families to participate in schools, reinvigorate tired and dissatisfied teachers, or guarantee a lower dropout rate.

Despite these caveats, when multicultural education is conceptualized as broad-based school reform, it can offer hope for real change. Multicultural education in a sociopolitical context is both richer and more complex than simple lessons on getting along or units on ethnic festivals. By focusing on major conditions contributing to underachievement, a broadly conceptualized multicultural education permits educators to explore alternatives to a system that promotes failure for too many of its students. Such an exploration can lead to the creation of a richer and more productive school climate and a deeper awareness of the role of culture and language in learning. Seen in this comprehensive way, educational success for all students is a realistic goal rather than an impossible ideal.

This chapter proposes a definition of multicultural education based on such a broad context and it analyzes the seven primary characteristics included in the definition. These characteristics underscore the role that multicultural education can play in reforming schools and providing an equal and excellent education for all students. This definition of multicultural education emerges from the reality of persistent problems in our nation's schools, especially the lack of achievement among students of diverse backgrounds. A comprehensive definition emphasizes the context and process of education rather than viewing multicultural education as an add-on or luxury disconnected from the everyday lives of students.

In spite of some differences among major theorists, during the past 30 years there has been remarkable consistency in the educational field about the goals, purposes, and reasons for multicultural education.[1] But no definition of multicultural education can truly capture all its complexities. The definition we present here reflects one way of conceptualizing the issues; it is based on our many years of experience as students, teachers, researchers, and teacher educators. We hope that it will serve to encourage further dialogue and reflection among readers. So, although we propose seven characteristics that we believe are essential in multicultural education, you might come up with just three, or with 15. The point is not to develop a definitive way to understand multicultural education but instead to start you thinking about the interplay of societal and school structures and contexts and how they influence learning.

What we believe *is* essential is an emphasis on the sociopolitical context of education and a rejection of the notion that multicultural education is either a superficial addition of content to the curriculum, or, alternatively, the magic pill that will do away with all educational problems. In the process of considering our definition of multicultural education, it is our hope that you will develop your own ideas, priorities, and perspective.

A Definition of Multicultural Education

We define multicultural education in a sociopolitical context as follows: Multicultural education is a process of comprehensive school reform and basic education for all students. It challenges and rejects racism and other forms of discrimination in schools and society and accepts and affirms the pluralism (ethnic, racial, linguistic, religious, economic, and gender, among others) that students, their communities, and teachers reflect. Multicultural education permeates schools' curriculum and instructional strategies as well as the interactions among teachers, students, and families and the very way that schools conceptualize the nature of teaching and learning. Because it uses critical pedagogy as its underlying philosophy and focuses on knowledge, reflection, and action (praxis) as the basis for social change, multicultural education promotes democratic principles of social justice.

The seven basic characteristics of multicultural education in this definition are as follows:

1   Multicultural education is antiracist education.
2   Multicultural education is basic education.
3   Multicultural education is important for all students.
4   Multicultural education is pervasive.
5   Multicultural education is education for social justice.
6   Multicultural education is a process.
7   Multicultural education is critical pedagogy.

Multicultural Education Is Antiracist Education

Antiracism, indeed antidiscrimination in general, is at the very core of a multicultural perspective. It is essential to keep the antiracist nature of multicultural education in mind because, in many schools, even some that espouse a multicultural philosophy, only superficial aspects of multicultural education are apparent. Celebrations of ethnic festivals are the extent of multicultural education programs in some schools. In others, sincere attempts to decorate bulletin boards with what is thought to be a multicultural perspective end up perpetuating the worst kind of stereotypes. Even where there are serious attempts to develop a truly pluralistic environment, it is not unusual to find incongruencies. In some schools, for instance, the highest academic tracks are overwhelmingly White, the lowest are populated primarily by students of color, and girls are nonexistent or invisible in calculus and physics classes. These are examples of multicultural education without an explicitly antiracist and antidiscrimination perspective.

Because many people erroneously assume that a school's multicultural program automatically takes care of racism, we stress that multicultural education *must be consciously antiracist.* Writing about multicultural education over 25 years ago, when the field was fairly new, Meyer Weinberg asserted:

> Most multicultural materials deal wholly with the cultural distinctiveness of various groups and little more. Almost never is there any sustained attention to the ugly realities of systematic discrimination against the same group that also happens to utilize quaint clothing, fascinating toys, delightful fairy tales, and delicious food. Responding to racist attacks and defamation is also part of the culture of the group under study.[2]

Being antiracist and antidiscriminatory means being mindful of how some students are favored over others in school policies and practices such as the curriculum, choice of materials, sorting policies, and teachers' interactions and relationships with students and their families. Consequently, to be inclusive and balanced, multicultural curricula must, by definition, be antiracist. Teaching does not become more honest and critical simply by becoming more inclusive, but this is an important first step in ensuring that students have access to a wide variety of viewpoints. Although the beautiful and heroic aspects of our history should be taught, so must the ugly and exclusionary. Rather than viewing the world through rose-colored glasses, antiracist multicultural education forces teachers and students to take a long, hard look at everything as it was and is, instead of just how we wish it were.

Too many schools avoid confronting in an honest and direct way the negative aspects of history, the arts, and science. Michelle Fine has called this the "fear of naming," and it is part of the system of silencing in public schools.[3] To name might become too messy, or so the thinking goes. Teachers often refuse to engage their students in discussions about racism because it might "demoralize" them. Too dangerous a topic, it is often left untouched.

Related to the fear of naming is the insistence of schools on "sanitizing" the curriculum, or what Jonathon Kozol many years ago called "tailoring" important men and women for school use. Kozol described how schools manage to take the most exciting and memorable heroes and bleed the life and spirit completely out of them because it can be dangerous, he wrote, to teach a history "studded with so many bold, and revolutionary, and subversive, and exhilarating men and women." He described how, instead, schools drain these heroes of their passions, glaze them over with an implausible veneer, place them on lofty pedestals, and then tell "incredibly dull stories" about them.[4] Although he wrote these words many years ago, Kozol could just as well be writing about education in today's U.S. schools.

The process of sanitizing is nowhere more evident than in depictions of Martin Luther King, Jr. In attempting to make him palatable to the U.S. mainstream, schools have made King a milquetoast. The only thing most children know about him is that he kept "having a dream." School bulletin boards are full of ethereal pictures of Dr. King surrounded by clouds. If children get to read or hear any of his speeches at all, it is his "I Have a Dream" speech. As inspirational as this speech is, it is only one of his notable accomplishments. Rare indeed are allusions to his early and consistent opposition to the Vietnam War; his strong criticism of unbridled capitalism; and the connections he made near the end of his life among racism, capitalism, and war. This sanitization of Martin Luther King, a man full of passion and life, renders him an oversimplified, lifeless figure, thus making him a "safe hero."

Most of the heroes we present to our children are either those in the mainstream or those who have become safe through the process of what Kozol referred to as "tailoring." Others who have fought for social justice are often downplayed, maligned, or ignored. For example, although John Brown's actions in defense of the liberation of enslaved people are considered noble by many, in our history books he is presented, at best, as somewhat of a crazed idealist. Nat Turner is another example. The slave revolt that he led deserves a larger place in our history, if only to acknowledge that enslaved people fought against their own oppression and were not simply passive victims. However, Turner's name and role in U.S. history are usually overlooked, and Abraham Lincoln is presented as the Great Emancipator as if he single-handedly was responsible for the abolition of slavery (and with little acknowledgment of his own inconsistent ideas about race and equality). Nat Turner is not considered a safe hero; Abraham Lincoln is.

To be antiracist also means to work affirmatively to combat racism. It means making antiracism and antidiscrimination explicit parts of the curriculum and teaching young people skills in confronting racism. A school that is truly committed to a multicultural philosophy will closely examine both its policies and the attitudes and behaviors of its staff to determine how these might discriminate against some students. The focus on school policies and practices makes it evident that multicultural education is about more than the perceptions and beliefs of individual teachers and other educators. Multicultural education is antiracist because it exposes racist and discriminatory practices in schools.

Racism is seldom mentioned in school (it is bad, a dirty word) and, therefore, is not dealt with. Unfortunately, many teachers think that simply having lessons in getting along or celebrating Human Relations Week will make students nonracist or nondiscriminatory in general. But it is impossible to be untouched by racism, sexism, linguicism, heterosexism, ageism, anti-Semitism, classism, and ethnocentrism in a society characterized by all of them. To expect schools to be an oasis of sensitivity and understanding in the midst of this stratification is unrealistic. Therefore, part of the mission of the school becomes creating the environment and encouragement that legitimates talk about inequality and makes it a source of dialogue. Teaching the missing or fragmented parts of our history is crucial to achieving this mission.

Although White students may be uncomfortable by discussions about race, Henry Giroux has suggested that bringing race and racism into full view can become a useful and positive pedagogical tool to help students locate themselves and their responsibilities concerning racism.[5] In addition, Beverly Daniel Tatum's ground-breaking work on bringing discussions of race out of the closet proposes discussing race and racism within the framework of racial and cultural identity theory. Doing so, she contends, can help students and teachers focus on how racism negatively affects all people and can provide a sense of hope for positive changes.[6]

What about teachers? Because many teachers have had little experience with diversity, discussions of racism often threaten to disrupt their deeply held ideals of fair play and equality. Many teachers are uneasy with these topics, and therefore fruitful classroom discussions about discrimination rarely happen. If this continues to be the case, neither unfair individual behaviors nor institutional policies and practices in schools will change. Students of disempowered groups will continue to bear the brunt of these kinds of inequities. The dilemma is how to challenge the silence about race and racism so that teachers can enter into meaningful and constructive dialogue with their students. In speaking specifically about confronting this issue in teacher education, Marilyn Cochran-Smith writes, "To teach lessons about race and racism in teacher education is to struggle to unlearn racism itself—to interrogate the assumptions that are deeply embedded in the curriculum, to our own complicity in maintaining existing systems of privilege and oppression, and to grapple with our own failure."[7]

For example, in research with teachers from around the country, Karen McLean Donaldson found that many teachers were in denial about racism and its effects in schools. On the other hand, those who became active in antiracist projects broadened their understanding and were able to use their new skills in creating affirming learning environments for all their students.[8]

One of the reasons schools are reluctant to tackle racism and discrimination is that these are disturbing topics for those who have traditionally benefited by their race, gender, and social class, among other advantageous differences. Because instruction in, and discussion of, such topics place people in the role of either the victimizer or the victimized, an initial and logical reaction, for example, of European American teachers and students in discussing race, is to feel guilty. But being antiracist does not mean flailing about in guilt and remorse. Although this reaction may be understandable, remaining at this level is immobilizing. Teachers and students need to move beyond guilt to a state of invigorated awareness and informed confidence in which they take personal and group action for positive change rather than hide behind feelings of remorse.

The primary victims of racism and discrimination are those who suffer its immediate consequences, but racism and discrimination are destructive and demeaning to everyone. Keeping this in mind, it is easier for all teachers and students to face these issues. Although not everyone is directly guilty of racism and discrimination, we are all responsible for it. What does this mean? Primarily, it means that working actively for social justice is everyone's business. Yet it is often the victims of racism and other kinds of discrimination who are left to act on their own. Everybody loses out when a particular group of students is scapegoated but confronting such scapegoating should be viewed as everyone's responsibility. Indeed, we will have come a long way when everybody feels this same obligation.

Multicultural Education Is Basic Education

Given the recurring concern for teaching the "basics," multicultural education must be understood as basic education. Multicultural literacy is just as indispensable for living in today's world as reading, writing, arithmetic, and computer literacy. When multicultural education is peripheral to the core curriculum, it is perceived as irrelevant to basic education. One of the major stumbling blocks to implementing a broadly conceptualized multicultural education is the ossification of the "canon" in our schools.

The canon, as understood in contemporary U.S. education, assumes that the knowledge that is most worthwhile is already in place. This notion explains the popularity of E. D. Hirsch's series *What Every [First, Second, Third . . .] Grader Needs to Know.*[9] Geared primarily to parents, this series builds on the fear that their children simply will not measure up if they do not possess the core knowledge (usually in the form of facts) that they need to succeed in school. According to this rather narrow view, the basics have, in effect, already been defined, and the knowledge taught is inevitably European, male, and upper class in origin and conception. In a recent response to Hirsch's view of cultural literacy, Eugene Provenzo faults Hirsch for a limited and rigid understanding of cultural literacy that is ultimately impoverished, elitist, antidemocratic, and even un-American in that it excludes so much that is uniquely American.[10]

The idea that there is a static and sacred knowledge that must be mastered is especially evident in the arts and social sciences. For instance, art history classes rarely consider other countries besides France's, Italy's, and sometimes England's Great Masters, yet surely other nations besides Europe have had great masters. "Classical music" is another example. What is called "classical music" is actually European classical music. Africa, Asia, and Latin America define their classical music in different ways. This same ethnocentrism is found in our history books, which portray Europeans and European Americans as the "actors" and all others as the recipients, bystanders, or bit players of history. The canon, as it currently stands, however, is unrealistic and incomplete because history is never as one-sided as it appears in most of our schools' curricula. We need to expand the definition of *basic* education by opening up curricula to a variety of perspectives and experiences.

This is not to say that the concern that the canon tries to address is not a genuine one. Modern-day knowledge is so dispersed and compartmentalized that our young people learn very little about commonalities in our history and culture. There is little core knowledge to which they are exposed and this can be problematic, but proposing static curricula, almost exclusively with European and European American referents, does little to expand our actual common culture.

At the same time, it is unrealistic, for a number of reasons, to expect perfectly "equal treatment" about all groups of people in school curricula and instruction. A "force-fit," which tries to equalize the number of African Americans, women, Jewish Americans, gays, and so on in the curriculum, is not what multicultural education is about. A great many groups have been denied access to participation in history. Thus, their role has not been equal, at least if we consider history in the traditional sense of great movers and shakers, monarchs and despots, and makers of war and peace. But, even within this somewhat narrow view of history, the participation of people of diverse backgrounds and social identities has nevertheless been appreciable. These heretofore ignored participants deserve to be included. The point is that those who have been important and/or prominent in the evolution of our history, arts, literature, and science, yet invisible, should be made visible. Recent literature anthologies are a good example of the inclusion of more voices and perspectives than ever before. Did these people become "great writers" overnight, or was it simply that they were "buried" for too long?

We are not recommending simply the "contributions" approach to history, literature, and the arts.[11] Such an approach can easily become patronizing by simply adding bits and pieces to a preconceived canon. Rather, missing from most curricula is a consideration of how generally excluded groups have made history and affected the arts, literature, geography, science, and philosophy on their own terms.

The alternative to multicultural education is monocultural education, which reflects only one reality and is biased toward the dominant group. Monocultural education is the order of the day in most of our schools. What students learn represents only a fraction of what is available knowledge, and those who decide what is most important make choices that are influenced by their own limited background, education, and experiences. Because the viewpoints of so many are left out, monocultural education is, at best, an incomplete education. It deprives all students of the diversity that is part of our world.

No school can consider that it is doing a proper or complete job unless its students develop multicultural literacy. What such a conception means in practice will no doubt differ from school to school, but at the very least, we should expect all students to be fluent in a language other than their own, aware of the literature and arts of many different peoples, and conversant with the history and geography not only of the United States but also of African, Asian, Latin American, and European countries. Through such an education, we should expect students to develop social and intellectual skills that help them understand and empathize with a wide diversity of people. Nothing can be more basic than this.

Multicultural Education Is Important for All Students

There is a widespread perception—or rather, misperception—that multicultural education is only for students of color, for urban students, or for so-called "disadvantaged" or "at-risk" students. This belief probably grew from the roots of multicultural education: the Civil Rights and Equal Education Movements of the 1960s. During that era, the primary objective of multicultural education was to address the needs of students who historically had been most neglected or miseducated by the schools, especially students of color. Those who first promoted multicultural education firmly believed that attention needed to be given to developing curriculum and materials that reflected these students' histories, cultures, and experiences. This thinking was historically necessary and is understandable even today, given the great curricular imbalance that continues to exist in most schools.

More recently, a broader conceptualization of multicultural education has gained acceptance. It is that all students are miseducated to the extent that they receive only a partial and biased education. Although it is true that the primary victims of biased education are those who are invisible in the curriculum, everyone misses out when education is biased. Important female figures, for example, are still largely absent in curricula, except in special courses on women's history that are few and far between. Working-class history is also absent in virtually all U.S. curricula. The children of the working class are deprived not only of a more forthright education but, more important, of a place in history, and students of all social class backgrounds are deprived of a more honest and complete view of our past. Likewise, there is a pervasive and impenetrable silence concerning gays and lesbians in most schools, not just in the curriculum but also in extracurricular activities. The result is that gay and lesbian students are placed at risk in terms of social well-being and academic achievement.[12]

Teachers in primarily White schools might think that multicultural education is not meant for their students. They could not be more wrong. White students receive only a partial education, which helps to legitimate their cultural blindness. Seeing only themselves, they may believe that they are the norm and thus most important and everyone else is secondary and less important. A recent book that challenges this perception (*What If All the Kids Are White?*) provides excellent strategies and resources for teachers working in mostly White communities.[13]

Males also receive an incomplete education because they (not to mention their female peers) learn little about women in their schooling. The children of the wealthy learn that the wealthy and the powerful are the real makers of history, the ones who have left their mark on civilization. Heterosexual students receive the message that gay and lesbian students should be ostracized because they are deviant and immoral. Only the able-bodied are reflected in most curricula, save for exceptions such as Helen Keller, who are presented as either bigger than life or as sources of pity. The humanity of all students is jeopardized as a result.

Multicultural education is, by definition, *inclusive*. Because it is *about* all people, it is also *for* all people, regardless of their ethnicity, ability, social class, language, sexual orientation, religion, gender, race, or other difference. It can even be convincingly argued that students from the dominant culture need multicultural education more than others because they are generally the most miseducated or uneducated about diversity. For example, European American youths often think that they do not even have a culture, at least not in the same sense that easily culturally identifiable youths do. At the same time, they feel that their ways of living, doing things, believing, and acting are "normal." Anything else is "ethnic" and exotic.

Feeling as they do, young people from dominant groups are prone to develop an unrealistic view of the world and of their place in it. These are the children who learn not to question, for example, the name of "flesh-colored" bandages, even though they are not the flesh color of 75 percent of the world's population. They do not even have to think about the fact that everyone, Christian or not, gets holidays at Christmas and Easter and that the holidays of other religions are given little attention in our calendars and school schedules. They may automatically assume that all children are raised by heterosexual biological parents and may be surprised to learn that many children are instead raised by just one parent, adoptive parents, grandparents, or lesbian or gay parents. As a result, whereas children from dominated groups may develop feelings of inferiority, dominant group children may develop feelings of superiority. Both responses are based on incomplete and inaccurate information about the complexity and diversity of the world, and both are harmful.

In spite of this, multicultural education continues to be thought of by many educators as education for the "culturally different" or the "disadvantaged." Teachers in predominantly European American schools, for example, may feel it is not important or necessary to teach their students anything about the Civil Rights Movement. Likewise, only in scattered bilingual programs in Mexican American communities are students exposed to literature by Mexican and Mexican American authors, and ethnic studies classes are often only offered at high schools with a high percentage of students of color. These are ethnocentric interpretations of multicultural education.

The thinking behind these actions is paternalistic as well as misinformed. Because anything remotely digressing from the "regular" (European American) curriculum is automatically considered soft by some educators, a traditional response to making a curriculum multicultural is to water it down. Poor pedagogical decisions are then based on the premise that so-called disadvantaged students need a watered-down version of the "real" curriculum, whereas more privileged children can handle the "regular" or more academically challenging curriculum. But, rather than dilute it, making a curriculum multicultural inevitably enriches it. All students would be enriched by reading the poetry of Langston Hughes or the stories of Gary Soto, by being fluent in a second language, or by understanding the history of Islam.

Multicultural Education Is Pervasive

Multicultural education is neither an activity that happens at a set period of the day nor another subject area to be covered. Having a "multicultural teacher" who goes from class to class in the same way as the music or art teacher is not what multicultural education should be about either. If this is a school's concept of multicultural education, it is little wonder that teachers sometimes decide that it is a frill they cannot afford.

A true multicultural approach is pervasive. It permeates everything: the school climate, physical environment, curriculum, and relationships among teachers and students and community.[14] It is apparent in every lesson, curriculum guide, unit, bulletin board, and letter that is sent home; it can be seen in the process by which books and audiovisual aids are acquired for the library, in the games played during recess, and in the lunch that is served. *Multicultural education is a philosophy, a way of looking at the world*, not simply a program or a class or a teacher. In this comprehensive way, multicultural education helps us rethink school reform.

What might a multicultural philosophy mean in the way that schools are organized? For one, it would probably mean the end of rigid forms of ability tracking, which inevitably favors some students over others. It would also mean that the complexion of the school, both literally and figuratively, would change. That is, schools would be integrated rather than segregated along lines of race and social class as they are now. In addition, there would be an effort to have the entire school staff be more representative of our nation's diversity. Pervasiveness would be apparent in the great variety and creativity of instructional strategies, so that students from all cultural groups, and females as well as males, would benefit from methods other than the traditional. The curriculum would be completely overhauled and would include the histories, viewpoints, and insights of many different peoples and both males and females. Topics usually considered "dangerous" could be talked about in classes, and students would be encouraged to become critical thinkers. Textbooks and other instructional materials would also reflect a pluralistic perspective. Families and other community people would be visible in the schools because they offer a unique and helpful viewpoint. Teachers, families, and students would have the opportunity to work together to design motivating and multiculturally appropriate curricula.

In other less global but no less important ways, the multicultural school would probably look vastly different. For example, the lunchroom might offer a variety of international meals, not because they are exotic delights but because they are the foods people in the community eat daily. Sports and games from all over the world might be played, and not all would be competitive. Letters would be sent home in the languages that the particular child's family understands. Children would not be punished for speaking their native language. On the contrary, they would be encouraged to do so, and it would be used in their instruction as well. In summary, the school would be a learning environment in which curriculum, pedagogy, and outreach are all consistent with a broadly conceptualized multicultural philosophy.

Multicultural Education Is Education for Social Justice

All good education connects theory with reflection and action, which is what Brazilian educator Paulo Freire defined as *praxis*.[15] Developing a multicultural perspective means learning how to think in more inclusive and expansive ways, reflecting on what is learned, and applying that learning to real situations. Nearly a century ago, educational philosopher John Dewey described what happens when education is not connected to reflection and action when he wrote "information severed from thoughtful action is dead, a mind-crushing load."[16] Multicultural education invites students and teachers to put their learning into action for social justice (for a definition of social justice, see Chapter 1). Whether debating a difficult issue, developing a community newspaper, starting a collaborative program at a local senior center, or organizing a petition for the removal of a potentially dangerous waste treatment plant in the neighborhood, students learn that they have power, collectively and individually, to make change.

This aspect of multicultural education fits in particularly well with the developmental level of young people who, starting in the middle elementary grades, are very conscious of what is fair and unfair. If their pronounced sense of justice is not channeled appropriately, the result can be anger, resentment, alienation, or dropping out of school physically or psychologically.

Preparing students for active membership in a democracy is also the basis of Deweyian philosophy and it has frequently been cited by schools as a major educational goal. But few schools serve as sites of apprenticeship for democracy. Policies and practices such as inflexible ability grouping, inequitable testing, monocultural curricula, and unimaginative pedagogy contradict this lofty aim. The result is that students in many schools perceive the claim of democracy to be a hollow and irrelevant issue. Henry Giroux, for example, has suggested that what he calls "the discourse of democracy" has been trivialized to mean such things as uncritical patriotism and mandatory pledges to the flag that the 9/11 disaster has exacerbated.[17] In some schools, democratic practices are found only in textbooks and confined to discussions of the American Revolution, and the chance for students to practice day-to-day democracy is minimal.

The fact that controversial topics such as power and inequality are rarely discussed in schools should come as no surprise. As institutions, schools are charged with maintaining the status quo, and discussing such issues might seem to threaten the status quo. But schools are also expected to promote equality. Exposing the contradictions between democratic ideals and actual manifestations of inequality makes many people uncomfortable, including some educators. Still, such matters are at the heart of a broadly conceptualized multicultural perspective because the subject matter of schooling is society, with all its wrinkles and warts and contradictions. Ethics and the distribution of power, status, and rewards are basic societal concerns; education *must* address them.

Although the connection between multicultural education and students' rights and responsibilities in a democracy is unmistakable, many young people do not learn about these responsibilities, about the challenges of democracy, or about the central role of citizens in ensuring and maintaining the privileges of democracy. Results from a recent study about the First Amendment, in which over 112,000 high school students were surveyed, provide a chilling example of how little students understand about democracy. The project, which was funded by the John S. and James L. Knight Foundation, found that when the First Amendment was quoted to students, more than one-third of them felt that it went too far in the rights it guarantees. The report concluded that "It appears, in fact, that our nation's high schools are failing their students when it comes to instilling in them appreciation for the First Amendment."[18] In this situation, social justice becomes an empty concept.

Multicultural education can have a great impact in helping to turn this situation around. A multicultural perspective presumes that classrooms should not simply allow discussions that focus on social justice, but also welcome them and even plan actively for such discussions to take place. These discussions might center on issues that adversely and disproportionately affect disenfranchised communities—poverty, discrimination, war, the national budget—and what students can do to address these problems. Because all of these problems are pluralistic, education must be multicultural.

Multicultural Education Is a Process

Curriculum and materials represent the content of multicultural education, but multicultural education is, above all, a process, that is, it is ongoing and dynamic. No one ever stops becoming a multicultural person, and knowledge is never complete. This means that there is no established canon that is set in stone. Second, multicultural education is a process because it primarily involves relationships among people. The sensitivity and understanding teachers show their students are more crucial in promoting student learning than the facts and figures they may know about different ethnic and cultural groups. Also, multicultural education is a process because it concerns such intangibles as expectations of student achievement, learning environments, students' learning preferences, and other cultural variables that are absolutely essential for schools to understand if they are to become successful with all students.

The dimension of multicultural education as a process is too often relegated to a secondary position, because content is easier to handle and has speedier results. For instance, staging an assembly program on Black History Month is easier than eliminating tracking: The former involves adding extracurricular content, and, although this is important and necessary, it is not as decisive at challenging fundamental perceptions about ability, social class, and race through the elimination of tracking. Another example: Changing a basal reader is easier than developing higher expectations for all students. The former involves substituting one book for another; the latter involves changing perceptions, behaviors, and knowledge, not an easy task. As a result, the processes of multicultural education are generally more complex, more politically volatile, and even more threatening to vested interests than introducing "controversial" content.

Because multicultural education is a process, it must debunk simplistic and erroneous conventional wisdom as well as dismantle policies and practices that are disadvantageous for some students at the expense of others. Through their teacher education programs, future teachers need to develop an awareness of the influence of culture and language on learning, the persistence of racism and discrimination in schools and society, and instructional and curricular strategies that encourage learning among a wide variety of students. Teachers' roles in the school also need to be redefined, because empowered teachers help to create learning environments in which students are empowered. Also, the role of families needs to be expanded so that the insights and values of the community can be accurately reflected in the school. Nothing short of a complete restructuring of curricula and the organization of schools is required. The process is complex, problematic, controversial, and time-consuming, but it is one in which teachers and schools must engage to make their schools truly multicultural.

Multicultural Education Is Critical Pedagogy

Knowledge is neither neutral nor apolitical, yet it is generally treated by teachers and schools as if it were. Consequently, knowledge taught in our schools tends to reflect the lowest common denominator—that which is sure to offend the fewest (and the most powerful) and is least controversial. Students may leave school with the impression that all major conflicts have already been resolved, but history, including educational history, is still full of great debates, controversies, and ideological struggles. These controversies and conflicts are often left at the schoolhouse door.

Every educational decision made at any level, whether by a teacher or by an entire school system, reflects the political ideology and worldview of the decision maker. Decisions to dismantle tracking, discontinue standardized tests, lengthen the school day, use one reading program rather than another, study literature from the Harlem Renaissance or Elizabethan period (or both), or use learning centers rather than rows of chairs, all reflect a particular view of learners and of education.

All the decisions we, as educators, make, no matter how neutral they seem, may have an impact on the lives and experiences of our students. This is true of the curriculum, books, and other materials we provide for them. State and local guidelines and mandates may limit what particular schools and teachers choose to teach, and this too is a political decision. What is excluded is often as revealing as what is included. Much of the literature taught at the high school level, for instance, is still heavily male-oriented, European, and European American. The significance of women, people of color, and those who write in other languages (even if their work has been translated into English) is diminished, unintentionally or not.

A major problem with a monocultural curriculum is that it gives students only one way of seeing the world. When reality is presented as static, finished and flat, the underlying tensions, controversies, passions, and problems faced by people throughout history and today disappear. To be informed and active participants in a democratic society, students need to understand the complexity of the world and the many perspectives involved. Using a critical perspective, students learn that there is not just one way (or even two or three) of viewing issues.

To explain what we mean by "using a critical perspective," we will be facetious and use the number 17 to explain it: Let's say there are at least 17 ways of understanding reality, and, until we have learned all of them, we have only part of the truth. The point is that there are multiple perspectives on every issue, but most of us have learned only the "safe" or standard ways of interpreting events and issues.

Textbooks in all subject areas exclude information about unpopular perspectives or the perspectives of disempowered groups in our society. These are the "lies my teacher told me" to which James Loewen refers in his powerful critique of U.S. history textbooks.[19] For instance, Thanksgiving is generally presented as an uncomplicated celebration in which Pilgrims and Indians shared the bounty of the harvest, but it is unlikely that the Wampanoags experienced Thanksgiving in this manner. One way to counter simplistic or one-sided views is to provide alternative or multiple views of the same topic. A good example is a book published by the Boston Children's Museum that presents a multiplicity of perspectives on Thanksgiving, including the Wampanoag perspective.[20] Likewise, few U.S. history texts include the perspective of working-class people, although they were and continue to be the backbone of our country. To cite another example, the immigrant experience is generally treated as a romantic and successful odyssey rather than the traumatic, wrenching, and often less-than-idyllic situation it was (and still is) for so many. The experiences of non-European immigrants or those forcibly incorporated into the United States are usually presented as if they were identical to the experiences of Europeans, which they have not at all been. We can also be sure that, if the perspectives of women were taken seriously, the school curriculum would be altered dramatically. The historian Howard Zinn provides one of the few examples of such a multifaceted, multicultural, and complex history. In his classic, *A People's History of the United States* (most recently updated in 2005), we clearly see a history full of passion and conflict with voices rarely included in traditional history texts.[21] All students need to understand these multiple perspectives and not only the viewpoints of dominant groups. Unless they do, students will continue to think of history as linear and fixed and to think of themselves as passive and unable to make changes in their communities and the larger society or even in their personal interactions.

According to James Banks, the main goal of a multicultural curriculum is to help students develop decision-making and social action skills.[22] By doing so, students learn to view events and situations from a variety of perspectives. A multicultural approach values diversity and encourages critical thinking, reflection, and action. Through this process, students are empowered. This is the basis of critical pedagogy. Its opposite is what Paulo Freire called "domesticating education,"—education that emphasizes passivity, acceptance, and submissiveness. According to Freire, education for domestication is a process of "transferring knowledge," whereas education for liberation is one of "transforming action."[23] Education that is liberating encourages students to take risks, to be curious, and to question. Rather than expecting students to repeat teachers' words, it expects them to seek their own answers.

How are critical pedagogy and multicultural education connected? They are what Geneva Gay has called "mirror images."[24] That is, they work together, according to Christine Sleeter, as "a form of resistance to dominant modes of schooling."[25] Critical pedagogy acknowledges rather than suppresses cultural and linguistic diversity. It is not simply the transfer of knowledge from teacher to students, even though that knowledge may challenge what students previously learned. Critical literacy, which developed from critical pedagogy and focuses specifically on language, has a similar goal. According to educational researcher Barbara Comber, "When teachers and students are engaged in critical literacy, they will be asking complicated questions about language and power, about people and lifestyles, about morality and ethics, about who is advantaged by the way things are and who is disadvantaged."[26]

A multicultural perspective does not simply operate on the principle of substituting one "truth" or perspective for another. Rather, it reflects on multiple and contradictory perspectives to understand reality more fully. The historian Ronald

Takaki expressed it best when he said, "The multiculturalism I have been seeking is a serious scholarship that includes all American peoples and challenges the traditional master narrative of American history." He concludes that "[t]he intellectual purpose of multiculturalism is a more accurate understanding of who we are as Americans."[27] This means that, in our pluralistic society, teachers and students need to learn to understand even those viewpoints with which they may disagree—not to practice "political correctness," but to develop a critical perspective about what they hear, read, or see. Individuals with this kind of critical perspective can use the understanding gained from mindful reflection to act as catalysts for change.

Ira Shor has proposed that critical pedagogy is more difficult precisely because it moves beyond academic discourse: "Testing the limits by practicing theory and theorizing practice in a real context is harder and more risky than theorizing theory without a context."[28] Yet the typical curriculum discourages students from thinking critically. In this sense, critical pedagogy takes courage. What does it mean to teach with courage? A few examples are in order. For teachers Darcy Ballentine and Lisa Hill, the purpose of teaching reading to their second, third, and fourth graders meant challenging the children to take up "brave books" that included what the teachers called "dangerous truths." These books broached topics such as racism and inequality, issues generally avoided in children's books (although certainly present in the lives of many children). Ballentine and Hill reflected on their experience in this way: "In the year that we taught these two texts, as well as many other brave books, our children's voices—in discussion, in explanations of their art, and in their dramatic enactments—continually reminded us that the risks we were taking in our teaching made sense."[29]

More recently, teacher Vivian Vasquez, in her book *Negotiating Critical Literacies with Young Children*, documented her experiences in using a critical literacy approach with three- to five-year-olds. Among the many examples she cites, one concerns what happened when the children in her class realized that a classmate had not eaten at the annual school barbecue because he was a vegetarian and only hot dogs and hamburgers had been served. On their own initiative—but having learned to think critically about social action—the students drew up a petition about providing vegetarian alternatives and gave it to the event committee. The next year, vegetarian alternatives were provided. In her beautiful and hopeful book, Vasquez demonstrates that critical literacy is not about despair and anger but rather about joy and inclusion. She also affirms that even the youngest children can learn to think critically and positively about their ability to effect change through their actions.[30]

History is generally written by the conquerors, not by the vanquished or by those who benefit least in society. The result is that history books are skewed in the direction of dominant groups in a society. When American Indian people write history books, they generally say that Columbus *invaded* rather than *discovered* this land, and that there was no heroic *westward expansion*, but rather an *eastern encroachment*. Mexican Americans often include references to Aztlán, the legendary land that was overrun by Europeans during this encroachment. Many Puerto Ricans remove the gratuitous word *granted* that appears in so many textbooks and explain that U.S. citizenship was instead *imposed*, and they emphasize that U.S. citizenship was opposed by even the two houses of the elected legislature that existed in Puerto Rico in 1917. African American historians tend to describe the active participation of enslaved Africans in their own liberation, and they often include such accounts as slave narratives to describe the rebellion and resistance of their people. Working class people who know their history usually credit laborers rather than Andrew Carnegie with the tremendous building boom that occurred in the United States, and the rapid growth of the U.S. economy, during the late 19th century and the 20th century. And Japanese Americans frequently cite racist hysteria, economic exploitation, and propaganda as major reasons for their internment in U.S. concentration camps during World War II.

Critical pedagogy is also an exploder of myths. It helps to expose and demystify as well as demythologize some of the truths that we take for granted and to analyze them critically and carefully. Justice for all, equal treatment under the law, and equal educational opportunity, although certainly ideals worth believing in and striving for, are not always the reality. The problem is that we teach them as if they are, and were always, real and true, with no exceptions. Critical pedagogy allows us to have faith in these ideals while critically examining the discrepancies between the ideal and the reality.

Because critical pedagogy begins with the experiences and viewpoints of students, it is by its very nature multicultural. The most successful education is that which begins with the learner and, when a multicultural perspective underpins education, students themselves become the foundation for the curriculum. However, a liberating education also takes students beyond their own particular and therefore limited experiences, no matter what their background.

Critical pedagogy is not new, although it has been referred to by other terms in other times. In our country, precursors to critical pedagogy can be found in the work of African American educators such as Carter Woodson and W. E. B. Du Bois.[31] In Brazil, the historic work of Paulo Freire influenced literacy and liberation movements throughout the world. Even before Freire, critical pedagogy was being practiced in other parts of the world. Almost half a century ago, Sylvia Ashton-Warner, teaching Maori children in New Zealand, found that the curriculum, materials, viewpoints, and pedagogy that had been used in educating them were all borrowed from the dominant culture. Because Maori children had been failed dismally by New Zealand schools, Ashton-Warner developed a strategy for literacy based on the children's experiences and interests. Calling it an "organic" approach, she taught children how to read by using the words they wanted to learn. Each child would bring in a number of new words each day, learn to read them, and then use them in writing. Because Ashton-Warner's approach was based on what children knew and wanted to know, it was extraordinarily successful. In contrast, basal readers, having little to do with Maori children's experiences, were mechanistic instruments that imposed severe limitations on the students' creativity and expressiveness.[32]

Other approaches that have successfully used the experiences of students are worth mentioning. The superb preschool curriculum developed nearly two decades ago by Louise Derman-Sparks and the Anti-Bias Curriculum Task Force is especially noteworthy. Another recent example is Mary Cowhey's approach. A first- and second-grade teacher, Cowhey has written about how she uses critical pedagogy to help create a strong community as well as to teach her students to question everything they learn. Catherine Compton-Lilly, in her role as a first-grade teacher and later a reading teacher, used a critical perspective to develop classroom strategies to "change the world" by confronting assumptions about race, poverty, and culture. Instructional strategies based on students' languages, cultures, families, and communities are also included in wonderful books by the educational organizations Rethinking Schools and Teaching for Change. Ira Shor's descriptions of the work he does in his own college classroom are further proof of the power of critical pedagogy at all levels. In the same category, Enid Lee, Deborah Menkart, and Margo Okazawa-Rey have developed an exceptional professional development guide for teachers and preservice teachers.[33]

Summary

Multicultural education represents a way of rethinking school reform because it responds to many of the problematic factors leading to school underachievement and failure. When implemented comprehensively, multicultural education can transform and enrich the schooling of all young people. Because multicultural education takes into account the cultures, languages, and experiences of all students, it can go beyond the simple transfer of skills to include those attitudes and critical, analytical abilities that have the potential to empower students for productive and meaningful lives.

This discussion leads us to an intriguing insight: In the final analysis, multicultural education as defined here is simply good pedagogy. That is, all good education takes students seriously, uses their experiences as a basis for further learning, and helps them to develop into informed, critically aware, and empowered citizens. What is multicultural about this? To put it simply, in our multicultural society, all good education needs to take into account the diversity of our student population. Multicultural education is good education for a larger number of our students. Is multicultural education just as necessary in a monocultural society? In response, we might legitimately ask whether even the most ethnically homogeneous society is truly monocultural, considering the diversity of social class, language, sexual orientation, physical and mental ability, and other human and social differences that exist in all societies. Our world is increasingly interdependent, and all students need to understand their role in a global society, not simply in their small town, city, or nation. Multicultural education is a process that goes beyond the changing demographics in a particular country. It is more effective education for a changing world.

Notes

1 A comprehensive resource on the history, goals, and concerns of multicultural education is *Handbook of Research on Multicultural Education*, 2nd ed., edited by James A. Banks and Cherry A. McGee Banks (San Francisco: Jossey-Bass, 2004).

2 Meyer Weinberg, "Notes from the Editor." *A Chronicle of Equal Education* 4, no. 3 (November 1982): 7.

3 Michelle Fine, *Framing Dropouts: Notes on the Politics of an Urban Public High School* (Albany: State University of New York Press, 1991).

4 Jonathan Kozol, "Great Men and Women (Tailored for School Use)." *Learning Magazine* (December 1975): 16–20.

5 Henry Giroux, "Rewriting the Discourse of Racial Identity: Towards a Pedagogy and Politics of Whiteness." *Harvard Educational Review* 67, no. 2 (Summer 1997): 285–320.

6 Beverly Daniel Tatum, *Why Are All the Black Kids Sitting Together in the Cafeteria? and Other Conversations About Race* (New York: Basic Books, 1997).

7 Marilyn Cochran-Smith, "Blind Vision: Unlearning Racism in Teacher Education." *Harvard Educational Review* 70, no. 2 (Summer 2000): 57–190.

8 Karen B. McLean Donaldson, *Shattering the Denial: Protocols for the Classrooms and Beyond* (Westport, CT: Bergin and Garvey, 2001).

9 Published by Delta beginning in 1994, these texts include the "core" knowledge that children are supposed to know at different grade levels in order to do well in school. As an example, see *What Your Fourth Grader Needs to Know: Fundamentals of a Good Fourth-Grade Education (The Core Knowledge)*, edited by E. D. Hirsch (New York: Delta, 1994).

10 Eugene F. Provenzo, Jr., *Critical Literacy: What Every American Ought to Know* (Boulder, CO: Paradigm, 2005).

11 For a discussion of different levels of curriculum integration in multicultural education, see James A. Banks, *Teaching Strategies for Ethnic Studies*, 7th ed. (Boston: Allyn and Bacon, 2003).

12 See, for example, Joan Roughgarden, *Evolution's Rainbow: Diversity, Gender, and Sexuality in Nature and People* (Berkeley: University of California Press, 2005); and Ian Ayres and Jennifer Gararda Brown, *Straightforward* (Princeton, NJ: Princeton University Press, 2005).

13 Louise Derman-Sparks, Patricia G. Ramsey, Julie Olsen Edwards, and Carol Brunson Day, *What If All The Kids Are White? Anti-Bias Multicultural Education With Young Children and Families* (New York: Teachers College Press, 2006).

14 A good example of how a multicultural approach includes educators, students, and families can be found in Patricia G. Ramsey, ed., *Teaching and Learning in a Diverse World: Multicultural Education for Young Children*, 3rd ed. (New York: Teachers College Press, 2004).

15 Paulo Freire, *Pedagogy of the Oppressed* (New York: Seabury Press, 1970).

16 John Dewey, *Democracy and Education* (New York: Free Press, 1966; first published 1916): 153.

17 Henry A. Giroux, "Democracy, Freedom, and Justice After September 11th: Rethinking the Role of Educators and the Politics of Schooling." *Teachers College Record* 104, no. 6 (September 2002): 1138–1162.

18 "Future of the First Amendment." John S. and James L. Knight Foundation, 2005. Available at: http://firstamendmentfuture.org

19 James W. Loewen, *Lies My Teacher Told Me: Everything Your American History Textbook Got Wrong* (New York: New Press, reissue edition, 2005).

20 Children's Museum, Boston, *Many Thanksgivings: Teaching Thanksgiving—Including the Wampanoag Perspective* (Boston: The Children's Museum, 2002).

21 Howard Zinn, *A People's History of the United States, 1492–Present* (New York: Harper Perennial, 2001; 1st ed., 1980).

22 James A. Banks, *Teaching Strategies for Ethnic Studies*, 7th ed. (Boston: Allyn and Bacon, 2003).

23 Paulo Freire, *The Politics of Education: Culture, Power, and Liberation* (South Hadley, MA: Bergen and Garvey, 1985).

24 Geneva Gay, "Mirror Images on Common Issues: Parallels Between Multicultural Education and Critical Pedagogy." In *Multicultural Education, Critical Pedagogy,*

and the Politics of Difference, edited by Christine E. Sleeter and Peter L. McLaren (Albany: State University of New York Press, 1996): 155–189.

25 Christine E. Sleeter, *Multicultural Education and Social Activism* (Albany, NY: State University of New York Press, 1996): 2.

26 Barbara Comber, "Critical Literacies and Local Action: Teacher Knowledge and a 'New' Research Agenda." In *Negotiating Critical Literacies in Classrooms*, edited by Barbara Comber and Anne Simpson. (Mahwah, NJ: Lawrence Erlbaum, 2001): 271.

27 Joan Montgomery, "A Different Mirror: A Conversation with Ronald Takaki," *Educational Leadership* 56, no. 7 (April 1999): 9–13.

28 Ira Shor, *When Students Have Power: Negotiating Authority in a Critical Pedagogy* (Chicago: University of Chicago Press, 1996): 3.

29 Darcy Ballentine and Lisa Hill, "Teaching Beyond Once Upon a Time." *Language Arts* 78, no. 1 (September 2000): 11–20.

30 Vivian Vasquez, *Negotiating Critical Literacies with Young Children* (Mahwah, NJ: Lawrence Erlbaum, 2004).

31 See, for instance, Carter G. Woodson, *The Miseducation of the Negro* (Washington, DC: Associated Publishers, 1933); W. E. B. Du Bois, "Does the Negro Need Separate Schools?" *Journal of Negro Education* 4, no. 3 (July 1935): 328–335. For a historical analysis of multicultural education and critical pedagogy, see James A. Banks, "Multicultural Education: Historical Development, Dimensions, and Practice." In *Handbook of Research on Multicultural Education*, 2nd ed., edited by James A. Banks and Cherry A. McGee Banks (San Francisco: Jossey-Bass, 2004).

32 Sylvia Ashton-Warner, *Teacher* (New York: Simon & Schuster, 1963).

33 See, for example, Louise Derman-Sparks and the A.B.C. Task Force, *Anti-Bias Curriculum: Tools for Empowering Young Children* (Washington, DC: National Association for the Education of Young Children, 1989); Mary Cowhey, *Black Ants and Buddhists: Thinking Critically and Teaching Differently in the Primary Grades* (Portland, ME: Stenhouse, 2006); Catherine Compton-Lilly, *Confronting Racism, Poverty, and Power: Classroom Strategies to Change the World* (Portsmouth, NH: Heinemann, 2004); Bill Bigelow, Linda Christensen, Stanley Karp, Barbara Miner, and Bob Peterson, eds., *Rethinking Our Classrooms: Teaching for Equity and Justice*, vol. 1 (Milwaukee, WI: Rethinking Schools, 1994); Bill Bigelow, Brenda Harvey, Stan Karp, and Larry Miller, eds., *Rethinking Our Classrooms: Teaching for Equity and Justice*, vol. 2 (Milwaukee, WI: Rethinking Schools, 2001); Ira Shor, *When Students Have Power: Negotiating Authority in a Critical Pedagogy* (Chicago: University of Chicago Press, 1997); and Enid Lee, Deborah Menkart, Margo Okazawa-Rey, *Beyond Heroes and Holidays: A Practical Guide to K-12 Anti-Racist, Multicultural Education and Staff Development* (Washington, DC: Network of Educators on the Americas [NECA], 1998). Also, two educational organizations, Teaching for Change and Rethinking Schools, have many excellent resources available.

Critical Questions

1 What do you see as the difference between a broadly conceptualized multicultural education and multicultural education defined in terms of "holidays and heroes"?

2 Do you believe it is important for anti-racism and anti-discrimination, in general, to be at the core of multicultural education? Why or why not?

3 Would you say that European American students are miseducated if they are not exposed to a multicultural curriculum? Similarly, are males miseducated if they do not learn about women in history? Why?

4 Think of a number of curriculum ideas that conform to the definition of multicultural education as social justice. How might students be engaged

through the curriculum to consider and act on issues of social justice? Give some specific examples.

5   How do *you* define multicultural education? Explain your definition.

Activities for Your Classroom

1   Think of some curriculum ideas that conform to the definition of multicultural education as social justice. How might students be engaged through the curriculum to consider and act on issues of social justice? Give specific examples.

2   With a group of colleagues, design an art, science, or math project that builds on multicultural education as critical pedagogy. How would it do this? In what activities would students be involved? How would these activities motivate them to think critically and become empowered?

3   Speak with your students about multicultural education. Do they know what it is? How do they define it? Do they think it is important? Why or why not? What can you learn from this discussion?

Community-Based Activities and Advocacy

1   Does your school have a mission statement? If so, is multicultural education included in a substantive way? If it is not, how might you revise the mission statement? Work with colleagues in your school or school system to suggest a change that emphasizes a multicultural perspective. Present it to your school council or to the central school board.

2   Prepare a workshop for the colleagues in your school in which you present the concepts of multicultural education as defined in this chapter. Work with a colleague or group of colleagues to design it. How would you present it? What materials might you include? What ideas would you focus on? If you feel confident enough to present it, consult with your principal about when it might be done.

Sources for a presentation on multicultural education:

Banks, J. & Banks, C. A. M. (2009). *Multicultural education: Issues and perspectives*, 7th ed. Boston: Allyn & Bacon.

National Association for Multicultural Education (NAME): http://www.nameorg.org

Nieto, S. & Bode, P. (2008). *Affirming diversity: The sociopolitical context of multicultural education*. Boston: Allyn & Bacon.

Supplementary Resources for Further Reflection and Study

Banks, J. A. & Banks, C. A. M. (Eds.). (2004). *Handbook of research on multicultural education*, 2nd ed. San Francisco: Jossey-Bass.

Written by many of the best-known scholars in the field, this volume includes almost 50 chapters devoted to the history, philosophy, and implications of multicultural education.

Nieto, S. (2009). Multicultural education in the United States: Historical realities, ongoing challenges, and transformative possibilities. In J. A. Banks (Ed.). *The Routledge international companion to multicultural education.* New York: Routledge.

A historical and conceptual overview of multicultural education in the United States, this chapter is part of a volume that places the field in an international context.

Sleeter, C. E. (2005). *Un-standardizing curriculum: Multicultural teaching in the standards-based classroom.* New York: Teachers College Press.

In this book, Christine Sleeter and a number of classroom teachers demonstrate how it is possible, even in times of rigid accountability and standardization, to develop curriculum with a multicultural perspective.

Spring, Joel (2006). *Deculturalization and the struggle for equality: A brief history of the education of dominated cultures in the United States,* 5th ed. New York: McGraw-Hill, Inc.

Spring provides short but compelling histories of the education of people of color in the United States that can help teachers understand the contemporary issues and problems of students from these groups in U.S. schools.

5   Public Education in the Twentieth Century and Beyond

High Hopes, Broken Promises, and an Uncertain Future

The following article, which first appeared in the *Harvard Educational Review* as part of its seventy-fifth anniversary issue in 2005, argues that the history of education in the United States is also the history of the struggle for equal educational opportunity. These two movements cannot be separated because although the nation has been defined from its very beginning by noble ideals of democracy and fair play, the reality has been quite different for marginalized segments of the population. These marginalized segments include the poor, African Americans, Latinos/as, girls and women, gay, lesbian, bisexual, and transgender (GLBT) communities, and more. As a result, nearly every significant educational movement in the nation has focused on expanding educational opportunities for these and other communities.

When the colonies first joined to become the United States of America over two centuries ago, formal education was largely reserved for the sons of wealthy White landowners and merchants. As the nation grew and developed, it became clear that formal education was a necessity for a broader segment of the population. With Horace Mann's appointment as Secretary of Education in Massachusetts in 1837, the idea that all students were entitled to a free, public, and compulsory education was born. The "common school" became the impetus for the belief that all children should be educated at public expense to reach their potential and become productive citizens of a democratic society. Of course, large segments of the population were still excluded, particularly people of color, as well as students with special needs, females, immigrants, and those too poor to attend school when their labor was needed at home. Many movements for expanding the benefits of education followed. The following chapter focuses on just three of those movements: desegregation, bilingual education, and multicultural education. Beginning with a review of the demographics of the nation, the article goes on to discuss various theories of achievement to explain why some segments of the population have been systematically excluded, and why these communities have nevertheless held high hopes for the benefits of education. Finally, the three movements are explored, along with the disappointments and possibilities they provide for the future of public education.

Public education and democracy have been firmly linked in the popular imagination since at least 1848, when Horace Mann, in his twelfth annual report to the Massachusetts State Board of Education, declared, "Education then, beyond all other devices of human origin, is a great equalizer of the conditions of men" (1868, p. 669). Half a century later, and just a few short years before the *Harvard Educational Review* published its inaugural issue, John Dewey's (1916) progressive notions about education cemented the link between education and democracy. According to Dewey, schools could serve not only to level the playing field, but also as an apprenticeship for civic life. Current proclamations about public education seem strangely at odds with these sentiments. Now the talk is more about testing and rubrics than about democracy and equality, making it clear that we have strayed far afield from the ideals articulated by Mann and Dewey.

In commemorating the *Harvard Educational Review*'s 75th anniversary, it is useful to reflect on how and why the goals of public education have seemingly shifted in such a dramatic way. In this article, I argue that the quintessential questions of public schooling over the past seventy-five years, and the answers to them, have emerged primarily from the changing demographics in our nation and schools. That is, changes in population in terms of race, ethinicity, social class, and other differences have helped to shape the educational experience of all students in our schools. I also suggest that the history of the past seventy-five years will influence how, as a nation, we view, design, and implement public education in the coming century.

In what follows, I present a broad overview of the hopes and disappointments of K-12 public education over the past seventy-five years, as well as the prospects for its future. Differences in race, ethnicity, social class, language, gender, sexual orientation, religion, and exceptionality, among others, have all defined inequality in public education. Each of these issues has also been the subject of important struggles for educational equality throughout the past century. One brief essay, however, cannot hope to address all these concerns fairly. Therefore, I have chosen to focus on race, ethnicity, social class, and language, and have selected as case studies three major efforts to equalize learning for all students that have responded to these four concerns and that have subsequently shifted the historical development of our public schools. These three efforts—desegregation, bilingual education, and multicultural education—will also no doubt influence future directions for school reform.

I begin with the changing nature of the student population and how it has affected the opportunities offered by public schools, and whether those opportunities have brought us any closer to public education as the democratic "equalizer." As part of this discussion, I review a number of theories advanced over the past century to explain the underachievement of students of diverse cultural, linguistic, and racial backgrounds. I then present brief case studies of the social and educational movements that responded to inequality as it has been manifested in various ways and in different communities: desegregation, bilingual education, and multicultural education. How these efforts have been thwarted is the subject of the next section, and I conclude with reflections on the need to renew the nation's commitment to public education and the public good in the coming century.

Changing Demographics, Changing Classrooms

Although the United States has always been a multiracial and multiethnic nation, it is far more diverse today than it was seventy-five years ago when the *Harvard Educational Review* was inaugurated. As of the year 2000, people of color made up 25 percent of our total population, a 5 percent increase from just a decade earlier. This growing racial and ethnic diversity has been accompanied by a growing linguistic diversity: Currently, 18 percent of U.S. residents speak a language other than English at home, with Spanish the language spoken by half of these (U.S. Census Bureau, 2000a). Also in 2000, the number of foreign-born or first-generation U.S. residents reached the highest level in U.S. history, 56 million, or triple the number in 1970. Unlike previous immigrants who were primarily from Europe, only 15 percent of recent immigrants come from Europe, with over half from Latin America and a quarter from Asia (U.S. Census Bureau, 2002).

It should come as no surprise, then, that the nation's public schools are also very different from what they were just a few decades ago. Although not yet a major-ity, the number of children in our public schools who represent backgrounds other than European American is growing rapidly: Whites still make up more than half of all students, but they are a dwindling majority, at just 61.2 percent. Blacks comprise 17.2 percent, Hispanics, 16.3 percent, Asian/Pacific Islanders, 4.1 percent, and American Indian/Alaska Natives, 1.2 percent of students in public schools (National Center for Education Statistics, 2002).

Besides differences in race/ethnicity and language, our nation is also character-ized by growing disparities in wealth, and it is especially bleak among people of color: while Whites represent just over 9 percent of the poor, Blacks are over 22 percent and Hispanics over 21 percent of those living in poverty (U.S. Census Bureau, 2000b).

Theories of Achievement: Changing Contexts, Changing Explanations

Given the changing demographics of students in U.S. schools, the discrepancy in academic achievement among various groups of students has been the subject of much speculation and research for several decades. Since almost the beginning of the twentieth century, competing theories have been advanced to explain what is now known as the "minority achievement gap," that is, the difference between the academic achievement of White, middle-class students and their peers of other social and cultural backgrounds, especially African Americans, Latinos, and Native Americans, as well as some Asian Pacific Americans. These theories have positioned students in various ways: as genetically inferior, culturally deprived, culturally different, economically disadvantaged, victims of structural inequality, and more. Because explanations of academic failure and success have been at the center of much educational policy and practice in K-12 education over the past century, I briefly review some of the more salient theories below.

Genetic and Cultural Inferiority

One of the most popular theories throughout the past several decades has been that students of racial minority and economically poor backgrounds are genetically or culturally inferior. This theory, which gained great momentum in the 1960s, was made by such researchers as Frank Reissman (1962), Carl Bereiter and Siegfried Engelmann (1966), and, most persuasively, by Arthur Jensen in a controversial but nevertheless influential 1969 *Harvard Educational Review* article, in which he posited that the poor achievement of African American students could be explained mostly by genetic differences. Although the terms used then (*culturally deprived, genetically inferior*) may be out of favor now, these viewpoints held great sway during the 1960s, and they were responsible for much of the social and educational policy made in the following decades. The assumption behind these theories was that students' failure to achieve could be explained by their so-called deficits, including their genetic makeup, poorly developed language skills, and inadequate mothering, among others.

William Ryan, an early critic of deficit theories, helped lay the groundwork to challenge such theories by arguing that they represented a strategy to "blame the victim." He wrote:

> We are dealing, it would seem, not so much with culturally deprived children as with culturally depriving schools. And the task to be accomplished is not to revise, amend, and repair deficient children, but to alter and transform the atmosphere and operations of the schools to which we commit these children.
>
> (1972, p. 61)

Ryan's eloquent argument against deficit theories notwithstanding, genetic and cultural inferiority theories are not a thing of the past. They survive, albeit couched in different terms. Current discourse continues to position marginalized groups as predetermined low achievers by using buzzwords such as "at risk" and "disadvantaged," terms reminiscent of the reasoning used as the basis of the theories made popular in the 1960s. In addition, such terms are based on a psychological framework that lays the blame primarily on students' individual and cultural characteristics rather than on structural inequality, social class inequality, and racism. This reasoning, in turn, supports questionable policies and practices that further jeopardize students of nonmajority backgrounds. For example, Catherine Banks (2004) points out that the imprecise and widely used label "at risk" became a funding category for state and federal educational agencies, making the terminology popular with bureaucrats and thus perpetuating a particular way for teachers and administrators to think about such students. Viewing these students and their families as being primarily responsible for student failure to learn has meant that more deep-seated issues of inequality and injustice have often been neglected.

Economic and Social Reproduction Theories

Beginning in the 1970s, activists, educators, and researchers challenged deficit theories by insisting that structural inequality, racism, and poverty—issues overlooked by deficit theories—could better explain students' poor academic achievement. Revisionist historians and economists such as Joel Spring (1972) and Samuel Bowles and Herbert Gintis (1976) suggested that schools tend to serve the interests of the dominant classes by reproducing the economic and social relations of society. Michael Katz (1975), for instance, demonstrated that from the start, public schools were "universal, tax-supported, free, compulsory, bureaucratically arranged, class-biased, and racist" (p. 106). According to Katz, these seemingly contradictory features derived from the very purpose of public schools, which was largely to train different segments of society for particular roles in life. As a result, these historians and economists claimed, schools reproduced the status quo and not only reflected structural inequalities based on class, race, and gender, but also helped to *create and maintain* these inequalities.

Economic and social reproduction theorists maintained that the "sorting" function of schools, to use a term coined by Spring (1972), is apparent in everything from physical structure to curriculum and instruction. For example, the schools of the poor are generally factory-like fortresses that operate with an abundance of bells and other controlling mechanisms, whereas the schools of the wealthy tend to be much more open physically and psychologically, thus giving students more autonomy and opportunities for creative thinking (Anyon, 1981). Moreover, relations between students and teachers in poor communities reflect a much more dominant-dominated relationship than in middle-class or wealthy communities (McDermott, 1977). Hence, the sorting function of the schools replicates the stratification of society. The benign, stated purpose of U.S. schools as an "equalizer" was seriously questioned by these theories.

The arguments of the social reproduction theorists have had a tremendous impact on educational thinking since the 1970s. But by concentrating primarily on the labor-market purpose of schooling, they tended to fall into a static and mechanistic explanation of school success or failure. Put in its most simplistic form, this analysis assumes that schooling is simply imposed from above and accepted from below. Yet because schools are complex and perplexing institutions, things are not always as neat or apparent as the theory of social and economic reproduction would suggest. The lengthy struggles over schooling in which many communities have been historically engaged—including desegregation, bilingual education, multicultural education, and access to education for females and students with special needs—are not accounted for in these theories. Some theorists, such as Michael Apple (1986), have suggested instead that schools are a product of conflicts among competing group interests, and that the purposes of the dominant class are never perfectly reflected in the schools, but rather are resisted and modified by the recipients of schooling.

Cultural Incompatibility Theory

Another explanation for school failure, the cultural mismatch or cultural difference theory, emerged in the early 1970s as a counterpoint to the cultural deprivation theory. According to this theory, because school culture and home culture are often at odds, the result is a "cultural clash" that gets in the way of student learning. As a result, the differing experiences, values, skills, expectations, and lifestyles with which children enter school, and whether these differences are consistent or not with the school environment, need to be considered. The more congruent home and school cultures are, the reasoning goes, the more successful students will be. Some of the theorists who promoted this line of thinking also identified institutional racism as being at the core of cultural mismatches. For example, the link between cultural mismatch and racism was eloquently articulated in an earlier *Harvard Educational Review* article by Baratz and Baratz (1970).

Cultural mismatch theories have continued to evolve, albeit with various names and subtle differences (cultural compatibility, cultural congruence, cultural competence, cultural responsiveness, culturally relevant and culturally appropriate instruction, among others). In the early 1980s, for example, Katherine Au (1980) was instrumental in identifying what she called *cultural congruence in instruction* as an important consideration in educating Hawaiian children. Gloria Ladson-Billings (1994), in coining the term *culturally relevant teaching*, has suggested that this kind of pedagogy is in sharp contrast to *assimilationist teaching*, whose main purpose is to transmit the dominant culture's beliefs and values in an uncritical way to all students. In the same vein, Geneva Gay's (2000) work in defining and explicating what she calls *culturally responsive teaching* has been significant.

The cultural mismatch theory has been a more hopeful explanation for school achievement than explanations based on genetic inferiority or economic reproduction because it assumes that teachers can learn to create environments in which all students can be successful learners. Hence, it respects teachers as creative intellectuals rather than simply as technicians.

Sociocultural Explanations for School Achievement

Another closely related theory links the cultural practices of particular communities with their students' learning in school settings. Shirley Brice Heath's (1983) classic research with a Black community that she called "Trackton" is a persuasive example of the power of aligning teaching to students' cultural practices. She found that the kinds of questioning rituals in which the parents and other adults engaged with children were not preparing the children adequately for school activities.

Middle-class parents, for example, usually speak Standard English, and they also tend to engage in school-like prereading activities much more regularly than do working-class parents. Also, in observing the White, middle-class teachers of these children, Heath found that the questions they asked students were qualitatively different from the kinds of questions the children were accustomed to at home. Teachers' questions concerned pulling attributes of things out of context and naming them (e.g., to identify size, shape, or color). In contrast, in their homes the children were asked questions about whole events or objects, as well as about their uses, causes, and effects. These questions, which were frequently linguistically complex and required children to have a sophisticated use of language, also required them to make analogical comparisons and understand complex metaphors. Usually there was no one "right" answer, because answers involved telling a story or describing a situation. The result of the different kinds of questions asked in the different contexts was a perplexing lack of communication between students and teachers.

Heath's work, although similar to notions of cultural incompatibility, was based primarily on differences in language practices that were made clear through ethnographic research. For example, through a research project with Heath, the teachers became aware of the differences in questioning rituals, and they began to study the kinds of questions that adults in Trackton asked. Teachers were then able to use these kinds of questions as a basis for asking more traditional "school" questions, to which children also needed to become accustomed if they were to be successful in school. The results were dramatic: Children became active and enthusiastic participants in these lessons, a notable change from their previous passive behavior. Heath's landmark research has been followed by many other studies based on sociocultural theories that explain student learning (e.g., Willis, Lintz, & Mehan, 2004).

Students as Caste-like Minorities

In an alternative explanation of school failure and success, in the 1970s anthropologist John Ogbu (1987) began developing a highly influential theory that goes beyond cultural discontinuities. He suggested that in order to understand academic outcomes it is necessary to look not only at a group's cultural background, but also at its situation in the host society and its perceptions of opportunities available in that society. Ogbu classified most European immigrants in the United States as voluntary immigrants, and racial minority group immigrants as either voluntary or involuntary minorities, that is, those who come of their own free will as opposed to those who were conquered or colonized. According to Ogbu, involuntary minorities are those who have been incorporated into the United States against their will and thus have a "caste-like" status in the society. These include American Indians, African Americans, Mexicans, and Puerto Ricans.

Ogbu concluded that voluntary minorities tend to do better in school than those born in the United States because their self-esteem and school success depend not just on their ethnicity, but also on their interaction with U.S. society.

Moreover, they tend to arrive in the United States with strong self-concepts developed in their home countries, where they are not seen as minorities. On the other hand, according to Ogbu, most voluntary minorities have a "folk theory" of school success that sees the United States as a land of opportunity, where one gets ahead through education and hard work.

According to Ogbu, given the long history of discrimination and racism in the schools, involuntary minority children and their families are often distrustful of the education system. It is not unusual for students from these groups to engage in what Ogbu called *cultural inversion*, that is, to resist acquiring and demonstrating the culture and cognitive styles identified with the dominant group. These behaviors, considered "White" by such students, include being studious and hardworking, speaking Standard English, listening to European classical music, going to museums, and getting good grades. Instead, involuntary minority students may choose to engage in what Ogbu called *oppositional behavior*, emphasizing cultural behaviors that differentiate them from the majority and are in opposition to it. These students must cope, in the words of Signithia Fordham and John Ogbu, "with the burden of acting White" (1986, p. 186). They see little benefit from academic success, at least in terms of peer relationships. Those who excel in school may feel both internal ambivalence and external pressures not to manifest behaviors and attitudes that would define them as academically successful.

John Ogbu's theories have been helpful in explaining the differences in the school experiences of students of various backgrounds. But they have also come under criticism for being incomplete, ahistorical, inflexible regarding individual differences, and rigid in defining immigrants as either voluntary or involuntary. Ogbu's theories may place an inordinate responsibility on students and families for improving academic performance without taking into account either institutional racism or what Claude Steele (2004) has called the *stereotype threat*, that is, how societal stereotypes about particular groups can influence their academic performance. In addition, his explanation of oppositional culture comes dangerously close to the old concept of the "culture of poverty" popularized in the 1960s.

Resistance Theory

Resistance theory, as articulated by scholars such as Henry Giroux (1983), Jim Cummins (1996), Herb Kohl (1994), and others, adds another layer to the explanation of school failure. According to this theory, *not* learning what schools teach can be interpreted as a form of political resistance. Frederick Erickson (1993) maintains that whereas cultural differences may cause some initial school failures and misunderstandings, it is only when they become entrenched over time that a consistent pattern of refusing to learn arises.

Resistance theory is helpful because it attempts to explain the complex relationship of disempowered communities with their schools. Students and their families are not only victims of the education system, but also actors in it. They learn to react to schools in ways that make perfect sense, given the reality of the schools, although some of these coping strategies may in the long run be self-defeating and counterproductive.

An extreme form of refusing education is dropping out. Michelle Fine's (1991) landmark ethnography of a large urban school found that most dropouts were actually stronger students than those who stayed in school. The dropouts she interviewed expressed two major reasons for their decisions to leave school: a political stance of resistance, and disappointment with the promise of education. Many were articulate in their resistance to school, and even some of those who stayed were unsure what benefits they would derive from their education.

Care, Student Achievement, and Social Capital

An issue that has received great attention since the early 1990s in explaining student success or failure is what Nel Noddings (1992) has called the "ethic of care." For her, care is just as—and in some cases, even more—important than entrenched structural conditions that influence student learning. In this theory, whether and how teachers and schools care for students can make an immense difference in how students experience schooling. However, care does not just mean giving students hugs or pats on the back. It also means loving them by having high expectations and making rigorous demands. Angela Valenzuela (1999), in a three-year exploration of academic achievement among Mexican and Mexican American students in a Texas high school, provides compelling examples of how care among a small number of teachers made a difference in students' engagement with schooling. This was the case in spite of the general context of the school that provided what Valenzuela called *subtractive schooling*, that is, a process that divested students of the social and cultural resources they brought to their education, making them vulnerable for academic failure. Her research led Valenzuela to locate the problem of underachievement not in students' identities or parents' economic situation, but in school-based relationships and organizational structures. Similarly, Nilda Flores-González (2002), in a study of Latino students in Chicago, came to the conclusion that school structures and climate help create either "school kids"—that is, those who connect with schooling and thus have a better chance to succeed—or "street kids"—those who have largely given up on school because they do not see it as a place where they belong.

Another theory closely connected with the ethic of caring is described by Ricardo Stanton-Salazar (1997) as a social capital networks framework. According to Stanton-Salazar, social networks reproduce or deny privilege and power, and they are of key importance between adults and youth, particularly vulnerable youth who rarely have access to the social capital that more privileged students take for granted. The networks and institutional supports he identifies include particular discourses and social capital; access to gatekeepers and to other opportunities usually closed to disenfranchised students; advocacy; role modeling; emotional and moral support; and advice and guidance. In the end, Stanton-Salazar argues, it is through the power of institutional agents such as teachers, counselors, and other adults who can manipulate the social and institutional conditions in and out of school that can determine who "makes it" and who does not. The support provided by these institutional agents is linked with caring because it is only through trusting and close relationships with teachers that students will gain access to such networks.

Newer Perspectives

This brief review of some of the many theories of school achievement to describe the experiences of students of diverse backgrounds makes it clear that there is no simple explanation for student success or failure. Many of the theories developed over the past century have been inadequate or incomplete: some have failed to consider the significance of culture in learning; others have not taken into account the social, cultural, and political context of schooling; still others have placed all the responsibility for academic failure or success solely on students and their families.

Newer perspectives concerning the education of new and old immigrant groups of color in the United States have emerged in the past several years, and they add significantly to our understanding. For example, Alejandro Portes and Rubén Rumbaut (2001), in a series of long-term, comprehensive studies of immigrant families of various backgrounds, concluded that the process of growing up as an immigrant in the United States ranges from smooth acceptance to traumatic confrontation. They found that race is a paramount factor in whether and how groups are accepted into the mainstream, and it can trump the influence of other factors such as social class, religion, or language. They found, for example, that immigrants fleeing from Communism are received more favorably than those fleeing economic exploitation. They cite Haitians, Nicaraguans, and Mexicans as economic refugees, who have significantly lower earnings than Cubans and Vietnamese, even after controlling for level of education, knowledge of English, and occupation. No matter how long they have been here or how hard they work, the earnings of Mexicans, Nicaraguans, and Haitians remain consistently low, while those of Vietnamese and Cubans, viewed as political refugees, increase for each additional year of residence in the United States. Portes and Rumbaut (2001) come to the startling conclusion that no matter how educated a Mexican or Haitian is, his or her chances of moving ahead economically are significantly constrained by the social environment in which their group has been incorporated into the United States. For these groups, a college degree yields no improvement in earnings. This conclusion flies in the face of conventional wisdom that education equals economic advancement. Clearly, other factors—race, context of incorporation, and others—are also at work.

High Hopes

The above discussion leads to the inevitable conclusion that school achievement, always difficult to explain, must be approached by taking into account multiple, competing, and dynamic conditions: the school's tendency to replicate society and its inequities; cultural and language incompatibilities; the unfair and bureaucratic structures of schools; the nature of the relationships among students, teachers, and the communities they serve; and the political relationship of particular groups to society and the schools. Given the complexity of the problem, it is not surprising that public education in the United States has been characterized by both extraordinary achievement and abysmal disappointments, and by everything in between. At the same time, public education has remained the best hope for personal fulfillment and a more productive life for most segments of our population. In fact, public schools have been the major battleground for many movements to extend civil rights and privileges, not only those having to do directly with education.

Expanding Equal Educational Opportunity

Since free public education first took hold in the late nineteenth century, expanding educational opportunities to benefit a greater number of children has been of paramount importance for many educators and citizens. With increasing racial, linguistic, and economic diversity in our nation and schools, the challenge to expand the dream of an equal education for more students has been even greater. In fact, calls for equal education have riveted the nation's attention during much of the twentieth century, whether through the civil rights movement led by African Americans and their allies, or other movements that resulted in school boycotts and takeovers, or court challenges and commission hearings. In what follows, I offer a brief review of some examples of these struggles, focusing on desegregation, bilingual education, and multicultural education.

Desegregation

The history of desegregation represents the greatest manifestation of the struggle for equal education in the twentieth century. African Americans in the South were especially victimized by the Jim Crow doctrine of "separate but equal" schools, a doctrine that made a sham of the promise of equal education. Black schools, always inferior to White schools in terms of infrastructure and resources, nevertheless often provided nurturing and academically supportive environments for African American children (Siddle Walker, 1996). But racially segregated schools were also evident in other parts of the country. Gloria Ladson-Billings (2004), for instance, has documented the long history of African Americans' attempts to desegregate public schools, beginning as early as 1849 in Boston. Until recently, segregation was firmly etched in the popular consciousness as being only a Black/White issue. Yet other groups also experienced segregated schooling. A number of historians, including leading scholars and activists such as W. E. B. Du Bois (2001), George Sánchez (1940), and Carter Woodson (1933), began unearthing the multiracial history of segregation based on race and ethnicity many years ago. Besides African Americans, Mexicans and Native Americans were especially negatively affected by segregation. Other groups denied an equal education, through either outright exclusion or segregation, included Chinese and Japanese children, primarily in California but in other states as well (Pang, Kiang, & Pak, 2004).

Dismantling *de jure* segregation did not happen overnight, of course. Although segregated schools were a fixture in many places around the country, it was not until the momentous 1954 *Brown v. Board of Education* decision that segregation by race in public schools was finally declared illegal. The *Brown* decision, universally recognized as the case that shot down the doctrine of "separate but equal," is also considered by some to be the most pivotal event since the Fifteenth Amendment of 1870, which granted all male Americans the right to vote (Ramsey & Williams, 2003).

Since the 1970s a new generation of historians has taken on the task of documenting the multiracial history of unequal education (Anderson, 1988; Donato, 1997; Ruiz, 2001; San Miguel, 2001; Spring, 2004; Tyack, 1995; Weinberg, 1977). The brutal history of boarding schools in the Native American community, for instance, has only recently been brought to light (Archuleta, Child, & Lomawaima, 2000; McBeth, 1983). Mexican Americans, the Latino group with the most extensive experience in the United States, also faced a long history of exclusion. Yet few people, even educators, recognize the less well known but also watershed moments of their struggle for equal education in such cases as *Independent School District v. Salvatierra* in Texas (1930), protesting the segregation of Mexican children; *Roberto Alvarez v. Lemon Grove* in California in 1931 (see Alvarez, 1986), the first successful desegregation case in U.S. history; and *Méndez v. Westminster* in California's Orange County (1945), which ended the segregation of Mexican children in California schools. Some of these cases, in fact, served as legal precedent for the *Brown* decision. More recent immigrants, including Central Americans and Asian Pacific Americans, have also faced unequal schooling and have engaged in numerous activities from legal challenges to demands for school reform to change the situation (Rumbaut & Portes, 2001; Suárez-Orozco & Suárez-Orozco, 2001).

The struggles for equity in the past seventy-five years that emerged from the civil rights movement provide a graphic illustration of the hope and promise that U.S. public schools hold, particularly for those communities that have been marginalized in our society. Yet it is a sad fact that segregation in public schools is on the rise today. The continuing struggle for desegregation and equal access highlights the certainty of challenges in the future.

Bilingual Education

In the United States, language use and patriotic loyalty have often been linked, and patriotism has been measured by how quickly one abandons a native language and replaces it with English (Crawford, 2000; Skutnabb-Kangas & Cummins, 1988). Consequently, in U.S. classrooms, linguistic diversity has commonly been viewed as a temporary, if troublesome, barrier to learning. The thinking has been that once students learned English, learning could proceed unhampered. As a result, forgetting their native language has generally been viewed as a regrettable but necessary price to pay for the benefits of citizenship. But U.S. language policies and practices have by no means been uniform. Instead, they have ranged from "sink-or-swim" policies (i.e., immersing language-minority students in

English-only classrooms where they must fend for themselves), to the imposition of English as the sole medium of instruction (sometimes with minimal English as a second language [ESL] support), all the way to allowing and even encouraging bilingualism.

The notion that students needed to lose their native language in order to succeed in school has been challenged since the 1960s, when language-minority communities began to demand bilingual education (Crawford, 2004; García, 2001; Nieto, 2001). The struggle for bilingual education, one of many struggles that emerged from the civil rights movement, was based on the premise that teaching children in their native language would help turn around the abysmal educational outcomes that were traditional for many immigrants, particularly Latinos. As a result, from the 1960s to the 1990s, many advocates took to the streets, legislatures, and courts to advocate for bilingual education. The results can be seen in such cases as the 1974 *Lau v. Nichols*, and in such legislation as the 1968 Bilingual Education Act. In *Lau*, the U.S. Supreme Court recognized the connection between native language rights and equal educational opportunity by ruling unanimously that the civil rights of students who did not understand the language of instruction were indeed being violated. The Court's decision reads, in part:

> There is no equality of treatment merely by providing students with the same facilities, textbooks, teachers, and curriculum; for students who do not understand English are effectively foreclosed from any meaningful education. Basic skills are at the very core of what these public schools teach. Imposition of a requirement that, before a child can effectively participate in the educational program he must already have acquired those basic skills, is to make a mockery of public education.
>
> (*Lau v. Nichols*, 1974)

Although the decision did not impose any particular remedy, its impact was immediate and extensive. By 1975, the U.S. Office for Civil Rights and the Department of Health, Education, and Welfare issued a document called "The *Lau Remedies*," which served as the basis for determining whether or not school systems throughout the United States were in compliance with the *Lau* decision. Bilingual programs became the common remedy of most school systems.

Bilingual programs may also have secondary salutary effects beyond teaching children English and allowing them to retain their native language. These include motivating students to remain in school rather than dropping out and, in general, making the school experience more meaningful and enjoyable (Nieto, 2004). A related phenomenon may be that bilingual education reinforces close relationships among children and their family members, promoting better communication than if they were instructed solely in English and became less able to use their native language at home (Baker & Jones, 1998; Crawford, 2004).

Although bilingual education has generally been shown to be more effective than programs such as English immersion or ESL only in teaching English and helping students keep up academically with other subject areas, it remains controversial (Crawford, 2004; Cummins, 1996; Nieto, 2001). However, a recent literature review of related research by James Crawford (2004) confirms once again the superiority of the bilingual education approach. Based on this review, Crawford concluded that successful bilingual programs have demonstrated that students can learn through their native language while learning English and achieving academically. In fact, fluency in English, although necessary, is no guarantee that language-minority students will succeed in school or later in life. Alejandro Portes and Rubén Rumbaut (2001) have found that students from nationalities that speak English best (including West Indians and Filipinos) are not necessarily those who earn the highest incomes or have the highest number of managers and professionals among their ranks. Chinese and other Asians, and Colombians and other Latin Americans, who have relatively low English fluency earn considerably more. Race and social status also play a key role.

The public has always been deeply divided over bilingual education, and this is truer today than ever before. Examples can be seen in California's passing of Proposition 227 in 1998, which resulted in the elimination of bilingual education, and in similar propositions in Arizona (2000) and Massachusetts (2002). These measures demonstrate a general reluctance to support bilingual education because it involves the use of languages other than English for instruction. The fact that one of the fundamental goals of bilingual education is the learning of English often goes unmentioned by opponents, who may perceive using languages of instruction other than English as a threat to national unity. But the myth that English has been a unifying force is just that. James Crawford (2000), who has exhaustively researched language policies in the United States, has suggested that such notions obscure a multilingual tradition unsurpassed in its variety while also inventing a unifying role for English that it has rarely enjoyed.

Multicultural Education

The history of what is now known as multicultural education is a long one, beginning early in the twentieth century with calls for the improvement of education among African Americans (Du Bois, 2001; Woodson, 1933). A precursor to multicultural education was the intergroup and intercultural education movement that began in the late 1920s and lasted until the late 1950s (C. Banks, 2004). These movements were the first educational attempts to acknowledge the multiracial and multicultural character of the United States by incorporating curriculum and material that promoted intercultural understanding and respect. But multicultural education as we now know it began in the early 1970s, and it too—like desegregation and bilingual education—emerged from the civil rights movement.

Multicultural education covers a broad range of approaches and definitions (Banks & Banks, 2004). Nevertheless, most proponents agree that it is based on the need to provide all students with a high-quality and equitable education. This is particularly crucial for those students who have been failed by the public schools because of differences such as race/ethnicity, language, immigrant status, social class, and others that are often positioned negatively in society.

Besides affirming the identities of all students through a more inclusive curriculum and culturally responsive pedagogy, multicultural education also takes into account the sociopolitical context in which education takes place by challenging institutional policies and practices, both in schools and society, that perpetuate inequality. As such, it is part of comprehensive school reform and a project in the larger struggle for social justice (Nieto, 2004). For example, the growing research on inequality in education begun in the 1960s and continuing through the present has highlighted the deleterious effects of such policies as tracking (Oakes, 1985), inequitable funding (Kozol, 1991), testing (Neill, 1997), and others.

As a result, from the beginning, multicultural education was viewed as a way to achieve the elusive goal of an equal educational opportunity for students of all backgrounds and circumstances. Consequently, it was based on a number of premises: that all children bring resources and strengths to their learning; that racism and other individual and institutional biases frequently get in the way of an equitable education; that other societal and school environments and structures can also hinder learning; that acknowledging and supporting the cultures, backgrounds, and communities of all children can be a positive ingredient in their education; and that schools can become places of affirmation and success for all children.

Christine Sleeter and Carl Grant (1987), in an early and influential analysis of the field published in the *Harvard Educational Review*, identified five approaches to multicultural education: *teaching the culturally different*, based on the notion that instruction needs to be adapted for students who are different from "mainstream" or dominant group students; *human relations*, an approach that emphasizes the need to treat all people fairly and equitably; *single-group studies*, in which one specific ethnic or racial group is the basis of study; *multicultural education*, an approach that acknowledges and celebrates the differences that students bring to their education; and *education that is multicultural and social reconstructionist*, an approach to transform an entire educational program while critiquing social structures and encouraging students to take an active stance in changing them. Although these versions of multicultural education often have competing aims and approaches, from the beginning of its development all advocates have agreed that multicultural education in any form was a more hopeful approach than the monocultural education that was in place in most schools. Moreover, according to Patricia Ramsey and Leslie Williams (2003), while many practitioners have initially been attracted to the "teaching the culturally different" approach, their experiences eventually lead them to embrace a more critical stance in which they begin to question institutional policies that discriminate against some students based on their social and cultural identities.

To counter the tendency to focus on superficial approaches to multicultural education in schools, James Banks (1991) developed what he called the *dimensions of multicultural education*. The dimensions include content integration, the extent to which content from a variety of cultures and groups is integrated into the curriculum; knowledge construction, the extent to which teachers and students understand how the perspectives, biases, and frames of reference in particular disciplines help shape knowledge in those disciplines; prejudice reduction, the way in which teachers help students develop positive and anti-biased attitudes about people of different backgrounds; equity pedagogy, in which pedagogical strategies are modified to help students of all backgrounds learn effectively; and empowering school culture and social structure, where the climate and organization of the school promote an equitable learning environment. These dimensions have been significant in defining the field, and they have led to the understanding that institutional changes in policies and practices are needed if multicultural education is to be a true and lasting reform. Thus, the "heroes and holidays" approach—characterized by such events as diversity dinners, celebrations of various nations or ethnicities, and other activities that do not consider the effects of structural inequality—has come under increasing criticism in the past decade (Bigelow, Christensen, Karp, Miner, & Peterson, 1994; Bigelow, Harvey, Karp, & Miller, 2001; Lee, Menkart, & Okazawa-Rey, 1998; Nieto, 2004).

Multicultural education has undergone a number of changes since its inception three decades ago. According to Ramsey and Williams (2003), two major changes are a broadening of the scope of multicultural education to include issues other than race and ethnicity, and a new focus on the identities and assumptions of White people and how these become normalized, to the detriment of others, throughout schools and society. The incorporation of critical pedagogy as a central tenet of multicultural education has also had a major impact on the field in several important ways: it affirms students' cultures without trivializing them by focusing on deeper dynamics of cultures rather than on surface characteristics; it challenges hegemonic knowledge; it complicates pedagogy so that there is no longer just one right way to teach; it challenges the simplistic focus on self-esteem as a way to break the bonds of oppression; it encourages "dangerous discourses" (Bigler, 1999, p. 119) that name and challenge inequities; and it recognizes that multicultural education is not a panacea for the problems of stratification and alienation (Nieto, 1999). In these ways, multicultural education has helped to challenge the assumption that all children have an equal chance at an excellent education, and it has been a cornerstone of the "high hopes" reflected in the title of this article.

In the final analysis, the multicultural education movement reflects the need to view school reform in a more comprehensive way. Rather than simply replacing some bureaucratic structures with others, multicultural education challenges the very structures themselves by suggesting that school policies and practices help create, maintain, and perpetuate inequality in the first place.

Broken Promises

Unfortunately, our public schools have never quite lived up to the high hopes envisioned by Mann and Dewey. In spite of John Dewey's (1916) idealistic assertion that "it is the aim of progressive education to take part in correcting unfair privilege and unfair deprivation, not to perpetuate them" (pp. 119–120), schools have too often served to uphold privilege. While the history of U.S. schools has been distinguished by the struggle for equality and by great moments of social justice and inclusion, it has also been characterized by segregation, exclusion, and racism.

School segregation has become an endemic problem in U.S. schools, reflecting residential and other patterns of social segregation. Regardless of the growing diversity in schools around the country, and despite the desegregation movement that began over fifty years ago, racial and ethnic segregation is on the rise. Students in U.S. schools are now more likely to be segregated from students of other races and backgrounds than at any time in the recent past. In fact, according to researcher Gary Orfield (2001), for Blacks, the 1990s witnessed the largest backward movement toward segregation since the 1954 *Brown v. Board of Education* decision, and the trend is continuing. Moreover, Latinos now have the dubious distinction of being the most segregated of all ethnic groups in terms of race, ethnicity, and poverty (Orfield & Yun, 1999).

Bilingual education has also been greatly dismantled. The 1968 Bilingual Education Law has been quietly, but almost completely, taken apart, and now emphasizes only English-language acquisition. And although fully forty-three states and the District of Columbia have legislative provisions for students with limited English proficiency, the number of students in bilingual classrooms has decreased over the past several years. In 2000, for instance, only 19 percent of language-minority students were receiving any instruction in their native language (Kindler, 2002). One reason is that bilingual education has been eliminated in a number of states since the late 1990s, often because of an entrenched ideological resistance to approaches based on native-language instruction.

Multicultural education too has been tremendously controversial since its beginnings. Reflecting as it does an opposition to a hegemonic education, and because it has been viewed by the Right as a threat to a common U.S. culture and by the Left as little more than "ethnic cheerleading," multicultural education has been criticized from all sides (Nieto, 1995; Sleeter, 1995). Yet the goals of multicultural education, when viewed within the context of a democratic society, have the potential to expand opportunities rather than limit them. According to Amy Gutmann (2004), "Multicultural education in democracies can help further civic equality in two important different ways: first, by expressing the democratic value of tolerating cultural differences that are consistent with civic quality, and second, by recognizing the role that cultural differences played in shaping society and the world in which children live" (p. 71).

The reemergence of extraordinarily segregated schools, the almost total dismantling of bilingual education, and the continuing vociferous backlash against multicultural education are vivid indications of the widespread resistance to social change in U.S. public education. As a result of the difficulties that these movements have had in becoming institutionalized or even accepted by the general public as essential to equalize the playing field for all children, the future of such efforts is uncertain.

Conclusion: An Uncertain Future

In our nation, access to an equal and high-quality education has long been regarded as the birthright of all children, regardless of station or rank. However, in spite of this cherished ideal, our educational history—as we have seen in this essay—is replete with examples of grossly uneven access and outcomes. These discrepancies are more often than not related to students' race/ethnicity, social class, gender, and other differences, and they are not new. Francesco Cordasco (1973, 1998), writing more than a quarter of a century ago, described the inequality in U.S. schools in this way: "In a multi-racial, ethnically variegated society, the American experience (certainly in its schools) has been an experience of cultural assault, discriminatory rejection of educational opportunity for many children, and the continuation of social and economic advantage for a white Anglo-Saxon, Protestant, middle-class partician elite" (p. 4). Many years later, Henry Giroux (1992), echoing this theme, characterized the situation in public education as "a retreat from democracy," an apt description for a system that was supposed to be at the core of democratic values.

In this article, I have argued that public education in the United States during the past seventy-five years has been the front line of the larger battle for equality and social justice. While many smaller skirmishes have been won, the outcome of the larger struggle is uncertain and, in some ways, it is in greater jeopardy than ever. The struggle has not been easy because public education has reflected both the high ideals of equality and the limited vested interests that challenge those high ideals; this tension has been critically evident in the area of race. According to educational historian David Tyack (1995), "Attempts to preserve white supremacy and to achieve racial justice have fueled the politics of education for more than a century" (p. 4). In spite of our society's passionate ideology of equality, as a nation we have a long way to go in reaching this goal.

The current policy climate at both the state and national levels is permeated by a profound distrust for public education and for teacher education, especially when the schools in question are for poor children (Cochran-Smith, 2003; Nieto, 2003). In spite of the rhetoric of equal education for all, there is no level playing field for children in our country, a situation that was vividly demonstrated a number of years ago by Jonathan Kozol's (1991) groundbreaking exposé of the discrepancies between urban and suburban schools. In his study, Kozol demonstrated that schools, sometimes adjacent to one another geographically, are as different as night and day in terms of funding and attention. Regrettably, the situation has not changed noticeably since the publication of Kozol's book; a child's zip code is still almost a sure indication of the kind of education he or she will receive. Recently, rather than being a paragon of educational equality, U.S. schools have consistently ranked among the most unequal in the industrialized world in terms of spending, curricular offerings, and teaching quality. The imbalanced support for children from different segments of society is invariably related to their social class, race, and ethnicity (Darling-Hammond, 2001).

Although education has been understood in our society as a major gateway out of poverty—and it has served this function admirably for some—academic success has been elusive for large numbers of young people who are economically poor, or culturally and racially different from the "mainstream," or both. Our schools cannot fulfill the ambitious and noble purpose they were purported to meet unless all of us—parents, policymakers, and the general public—commit ourselves to sustaining education as a public trust for future generations. It is time once again to direct our attention to the institutional and structural barriers that impede educational equality. As we commemorate the seventy-fifth anniversary of the *Harvard Educational Review*, we would do well to remember the vision articulated by such visionaries as Horace Mann (1868), John Dewey (1916), W.E. B. Du Bois (2001), George Sanchez (1940), and other advocates of public education, because it is far from evident today. What will it take for our schools to become the beacon of hope that they once were? I believe it will take committing the nation's full moral and economic resources to all schools and students, but particularly to those who have been most jeopardized by broken promises. Our response to this dilemma may well determine the future of public education in our nation.

References

Alvarez, R. R., Jr. (1986). The Lemon Grove incident: The nation's first successful desegregation court case. *Journal of San Diego History, 32*, 116–135.

Anderson, J. D. (1988). *The education of Blacks in the south, 1869–1935.* Chapel Hill: University of North Carolina Press.

Anyon, J. (1981). Social class and school knowledge. *Curriculum Inquiry, 11*(1), 3–41.

Apple, M. W. (1986). *Teachers and texts: A political economy of class and gender relations in education.* Boston: Routledge-Kegan Paul.

Archuleta, M. L., Child, B. J., & Lomawaima, K. T. (2000). *Away from home: American Indian boarding school experiences, 1879–2000.* Phoenix: Heard Museum.

Au, K. H. (1980). Participant structures in a reading lesson with Hawaiian children. *Anthropology and Education Quarterly, 11*(2), 91–115.

Baker, C., & Jones, S. P. (1998). *Encyclopedia of bilingualism and bilingual education.* Clevedon, England: Multilingual Matters.

Banks, C. A. M. (2004). *Improving multicultural education: Lessons from the Intergroup Education movement.* New York: Teachers College Press.

Banks, J. A. (1991). The dimensions of multicultural education. *Multicultural Leader, 4*, 5–6.

Banks, J. A. (2004). Multicultural education: Historical development, dimensions, and practice. In J. A. Banks & C. A. M. Banks (Eds.), *Handbook of research on multicultural education* (2nd ed.) (pp. 3–29). San Francisco: Jossey-Bass.

Banks, J. A., & Banks, C. A. M. (Eds.). (2004). *Handbook of research on multicultural education* (2nd ed.). San Francisco: Jossey-Bass.

Baratz, S. S., & Baratz, J. C. (1970). Early childhood intervention: The social science base of institutional racism. *Harvard Educational Review, 40*, 29–50.

Bereiter, C., & Englemann, S. (1966). *Teaching disadvantaged children in the preschool.* Englewood Cliffs, NJ: Prentice-Hall.

Bigelow, B., Christensen, L., Karp, S., Miner, B., & Peterson, B. (Eds.). (1994). *Rethinking our classrooms: Teaching for equity and justice (vol. 1).* Milwaukee: Rethinking Schools.

Bigelow, B., Harvey, B., Karp, S., & Miller, L. (Eds.). (2001). *Rethinking our classrooms: Teaching for equity and justice (vol. 2).* Milwaukee: Rethinking Schools.

Bigler, E. (1999). *American conversations: Puerto Ricans, White ethnics, and multicultural education.* Philadelphia: Temple University Press.

Bowles, S., & Gintis, H. (1976). *Schooling in capitalist America: Economic reform and the contradictions of economic life.* New York: Basic Books.

Brown v. Board of Educ., 347 U.S. 483 (1954).

Cochran-Smith, M. (2002). Editorial: Reporting on teacher quality: The politics of politics. *Journal of Teacher Education*, 53(5).

Cordasco, F. (1998). *America and the quest for equal educational opportunity: The schools and the children of the poor. Selected documents in social policy*. New York: Edna Vaughn. (Reprinted from *British Journal of Educational Studies*, 21, February, 1973, 0–63).

Crawford, J. (2000). *At war with diversity: U.S. language policy in an age of anxiety*. Clevedon, England: Multilingual Matters.

Crawford, J. (2004). *Educating English learners: Language diversity in the classroom*. Los Angeles: Bilingual Education Services.

Cummins, J. (1996). *Negotiating identities: Education for empowerment in a diverse society*. Ontario: California Association for Bilingual Education.

Darling-Hammond, L. (2001). *The right to learn: A blueprint for creating schools that work*. San Francisco: Jossey-Bass.

Del Rio Independent School District v. Salvatierra, 33 S. W. 2d 790 (Texas 1930).

Dewey, J. (1916). *Democracy and education*. New York: Free Press.

Donato, R. (1997). *The other struggle for equal schools: Mexican Americans during the civil rights movement*. Albany: State University of New York Press.

Du Bois, W. E. B., & Aptheker, H. (2001). *The education of Black people: Ten critiques 1906–1960*. New York: Monthly Review Press.

Erickson, F. (1993). Transformation and school success: The politics and culture of educational achievement. In E. Jacob & C. Jordan (Eds.), *Minority education: Anthropological perspectives* (pp. 27–51). Norwood, NJ: Ablex.

Fine, M. (1991). *Framing dropouts: Notes on the politics of an urban high school*. Albany: State University of New York Press.

Flores-González, N. (2002). *School kids, street kids: Identity and high school completion among Latinos*. New York: Teachers College Press.

Fordham, S., & Ogbu, J. U. (1986). Black students' school success: Coping with the "burden of acting White." *Urban Review*, 18, 176–206.

García, E. E. (2001). *Hispanic education in the United States: Raíces y alas*. New York: Rowman & Littlefield.

Gay, G. (2000). *Culturally responsive teaching: Theory, research, and practice*. New York: Teachers College Press.

Giroux, H. A. (1983). *Theory and resistance in education: A pedagogy for the opposition*. South Hadley, MA: Bergin & Garvey.

Giroux, H. A. (1992). Educational leadership and the crisis of democratic government. *Educational Researcher*, 21(4), 4–11.

Gutmann, A. (2004). Unity and diversity in democratic multicultural education: Creative and destructive tensions. In J. A. Banks (Ed.), *Diversity and citizenship education* (pp. 71–96). San Francisco: Jossey-Bass.

Heath, S. B. (1983). *Ways with words*. New York: Cambridge University Press.

Jensen, A. R. (1969). How much can we boost IQ and scholastic achievement? *Harvard Educational Review*, 39, 1–123.

Katz, M. B. (1975). *Class, bureaucracy, and the schools: The illusion of educational change in America*. New York: Praeger.

Kindler, A. L. (2002). *Survey of the states' limited English proficient students and available educational programs and services, 1999–2000 summary report*. Washington, DC: U.S. Department of Education, Office of English Language Acquisition, Language Enhancement, and Academic Achievement for Limited English Proficient Students.

Kohl, H. (1994). *"I won't learn from you" and other thoughts on creative maladjustment*. New York: New Press.

Kozol, J. (1991). *Savage inequalities: Children in America's schools*. New York: Crown.

Ladson-Billings, G. (1994). *The dreamkeepers: Successful teachers of African American children*. San Francisco: Jossey-Bass.

Ladson-Billings, G. (2004). Landing on the wrong note: The price we paid for Brown. *Educational Researcher*, 33(7), 3–13.

Lau v. Nichols, 414 U.S. 563 (1974).

Lee, E., Menkart, D., & Okazawa-Rey, M. (1998). *Beyond "heroes and holidays": A practical guide to K-12 anti-racist, multicultural education and staff development*. Washington, DC: Teaching for Change.

Mann, H. (1868). Twelfth annual report to the Massachusetts State Board of Education, 1848. In M. Mann (Ed.), *Life and works of Horace Mann* (vol. 3, p. 669). Boston: Walker, Fuller.

McBeth, S. (1983). *Ethnic identity and the boarding school experience of west-central Oklahoma American Indians*. Washington, DC: University Press of America.

McDermott, R. P. (1977). Social relations as contexts for learning in school. *Harvard Educational Review*, 47(2), 198–213.

National Center for Education Statistics. (2002). State nonfiscal survey of public elementary/secondary education, 2000–2001. Common Core of Data (CCD).

Neill, M. (1997). *Testing our children: A report card on state assessment systems*. Cambridge, MA: FairTest.

Nieto, S. (1995). From Brown heroes and holidays to assimilationist agendas: Reconsidering the critiques of multicultural education. In C. E. Sleeter & P. L. McLaren (Eds.), *Multicultural education, critical pedagogy, and the politics of difference* (pp. 191–220). Albany: State University of New York Press.

Nieto, S. (1999). Critical multicultural education and students' perspectives. In S. May (Ed.), *Rethinking multicultural and antiracist education: Towards critical multiculturalism* (pp. 191–215). London: Falmer Press.

Nieto, S. (2001). We speak in many tongues: Linguistic diversity and multicultural education. In C. P. Díaz (Ed.), *Multicultural education for the twenty-first century* (pp. 152–170). New York: Longman.

Nieto, S. (2003). *What keeps teachers going?* New York: Teachers College Press.

Nieto, S. (2004). *Affirming diversity: The sociopolitical context of multicultural education* (4th ed.). Boston: Allyn & Bacon.

Noddings, N. (1992). *The challenge to care in schools: An alternative approach to education*. New York: Teachers College Press.

Oakes, J. (1985). *Keeping track: How schools structure inequality*. New Haven, CT: Yale University Press.

Ogbu, J. U. (1987). Variability in minority school performance: A problem in search of an explanation. *Anthropology and Education Quarterly*, 18, 312–334.

Orfield, G. (2001). *Schools more separate: Consequences of a decade of resegregation*. Cambridge, MA: Civil Rights Project at Harvard University.

Orfield, G., & Yun, J. T. (1999). *Resegregation in American schools*. Cambridge, MA: Civil Rights Project at Harvard University.

Pang, V. O., Kiang, P. N., & Pak, Y. K. (2004). Asian Pacific American students. In J. A. Banks & C. A. M. Banks (Eds.), *Handbook of research on multicultural education* (2nd ed., pp. 542–563). San Francisco: Jossey-Bass.

Portes, A., & Rumbaut, R. G. (2001). *Legacies: The story of the immigrant second generation*. Berkeley: University of California Press.

Ramsey, P. G., & Williams, L. R. (2003). *Multicultural education: A source book* (2nd ed.) New York: Routledge Falmer.

Reissman, F. (1962). *The culturally deprived child.* New York: Harper & Row.

Ruiz, V. L. (2001). South by southwest: Mexican Americans and segregated schooling: 1900–1950. *Magazine of History*, 15(2), 23–27.

Ryan, W. (1972). *Blaming the victim.* New York: Vintage Books.

Sánchez, G. I. (1940). *Forgotten people: A study of New Mexicans.* Albuquerque: University of New Mexico Press.

San Miguel, G., Jr. (2001). *Brown, not White: School integration and the Chicano movement in Houston.* College Station: Texas A & M University Press.

Siddle Walker, V. (1996). *Their highest potential: An African American community school in the segregated south.* Chapel Hill: University of North Carolina Press.

Skutnabb-Kangas, T., & Cummins, J. (Eds.). (1988). *Minority education: From shame to struggle.* Clevedon, England: Multilingual Matters.

Sleeter, C. E. (1995). An analysis of the critiques of multicultural education. In J. A. Banks & C. A. M. Banks (Eds.), *Handbook of research on multicultural education* (pp. 81–94). New York: Macmillan.

Sleeter, C. E., & Grant, C. A. (1987). An analysis of multicultural education in the United States. *Harvard Educational Review*, 57, 421–444.

Spring, J. (1972). *The rise and fall of the corporate state.* Boston: Beacon Press.

Spring, J. (2004). *Deculturalization and the struggle for equality: A brief history of the education of dominated cultures in the United States* (4th ed.). New York: McGraw-Hill.

Stanton-Salazar, R. (1997). A social capital framework for understanding the socialization of racial minority children and youth, *Harvard Educational Review*, 67, 1–40.

Steele, C. M. (2004). A threat in the air: How stereotypes shape intellectual identity and performance. In J. A. Banks & C. A. M. Banks (Eds.), *Handbook of research on multicultural education* (pp. 682–698). San Francisco: Jossey-Bass.

Suárez-Orozco, C., & Suárez-Orozco, M. (2001). *Children of immigration.* Cambridge, MA: Harvard University Press.

Tyack, D. (1995). Schooling and social diversity: Historical reflections. In W. D. Hawley & A. W. Jackson (Eds.), *Toward a common destiny: Improving race and ethnic relations in America* (pp. 3–38). San Francisco: Jossey-Bass.

U.S. Census Bureau. (2000a). *USA Statistics in brief: Population and vital statistics.* Washington, DC: U.S. Department of Commerce. Available online at http://www.census.gov/statab/www/popppart.htm

U.S. Census Bureau. (2000b). *Poverty in the United States: 2000.* Washington, DC: U.S. Government Printing Office.

U.S. Census Bureau. (2002). *Profile of the foreign-born population in the United States: 2000.* Washington, DC: U.S Department of Commerce.

Valenzuela, A. (1999). *Subtractive schooling: U.S.-Mexican youth and the politics of caring.* Albany: State University of New York Press.

Weinberg, M. A. (1977). *A chance to learn: A history of race and education.* Cambridge, England: Cambridge University Press.

Westminster School District of Orange County v. Mendez, 161 F. 2d 774 (9th Cir. 1947).

Willis, J. S., Lintz, A., & Mehan, H. (2004). Ethnographic studies of multicultural education in U.S. classrooms and schools. In J. A. Banks & C. A. M. Banks (Eds.), *Handbook of research on multicultural education* (2nd ed., pp. 163–183). San Francisco: Jossey-Bass.

Woodson, C. G. (1933). *The mis-education of the Negro.* Washington, DC: Associated Publishers.

I am grateful to the editors of the *Harvard Educational Review* for their thoughtful suggestions on an earlier draft of this article, and to Patty Bode for invaluable editorial assistance.

Critical Questions

1   How would you describe the link between public education and democracy? Do you believe they need to be connected? Why or why not?

2   Genetic and cultural inferiority, economic and social reproduction, cultural incompatibility, sociocultural theory, resistance, and other theories have all been used as explanations as to why some students succeed in school and others fail. What are your thoughts on these theories? Which, if any, does a better job of explaining the variability in student achievement?

3   As you read in this article, sociologists Alejandro Portes and Ruben Rumbaut have found through their research that "no matter how educated a Mexican or Haitian is, his or her chances of moving ahead economically are significantly constrained by the social environment in which their group has been incorporated into the United States." They also found that for these groups, a college education yields no significant benefit compared to other immigrants. Are you surprised by their conclusions? Why or why not?

4   In this article, I argue that desegregation, bilingual education, and multicultural education have all been based on "high hopes" that have led, in one way or another, to "broken promises." Do you agree? If so, why do you think the high hopes have been dashed? If not, do you believe that the promise of these movements has been fulfilled?

Community-Based Activities and Advocacy

1   Investigate the history of desegregation in your school district by interviewing some of the community's leaders. Do they think that desegregation worked? Why or why not? Do they have other ideas that they believe would close the achievement gap? Write a research paper with your results.

2   Do research on the status of bilingual education in your community and state. If bilingual education is permissible, find out how it is implemented in your district. Is it through a pull-out program, a transitional bilingual program, or two-way bilingual education? Once you have found out which approach is used, write a brief Op-ed (opinion) piece for the local newspaper on which approach is best and why.

Supplementary Resources for Further Reflection and Study

Banks, J. A. & Banks, C. A. M. (Eds.). (2004). *Handbook of research on multicultural education*, 2nd ed. San Francisco: Jossey-Bass.

   The definitive handbook on multicultural education, this volume encompasses 49 chapters and covers issues ranging from the history of the field to research issues and trends and developments in the field. Contributors include experts who focus on multicultural education and whose work centers on such areas as ethnic studies, language and culture, research methods, school reform, and higher education.

Darling-Hammond, L. (2005). *Preparing teachers for a changing world: What teachers should learn and be able to do.* San Francisco: Jossey-Bass.

Well organized, meticulously researched, and well written, this collection of chapters by various authors captures the major trends, differing perspectives, and many challenges of teacher education today, while putting forth a vision for the future that is solidly grounded in research and current and evolving knowledge.

García, O. (2009). *Bilingual education in the 21st century: A global perspective.* Hoboken, NJ: Wiley/Blackwell.

This international overview of bilingual education offers educators a comprehensive and rich understanding of the field. With a focus on theory, history, policy, practice, and legal issues, it provides a sound rationale for bilingual education both in the United States and in other nations.

Orfield, G. & Lee, C. (2005). *Why segregation matters: Poverty and educational inequality.* Cambridge: The Civil Rights Project, Harvard University.

According to researchers Orfield and Lee, U.S. schools are now more separate and unequal than at any time since the celebrated 1954 Brown v. Board of Education decision, and this segregation has led to, among other problems, poor urban schools having the highest dropout rates in the nation. This research report from the Civil Rights Project presents data on the deepening segregation of schools since the 1980s and chronicles the deleterious effects of segregation on both schools and society.

6 We Speak in Many Tongues

Language Diversity and Multicultural Education

Linguistic diversity is a fact of life in many countries around the world, including our own. As a matter of fact, if all native Spanish-speakers in the United States were considered a country, it would be the fourth-largest Spanish-speaking country in the world! Yet our society is also among the most monolingual on the globe, with a great many people able to speak English only. Because it is the language of power, it is still possible to remain monolingual in the United States and be successful in life. This is not so in many other countries, where being bilingual or multilingual is essential.

In spite of the fact that language diversity is obvious everywhere in our nation—from factories to subways to radio and television stations—schools have been slow to catch up to this reality. As a result, in our country there is a stigma attached to speaking a language other than English, particularly in public, if it is one's native language. (If, however, it is one's second language, the stigma is not as great and, in fact, it can be seen as "cool.") Because of the negative pressure to speak only English, children who speak another language and have the potential to become bilingual frequently end up as monolingual speakers of English. Both individually and collectively, we lose a great national resource when this happens.

The field of multicultural education was slow to embrace linguistic diversity as a central focus of its work and until recently, most conceptualizations of multicultural education did not consider the significance of language in teaching and learning. This has changed in the past couple of decades, especially because the growing immigrant and refugee populations in the United States makes it more apparent than ever that linguistic diversity is a vital component of an overall understanding of diversity.

In the chapter that follows, I analyze language as a major area of diversity in the United States and address the responsibility that *all* teachers—not just bilingual or ESL teachers—have in teaching students who speak native languages other than English.

The United States is becoming a more multilingual nation than ever, if not in policy, at least in practice. The number of immigrants entering the United States during the 1970s and 1980s was among the largest in history. Between 1981 and 1990 alone, over 7,300,000 people immigrated to the United States legally, increasing immigration by 63% over the previous decade (U.S. Bureau of the Census 1994). The new immigrants of 1990 equaled in numbers those of the peak immigration decade in U.S. history, 1900 to 1910 (Portes and Rumbaut 1996), although the percentage was much smaller (14.7%, compared with 7.9% in 1990). Unlike previous immigrants who were overwhelmingly from Europe, about one-third of the newest immigrants were from Asia and another third from Latin America (U.S. Immigration and Naturalization Service 1995). The growing immigration has resulted in a concomitant increase in the number of people who speak a native language other than English: according to the 1990 Census, almost 32 million people speak a language other than English at home, with almost half of those speaking Spanish. Not coincidentally, the total number of people claiming to speak a language other than English increased from 23 million (11%) in 1980 to almost 32 million (14%) in 1990 (Portes and Rumbaut 1996).

Notwithstanding the widespread perspective that English is the sole language of communication in our society, U.S. classrooms, communities, and workplaces are very linguistically diverse. For example, of the nearly 46,000,000 students in public and private schools in the United States, over 3,000,000 (7.4%) are limited in their English proficiency (Macías 1998). Language minority students are no longer confined to large urban school systems but are also found in small town, suburban, and rural schools throughout the nation. This means that all teachers, not just those who specialize in bilingual and ESL education, need to be prepared to teach students of diverse language backgrounds.

The purpose of this chapter is to propose productive ways that teachers and schools can approach linguistic diversity so that they can teach language minority students to high levels of achievement. Rather than continuing to view linguistic diversity as a problem to be corrected, teachers can learn to think of it as an asset for classrooms and society in general. For that reason, I focus on the importance of native and second language development, and on strategies that all teachers—not simply those who specialize in the education of language minority students—can use to teach them effectively.

Language Diversity and Multicultural Education: Expanding the Framework

To understand language diversity in a comprehensive and positive way, we need to reconceptualize how we view it. This reconceptualization includes:

- perceiving language diversity as a resource rather than as a deficit;
- understanding the key role that language discrimination has played in U.S. educational history;
- placing language diversity within a multicultural education framework and redefining the benefits of linguistic diversity for all students;

- understanding the crucial role of native language development in school achievement;
- making the education of language minority students the responsibility of *all teachers.*

Viewing Bilingualism as a Resource

In the United States, we have generally been socialized to think of language diversity as a negative rather than positive condition (Crawford 1992). Yet in most other countries in the world, bilingualism and multilingualism are the order of the day. The prestige accorded to language diversity is a highly complex issue that depends on many factors: the country in question, the region of the country one resides in, the language variety spoken, where and when one has learned to speak specific languages, and of course, the race, ethnicity, and class of the speaker. Sometimes bilingualism is highly valued. This is usually the case with those who are formally educated and have status and power in society. At other times, bilingualism is seen as a sign of low status. This is usually the case with those who are poor and powerless within their society, even if they happen to speak a multitude of languages (Fairclough 1989; Phillipson 1992; Corson 1993). It is evident that issues of status and power must be taken into account in reconceptualizing language diversity. This means developing an awareness that privilege, ethnocentrism, and racism are at the core of policies and practices that limit the use of languages other than officially recognized high-status languages allowed in schools and in the society in general. When particular languages are prohibited or denigrated, the voices of those who speak them are silenced and rejected as well.

English is the language of power in the United States. For those who speak it as a native language—especially if they are also at least middle class and have access to formal education—monolingualism is an asset. At times, bilingualism is considered an asset, but commonly only in the case of those who are native English speakers and have learned another language as a *second* language. Those who speak a native language associated with low prestige and limited power—especially if they do not speak English well, or speak it with an accent—are often regarded as deficient. The *kind* of accent one has is also critical. Speaking French with a Parisian accent, for example, may be regarded as a mark of high status in some parts of the country, while speaking Canadian French or Haitian Creole usually is not. Likewise, speaking Castilian Spanish is regarded more positively than speaking Latin American or Caribbean Spanish, which are generally viewed in our society as inferior varieties of the Spanish language.

For some people, then, bilingualism is perceived to be a handicap. This is usually the case with Latino, American Indian, Asian, and other Caribbean students, those who are also the majority of the language-minority students in our classrooms. Linguistically, there is nothing wrong with the languages they speak; for purposes of communication, one language is as valid as any other. But socially and politically, the languages spoken by most language minority students in the United States are accorded low status. Students who speak these languages are perceived to have a problem, and the problem is defined as fluency in a language other than English. In this case, the major purpose of education becomes the elimination of all signs of the native language. Even well-meaning educators may perceive their students' fluency in another language as a handicap to their learning English.

Developing an Awareness of Linguicism

U.S. educational history is replete with examples of language discrimination or what Tove Skutnabb-Kangas (1988) has called *linguicism*. Specifically, she defines linguicism as "ideologies and structures that are used to legitimate, effectuate, and reproduce an unequal division of power and resources (both material and nonmaterial) between groups that are defined on the basis of language" (p. 13). Entire communities, starting with American Indian nations and enslaved African Americans, have been denied the use of their native languages for either communication or education. This is evident in policies that forbid the use of other languages in schools as well as in the lack of equal educational opportunity for youngsters who cannot understand the language of instruction (Crawford 1992; Cummins 1996; Spring 1997). While linguicism has been particularly evident in racially and economically oppressed communities, it has not been limited to these groups historically, but has in fact been a widespread policy with all languages other than English in our society. The massive obliteration of the German language is a case in point. German was almost on a par with English as a language of communication during the 18th and 19th centuries, and was one of the most common languages used in bilingual programs during parts of our history. But the use of German as a language of instruction was effectively terminated by xenophobic policies immediately prior to and after World War I (Crawford 1992).

The tremendous pressures to conform to an English-only environment meant that giving up one's native language, although a terrible sacrifice, was accepted as a necessary and inevitable price to pay for the benefits of U.S. citizenship. Educators by and large accepted as one of their primary responsibilities the language assimilation of their students. Even today, it is not uncommon to hear of children punished for speaking their native language, or of notes sent home to parents who barely speak English that ask them not to speak their native language with their children. While today there is more of an awareness of the ethnocentrism of such practices, the fact that they continue to exist is an indication of an ingrained reluctance to perceive language diversity in positive terms. In developing a more accurate understanding of language diversity, it is critical to review how language discrimination has been used to disempower those who speak languages other than English. One implication of this understanding is that language diversity needs to be viewed using the lens of educational equity. That is, it is not simply a question of language difference, but rather of power difference. As such, language diversity is a key part of a multicultural education framework.

The Role of Linguistic Diversity in Multicultural Education

Expanding the framework for language diversity means redefining it as part of multicultural education. Just as race, class, and gender are usually considered integral to multicultural education, language diversity—although it does not fit neatly into any of these categories—should also be taken into account. One of the primary goals of multicultural education is to build on the strengths that students bring to school, but even in multicultural education, language diversity is not always considered an asset. Currently, the most enlightened and inclusive frameworks for multicultural education consider the significance of language differences (Banks and Banks 1995; Macedo and Bartolomé 1999), but this was not always the case. While it is true that most language minority students in United States schools are also from racial minority and poor backgrounds, language issues cannot be relegated to either racial or class distinctions alone. Language diversity in and of itself needs to be considered an important difference.

The failure of some supporters of multicultural education to seriously consider linguistic diversity, and the inclination of those in bilingual education to view multicultural education simply as a watering down of bilingual and ethnic studies programs, leads to an artificial separation. This separation often results in the perception that multicultural education is for African American and other students of color who speak English, while bilingual education is only for Latino and other students who speak a language other than English as their native language. These perceptions are reinforced by the fact that each of these fields has its own organizations, publications, conferences, political and research agendas, and networks. This kind of specialization is both necessary and desirable because the concerns of each field are sometimes unique. But the implication that bilingual and multicultural education are fundamentally different and unconnected domains denies their common historical roots and complementary goals. As a result, proponents of bilingual and multicultural education sometimes see one another as adversaries with distinct objectives and agendas. Ignorance and hostility may arise, with each scrambling for limited resources.

Language is one of the most salient aspects of culture. Hence, the education of language minority students is part and parcel of multicultural education. The fields of bilingual and multicultural education are inextricably connected, both historically and functionally. If the languages students speak, with all their attendant social meanings and affirmations, are either negated or relegated to a secondary position in their schooling, the possibility of school failure is increased. Because language and culture are intimately connected, and because both bilingual and multicultural approaches seek to involve and empower the most vulnerable students in our schools, it is essential that their natural links be fostered.

Native Language and School Achievement

Effective teaching is based on the fact that learning builds on prior knowledge and experiences. But in the case of language minority students, we seem to forget this fact as schools regularly rob students of access to their prior learning through languages other than English. That this process contradicts how learning takes place and the crucial role of language is well articulated by Jim Cummins (1996), who maintains that "there is general agreement among cognitive psychologists that we learn by integrating new input into our existing cognitive structures or schemata. Our prior experience provides the foundation for interpreting new information. No learner is a blank slate" (p. 17).

When teachers and schools disregard language minority students' native languages and cultures, it is generally for what they believe to be good reasons. Schools often link students' English-language proficiency with their prospective economic and social mobility: that is, students who speak a language other than English are viewed as "handicapped" and they are urged, through subtle and direct means, to abandon their native language. The schools ask parents to speak English to their children at home, they punish children for using their native language, or they simply withhold education until the children have learned English sufficiently well, usually in the name of protecting students' futures. The negative impact of these strategies on language minority students is incalculable. For instance, in her research concerning factors that promoted or impeded academic success for Mexican-descent students in a California high school, Margaret Gibson (1995) found that the school environment stressed English-language monolingualism as a goal, in the process overlooking the benefits of bilingualism. Rather than focus on the native language abilities of students, teachers encouraged them to speak English as much as possible to the exclusion of Spanish. Gibson defined this perception on the part of teachers as "English only attitudes" (Gibson 1995). David Corson (1993) has suggested that when these kinds of attitudes prevail, students quickly pick up disempowering messages: "The members of some social groups, as a result, come to believe that their educational failure, rather than coming from their lowly esteemed social or cultural status, results from their natural inability: their lack of giftedness" (p. 11).

It is sometimes tempting to point to strategies such as English immersion programs as the solution to the educational problems of language minority students. But the lack of English skills alone cannot explain the poor academic achievement of language minority students. Equating English language acquisition with academic achievement is simplistic at best. For example, a large-scale study of the academic achievement of Mexican American and Puerto Rican students of varying English-language abilities concluded that contrary to the conventional wisdom, Spanish was *not* an impediment to achievement. On the contrary, the researchers found that in some cases, *better English proficiency meant lower academic performance* (Adams et al. 1994). In this case, the researchers theorized that peer pressure mitigated the traditional relationship between English proficiency and academic performance.

In contrast to negative perceptions of bilingualism, a good deal of research confirms the positive influence of knowing another language. Native language maintenance can act as a buffer against academic failure by promoting literacy in children's most developed language. This was the conclusion reached by researchers studying the case of Black English, also called *Ebonics* or *Black dialect*.

dialect-speaking four-year olds enrolled in a Head Start program were able to recall more details with greater accuracy when they retold stories in their cultural dialect rather than in standard English (Williams 1991). Lourdes Díaz Soto's (1997) research concerning Hispanic families of young children with low and high academic achievement found that parents of the higher achieving children provided native-language home environments more often than did the parents of the lower achieving youngsters. Likewise, Patricia Gándara (1995), in analyzing the impressive academic achievements of Mexican American adults who grew up in poverty, found that only 16% of them came from homes where English was the primary language. The largest percentage of these successful adults grew up in households where *only* Spanish was spoken, and a remarkable two-thirds of them began school speaking *only* Spanish. A similar finding was reported by Ana Celia Zentella (1997) in a study of Puerto Rican families in El Barrio, a low-income community in New York City. She found that the most successful students were enrolled in bilingual programs and they were also the most fluent bilinguals. Moreover, in their review of several research studies concerning the adaptation and school achievement of immigrants of various backgrounds, Alejandro Portes and Rubén Rumbaut (1996) came to a striking conclusion: *students with limited bilingualism are far more likely to leave school than those fluent in both languages.* Rather than an impediment to academic achievement, bilingualism can actually promote learning.

Conclusions such as these contradict the common advice given to language minority parents to "speak English with your children at home." Challenging the prevailing wisdom of this advice, Virginia Collier (1995) has suggested that speaking English only at home among students who are more proficient in another language can slow down cognitive development because it is only when parents and their children speak the language they know best that they are working at their "level of cognitive maturity" (p. 14). Catherine Snow (1997), another respected researcher in literacy and language acquisition, agrees, stating that "the greatest contribution immigrant parents can make to their children's success is to ensure they maintain fluency and continue to develop the home language" (p. 29).

The major problem facing language minority children has often been articulated as one of not knowing English. But the real problem may be what Luis Moll (1992, p. 20) has labeled the "obsession with speaking English," as if learning English would solve all the other dilemmas faced by language minority students, including poverty, racism, poorly financed schools, and the lack of access to excellent education. Rather than supporting the suppression or elimination of native language use at home and school, the research reviewed here supports developing and maintaining native language literacy. If this is the case, then the language dominance of students is not the real issue; rather, *the way in which teachers and schools view students' language may have an even greater influence on their achievement.*

Articulating the issue of the education of language minority students in this way leads to the conclusion that language diversity must be placed within a *sociopolitical context.* That is, more consequential than language difference itself are questions of how language diversity and language use are perceived by schools, and whether or not modifications are made in the curriculum. The prevailing view that bilingualism is a deficit for language minority students but an asset for students from wealthy and privileged backgrounds has to do *not* with the relative merits of the different languages involved, but with the sociopolitical context of education. For example, it is not unusual to find in the same high school the seemingly incongruous situation of one group of students having their native language wiped out while another group of students struggles to learn a foreign language in a contrived and artificial setting. There are more affirming approaches to teaching language minority students, and they need to be used more widely than is currently the case.

Approaches to Teaching Language Minority Students

In the United States, most of the pedagogical approaches currently used with students who speak a language other than English are compensatory in nature. That is, they are premised on the assumption that language diversity is an illness that needs to be cured. As a result, traditional approaches emphasize using the native language as little as possible, if at all, and then only as a bridge to English. When English is learned sufficiently well, the reasoning goes, the bridge can be burned and the students are well on their way to achieving academic success.

There are several problems with this reasoning. First, a compensatory approach assumes that students are only *lacking* in something, rather than that they also possess certain skills and talents. Instead of perceiving fluency in another language as an asset to be cherished, it is seen as something that needs repair. In many schools, using native language literacy as a basis for English language development is not considered a viable option. As a result, students are expected to start their education all over again. Not only do they flounder in English, but they often forget their native language in the process. Even when language minority students are in bilingual programs where their native language is used as a medium of instruction, they are frequently removed too quickly and end up in special education classes (Cummins 1984).

The most common approaches to teaching language minority students in the past quarter century have been ESL (English as a Second Language) and bilingual education, the latter being far more controversial than the former. In spite of the controversy surrounding it, bilingual education and other programs that support native-language use, even if only as a transition to English, are generally more effective than programs such as ESL alone. This is true not only in terms of learning content in the native language, but in learning English as well. This seeming contradiction can be understood if one considers the fact that students in bilingual programs are provided with continued education in content areas along with structured instruction in English. In addition, these programs build on students' previous literacy so that it becomes what W. E. Lambert (1975) has called an *additive* form of bilingual education. *Subtractive* bilingual education, on the other hand, frequently occurs when one language is substituted for another; as a result, true literacy is not achieved in either. This may happen in programs where the students' native language is eliminated and English grammar, phonics, and other language features are taught out of context with the way in which real day-to-day language is used.

There is a substantial relationship between bilingual education and equity. That is, bilingual education is viewed by many language-minority communities as vital to the educational achievement of their children. Although frequently addressed as simply an issue of language, it can be argued that bilingual education is a civil rights issue because it is the only guarantee that children who do not speak English will be provided education in a language they understand. Without it, millions of children may be doomed to educational underachievement and limited occupational choices in the future.

This connection was recognized by the U.S. Supreme Court in 1974. Plaintiffs representing 1,800 Chinese-speaking students sued the San Francisco Unified School District in 1969 for failing to provide students who did not speak English with an equal chance to learn. They lost their case in San Francisco, but by 1974 they had taken it all the way to the Supreme Court. In the landmark *Lau v. Nichols* case, the Court ruled unanimously that the civil rights of students who did not understand the language of instruction were indeed being violated. The Court stated, in part: "There is no equality of treatment merely by providing students with the same facilities, textbooks, teachers, and curriculum; for students who do not understand English are effectively foreclosed from any meaningful education" (*Lau v. Nichols*, 414, U.S. 563, 1974).

Although the decision did not impose any particular remedy, its results were immediate and extensive. By 1975, the Office for Civil Rights and the Department of Health, Education, and Welfare issued a document called "The *Lau* Remedies," which then served as the basis for providing school systems with guidance in identifying students with a limited proficiency in English, assessing their language abilities, and providing appropriate programs. Bilingual programs have been the common remedy in many school systems.

There are numerous program models and definitions of bilingual education (Ovando and Collier 1998), but in general terms, bilingual education can be defined as *an educational program that involves the use of two languages of instruction at some point in a student's school career.* This definition is broad enough to include many program variations. A primary objective of all bilingual programs is to develop proficiency and literacy in the English language. ESL is an integral and necessary component of all bilingual programs, but when provided in isolation, it is not bilingual education because the child's native language is not used in instruction. While they are learning to communicate in English, students in ESL programs may be languishing in their other subject areas because they do not understand the language of instruction.

Probably the most common model of bilingual education in the United States is the *transitional bilingual education* approach. In this approach, students are taught content area instruction in their native language while also learning English as a second language. As soon as they are thought to be ready to benefit from the monolingual English-language curriculum, they are "exited" or "mainstreamed" out of the program. The rationale behind this model is that native-language services should serve only as a transition to English. Therefore, there is a limit on the time a student may be in a bilingual program, usually three years. *Developmental* or *maintenance bilingual education* is a more comprehensive and long-term model. As in the transitional approach, students receive content area instruction in their native language while learning English as a second language. The difference is that generally no limit is set on the time students can be in the program. The objective is to develop fluency in both languages by using both for instruction.

Two-way bilingual education (Christian 1994) is a program model that integrates students whose native language is English with students for whom English is a second language. Two-way bilingual programs validate both languages of instruction, and their primary goals are to develop bilingual proficiency, academic achievement, and positive cross-cultural attitudes and behaviors among all students. Students in these programs not only learn through two languages, but they also learn to appreciate the language and culture of others, and to empathize with their peers in the difficult process of developing fluency in a language not their own (Christian et al. 1997). This approach lends itself to cooperative learning and peer tutoring, and it holds the promise of expanding our nation's linguistic resources and improving relationships between majority and minority language groups.

What Works With Language Minority Students?

Research concerning the most effective programs for language minority students points to the benefits of native language development. Students generally need between five and seven years to make a successful transition from their native language to English (Cummins 1981; Thomas and Collier 1997). But because bilingual education, and especially native-language instruction, challenges the assimilationist nature of education in our society, it has been the most controversial program. Ironically, when students fail to achieve after being removed from bilingual programs too early, the blame is placed on bilingual programs, rather than on their premature exit from those very programs that could have helped them.

The fact is that bilingual education has generally been found to be more effective than other programs such as ESL alone, even for English language development. This finding has been reiterated in many studies over the years, most recently in a 1998 summary of research conducted by the Center for Research on Education, Diversity, and Excellence (National Association for Bilingual Education 1998). Even in the anti-bilingual climate of California in 1998, surprising results were found: achievement test scores from San Francisco and San Jose found that students who completed bilingual education generally performed better than native English-speaking children in reading, math, language, and spelling (Asimov 1998). Many of the gains were impressive. This situation was reported just one month after the passage of Proposition 227, which virtually outlawed the use of bilingual education in the state.

Research by Wayne Thomas and Virginia Collier (1997) has confirmed once again the benefits of bilingual education. In a comprehensive investigation of the records of 700,000 language minority students in five large school systems from 1982 to 1996, the researchers found that language minority students who received bilingual education finished their schooling with average scores that reached or exceeded the 50th national percentile in all content areas. In contrast, language minority students who received even well-implemented ESL-pullout instruction—a very common program type—typically finished school, if they graduated at all, with average scores between the 10th and 18th national percentiles. Thomas and Collier also found that two-way developmental bilingual education was the most successful program model of all. Unfortunately, this is the least common program model in the United States.

Bilingual programs also may have secondary salutary effects, such as motivating students to remain in school rather than dropping out, making school more meaningful, and in general making the school experience more enjoyable. A related phenomenon is that bilingual education may reinforce close relationships among children and their family members, promoting more communication than would be the case if they were instructed solely in English and lost their native language. This is what Lily Wong Fillmore (1991) found through interviews with immigrant parents when their preschool children were placed in English-only settings. Not only did the children lose their first language, but more significantly, they lost the ability to communicate with their parents and families. In the process, they also lost the academic advantage that fluency and literacy in a language would give them when they begin school.

In my own research with academically successful students (Nieto 2000a), I found that maintaining language and culture were essential in supporting and sustaining academic achievement. In a series of in-depth interviews with linguistically and culturally diverse students, one of the salient features that accounted for school success was a strong-willed determination to hold onto their culture and native language. Although their pride in culture and language was not without conflict, the steadfastness with which they maintained their culture and language in spite of widespread negative messages about them was surprising.

An intriguing conclusion from research on the importance of language and culture on academic achievement is that cultural and linguistic maintenance seem to have a positive impact on academic success. This is obviously not true in all cases, and it cannot be overstated. But the benefits of cultural and linguistic maintenance challenge the "melting pot" ideology that has dominated U.S. schools and society throughout the last century. We can even say that when their language and culture are reinforced both at home and school, students seem to develop less confusion and ambiguity about their ability to learn. Regardless of the sometimes harsh attacks on their culture and language—as is the case in communities that have strident campaigns to pass English-only legislation —students whose language and culture are valued in the school setting pick up affirming messages about their worth. The notion that assimilation is a necessary prerequisite for success in school and society is severely tested by current research.

In spite of the evidence that some form of bilingual education is most effective for teaching language minority students, most students who could benefit are not in such programs. This is due to both political and pragmatic considerations. For one, in many school systems, there are not enough trained teachers for such programs. In addition, the numbers of students who speak the same language is generally too small to require an entire program. Furthermore, the segregation that bilingual education presupposes poses a genuine dilemma. It is also true, however, that every bilingual program has numerous opportunities for integrating students more meaningfully than is currently the case. Moreover, the bilingual program can be more structurally integrated into the school instead of separated in a wing of the building so that teachers from both bilingual and nonbilingual classrooms can work on collaborative projects with their students. This kind of collaboration does not happen often enough. Besides being physically separated from other teachers—often in the basement, an apt metaphor (Nieto 2000b)— bilingual teachers bear the burden of the "bilingual" label in the same way as their students: They may be seen as less intelligent, less academically prepared, and less able than nonbilingual teachers—this in spite of the fact that they are usually fluent in two languages and have a wide range of pedagogical approaches for teaching a diverse student body. Because many bilingual teachers are from the same cultural and linguistic backgrounds as the students they teach, they bring a necessary element of diversity into the school. But many schools have not found a way to benefit from their presence.

Two-way bilingual programs provide another opportunity for integration and enhanced academic achievement for all students. For example, research on a Spanish–English two-way program in Cambridge, Massachusetts, found both groups of children progressing well in all subject matters and neither group declining in its native language development. Researchers also found that children at all grade levels selected their best friend without an ethnic or racial bias, that the self-esteem of children from both groups was enhanced, and that there was much less segregation than before the program—all worthy social and educational goals (Cazabon, Lambert, and Hall 1993). But two-way bilingual education is not always an option. This is because not all languages have the same appeal of Spanish, which is spoken in many places in the world, for English-speaking students and their families.

Other approaches for integrating students of diverse language backgrounds include setting aside times for joint instruction and developing bilingual options in desegregation plans and magnet schools. But much remains to be done in expanding options such as these. Perhaps the most noteworthy change that can take place is a shift in thinking so that bilingual classrooms, teachers, and students are seen as rich resources for nonbilingual classrooms, teachers, and students. When this shift happens, schools will have taken the first step in making bilingualism and even multilingualism central educational goals for all students. This is hardly the case right now. On the contrary, English language acquisition for language minority students is often pursued at the expense of native language development. Even for monolingual English students, the goal of bilingualism is an elusive one because foreign language courses are ineffective in that they are usually delayed until secondary school. But if language diversity were to become an option for all students, the low status and persistent underfunding of bilingual education might be eliminated.

Implications for Teaching Language Minority Students

The dramatic increase in the number of language minority students in our country in the past three decades means that every classroom in every city and town has already been or will soon be affected. The responsibility for educating language minority students can no longer fall only on those teachers who have been trained specifically to provide bilingual education and ESL services; this responsibility needs to be shared by *all* teachers and *all* schools. Yet most teachers have had little training in language acquisition and other language-related issues: even in bilingual classrooms, only 10% of teachers serving English language learners are certified in bilingual education (August and Hakuta 1998).

In what follows, I suggest a number of steps that all educators can take to more effectively educate language minority students. But first let me emphasize that while learning new approaches and techniques may be very helpful, *teaching language minority students successfully means above all changing one's attitudes towards the students, their languages and cultures, and their communities* (Cummins 1996; Nieto 1999). Having said this, however, there are necessary bodies of knowledge and approaches that all teachers need to develop if they are to be successful with the growing number of language minority students in our schools: (1) All teachers need to understand how language is learned. (2) Teachers need to develop an additive perspective concerning bilingualism. (3) Teachers and schools can learn to consciously foster native language literacy.

All Teachers Need to Understand How Language Is Learned

This includes both native and subsequent languages. For example, Stephen Krashen's (1981) theories of second language acquisition and his recommendations that teachers provide students for whom English is a second language with *comprehensible input* by including engaging and contextualized cues in their instruction is useful for all teachers who have language minority students in their classrooms. Likewise, related knowledge in curriculum and instruction, linguistics, sociology, and history are all critical for teachers of language minority students.

The following knowledge base should be helpful for all teachers. (For a more detailed discussion, see Nieto, 2000b.)

- First and second language acquisition.
- The sociocultural and sociopolitical context of education for language minority students.
- The history of immigration in the United States, with particular attention to language policies and practices throughout that history.

- The history and experiences of specific groups of people, especially those who are residents of the city, town, and state where they are teaching.
- The ability to adapt curriculum for students whose first language is other than English.
- Competence in pedagogical approaches suitable for culturally and linguistically heterogeneous classrooms.
- Experience with teachers of diverse backgrounds and the ability to develop collaborative relationships with colleagues that promote the learning of language minority students.
- The ability to communicate effectively with parents of diverse language, culture, and social class backgrounds.

Because many teachers have not had access to this kind of knowledge during their teacher preparation, they may need to acquire it on their own. They can do this by attending conferences in literacy, bilingual education, multicultural education, and ESL; participating in professional development opportunities in their district and beyond; subscribing to journals and newsletters in these fields; setting up study groups with colleagues to discuss and practice different strategies; and returning to graduate school to take relevant courses or seek advanced degrees.

Teachers Need to Develop an Additive Perspective Concerning Bilingualism

An additive perspective (Lambert 1975) is radically different from the traditional expectation that immigrants need to exchange their native language for their new language, English. The terrible psychic costs of abandoning one's native language, not to mention the concurrent loss of linguistic resources to the nation, is now being questioned. An additive bilingualism supports the notion that English *plus* other languages can make us stronger individually and as a society.

In their research, María Fránquiz and María de la luz Reyes (1998) set out to answer the question, "If I am not fluent in the languages my students speak, how can I effectively teach English language arts to a linguistically diverse class?" They found that teachers do not have to be fluent in the native languages of their students to support their use in the classroom. Rather, they discovered that encouraging students to use their native languages and cultural knowledge as resources for learning is frequently more important than knowing the students' languages. What does this mean in practice? In their research, Fránquiz and Reyes provide examples of teachers "who are not paralyzed by their own monolingualism" (p. 217). They document, for example, the positive results of teachers' acceptance of a range of language registers and codes, from standard to more colloquial forms of speech, and from monolingual to more mixed language speech. These language forms are often prohibited in classroom discourse, but allowing them to flourish is a way of using students' current knowledge to build future knowledge.

Teachers and Schools Can Learn to Consciously Foster Native Language Literacy

Teachers can actively support the native language literacy of their students by providing them the time and space to work with their peers, or with tutors or mentors, who speak the same native language. In her work with immigrant students, for instance, Cristina Igoa (1995) reserves the last period of the day three times a week for students to listen to stories or to read in their native languages. Because she does not speak all the languages of her students who come from numerous language backgrounds, she recruits college students who are fluent in various languages to help out.

Teachers can also make a commitment to learn at least one of the languages of their students. When they become second language learners, teachers develop a new appreciation for the struggles experienced by language minority students—including exhaustion, frustration, and withdrawal—when they are learning English. This was what happened to Bill Dunn, a doctoral student of mine and a veteran teacher who decided to "come out of the closet as a Spanish speaker" (Nieto 1999). He realized that, after teaching for 20 years in a largely Puerto Rican community, he understood a great deal of Spanish, so he decided to study it formally and to keep a journal of his experiences. Although he had always been a wonderful and caring teacher, putting himself in the place of his students helped him understand a great many things more clearly, from students' grammatical errors in English to their boredom and misbehavior when they could not understand the language of instruction.

The responsibility to create excellent learning environments for language minority students should not rest with individual teachers alone, however. Entire schools can develop such environments. Catherine Minicucci and her associates (1995) analyzed eight exemplary school reform efforts for language minority students and they found that all of the schools shared the following common characteristics, among others:

- They had a schoolwide vision of excellence that incorporated students of limited English proficiency.
- They created a community of learners engaged in active discovery.
- They designed programs to develop both the English and native-language skills of language minority students.
- They made a conscious effort to recruit and hire bilingual staff members.
- They communicated frequently with parents in their native languages.
- They honored the multicultural quality of the student population.

The researchers concluded that the success of schools with these attributes challenges the conventional assumption that students need to learn English *before* they can learn grade-level content in social studies, math, or anything else.

Conclusion

Language is one of the fundamental signs of our humanity. It is "the palette from which people color their lives and culture" (Allman 1990). Although linguistic diversity is a fact of life in American schools and society, many languages are not accorded the respect and visibility they deserve. But given recent trends in immigration, the shrinking of our world, and the subsequent necessity to learn to communicate with larger numbers of people, a reconceptualization of the role of languages other than English in our schools and society is in order. Given this kind of reconceptualization, current school policies and practices need to be reexamined. Those that build on students' diversity need to be strengthened, while those that focus on differences as deficits must be eliminated. This means, at the very least, that bilingual and multicultural programs for all students have to be comprehensively defined, adequately funded, and strongly supported.

The issue of what to do about language minority students goes much deeper than simple language diversity. Above all, it is an issue of educational equity. Whether bilingual education, ESL, or other approaches and support services are offered, they need to be developed with an eye toward promoting, rather than limiting, educational opportunities for all students. Given the increasing number of students who enter schools speaking a native language other than English, it is clear that attending to the unique condition of language minority students is the responsibility of all educators. For students with limited English proficiency, suitable approaches geared to their particular situation are not frills, but basic education. For English monolingual students, too, learning to appreciate and communicate in other languages is a gift to be cherished. When we approach language diversity as a resource that is respected and fostered, all students benefit.

References

Adams, D., Astone, B., Nuñez-Wormack, E., and Smodlaka, I. (1994). Predicting the academic achievement of Puerto Rican and Mexican-American ninth-grade students. *The Urban Review, 26*(1), 1–14.

Allman, W. F. (1990, November 5). The mother tongue. *U.S. News and World Report.*

Asimov, N. (1998, July 7). Bilingual surprise in state testing. *San Francisco Chronicle,* A1.

August, D., and Hakuta, K. (Eds.). (1998). *Educating language-minority children.* Commission on Behavioral and Social Sciences and Education, National Research Council, Institute of Medicine. Washington, DC: National Academy Press.

Banks, J. A., and Banks, C. A. M. (Eds.). (1995). *Handbook of research on multicultural education.* New York: Macmillan.

Cazabon, M., Lambert, W. E., and Hall, G. (1993). *Two-way bilingual education: A progress report on the Amigos Program.* Santa Cruz, CA: National Center for Research in Cultural Diversity and Second Language Learning.

Christian, D. (1994). *Two-way bilingual education: Students learning through two languages.* Santa Cruz, CA: National Center for Research on Cultural Diversity and Second Language Learning.

Christian, D., Montone, C., Lindholm, K. J., and Carranza, I. (1997). *Profiles in two-way immersion education.* McHenry, IL: Delta Systems.

Collier, V. P. (1995). *Promoting academic success for ESL students: Understanding second language acquisition at school.* Elizabeth, NJ: New Jersey Teachers of English to Speakers of Other Languages-Bilingual Educators.

Corson, D. (1993). *Language, minority education and gender: Linking social justice and power.* Clevedon, England: Multilingual Matters.

Crawford, J. (1992). *Hold your tongue: Bilingualism and the politics of "English only."* Reading, MA: Addison-Wesley.

Cummins, J. (1981). The role of primary language development in promoting educational success for language minority students. In Office of Bilingual Bicultural Education, *Schooling and language minority students: A theoretical framework.* Sacramento, CA.: Evaluation, Dissemination, and Assessment Center, California State University, Los Angeles.

Cummins, J. (1984). *Bilingualism and special education.* Clevedon, England: Multilingual Matters.

Cummins, J. (1996). *Negotiating identities: Education for empowerment in a diverse society.* Ontario: California Association for Bilingual Education.

Fairclough, N. (1989). *Language and power.* New York: Longman.

Fránquiz, M. E., and de la luz Reyes, M. (1998). Creating inclusive learning communities through English language arts: From *chanclas* to *canicas. Language Arts, 75*(3), 211–220.

Gándara, P. (1995). *Over the ivy walls: The educational mobility of low-income Chicanos.* Albany: State University of New York Press.

Gibson, M. A. (1995). Perspectives on acculturation and school performance. *Focus on Diversity* (Newsletter of the National Center for Research on Cultural Diversity and Second Language Learning), *5*(3), 8–10.

Igoa, C. (1995). *The inner world of the immigrant child.* New York: St. Martin's.

Krashen, S. (1981). *Second language acquisition and second language learning.* New York: Pergamon.

Lambert, W. E. (1975). Culture and language as factors in learning and education. In A. Wolfgang (Ed.), *Education of immigrant students.* Toronto: OISE.

Lau v. Nichols, 414 U.S. 563 (1974).

Macedo, D., and Bartolomé, L. I. (1999). *Dancing with bigotry: Beyond the politics of difference.* New York: St. Martin's.

Macías, R. R., et al. (1998). *Summary report of the survey of the states' limited English proficient students and available educational programs and services, 1996–97.* Washington, DC: National Clearinghouse of Bilingual Education.

Minicucci, C., Berman, P., McLaughlin, B., McLeod, B., Nelson, B., and Woodworth, K. (1995). School reform and student diversity. *Phi Delta Kappan, 77*(1), 77–80.

Moll, L. C. (1992). Bilingual classroom studies and community analysis: Some recent trends. *Educational Researcher, 21*(2), 20–24.

National Association for Bilingual Education. (1998, May 1). Findings of the Effectiveness of Bilingual Education. *NABE News,* 5.

Nieto, S. (1999). *The light in their eyes: Creating multicultural learning communities.* New York: Teachers College Press.

Nieto, S. (2000a). *Affirming diversity: The sociopolitical context of multicultural education* (3rd ed.). New York: Longman.

Nieto, S. (2000b). Bringing bilingual education out of the basement, and other imperatives for teacher education. In Z. Beykont (Ed.), *Lifting every voice: Pedagogy and politics of bilingual education* (pp. 187–207). Cambridge, MA: Harvard Education Publishing Group.

Ovando, C. J., and Collier, V. P. (1998). *Bilingual and ESL classrooms: Teaching in multi-cultural contexts* (2nd ed.). New York: McGraw-Hill.

Phillipson, R. (1992). *Linguistic imperialism.* Oxford, England: Oxford University Press.

Portes, A., and Rumbaut, R. G. (1996). *Immigrant America: A portrait* (2nd ed.). Berkeley: University of California Press.

Skutnabb-Kangas, T. (1988). Multilingualism and the education of minority children. In T. Skutnabb-Kangas and J. Cummins (Eds.), *Minority language: From shame to struggle.* Clevedon, England: Multilingual Matters, pp. 9–44.

Snow, C. (1997). The myths around bilingual education. *NABE News, 21*(2), 29.

Soto, L. D. (1997). *Language, culture, and power: Bilingual families and the struggle for quality education.* Albany: State University of New York Press.

Spring, J. (1997). *Deculturalization and the struggle for equality: A brief history of the education of dominated cultures in the United States* (2nd ed.). New York: McGraw-Hill.

Thomas, W. P., and Collier, V. P. (1997). *School effectiveness for language minority students.* Washington, DC: National Clearinghouse for Bilingual Education.

U.S. Bureau of the Census. (1994). *Statistical abstract of the United States* (114th ed.). Washington, DC: U.S. Government Printing Office, p. 11.

U.S. Immigration and Naturalization Service. (1995). *Statistical yearbook of the immigration and naturalization service.* Washington, DC: U.S. Government Printing Office.

Williams, S. W. (1991). Classroom use of African American Language: Educational tool or social weapon? In C. E. Sleeter (Ed.), *Empowerment through multicultural education* (pp. 199–215). Albany: State University of New York Press.

Wong Fillmore, L. (1991). When learning a second language means losing the first. *Early Childhood Research Quarterly, 6*, 323–346.

Zentella, Ana Celia (1997). *Growing up bilingual: Puerto Rican children in New York.* Malden, MA: Blackwell.

Critical Questions

1   Research the English-Only movement. Do you consider it an example of linguicism? Why or why not?

2   The argument that "My folks made it without bilingual education; why give other folks special treatment?" has often been made, particularly by descendants of European American immigrants. Do you think this is a compelling argument? Why or why not? (You may want to do some research on the Nativist movement of the nineteenth century as background for this discussion.)

3   If you were the principal of a school with a large population of language-minority students, what would you do to address this situation? What if you were a parent or teacher of one of those children? If you were one of the students, what kind of help might you need?

4   What preparation have you had to teach students of linguistically diverse backgrounds in your teacher education program? What would you like to have learned? What would have most helped you be effective with students who speak languages other than English?

Activity for Your Classroom

Although about a fifth of all U.S. citizens are either immigrants or the children of an immigrant, and many of them speak a language other than English in addition to English, the U.S. is thought of as a fairly monolingual society. To help your students understand the important role that language diversity has in our history and current society, engage them in a family and community language survey. Help your students create an interview instrument concerning the language backgrounds, histories, and speaking abilities of their families. (The interview can range from simple to complex questions and issues, depending on the ages, grade levels, and abilities of your students.) Ask them to interview their family members from parents/guardians to grandparents and neighbors. Discuss the results in class. If possible, have your students audiotape responses from family members and neighbors who speak another language and play these in class. What was surprising to them about what they learned?

Community-Based Activity and Advocacy

What are the policies and practices concerning language-minority students in your school? How could language-minority students be better served? Along with a group of interested parents and teachers, think about policies and practices that would be most appropriate and beneficial for these students (and might also benefit English-speaking monolingual students). Draw up a list of suggestions that you can give to the school council, parent group, or principal.

Supplementary Resources for Further Reflection and Study

Crawford, J. (2004). *Educating English learners: Language diversity in the classroom*, 5th ed. Los Angeles: Bilingual Education Services.
  A comprehensive treatment of the education of linguistic-minority students in the United States, this book includes the history of language diversity and education policies, theories on the best way to learn English, analysis of English-only policies in several states, and a guide to ELL program models from structured English immersion to two-way bilingual education.

Cummins, J. (2001). *Language, Power, and Pedagogy: Bilingual Children in the Crossfire*. Clevedon, England: Multilingual Matters.
  Cummins not only reviews the research and theory relating to instruction and assessment of bilingual students, but also offers a detailed discussion on the ways in which power relations in the wider society affect patterns of teacher–student interaction in the classroom.

Delpit, L. & Doudy, J. K. (Eds.). (2002). *The skin that we speak: Thoughts on language and culture in the classroom*. New York: The New Press.
  The editors bring the discussion of language in the classroom beyond the highly contentious arena of Ebonics and bilingual education to present a thoughtful

exploration of the varieties of English that we speak. Authors include Lisa Delpit, Herbert Kohl, Gloria Ladson-Billings, Victoria Purcell-Gates, Geneva Smitherman, Asa Hilliard, and others.

Fecho, B. (2003). *"Is this English?" Race, language, and culture in the classroom.* New York: Teachers College Press.

This is the story of a White high school English teacher, Bob Fecho, and his students of color who mutually engage issues of literacy, language, learning, and culture. Through his journey, Fecho presents a method of "critical inquiry" that allows students and teachers to take intellectual and social risks in the classroom to make meaning together and, ultimately, transform literacy education.

Harmon, M. R. & Wilson, M. J. (2006). *Beyond grammar: Language, power, and the classroom.* Mahwah, NJ: Lawrence Erlbaum.

In this highly readable book, the authors link issues of language with ethnicity, gender, and power. They discuss why all teachers, especially teachers of English, need to understand these issues within a social justice framework.

Part II

Identity and Belonging

One might well ask what a student's identity has to do with learning. After all, isn't learning neutral with respect to students' ethnicities and native languages? Although many approaches to learning have been based on just such a universal approach, the previous chapters have made clear that who students are and the sociopolitical context in which students live can indeed be crucial factors in promoting or hindering learning. As much as we may resist the idea, students' identities play a role in whether they are welcomed or rejected as learners in schools and, consequently, whether they do or do not benefit from their schooling.

The chapters that follow center on identity and belonging as key issues in learning and teaching. Chapter 7 tackles the complex question of culture: what it means, how it is made visible in our beliefs and daily actions, and what it has to do with schooling. Chapter 8 is based on research I did a number of years ago on young peoples' responses to interviews that centered on culture, identity, and learning. Young people of diverse backgrounds have many lessons for teachers and schools, and these lessons have implications that reach far beyond their own identities. In Chapter 9, my colleague John Raible and I discuss the complex identities of young people of various backgrounds, thus challenging simplistic ways of understanding identity and culture.

7   Culture and Learning

> [We] are not simply bearers of cultures, languages, and histories, with a duty to reproduce them. We are the products of linguistic-cultural circumstances, actors with a capacity to resynthesize what we have been socialized into and to solve new and emerging problems of existence. We are not duty-bound to conserve ancestral characteristics which are not structurally useful. We are both socially determined and creators of human futures.
>
> Mary Kalantzis, Bill Cope, and Diana Slade, *Minority Languages*, 18.

The term "culture" can be problematic because it can mean different things to different people in different contexts. For instance, culture is sometimes used as if it pertains only to those with formal education and privileged social status, implying activities such as attending the opera once a month. In the present day, it generally is acknowledged that culture is not just what an elite group of people may do in their spare time, but there are still various and conflicting ideas of what culture actually means in everyday life. Among many Whites in the United States, for instance, culture is thought to be held exclusively by those different from them. As a consquence, it is not unusual to hear people, especially those of European background, lament that they do not "have" culture in the same way that African Americans, Asian Americans, Native Americans, or other groups visibly different from the dominant group "have" it. In other cases, culture is used interchangeably with ethnicity as if both were simply passed down, constant and eternal, from one generation to the next. At still other times, culture can mean the traditions one celebrates within the family, in which case it is reduced to foods, dances, and holidays. Less often is culture thought of as the values one holds dear, or the way one looks at and interacts with the world.

In this chapter, I explore the complex relationship between culture and learning. I define culture through a number of interrelated characteristics that make it clear that culture is more than artifacts, rituals, and traditions. In fact, it is becoming increasingly indisputable that culture and cultural differences, including language, play a discernible—although complicated—role in learning. I consider how culture and language influence learning by looking at some of the cutural discontinuities between school and home expectations of students from various backgrounds.

Defining Culture

Elsewhere, I have defined culture as "the ever-changing values, traditions, social and political relationships, and worldview created, shared, and transformed by a group of people bound together by a combination of factors that can include a common history, geographic location, language, social class, and religion" (Nieto, 1992). As is clear from this definition, culture is complex and intricate; it includes content or product (the *what* of culture), process (*how* it is created and transformed), and the agents of culture (*who* is responsible for creating and changing it). Culture cannot be reduced to holidays, foods, or dances, although these are, of course, elements of culture. This definition also makes it clear that everyone has a culture because all people participate in the world through social and political relationships informed by history as well as by race, ethnicity, language, social class, gender, sexual orientation, and other circumstances related to identity and experience.

At least two issues need to be kept in mind if culture is to have any meaning for educators who want to understand how it is related to learning. First, culture needs to be thought of in an unsentimental way. Otherwise, it is sometimes little more than a yearning for a past that never existed, or an idealized, sanitized version of what exists in reality. The result may be an unadulterated, essentialized "culture on a pedestal" that bears little resemblance to the messy and contradictory culture of real life. The problem of viewing some aspects of culture as indispensable attributes that must be shared by all people within a particular group springs from a romanticized and uncritical understanding of culture. For instance, I have heard the argument that poetry cannot be considered Puerto Rican unless it is written in Spanish. Thus, the Spanish language becomes a *constitutive characteristic* of being Puerto Rican. While there is no argument that speaking Spanish is an important and even major aspect of Puerto Rican culture, it is by no means a prerequisite for Puerto Ricanness. There are hundreds of thousands of Puerto Ricans who identify themselves first and foremost as Puerto Rican but who do not speak Spanish due to the historical conditions in which they have lived.

The second consideration to be kept in mind is that the sociopolitical context of culture needs to be acknowledged. That is, cultures do not exist in a vacuum, but rather are situated in particular historical, social, political, and economic conditions, and therefore they are influenced by issues of power. The claim of Whites that they do not have a culture is a case in point. Whites frequently do not experience their culture *as a culture* because as the officially sanctioned and high-status culture, it "just is." Therefore, when Whites say that they do not "have" a culture, they in effect relegate culture to no more than quaint customs or colorful traditions. This stance is disingenuous at best because it fails to observe that Whites as a group participate disproportionately in a *culture of power* (Delpit, 1988) simply based on their race, although access to this power is not available to those who are not White (nor, it should be stressed, is it shared equally among Whites).

In what follows, I describe a set of attributes that are key to understanding how culture is implicated in learning, and how these notions of culture complicate a facile approach to multicultural education. These characteristics are complementary and interconnected, so much so that it is difficult to disentangle them from one another. I do so here only for purposes of clarity, not to suggest that they exist in isolation. The characteristics I review here include culture as *dynamic; multifaceted; embedded in context; influenced by social, economic, and political factors; created and socially constructed; learned;* and *dialectical.*

Culture Is Dynamic

Culture does not exist outside of human beings. This means that cultures are not static relics, stagnant behaviors, or sterile values. Steven Arvizu's (1994) wonderful description of culture as a *verb* rather than a *noun* captures this essence of culture beautifully. That is, culture is dynamic, active, changing, always on the move. Even within their native contexts, cultures are always changing as a result of political, social, and other modifications in the immediate environment. When people with different backgrounds come in contact with one another, such change is to be expected even more.

But cultural change is not simply a one-way process. The popular conception of cultural change is that it is much like a transfusion: As one culture is emptied out of a person, a new one is poured in. In this conception, each culture is inert and permanent, and human beings do not influence the process to any significant degree. But the reality is that cultures are always hybrids, and that people select and reject particular elements of culture as suitable or not for particular contexts. Cultural values are not gotten rid of as easily as blood, nor are new ones simply infused. For instance, there is ample ethnographic evidence that in spite of the enormous political, social, and economic changes among American Indians in the past 100 years, their child.-rearing practices, although they have, of course, changed, have also remained quite stable (Deyhle & Swisher, 1997). Likewise, among immigrants to the United States, there are indications that ethnic values and identities are preserved to some extent for many generations (Greenfield, 1994; McGoldrick, Pearce, & Giordano, 1982).

In some ways, we can think of culture as having both *surface* and *deep structure*, to borrow a concept from linguistics (Chomsky, 1965). For instance, in previous research (Nieto, 1992), when interviewing young people of diverse backgrounds I was initially surprised by the seeming homogeneity of the youth culture they manifested. That is, regardless of racial, ethnic, or linguistic background, or time in the United States—but usually intimately connected to a shared urban culture and social class—the youths often expressed strikingly similar tastes in music, food, clothes, television viewing habits, and so on. Yet, when I probed more deeply, I also found evidence of deeply held values from their ethnic heritage. For example, Marisol, a young Puerto Rican woman whom I interviewed, loved hip hop and rap music, pizza, and lasagna. She never mentioned Puerto Rican food, and Puerto Rican music to her was just the "old-fashioned" and boring music her parents listened to. Nonetheless, in her everyday interactions with her parents and siblings, and in the answers she gave to my interview questions, she reflected deep aspects of Puerto Rican culture such as respect for elders, a profound kinship with and devotion to family, and a desire to uphold important traditions such as staying with family rather than going out with friends on important holidays. Just as there is no such thing as a "pure race," there is likewise no "pure culture." That is, cultures influence *one another*, and even minority cultures and those with less status have an impact on majority cultures, some-times in dramatic ways. Rap music, with its accompanying style of talk, dress, and movement, is a notable example among young people of diverse backgrounds in urban areas.

In terms of schooling, the problem with thinking of culture as static is that curriculum and pedagogy are designed as if culture indeed were unchanging. This issue was well expressed by Frederick Erickson (1990), who has argued that when culture is thought of as fixed, or simply as an aesthetic, the educational practice derived from it supports the status quo. This is because reality itself can then be perceived as inherently static.

Erickson goes on to say, "When we think of culture and social identity in more fluid terms, however, we can find a foundation for educational practice that is transformative" (p. 22). The view of culture as dynamic rather than fixed is unquestionably more befitting a conception of multicultural education as liberat-ing pedagogy based on social justice.

Culture Is Multifaceted

Closely related to the dynamic nature of culture is that cultural identifications are multiple, eclectic, mixed, and heterogeneous. This means, for one thing, that culture cannot be conflated with just ethnicity or race. As an example, Mexican or Mexican American culture may be familiar to us because it concerns an identity based primarily on ethnicity, the best-known site of culture. But one also can speak, for instance, of a lesbian culture because as a group, lesbians share a history and identity, along with particular social and political relationships. Thus, one can be culturally Mexican American and a lesbian at the same time. But having multiple cultural identities does not imply that each identity is claimed or mani-fested equally. A wealthy light-skinned Mexican American lesbian and a working-class dark-skinned Mexican American lesbian may have little in common other than their ethnic heritage and sexual orientation, and the oppression that comes along with these identities. People create their identities in different ways: While one Mexican American lesbian may identify herself first and foremost ethnically, another may identify herself as a lesbian, a third as both, and a fourth primarily as a member of the working class.

Because culture is not simply ethnicity, even among specific cultural groups there are many and often conflicting cultural identities. Skin color, time of arrival in the United States, language use, level of education, family dynamics, place of residence, and many other differences within groups may influence how one interprets or "lives" a culture. Further, the intersection of ethnicity and social class, or what Milton Gordon (1964) termed *ethclass*, is a key factor in defining culture. For instance, as a young girl I was surprised to meet middle-class Puerto Ricans when I spent a summer in Puerto Rico. Given my experiences until that time as a member of an urban U.S. Puerto Rican family that could best be described as working poor, I had thought that only Whites could be middle-class. Although I spoke Spanish fairly well and thought of myself as Puerto Rican, I discovered that in some ways I had more in common with my African American peers in my Brooklyn neighborhood and school than with the middle-class Puerto Ricans I met on the island. I began to see that my Puerto Rican culture was in fact quite different from Puerto Rican culture as defined on the island. Years later I understood that these differences had to do with location, experience, and social class.

Another important aspect of identity has to do with how interactions with people of other cultural groups may influence culture and identity. This is certainly the case in urban areas, where the identities of young people of many diverse ethnic and racial backgrounds defy easy categorization. Shirley Brice Heath (1995) has suggested that young urban dwellers in the United States are creating new cultural categories based on shared experiences because, according to her, these young people "think of themselves as a *who* and not a *what*" (p. 45). They engage not only in border crossings, but also in what Heath called "crossings and crisscrossings" (p. 48). Given the growing presence of people in the United States who claim a biracial, multiracial, or multiethnic identity, ethnicity alone is unable to fully define culture. The multiple identities of youths have important and far-reaching implications for the development and implementation of multicultural education: It is evident that simplistic and bounded conceptions that focus just on specific racial or ethnic groupings fail to capture the realities of many urban youths who live with complicated and heterogeneous realities.

Culture Is Embedded in Context

To say that culture is embedded in context is to say that it invariably is influenced by the environment in which it exists. The culture of Japanese students in Japan is of necessity different from that of Japanese immigrant students in the United States or of Japanese immigrant students in Peru or Brazil. When culture is presented to students as if it were context-free, they learn to think of it as quite separate from the lives that people lead every day. It is what Frederick Erickson (1990) has described as the fragmenting of people's lives "as we freeze them outside time, outside a world of struggle in concrete history" (p. 34). Culture is commonly decontextualized. In the United States, decontextualization typically occurs in the school curriculum and in media images outside of school. A notable case is that of American Indians, who customarily have been removed from their cultural and historical rootedness through images that eternalize them as either noble heroes or uncivilized savages, and typically as a combination of both (Churchill, 1992). On the other hand, the history of oppression, dehumanization, resistance, and struggle of the many Indigenous Nations rarely is studied in schools. If there is any doubt about the image of American Indians held by most non-Indian children in the United States, ask even 6-year-olds and they will provide in precise detail the most stereotypical and ahistorical portrait of Indians, as Erickson (1990) noted, "outside time" (p. 34). If these children happen to live in a geographic region where there are no reservations or large concentrations of Indians, they often are shocked to learn that Indians are still around today and that they are teachers, or truck drivers, or artists. Even when American Indians are included in the curriculum as existing in the present, the idyllic images of them tend to reinforce common stereotypes. For instance, while we may be happy to show students pictures of powwows, we are less likely to discuss how reservations have been used as toxic dumping sites.

A further example of how culture is influenced by context will suffice. Puerto Ricans generally eat a great deal of rice in many different manifestations. Rice is a primary Puerto Rican staple. There is even a saying that demonstrates how common it is: "Puertorriqueños somos como el arroz blanco: Estamos por todas partes" (Puerto Ricans are like white rice: We are everywhere), an adage that says as much about rice as it does about the diaspora of the Puerto Rican people, almost half of whom live outside the island. As a rule, Puerto Ricans eat short-grained rice, but I prefer long-grained rice, and other Puerto Ricans often made me feel practically like a cultural traitor when I admitted it. I remember my amazement when a fellow academic, a renowned Puerto Rican historian, explained the real reason behind the preference for short-grained rice. This preference did not grow out of the blue, nor does any particular quality of the rice make it inherently better. On the contrary, the predilection for short-grained rice was influenced by the historical context of Puerto Ricans as a colonized people.

It seems that near the beginning of the twentieth century when Puerto Rico was first taken over by the United States as spoils of the Spanish-American War, there was a surplus of short-grained rice in the United States. Colonies frequently have been the destination for unwanted or surplus goods from the metropolis, so Puerto Rico became the dumping ground for short-grained rice, which had lower status than long-grained rice in the United States. After this, of course, the preference for short-grained rice became part of the culture. As is true of all cultural values, however, this particular taste was influenced by history, economics, and power, which will be further elaborated in what follows.

Culture Is Influenced by Social, Economic, and Political Factors

As is evident from the above, intimately related to the fact that culture is bound to a particular context, is that it is greatly influenced by the political, historical, and economic conditions in which it is found. It exists not in isolation but through concrete relationships characterized by differential access to power. As a result, dominant social groups in a society often determine what counts as culture. This is why, for example, a dominant cultural group unabashedly can designate itself as "the norm" and others as "culturally deprived" (Lewis, 1965; Reissman, 1962). Those who are so designated may not necessarily see them-selves in this way, but naming by others takes on great power; eventually many of those who are designated as "culturally deprived" may learn to believe it. Yet "culturally deprived" actually means simply that the group in question does not share in the culture—and consequently in the power—of the dominant group. The paradox of this stance is that while Whites see themselves as culturally neutral or "cultureless," at the same time they insist, through constant messages in the dominant ideology, that theirs is the valued and valuable culture.

The theories of sociologist Pierre Bourdieu (1986) are significant here. According to him, it is not simply money, or *economic capital,* that determines one's standing in the social structure; equally important are what he has termed *social capital* and *cultural capital.* Social capital is made up of social obligations and networks that are convertible into economic capital. Cultural capital, which is more immediately important to us here, can be defined as the acquired tastes, values, languages, and dialects, or the educational qualifications, that mark a person as belonging to a privileged social and cultural class. Just as in the case of learning one's native culture and language, cultural capital is acquired in the absence of any deliberate or explicit teaching; it is therefore unconsciously learned. The initial accumulation of cultural capital, in the words of Bourdieu (1986), is "the best hidden form of hereditary transmission of capital" (p. 246).

In essence, then, culture is deeply entangled with economic and political privilege. That is, the tastes, values, languages, and dialects that have the greatest status are associated with the dominant social class *not because these tastes, values, languages, or dialects are inherently better but because they have higher social prestige as determined by the group with the greatest power.* As a case in point, for many years linguists have proposed that Black English is a rich and creative variety of English, as logical and appropriate as standard English for purposes of communication (Labov, 1972; Smitherman, 1977). Yet the conventional wisdom still common among teachers is that Black English is simply "bad English." Thus, rather than building on students' native discourse— what has been termed *additive bilingualism* (Lambert, 1975)—most teachers simply attempt to eradicate Black English and replace it with standard English, a *subtractive* form of bilingualism. On the other hand, when expressions from Black English make their way into standard English because they are used by middle-class Whites, they immediately take on a higher social status and thus become acceptable.

The example of Black English underscores the impact that culture may have on learning and academic achievement. Most schools are organized to reflect and support the cultural capital of privileged social and cultural groups; in the United States, that group is middle-class or upper-class, English-speaking Whites. As a result of their identity and upbringing, some children arrive at the schoolhouse door with a built-in privilege because they have learned this cultural capital primarily in the same way as they have learned to walk, that is, unconsciously and effortlessly. Their culture, in this case, the variety of English that they speak, seems both natural and correct. Yet as suggested by Carol Lee and Diana Slaughter-Defoe (1995), because of the low prestige of Black English, "the influences of language on learning for African Americans are both complex and problematic" (p. 357).

This example also places in bold relief the arbitrary nature of cultural capital. Paulo Freire (Shor & Freire, 1987) captured the frivolous essence of such designations when he asked, "When did a certain form of grammar become 'correct'? Who named the language of the elite as 'correct,' as the standard?" He answered his own question by stating, "They did, of course. But, why not call it 'upper-class dominating English' instead of 'Standard English.' That authentic naming would reveal, instead of obscure, the politics of power and language in society" (p. 45). Further on, in discussing the same topic, he added, "This so-called 'standard' is a deeply *ideological* concept, but it is necessary to teach correct usage while also criticizing its political implications" (p. 71).

One could envision another, quite different, scenario. If, for instance, through some extraordinary turn of events, working-class African Americans were to become the esteemed social group in the United States, Black English probably would become the new standard. In turn, schools would make certain that the curriculum, texts, and other materials would reflect this new form of cultural capital; in addition, only those teachers who were intimately familiar with Black English and who considered it an innately superior variety of English would be hired. Accordingly, the children of working-class African American homes would enter school with a built-in advantage compared with other children, who would be considered "culturally deprived" because they did not have the cultural capital of Black English. As far-fetched as this scenario is, given current economic and political realities in the United States, it serves as a graphic example of the capricious nature of determining whose culture becomes highly valued.

Culture Is Created and Socially Constructed

As discussed previously, culture often is thought of as a product-in-place, and as something handed down that must be kept the way it is. Not only does this result in a static view of culture, but it also implies that culture is already finished. As we have seen, culture is constantly evolving, and the reason that it evolves is because *human beings change it*. The action of people on culture takes place in big ways and small, by everyday people and by those who have power. When Jonathan Kozol (1978) went to Cuba to research the successful massive literacy campaign that had just taken place, he spoke with young people in schools, many of whom had been the teachers of the peasants who learned to read. He was awed by the young people's responses when he asked them what was meant by *history*. He recounted that when he had asked that same question of students in Schenectady, New York, the answers had been fairly uniform: "History is everything that happened in the past and is now over. . . . History is what is done by serious and important people" (p. 176). In contrast, when he asked young people in Cuba the same question, their answers were starkly different: "It is the past, but there are things that we do now which will be part of history someday" (p. 176). These young people saw that history was not just what was written in history books, or the actions of "important people" in conquest, war, or politics. What they had done in the literacy campaign was also history.

In the same way, culture is what we do every day. Cultures change as a result of the decisions that we, as cultural agents, make about our traditions, attitudes, behaviors, and values. Were it not so, we would forever be mere pawns or victims of the actions of others. Sometimes, of course, cultural values develop as a result of victimization. The previous example of short-grained rice is a case in point. But even here, people took what they were given and made it a positive value. Without such valuing, short-grained rice would not have become part of the culture. The cuisine of poor people throughout the world is another illustration of how culture is created. Poor people often get nothing but leftovers, the parts of animals or plants that nobody else wants. What they have done with these remains has sometimes been nothing short of extraordinary. This is cultural creation in action. Put another way, in the words of Frederick Erickson (1997): "Culture can be thought of as a construction—it constructs us and we construct it" (p. 39). Culture, then, is not a passive legacy, but an active operation that takes place through contact and interactions with others. Culture is a social construction because it cannot exist outside of social contact and collaboration.

Culture Is Learned

Closely related to the fact that culture is created and socially constructed is the fact that it is *learned*. That is, culture is not handed down through our genes, nor is it inherited. This is very clear to see, for example, when children from a particular ethnic group (for instance, Korean) are adopted by families from another ethnic group (usually European American). Although the children may still be considered ethnically and racially Korean, they will in all likelihood be *culturally* European American, unless their parents made a conscious and determined effort to teach them the culture and history of their heritage while raising them, or the children themselves later decide to do so.

Culture, especially ethnic and religious culture, is learned through interactions with families and communities. It usually is not consciously taught, or consciously learned. That is why it seems so natural and effortless. Although this process does not hold true of all cultures—for example, deaf or gay culture—we predictably learn culture while sitting on our mothers' or grandmothers' laps, standing by our fathers, listening to the conversations of family members around us, and modeling our behavior on theirs. In fact, most people do not even think about their culture unless it is in a subordinate position to another culture or—if they belong to a majority culture—when they leave the confines of home and are no longer part of the cultural norm.

That culture is learned is also apparent in the very concept of *biculturalism*. Bilingual education, for instance, very often is called *bilingual/bicultural education* because it is based on the principle that one can learn two languages and two cultural systems in order to function and even to succeed in different linguistic and cultural contexts. This point was made in research by Gloria Ladson-Billings (1994). Of the eight teachers she identified as successful with African American youths, three were White, and of them, one had a White culture of reference, another a bicultural culture of reference, and the third an African American culture of reference. However, becoming bicultural is not as simple as discarding one set of clothes for another. Because culture is complex, "learning" a culture that is not one's native culture is an exceedingly difficult task, one accomplished only through direct, sustained, and profound involvement with it. Because most teachers in the United States have not been through this process, it can be difficult for them to understand how excruciating the process is for their students. Furthermore, it is difficult to become bicultural in an untroubled sense because it means internalizing two cultural systems whose inherent values may be diametrically opposed.

In the United States, it is generally only students from dominated cultures who need to become bicultural as a requirement for academic and societal success. That they do so is a testament to great strength and resiliency. The fact that these students, in spite of being young, feeling isolated, and facing what can be terrifying situations in unfamiliar environments, nonetheless can incorporate the cultural motifs of disparate values and behaviors says a great deal about human tenacity. What they accomplish might best be thought of as *critical biculturalism*, a biculturalism that is neither facile nor uncomplicated, but full of inconsistencies and challenges.

Culture Is Dialectical

Culture often is thought of as a seamless web of interrelated and mutually supportive values and behaviors, yet nothing could be further from the truth. Because they are complex systems that are created by people and influenced by social, economic, and political factors, cultures are also dialectical, conflicted, and full of inherent tensions. A culture is neither "good" nor "bad" in general, but rather embodies values that have grown out of historical and social conditions and necessities. As individuals, we may find elements of our own or others' cultures uplifting or repugnant. That culture is dialectical does not mean that we need to embrace all of its contradictory manifestations in order to be "authentic" members of the culture.

Young people whose cultures are disparaged by society sometimes feel that they have to accept either one culture or the other wholly and uncritically. This was found to be the case, for instance, among Romani (Gypsy) youth in research carried out in Hungary (Forray & Hegedüs, 1989). Prevalent gender expectations of Romani boys and girls tend to be fairly fixed and stereotypical. Yet because the family is often the only place where culturally dominated young people can positively strengthen their self-image, Romani girls may correctly perceive that breaking free of even limited expectations of their future life options also results in giving up their ethnic identity and abandoning their families. Through questionnaires collected from elementary school teachers of Romani children, it became clear that teachers' negative attitudes and behaviors concerning the fixed gender roles in the Romani culture were at least partly responsible for strengthening the expected gender-based behavior among girls in school. Had teachers been able to develop a more culturally balanced and sensitive approach, it is conceivable that the Romani girls might have felt safe to explore other options without feeling that they were cultural traitors.

That culture is dialectical also leads to an awareness that there is no special virtue in preserving particular elements of culture as if they existed outside of social, political, and historical spaces. Mary Kalantzis and her colleagues (1989) have described this contradiction eloquently:

> Preserving "communities" is not a good for its own sake, as if peoples should be preserved as museum pieces, so that they are not lost to posterity. "Communities" are always mixed, contradictory, conflict-ridden and by no means socially isolated entities. Active cultural re-creation, if people so wish, might involve consciously dropping one language in preference for another or abandoning some cultural tradition or other—such as sexism.
>
> (p. 12)

The work of the Puerto Rican sociologist Rafael Ramírez (1974) is particularly relevant here. Ramírez has suggested that we can think of every culture as a coin that has two contradictory faces or subsystems. He calls these the *culture of survival* and the *culture of liberation*, and each is important in defining the complexity of culture. The culture of survival embodies those attitudes, values, traditions, and behaviors that are developed in response to political, economic, or social forces, some of which may be interpreted as a threat to the survival of the culture in some way. They can either limit (e.g., the unequal treatment of women) or expand. (i.e., mutual cooperation) people's perspectives within a particular culture. In the case of the role of women, values and behaviors of both males and females grew out of the necessity to view women, because of their unique biology, as primary caregivers. The need to survive is thus manifested in many cultures in perfectly understandable, although not always ethical or equitable ways, given the history of the species. According to Ramírez:

> The culture of survival is characterized mainly by the contradiction that it sustains, affirms, and provides certain power but, at the same time, does not confront or alter the oppressive elements and institutions nor affect the structure of political and economic power that controls the system.
>
> (p. 86)

Ramírez has defined the culture of liberation as the values, attitudes, traditions, and behaviors that embody liberatory aspects of culture. This face of culture, according to Ramírez, is part of the process of decolonization, and of questioning unjust structures and values, and it "comprises those elements that promote a new social order in which the democratization of the sociopolitical institutions, economic equality and cooperation and solidarity in interpersonal relations predominate" (p. 88). In this way, Ramírez says, authoritarianism is contrasted with democracy, racism with consciousness of racial and ethnic identity, and sexism with gender equality. Human rights that are generally accepted by most societies can be included in the framework of the culture of liberation. As we shall see later, understanding the contradictory nature of culture is important if students and teachers are to develop a critical, instead of a romantic, perspective of their own and other people's cultures.

Language as Culture

As we have seen in several examples above, language is deeply implicated with culture and an important part of it. That is, the language, language variety, or dialect one speaks is culture made manifest, although it is not, of course, all there is to culture. This explains why, for instance, so many assimilationist movements both inside and outside of schools—from the forced removal of American Indian children to boarding schools beginning in the nineteenth century, to the recent English-Only Movement—have had native-language devaluation and elimination as major themes. In a very real sense, language is power, and this truth has been at the core of such movements. In the words of Richard Ruiz (1991), "A major dimension of the power of language is the power to define, to decide the nature of lived experience" (p. 218). Doing away with a language, or prohibiting its use, tears away at the soul of a people. Consequently, it is not surprising that language often has served as a powerful symbol and organizing tool for language-minority groups. For instance, using the example of four Indigenous minority cultures (Navajo, Huala Pai, Maori, and Hawaiian), Carlos Ovando and Karen Gourd (1996) have shown how language maintenance and revitalization movements have been used by marginalized groups as major vehicles to attain power within society, to create a sense of peoplehood, and to challenge officially sanctioned structures and languages.

In the United States, attitudes about languages and language varieties other than the mainstream language have oscillated between grudging acceptance and outright hostility. These attitudes have been rationalized as necessary for political and social cohesion and for academic success (Crawford, 1992). Laws as well as school policies have reflected for the most part negative attitudes about native-language maintenance: Examples include the virtual disappearance of native-language instruction between the two world wars, recent court cases involving workers who dared to speak their native language among themselves, and even mothers who, in the privacy of their own homes, speak with their children in their own language, the language that reflects their nurture and love. This was the case of a young mother chastised by a judge for speaking Spanish to her child (cited in Cummins, 1996). Marta Laureano, who was involved in a child custody case in Texas, was admonished by Judge Samuel Kiser that she was relegating her daughter to a future as a housemaid if she continued speaking Spanish to her. He also charged that speaking Spanish to her was "bordering on abuse" and ordered her to speak only English at home (Cummins, 1996, p. 21).

If research were to prove that maintaining native-language use was a detriment to learning, there might be some reason to consider assimilation as a positive process. This has not proven to be the case, however. David Dolson's (1985) research on the home language use and academic performance of Latino students, for instance, found that those from *additive* bilingual home contexts—that is, homes where Spanish continued to be used even after children learned English—significantly outperformed their peers from *subtractive* homes—where the Spanish was replaced by English. Moreover, he discovered that more Spanish at home usually resulted in better *English* skills as well, supporting the idea that Spanish-language use in the home fosters improved academic performance. Lourdes Díaz Soto's (1993) research among 30 Hispanic families of young children with low and high academic achievement found that parents of the higher-achieving children inevitably favored a native-language environment to a greater extent than those of lower-achieving youngsters. Her findings, rather than suggesting the suppression or elimination of native-language use at home and school—an attitude that is all too common in schools—support just the opposite.

Similar conclusions have been reached by researchers using the case of Black English or Black dialect. In one study, for example, dialect-speaking 4-year-olds enrolled in a Head Start program were able to recall more details with greater accuracy when they retold stories in their cultural dialect rather than in standard English (Hall, Reder, & Cole, 1979). A more recent research study by Geneva Smitherman (1994) concerning the impact of Black English Vernacular (BEV) on the writing of African American students echoed this finding among older students. Using essays written by African American students for the National Assessment of Educational Progress (NAEP), Smitherman demonstrated that the use of African American discourse style correlated positively with higher scores.

There is even some evidence to support the hypothesis that speaking only English may act as a *barrier* to academic success for bicultural students. Research by David Adams and his colleagues (Adams, Astone, Nuñez-Wormack, & Smodlaka, 1994) examining the predictive value of English proficiency, Spanish proficiency, and the use of each at home relative to the academic achievement of Latino students in five cities, found that recent immigrants who were *more* fluent in Spanish performed better than did second- or third-generation Latinos. They also found a small but negative influence of English-language proficiency on the academic performance of the Mexican American students in the sample; that is, better English proficiency meant lower academic performance among Mexican American youths. How to analyze this finding? The researchers conjectured that there might be what they called a "counterforce" against the traditional relationship between English proficiency and academic performance. They continued, "This counterforce may very well be the peer pressure students experience which works against school achievement, in spite of the students' English-language proficiency" (Adams et al., 1994, pp. 11–12).

This research confirms that simply speaking English is no guarantee that academic success will follow. There seem to be several reasons for this. First, when children are able to keep up with their native language at home, they develop *metalinguistic awareness*, that is, a greater understanding of how language itself works, and of how to use language for further learning. Based on her extensive research concerning second language acquisition, Virginia Collier (1995) has suggested that practicing English at home among students who are more proficient in another language actually can slow down cognitive development because it is only when parents and their children speak the language they know best that they are working at their "level of cognitive maturity" (p. 14). Furthermore, given the negative attitudes that we have seen among teachers about languages and language varieties other than standard English, and especially about languages they consider to have a low status, children who speak these languages may become further alienated from school and what it represents. In essence, students may disidentify with school. For example, the research by Adams and his colleagues (1994) supports the hypothesis that the identification of second- and third-generation Americans with school and academic achievement is weak owing to the repeated and consistent school failure among some groups (Ogbu, 1987). Knowing English may not be sufficient to defy the weak identification with schooling.

Links among Culture, Language, and Learning

Given the preceding discussion, it is indisputable that culture, language, and learning are connected. In what follows, some of the links will be made more explicit, beginning with a discussion of child-rearing practices.

Child-Rearing Practices and Learning

Child-rearing is above all a teaching and learning process, making the home the first context for learning. The earliest and most significant socialization of children takes place within their families and communities. Just as they learn to walk and talk, children also learn *how to learn as* defined within their particular cultural contexts. Children's interactions with parents or other caregivers thus pave the way for how they may fare in school. That is, where students' cultural values and behaviors "fit" with school policies and practices, learning can take place in a fairly straightforward manner; where they clash, learning may be experienced in a negative way.

Early research on child-rearing practices often focused on maladaptive responses to school and helped explain the relative lack of success of children from nonmainstream families. A more positive approach was proposed by Manuel Ramirez and Alfredo Castañeda (1974). While granting that families of different cultural groups employ different child-rearing practices and that these practices influence children's learning in school, Ramirez and Castañeda suggested that, rather than expect families to do all the changing, schools too needed to change by responding to the different ways of learning that children bring to school. The child-rearing styles of caregivers from diverse cultures, according to these researchers, resulted in different *learning styles*, or diverse ways of receiving and processing information. They concluded that the only appropriate response of schools in a pluralistic and democratic society was to develop learning environments that were, in their words, "culturally democratic," that is, environments that reflect the learning styles of all students within them. This perspective was radically different from the usual expectation that all children arrive at school with the same ways of learning. Given the notion that schools create and perpetuate inequality through policies and practices, including the pressure to assimilate, the perspective suggested by Ramirez and Castañeda makes a good deal of sense.

Ramirez and Castañeda were among the first researchers to suggest that all learning styles, not just the analytic style generally favored by majority-group students and. practiced in most schools, are suitable for academic work. They built on the theories of Herman Witkin (1962) that people have either a *field independent* learning style (usually defined as preferring to learn in an analytic matter with materials devoid of social context) or a *field dependent* learning style (understood as favoring highly social and contextualized. settings). Based on their research with children of various cultural backgrounds, they concluded that European American children tend to be field independent, and Mexican American, American Indian, and African American children tend to be field *sensitive*, the term they substituted for the more negatively charged *dependent*. They suggested that students need to be provided environments where they can learn according to their preferred style, while also becoming *bicognitive*, that is, comfortable and proficient in both styles.

The proposition that students from diverse backgrounds use various approaches to learning and that schools need to make accommodations for them represented a considerable advance in both the theory and practice of education. Nevertheless, much of the learning style research can be criticized on a number of grounds. First, there is no agreement on the number or range of learning styles that actually exist. Second, this research has inclined toward overdetermination, basing students' learning styles almost exclusively on their culture when in fact we know that learning is a much more complex matter. Third, some assessment and instructional strategies and adaptations developed as a result of the learning style research have been overly mechanical and technical, although they might never have been intended to be used as such. For instance, one of the few reviews that looked seriously at the outcomes of adapting instruction to the visual learning style presumably favored by American Indian children concluded that there was virtually no evidence that such adaptations resulted in greater learning (Kleinfeld & Nelson, 1991).

An example of how this kind of research has been poorly used can be found in professional development workshops or education texts that provide lists of "attributes" of students of particular cultural backgrounds based on the learning styles they are reputed to have ("Vietnamese children are . . ." or "African American children learn best when . . ."). All too often, the effect of such categorizations is that the existing stereotypes of children from particular backgrounds become even more rigid. Moreover, categorizing students' learning styles based on race or ethnicity can veer dangerously close to the racist implications drawn from distinctions on IQ tests (Herrnstein & Murray, 1994; Jensen, 1969). For instance, Asa Hilliard (1989) has voiced grave reservations about the use of the term *learning style* as an excuse for low expectations on the part of teachers, and on poor instruction based on these expectations. In this case, the remedy can be worse than the illness itself.

In spite of the theoretical and implementation problems with learning style research, Donna Deyhle and Karen Swisher (1997) suggest that ethnographic studies can prove to be insightful in providing evidence concerning the significance of child-rearing values on learning styles. In these studies, students' learning styles are gleaned from many hours of observation and analysis. Deyhle and Swisher believe that becoming aware of students' preferred ways of learning can be useful, although it is by no means sufficient to guarantee that appropriate environments are created for student learning. Their reasonable conclusion is: "Knowledge of group tendencies presents a framework through which to observe and understand individual behaviors" (p. 151). Cross-cultural psychologists have developed a more conceptually sophisticated explanation for how families of diverse cultural backgrounds influence learning and the cognitive development of their children through their child-rearing practices and interactions, and based on the kind of ecological system in which they live (Greenfield, 1994; Greenfield & Cocking, 1994).

Although research in learning styles has brought the issue of culture and its possible impact on learning to the forefront, the field is fraught with conflict due to criticisms such as those mentioned above, among others (for an analysis of these, see Irvine & York, 1995). One way to ameliorate what can be the overly deterministic tone of this research is to speak of *learning preferences* instead of *styles*. In this case, the implication is that numerous factors influence how people learn, and that in fact all individuals differ in some ways from one another in how they learn. In any event, learning styles or preferences by themselves, although providing an important piece of the puzzle for understanding student learning, do not adequately explain the vastly different outcomes of student achievement. Others have suggested a shift in focus from *learning style* to *cultural style* or *teaching style* (Hilliard, 1989/90; Ladson-Billings, 1992).

Cultural, Linguistic, and Communication Discontinuities Between Home and School

The discontinuities experienced by students whose cultures and/or languages differ substantially from the mainstream, and how these might interfere with learning, are questions that have gained enormous significance in the past 2 decades, especially by educators using an anthropological perspective. One such theory, the *communication process explanation* (Erickson, 1993), is based on the fact that although students may be socialized to learn in particular ways at home, these cultural and communication patterns may be missing in the school setting. The research undergirding this argument has generally been ethnographic in nature, and it has been based on months, and sometimes years, of extensive fieldwork and analysis.

Two significant early studies were groundbreaking in the field and serve as examples of this theory. Susan Philips's (1982) ethnographic research among American Indian schoolchildren on the Warm Springs Reservation in Oregon concluded that the core values with which the children were raised—including harmony, internal locus of control, shared authority, voluntary participation, and cooperation—often were violated in the school setting. For instance, she found that the children did poorly in classroom contexts that demanded individualized performance and emphasized competition. However, they became motivated learners when the context did not require them to perform in public and when cooperation was valued over competition, as in student-directed group projects. Given the assessment practices of most schools, these students were at a disadvantage because their learning was not always demonstrated in the kinds of behaviors expected of them, such as individual performance and recitation.

Philips's insights were a powerful challenge to previous deficit-based conclusions that American Indian children were "slow," "inarticulate," or "culturally deprived," and that they were therefore incapable of learning. Her research provided an alternative, culturally based explanation for the apparent discontinuities between home and school. In a similar vein, Shirley Brice Heath's (1983) research in a working-class African American community she called "Trackton" is a compelling example of cultural and communication discontinuities. In her research, she discovered that the questioning rituals in which parents and other adults in the community engaged with children were not preparing them adequately for the kinds of activities they would face in schools. Furthermore, when Heath observed White middle-class teachers in their own homes, she found that their questions, both to their own children and to their students, differed a great deal from the kinds of questions that the parents of children in Trackton asked. Teachers' questions invariably pulled attributes such as size, shape, or color out of context and asked children to name them. Hugh Mehan (1991) has called these questions "mini-lessons" that prepare children from middle-class homes for the kinds of questions they will hear in school.

On the other hand, the parents of the children from Trackton asked them questions about whole events or objects, and about their uses, causes, and effects. Parents often asked their children questions that were linguistically complex and that required analogical comparisons and complex metaphors rather than "correct" answers out of context. The result of these differences was a lack of communication among teachers and students in the school. Students who at home would be talkative and expressive would become silent and unresponsive in school because of the nature of the questions that teachers asked; this behavior led teachers to conclude that the children were slow to learn or deficient in language skills. It was only through their fieldwork as ethnographers of their own classrooms that the teachers became aware of the differences in questioning rituals and of the kinds of questions that their students' families and other adults in the community asked. Teachers were then able to change some of their questioning procedures to take advantage of the skills that the children already had, building on these skills to then ask more traditional "school" questions. The results were striking, as students became responsive and enthusiastic learners, a dramatic departure from their previous behavior.

A. Wade Boykin (1994) also has reviewed the implications of cultural discontinuities for African American students. According to him, in general Black students in the United States practice a cultural style that he calls *Afrocultural expression.* This style emphasizes spirituality, harmony, movement, verve, communalism, oral tradition, and expressive individualism, elements that are either missing, downplayed, or disparaged in most mainstream classrooms. As a result, there are often incompatibilities between Black students' cultural styles and the learning environment in most schools, and Black students may end up losing out. The problem is not that their styles are incompatible with learning, but rather that these styles are not valued in most classrooms as legitimate conduits for learning.

These examples provide evidence that home cultures and native languages sometimes get in the way of student learning not because of the nature of the home cultures or native languages themselves, but rather because they do not conform to the way that schools define learning. On the other hand, this cultural mismatch is not inevitable: There are numerous examples of research in the past two decades that has concluded that culture and language can work in a mutual and collaborative manner to promote learning rather than obstruct it. Teachers and schools, not only students, need to accommodate to cultural and linguistic differences. According to Margaret Gibson (1991), schooling itself may contribute unintentionally to the educational problems of bicultural students by pressuring them to assimilate against their wishes. Maintaining their language and culture is a far healthier response on the part of young people than adopting an oppositional identity that may effectively limit the possibility of academic achievement.

Other research has confirmed the benefits of maintaining a cultural identification. For instance, in her research among Navajo students, Donna Deyhle (1992) found that those who came from the most traditional Navajo homes, spoke their native language, and participated in traditional religious and social activities were among the most academically successful students in school. Similar findings have been reported for students from other cultural groups as well. A study of Cambodian refugee children by the Metropolitan Indochinese Children and Adolescent Service found that the more they adapted their behavior to fit in with mainstream U.S. culture, the more their emotional adjustment suffered (National Coalition, 1988). Another study of Southeast Asian students found a significant connection between grades and culture: that is, higher grade point averages correlated with the maintenance of traditional values, ethnic pride, and close social and cultural ties with members of the same ethnic group (Rumbaut & Ima, 1987). Likewise, based on her extensive research with adolescent students of color of diverse ethnic backgrounds, Jean Phinney (1993) determined that adolescents who have explored their ethnicity and are clear about its importance in their lives are more likely to be better adjusted than those who have not.

Responses to Cultural Discontinuities

Because many children from diverse cultural backgrounds experience school failure, we need to address how cultural discontinuities between students' homes and their schools affect learning. There have been a number of attempts to adapt learning environments to more closely match the native cultures of students.

Responding to cultural discontinuities takes many forms and can mean anything from developing specific instructional strategies to providing environments that are totally culturally responsive.

Culturally responsive education, an approach based on using students' cultures as an important source of their education, can go a long way in improving the education of students whose cultures and backgrounds have been maligned or omitted in schools. This approach offers crucial insights for understanding the lack of achievement of students from culturally subordinated groups. One of the best known of these is KEEP (the Kamehameha Elementary Education Program) in Hawaii (Au, 1980). KEEP was established because cultural discontinuities in instruction were identified as a major problem in the poor academic achievement of Native Hawaiian children. Educational modifications in KEEP included changing from a purely phonics approach to one emphasizing comprehension, from individual work desks to work centers with heterogeneous groups, and from high praise to more culturally appropriate practices, including indirect and group praise. The KEEP culturally compatible K-3 language arts approach met with great success in student learning and achievement. Similar positive conclusions were reached when the cultures of students of diverse backgrounds were used as a bridge to the dominant culture (Abi-Nader, 1993; Hollins, King, & Hayman, 1994; Irvine, 1997; Ladson-Billings, 1994).

In spite of the promising approaches highlighted by this research, a number of serious problems remain. For one, culturally responsive pedagogy sometimes is based on a static view of culture that may even verge on the stereotypical. Students of particular backgrounds may be thought of as walking embodiments of specific cultural values and behaviors, with no individual personalities and perspectives of their own. An unavoidable result is that entire cultures are identified by a rigid set of characteristics. Culturally congruent approaches, applied uncritically and mechanistically, fall into the same trap as monocultural education; that is, they may be based on an essentialist notion of culture that assumes that all students from the same cultural background learn in the same way. If this is the case, pedagogy and curriculum become, in the words of Erickson (1990), "cosmetically relevant" rather than "genuinely transformative" (p. 23).

A result of essentialist notions is that the diversity of individual students' experiences and identities may be overlooked, and their culture may be used to homogenize all students of the same group. This happens, for instance, when teachers make comments such as, "Korean children prefer to work on their own," because such statements deny the individual idiosyncrasies, preferences, and outlooks of particular students and their families. All cultures operate in synergy, creating new and different forms that borrow from and lend substance to one another. In other words, the multifaceted, contested, and complex nature of culture sometimes is not taken into consideration in culturally responsive pedagogy. Because cultures never exist in a pristine state, untouched by their context, any approach to meaningful and effective pedagogy needs to take into account how students' languages, cultures, and other differences exist within, and are influenced by, mainstream U.S. culture as well as by other subcultures with which they come in contact.

A culturally responsive stance sometimes considers those of nonmajority backgrounds to exist in complete contrast to the majority population, but this is rarely true. I recall, for example, the reaction of a young African American student after he visited an American Indian community in the Northeast: "They have VCRs!" he exclaimed in surprise tinged with disappointment. This young man attended a progressive alternative school with a multicultural curriculum with which I was associated many years ago. The school was a wonderful place in many ways, and the curriculum emphasized positive and liberatory aspects of the histories and cultures of people of color. Nevertheless, we were not immune from falling victim to developing our own static, albeit more positive, romanticized vision of what people of diverse cultures were like. In this case, in preparing students for the trip, we somehow had managed to remove all vestiges of materialistic contemporary life from Indigenous people, and the result was that the children developed an unrealistic and partial view of an entire group of people.

These caveats concerning cultural discontinuities also were explored in research with a Mexicano community by Olga Vasquez, Lucinda Pease-Alvarez, and Sheila Shannon (1994). In a number of case studies of children from this community, they found that a great deal of convergence existed between the children's home and school language interaction patterns. Although these researchers did not question that cultural discontinuities exist, they rejected the suggestion that home-school discontinuity can predict the success or failure of an entire cultural group. Instead, based on research in which they saw firsthand the students' multiple linguistic and cultural skills, they urged educators to consider "the complexity of their students' experiences in a multilayered network of cultures and reference groups" (p. 187).

Finally, a focus on cultural discontinuities alone may hide the structural inequalities with which so many students, especially those who live in poverty, contend on a daily basis. It is therefore necessary to look beyond cultural responsiveness alone to help explain student academic success.

Conclusion: Implications

What are the implications for teachers and schools concerning the links among language, culture, and learning? I would suggest that at least three issues need to be emphasized.

1. *Students' identification with, and maintenance of, their native culture and language can have a positive influence on learning.* The judgment that cultural identification and maintenance are important for academic achievement is not new, but it bears repeating because it is still far from accepted in most schools and classrooms. Research in the past two decades consistently has found that students who are allowed and encouraged to identify with their native languages and cultures in their schools and communities can improve their learning. This finding is also a direct and aggressive challenge to the assimilationist perspective that learning can take place only after one has left behind the language and culture of one's birth. Research in this area has made it clear that students' cultures are important to them and their families. However, maintaining them is also

problematic because the identities of bicultural students generally are disparaged or dismissed by schools.

2. *The role of the teacher as cultural accommodator and mediator is fundamental in promoting student learning.* In much of the research reviewed, it has become apparent that teachers have a great deal to do with whether and how students learn. Consequently, teachers' role as cultural mediators in their students' learning becomes even more urgent. In many cases, teachers need to teach children how to "do school" in order to be academically successful. This kind of mediation may not be necessary for the children of middle-class and culturally mainstream families, but very often it is required for students whose families do not have the high-status cultural capital required for academic success. Teachers need to support this kind of learning while at the same time affirming the cultures and languages that children bring to school as viable and valuable resources for learning.

3. *A focus on cultural differences in isolation from the broader school and societal context will likely not lead to increased learning or empowerment.* Personal and institutional accommodations to student differences need to be in place in order for students to become successful learners. Obviously, these accommodations require drastic shifts in teachers' beliefs and attitudes, and in schools' policies and practices: Instead of simply tinkering with a few cultural additions to the curriculum or adopting a new teaching strategy, a wholesale transformation of schools is in order if we are serious about affording all students an equal chance to learn.

References

Arvizu, S. F. (1994). Building bridges for the future: Anthropological contributions to diversity and classroom practice. In R. A. DeVillar, C. J. Faltis, & J. Cummins (Eds.). *Cultural diversity in schools: From rhetoric to reality* (pp. 75–97). Albany: State University of New York Press.

Bourdieu, P. (1986). The forms of capital. In J. G. Richardson (Ed.). *Handbook of theory and research for the sociology of education* (pp. 241–248). Westport, CT: Greenwood Press.

Chomsky, N. (1965). *Aspects of the theory of syntax.* Cambridge, MA: MIT Press.

Churchill, W. (1992). *Fantasies of the master race: Literature, cinema and the colonization of American Indians.* Monroe, ME: Common Courage Press.

Delpit, L. D. (1988). The silenced dialogue: Power and pedagogy in educating other people's children. *Harvard Educational Review, 58,* 280–298.

Deyhle, D. & Swisher, K. (1997). Research in American Indian and Alaska Native education: From assimilation to self-determination. In M. W. Apple (Ed.), *Review of research in education* (v. 22, pp. 113–194). Washington, DC: American Educational Research Association.

Erickson, F. (1990). Culture, politics, and educational practice. *Educational Foundations, 4* (2), 21–45.

Erickson, F. (1997). Culture in society and in educational practices. In J. A. Banks & C. A. M. Banks (Eds.), *Multicultural education: Issues and perspectives,* 3rd ed. (pp. 32–60). Boston: Allyn & Bacon.

Forray, K. R. & Hegedüs, A. T. (1989). Differences in the upbringing and behavior of

Romani boys and girls, as seen by teachers. *Journal of Multilingual and Multicultural Development, 10* (6), 515–528.

Gordon, M. (1964). *Assimilation in American life: The role of race, religion, and national origins.* New York: Oxford University Press.

Greenfield, P. M. (1994). Independence and interdependence as developmental scripts: Implications for theory, research, and practice. In P. M. Greenfield & R. R. Cocking (Eds.), *Cross-cultural roots of minority child development* (pp. 1–37). Hillsdale, NJ: Lawrence Erlbaum.

Greenfield, P. M. & Cocking, R. R. (Eds.). (1994). *Cross-cultural roots of minority child development.* Hillsdale, NJ: Lawrence Erlbaum.

Hall, W. S., Reder, S., & Cole, M. (1979). Story recall in young black and white children: Effects of racial group membership, race of experimenter, and dialect. In A. W. Boykin, A. J. Franklin, & Y. F. Yates (Eds.), *Research directions of black psychologists* (pp. 253–265). New York: Russell Sage Foundation.

Heath, S. B. (1995). Race, ethnicity, and the defiance of categories. In W. D. Hawley & A. W. Jackson (Eds.), *Toward a common destiny: Improving race and ethnic relations in America* (pp. 39–70). San Francisco: Jossey-Bass.

Herrnstein, R. J. & Murray, C. (1994). *The bell curve: Intelligence and class structure in American life.* New York: Free Press.

Hilliard, A. (1989). Teachers and cultural style in a pluralistic society. *NEA Today, 7* (6), 65–69.

Irvine, J. J. & York, D. E. (1995). Learning styles and culturally diverse students: A literature review. In J. A. Banks & C. A. M. Banks (Eds.), *Handbook of research on multicultural education* (pp. 484–479). New York: Macmillan.

Jensen, A. R. (1969). How much can we boost I.Q. and scholastic achievement? *Harvard Educational Review, 39,* 1–123.

Kalantzis, M., Cope, B., & Slade, D. (1989). *Minority languages.* London: Falmer Press.

Kleinfeld, J. & Nelson, P. (1991). Adapting instruction to Native Americans' learning styles: An iconoclastic view. *Journal of Cross-Cultural Psychology, 22,* 273–282.

Kozol, J. (1978). *Children of the revolution: A Yankee teacher in the Cuban schools.* New York: Delacorte Press.

Labov, W. (1972). *Language in the inner city: Studies in the black English vernacular.* Philadelphia: University of Pennsylvania Press.

Ladson-Billings, G. (1992). Culturally relevant teaching: The key to making multicultural education work. In C. A. Grant (Ed.), *Research and multicultural education: From the margins to the mainstream* (pp. 106–121). Bristol, PA: Falmer Press.

Ladson-Billings, G. (1994). *The dreamkeepers: Successful teachers of African American children.* San Francisco: Jossey-Bass.

Lambert, W. E. (1975). Culture and language as factors in learning and education. In A. Wolfgang (Ed.), *Education of immigrant students* (pp. 55–83). Toronto: Ontario Institute for Studies in Education.

Lee, C. D. & Slaughter-Defoe, D. T. (1995). Historical and sociocultural influences on African American education. In J. A. Banks & C. A. M. Banks (Eds.), *Handbook of research on multicultural education* (pp. 348–371). New York: Macmillan.

Lewis, O. (1965). *La vida: A Puerto Rican family in the culture of poverty—San Juan and New York.* New York: Random House.

McGoldrick, M., Pearce, J. K., & Giordano, J. (1982). *Ethnicity and family therapy.* New York: Guilford Press.

Nieto, S. (1992). *Affirming diversity: The sociopolitical context of multicultural education.* New York: Longman.

Ogbu, J. U. (1987). Variability in minority school performance: A problem in search of an explanation. *Anthropology and Education Quarterly, 18* (4), 312–334.

Ramirez, R. (1974). Culture of liberation and the liberation of culture. In Centro de Estudios Puertorriqueños, *Taller de cultura: Cuaderno 6, Conferencia de historiografía* (pp. 81–99). New York: Puerto Rican Studies Research Center, City University of New York.

Ramirez, M. & Castañeda, A. (1974). *Cultural democracy, bicognitive development and education.* New York: Academic Press.

Reissman, F. (1962). *The culturally deprived child.* New York: Harper & Row.

Shor, I. & Freire, P. (1987). *A pedagogy for liberation: Dialogues on transforming education.* New York: Bergin & Garvey.

Smitherman, G. (1977). *Talkin and testifyin: The language of black America.* Boston: Houghton Mifflin.

Smitherman, G. (1994). The blacker the berry, the sweeter the juice: African American student writers. In A. H. Dyson & C. Genishi (Eds.), *The need for story: Cultural diversity in classroom and community* (pp. 89–101). Urbana, IL: National Council of Teachers of English.

Witkin, H. A. (1962). *Psychological differentiation.* New York: Wiley.

Critical Questions

1   Define culture.
2   Define your culture. How do you identify yourself? What is important to you about your culture? How does your culture influence your choice of friends, your choice of activities, your taste in food or fashion, important decisions that you make in your life?
3   As you saw in this chapter, power is implicated in culture. Give some examples of this from your own experience.

Activity for Your Classroom

Have a discussion about culture with your students. Ask them to research something about their cultural heritage and identity. Depending on their ages and grade levels, they can make a "culture bag" (a bag filled with items that help describe their culture), an oral history of a family member, or library research on their heritage.

Community-Based Activities and Advocacy

1   Research the community in which you teach (or plan to teach). Find out something about the racial/ethnic/cultural make-up of the community. Explore the community organizations and agencies, particularly those that focus on culture. What activities do they sponsor? How relevant are these activities to the life of the community? Present your findings to your peers in this course.
2   How is culture either affirmed or disparaged in your school? Think about school policies and practices such as curriculum, outreach to families, school

traditions and rituals, and others. How might your school change some of these policies and practices to be more inclusive of all families? Come up with some suggestions and present them to your school council.

Supplementary Resources for Further Reflection and Study

Ballenger, C. (1999). *Teaching other people's children: Literacy and learning in a bilingual classroom.* New York: Teachers College Press.

Cynthia Ballenger, a teacher in Boston, describes her three years teaching Haitian children in an inner-city preschool. Based on ethnographic research in her own classroom, she explores how teachers who listen closely to children from cultures other than their own can understand the approaches to literacy that these children bring with them to school. Focusing on three areas crucial to early childhood education (classroom behavior, concepts of print, and storybook reading), she challenges many widely held assumptions and cultural perspectives about the education of young children.

Carter, P. L. (2005). *Keepin' it real: School success beyond black and white.* New York: Oxford University Press.

In this book, Prudence Carter argues for a broader recognition of the unique cultural styles and practices that non-White students bring to the classroom. Based on extensive interviews and surveys of students in New York, she demonstrates that students who are successful negotiators of school systems are what she calls "multicultural navigators." Multicultural navigators are culturally-savvy teens who draw from multiple traditions, whether it be knowledge of hip hop or of classical music, to achieve their high ambitions.

Gonzalez, N. E., Moll, L., & Amanti, C. (Eds.). (2005). *Funds of knowledge: Theorizing practices in households and classrooms.* Mahwah, NJ: Lawrence Erlbaum.

The concept of "funds of knowledge" is based on a simple premise: People are competent and have knowledge, and their life experiences have given them that knowledge. The editors and authors in this book suggest that teachers who have first-hand research experiences with families are able to document families' competence and knowledge, and that such engagement provides many possibilities for positive pedagogical practices in classrooms.

Gutierrez, K. & Rogoff, B. (2003). Cultural ways of learning: Individual traits or repertoires of practice. *Educational Researcher, 32* (5), 19–25.

In this important article, Kris Gutierrez and Barbara Rogoff challenge the more static conceptions of culture by both eschewing simplistic notions that center on specific traits and focusing on repertoires of practice that better define families and communities.

Hollins, E. R., King, J. E., & Hayman, W. C. (1994). *Teaching diverse populations: Formulating a knowledge base.* Albany: State University of New York Press.

This book approaches the challenge of teaching students of diverse backgrounds in a variety of ways, including relating of cultural and experiential knowledge to classroom instruction, examining the behaviors of teachers who are effective with culturally diverse populations, analyzing effective school models, reviewing models of effective instruction, and exploring ethnic identity as a variable in the formula for school success.

8 Lessons From Students on Creating a Chance to Dream

For the most part, discussions about developing strategies to solve educational problems lack the perspectives of one of the very groups they most affect: students, especially those students who are categorized as "problems" and are most oppressed by traditional educational structures and procedures. In this article, which is based on interviews of young people from a wide variety of ethnic, racial, linguistic, and social-class backgrounds, I present their ideas about the kinds of schools that would have been most affirming for them.

By focusing on students' thoughts about school policies and practices and the effects of racism and other kinds of discrimination on their education, the article explores what characteristics of these students' specific experiences helped them remain and succeed in school, despite the obstacles. In essence, these are lessons from students because they illustrate that students need to be included in the dialogue in order for school reform efforts to be successful.

> How does it come about that the one institution that is said to be the gateway to opportunity, the school, is the very one that is most effective in perpetuating an oppressed and impoverished status in society?
>
> (Stein, 1971, p. 178)

The poignant question above was posed in the *Harvard Educational Review* in 1971 by Annie Stein, a consistent critic of the schools and a relentless advocate for social justice. This question shall serve as the central motif of this article because, in many ways, it remains to be answered and continues to be a fundamental dilemma standing in the way of our society's stated ideals of equity and equal educational opportunity. Annie Stein's observations about the New York City public schools ring true today in too many school systems throughout the country and can be used to examine some of the same policies and practices she decried in her 1971 article.

It is my purpose in this article to suggest that successfully educating all students in U.S. schools must begin by challenging school policies and practices that place roadblocks in the way of academic achievement for too many young people. Educating students today is, of course, a far different and more complex proposition than it has been in the past. Young people face innumerable personal, social, and political challenges, not to mention massive economic structural changes not even dreamed about by other generations of youth in the twentieth century. In spite of the tensions that such challenges may pose, U.S. society has nevertheless historically had a social contract to educate *all* youngsters, not simply those who happen to be European American, English speaking, economically privileged, and, in the current educational reform jargon, "ready to learn."[1] Yet, our schools have traditionally failed some youngsters, especially those from racially and culturally dominated and economically oppressed backgrounds. Research over the past half century has documented a disheartening legacy of failure for many students of all backgrounds, but especially children of Latino, African American, and Native American families, as well as poor European American families and, more recently, Asian and Pacific American immigrant students. Responding to the wholesale failure of so many youngsters within our public schools, educational theorists, sociologists, and psychologists devised elaborate theories of genetic inferiority, cultural deprivation, and the limits of "throwing money" at educational problems. Such theories held sway in particular during the 1960s and 1970s, but their influence is still apparent in educational policies and practices today.[2]

The fact that many youngsters live in difficult, sometimes oppressive conditions is not at issue here. Some may live in ruthless poverty and face the challenges of dilapidated housing, inadequate health care, and even abuse and neglect. They and their families may be subject to racism and other oppressive institutional barriers. They may have difficult personal, psychological, medical, or other kinds of problems. These are real concerns that should not be discounted. But, despite what may seem to be insurmountable obstacles to learning and teaching, some schools are nevertheless successful with young people who live in these situations. In addition, many children who live in otherwise onerous situations also have loving families willing to sacrifice what it takes to give their children the chance they never had during their own childhoods. Thus, poverty, single-parent households, and even homelessness, while they may be tremendous hardships, do not in and of themselves doom children to academic failure (see, among others, Clark, 1983; Lucas, Henze, & Donato, 1990; Mehan & Villanueva, 1993; Moll, 1992; Taylor & Dorsey-Gaines, 1988). These and similar studies point out that schools that have made up their minds that their students deserve the chance to learn do find the ways to educate them successfully in spite of what may seem to be overwhelming odds.

Educators may consider students difficult to teach simply because they come from families that do not fit neatly into what has been defined as "the mainstream." Some of them speak no English; many come from cultures that seem to be at odds with the dominant culture of U.S. society that is inevitably reflected in the school; others begin their schooling without the benefit of early experiences that could help prepare them for the cognitive demands they will face. Assumptions are often made about how such situations may negatively affect student achievement and, as a consequence, some children are condemned to failure before they begin. In a study by Nitza Hidalgo, a teacher's description of the students at an urban high school speaks to this condemnation: "Students are generally poor, uneducated and come from broken families who do not value school. Those conditions that produce achievers are somewhere else, not here. We get street people" (Hidalgo, 1991, p. 58). When such viewpoints guide teachers' and schools' behaviors and expectations, little progress can be expected in student achievement.

On the other hand, a growing number of studies suggest that teachers and schools need to build on rather than tear down what students bring to school. That is, they need to understand and incorporate cultural, linguistic, and experiential differences, as well as differences in social class, into the learning process (Abi-Nader, 1993; Hollins, King, & Hayman, 1994; Lucas et al., 1990; Moll & Díaz, 1993). The results of such efforts often provide inspiring examples of success because they begin with a belief that all students deserve a chance to learn. In this article, I will highlight these efforts by exploring the stories of some academically successful young people in order to suggest how the policies and practices of schools can be transformed to create environments in which all children are capable of learning.

It is too convenient to fall back on deficit theories and continue the practice of blaming students, their families, and their communities for educational failure. Instead, schools need to focus on where they *can* make a difference, namely, their own instructional policies and practices. A number of recent studies, for example, have concluded that a combination of factors, including characteristics of schools as opposed to only student background and actions, can explain differences between high- and low-achieving students. School characteristics that have been found to make a positive difference in these studies include an enriched and more demanding curriculum, respect for students' languages and cultures, high expectations for all students, and encouragement for parental involvement in their children's education (Lee, Winfield, & Wilson, 1991; Lucas et al., 1990; Moll, 1992). This would suggest that we need to shift from a single-minded focus on low- or high-achieving students to the conditions that create low- or high-achieving schools. If we understand school policies and practices as being enmeshed in societal values, we can better understand the manifestations of these values in schools as well. Thus, for example, "tracked" schools, rather than reflecting a school practice that exists in isolation from society, reflect a society that is itself tracked along racial, gender, and social-class lines. In the same way, "teacher expectations" do not come from thin air, but reflect and support expectations of students that are deeply ingrained in societal and ideological values.

Reforming school structures alone will not lead to substantive differences in student achievement, however if such changes are not also accompanied by profound changes in how we as educators think about our students; that is, in what we believe they deserve and are capable of achieving. Put another way, changing policies and practices is a necessary but insufficient condition for total school transformation. For example, in a study of six high schools in which

Latino students have been successful, Tamara Lucas, Rosemary Henze, and Rubén Donato (1990) found that the most crucial element is a shared belief among teachers, counselors, and administrators that all students are capable of learning. This means that concomitant changes are needed in policies and practices *and* in our individual and collective will to educate all students. Fred Newmann (1993), in an important analysis of educational restructuring, underlines this point by emphasizing that reform efforts will fail unless they are accompanied by a set of particular commitments and competencies to guide them, including a commitment to the success of all students, the creation of new roles for teachers, and the development of schools as caring communities.

Another crucial consideration in undertaking educational change is a focus on what Jim Cummins (1994) has called the "relations of power" in schools. In proposing a shift from coercive to collaborative relations of power, Cummins argues that traditional teacher-centered transmission models can limit the potential for critical thinking on the part of both teachers and students, but especially for students from dominated communities whose cultures and languages have been devalued by the dominant canon.[3] By encouraging collaborative relations of power, schools and teachers can begin to recognize other sources of legitimate knowledge that have been overlooked, negated, or minimized because they are not part of the dominant discourse in schools.

Focusing on concerns such as the limits of school reform without concomitant changes in educators' attitudes towards students and their families, and the crucial role of power relationships in schools may help rescue current reform efforts from simplistic technical responses to what are essentially moral and political dilemmas. That is, such technical changes as tinkering with the length of the school day, substituting one textbook for another, or adding curricular requirements may do little to change student outcomes unless these changes are part and parcel of a more comprehensive conceptualization of school reform. When such issues are considered fundamental to the changes that must be made in schools, we might more precisely speak about *transformation* rather than simply about reform. But educational transformation cannot take place without the inclusion of the voices of students, among others, in the dialogue.

Why Listen to Students?

One way to begin the process of changing school policies and practices is to listen to students' views about them; however, research that focuses on student voices is relatively recent and scarce. For example, student perspectives are for the most part missing in discussions concerning strategies for confronting educational problems. In addition, the voices of students are rarely heard in the debates about school failure and success, and the perspectives of students from disempowered and dominated communities are even more invisible. In this article, I will draw primarily on the words of students interviewed for a previous research study (Nieto, 1992). I used the interviews to develop case studies of young people from a wide variety of ethnic, racial, linguistic, and social-class backgrounds who were at the time students in junior or senior high school. These ten young people lived in communities as diverse as large urban areas and small rural hamlets, and belonged to families ranging from single-parent households to large, extended families. The one common element in all of their experiences turned out to be something we as researchers had neither planned nor expected: they were all successful students.[4]

The students were selected in a number of ways, but primarily through community contacts. Most were interviewed at home or in another setting of their choice outside of school. The only requirement that my colleagues and I determined for selecting students was that they reflect a variety of ethnic and racial backgrounds, in order to give us the diversity for which we were looking. The students selected self-identified as Black, African American, Mexican, Native American, Black and White American (biracial), Vietnamese, Jewish, Lebanese, Puerto Rican, and Cape Verdean. The one European American was the only student who had a hard time defining herself, other than as "American" (for a further analysis of this issue, see Nieto, 1992). That these particular students were academically successful was quite serendipitous. We defined them as such for the following reasons: they were all either still in school or just graduating; they all planned to complete at least high school, and most hoped to go to college; they had good grades, although they were not all at the top of their class; they had thought about their future and had made some plans for it; they generally enjoyed school and felt engaged in it (but they were also critical of their own school experiences and that of their peers, as we shall see); and most described themselves as successful. Although it had not been our initial intention to focus exclusively on academically successful students, on closer reflection it seemed logical that such students would be more likely to want to talk about their experiences than those who were not successful. It was at that point that I decided to explore what it was about these students' specific experiences that helped them succeed in school.

Therefore, the fact that these students saw themselves as successful helped further define the study, whose original purpose was to determine the benefits of multicultural education for students of diverse backgrounds. I was particularly interested in developing a way of looking at multicultural education that went beyond the typical "Holidays and Heroes" approach, which is too superficial to have any lasting impact in schools (Banks, 1991; Sleeter, 1991).[5] By exploring such issues as racism and low expectations of student achievement, as well as school policies and practices such as curriculum, pedagogy, testing, and tracking, I set about developing an understanding of multicultural education as antiracist, comprehensive, pervasive, and rooted in social justice. Students were interviewed to find out what it meant to be from a particular background, how this influenced their school experience, and what about that experience they would change if they could. Although they were not asked specifically about the policies and practices in their schools, they nevertheless reflected on them in their answers to questions ranging from identifying their favorite subjects to describing the importance of getting an education. In this article, I will revisit the interviews to focus on students' thoughts about a number of school policies and practices and on the effects of racism and other forms of discrimination on their education.

The insights provided by the students were far richer than we had first thought. Although we expected numerous criticisms of schools and some concrete suggestions, we were surprised at the depth of awareness and analysis the students shared with us. They had a lot to say about the teachers they liked, as well as those they disliked, and they were able to explain the differences between them; they talked about grades and how these had become overly important in determining curriculum and pedagogy; they discussed their parents' lack of involvement, in most cases, in traditional school activities such as P.T.O. membership and bake sales, but otherwise passionate support for their children's academic success; they mused about what schools could do to encourage more students to learn; they spoke with feeling about their cultures, languages, and communities, and what schools could do to capitalize on these factors; and they gave us concrete suggestions for improving schools for young people of all backgrounds. This experience confirmed my belief that educators can benefit from hearing students' critical perspectives, which might cause them to modify how they approach curriculum, pedagogy, and other school practices. Since doing this research, I have come across other studies that also focus on young people's perspectives and provide additional powerful examples of the lessons we can learn from them. This article thus begins with "lessons from students," an approach that takes the perspective proposed by Paulo Freire, that teachers need to become students just as students need to become teachers in order for education to become reciprocal and empowering for both (Freire, 1970).

This focus on students is not meant to suggest that their ideas should be the final and conclusive word in how schools need to change. Nobody has all the answers, and suggesting that students' views should be adopted wholesale is to accept a romantic view of students that is just as partial and condescending as excluding them completely from the discussion. I am instead suggesting that if we believe schools must provide an equal and quality education for all, students need to be included in the dialogue, and that their views, just as those of others, should be problematized and used to reflect critically on school reform.

Selected Policies and Practices and Students' Views about Them

School policies and practices need to be understood within the sociopolitical context of our society in general, rather than simply within individual schools' or teachers' attitudes and practices. This is important to remember for a number of reasons. First, although "teacher bashing" provides an easy target for complex problems, it fails to take into account the fact that teachers function within particular societal and institutional structures. In addition, it results in placing an inordinate amount of blame on some of those who care most deeply about students and who struggle every day to help them learn. That some teachers are racist, classist, and mean-spirited and that others have lost all creativity and caring is not in question here, and I begin with the assumption that the majority of teachers are not consciously so. I do suggest, however, that although many teachers are hardworking, supportive of their students, and talented educators, many of these same teachers are also burned out, frustrated, and negatively influenced by societal views about the students they teach. Teachers could benefit from knowing more about their students' families and experiences, as well as about students' views on school and how it could be improved.

How do students feel about the curriculum they must learn? What do they think about the pedagogical strategies their teachers use? Is student involvement a meaningful issue for them? Are their own identities important considerations in how they view school? What about tracking and testing and disciplinary policies? These are crucial questions to consider when reflecting on what teachers and schools can learn from students, but we know very little about students' responses. When asked, students seem surprised and excited about being included in the conversation, and what they have to say is often compelling and eloquent. In fact, Patricia Phelan, Ann Locke Davidson, and Hanh Thanh Cao (1992), in a two-year research project designed to identify students' thoughts about school, discovered that students' views on teaching and learning were remarkably consistent with those of current theorists concerned with learning theory, cognitive science, and the sociology of work. This should come as no surprise when we consider that students spend more time in schools than anybody else except teachers (who are also omitted in most discussions of school reform, but that is a topic for another article). In the following sections, I will focus on students' perceptions concerning the curriculum, pedagogy, tracking, and grades in their schools. I will also discuss their attitudes about racism and other biases, how these are manifested in their schools and classrooms, and what effect they may have on students' learning and participation in school.

Curriculum

The curriculum in schools is at odds with the experiences, backgrounds, hopes, and wishes of many students. This is true of both the tangible curriculum as expressed through books, other materials, and the actual written curriculum guides, as well as in the less tangible and "hidden" curriculum as seen in the bulletin boards, extracurricular activities, and messages given to students about their abilities and talents. For instance, Christine Sleeter and Carl Grant (1991) found that a third of the students in a desegregated junior high school they studied said that *none* of the class content related to their lives outside class. Those who indicated some relevancy cited only current events, oral history, money and banking, and multicultural content (because it dealt with prejudice) as being relevant. The same was true in a study by Mary Poplin and Joseph Weeres (1992), who found that students frequently reported being bored in school and seeing little relevance in what was taught for their lives or their futures. The authors concluded that students became more disengaged as the curriculum, texts, and assignments became more standardized. Thus, in contrast to Ira Shor's (1992) suggestion that "What students bring to class is where learning begins. It starts there and goes places" (p. 44), there is often a tremendous mismatch between students' cultures and the culture of the school. In many schools, learning starts not with what students bring to class, but with what is considered high-status knowledge; that is, the "canon," with its overemphasis on European and European American history, arts, and values. This seldom includes the backgrounds, experiences, and talents of the majority of students in U.S. schools. Rather than "going elsewhere," their learning therefore often goes nowhere.

That students' backgrounds and experiences are missing in many schools is particularly evident where the native language of most of the students is not English. In such settings, it is not unusual to see little or no representation of those students' language in the curriculum. In fact, there is often an insistence that students "speak only English" in these schools, which sends a powerful message to young people struggling to maintain an identity in the face of overpowering messages that they must assimilate. This was certainly the case for Marisol, a Puerto Rican girl of sixteen participating in my research, who said:

> I used to have a lot of problems with one of my teachers 'cause she didn't want us to talk Spanish in class and I thought that was like an insult to us, you know? Just telling us not to talk Spanish, 'cause they were Puerto Ricans and, you know, we're free to talk whatever we want, . . . I could never stay quiet and talk only English, 'cause sometimes . . . words slip in Spanish. You know, I think they should understand that.

Practices such as not allowing students to speak their native tongue are certain to influence negatively students' identities and their views of what constitutes important knowledge. For example, when asked if she would be interested in taking a course on Puerto Rican history, Marisol was quick to answer: "I don't think [it's] important. . . . I'm proud of myself and my culture, but I think I know what I should know about the culture already, so I wouldn't take the course." Ironically, it was evident to me after speaking with her on several occasions that Marisol knew virtually nothing about Puerto Rican history. However, she had already learned another lesson well: given what she said about the courses she needed to take, she made it clear that "important" history is U.S. history, which rarely includes anything about Puerto Rico.

Messages about culture and language and how they are valued or devalued in society are communicated not only or even primarily by schools, but by the media and community as a whole. The sociopolitical context of the particular city where Marisol lived, and of its school system, is important to understand: there had been an attempt to pass an ordinance restricting the number of Puerto Ricans coming into town based on the argument that they placed an undue burden on the welfare rolls and other social services. In addition, the "English Only" debate had become an issue when the mayor had ordered all municipal workers to speak only English on the job. Furthermore, although the school system had a student body that was 65 percent Puerto Rican, there was only a one-semester course on Puerto Rican history that had just recently been approved for the bilingual program. In contrast, there were two courses, which although rarely taught were on the books, that focused on apartheid and the Holocaust, despite the fact that both the African American and Jewish communities in the town were quite small. That such courses should be part of a comprehensive multicultural program is not being questioned; however, it is ironic that the largest population in the school was ignored in the general curriculum.

In a similar vein, Nancy Commins's (1989) research with four first-generation Mexican American fifth-grade students focused on how these students made decisions about their education, both consciously and unconsciously, based on their determination of what counted as important knowledge. Her research suggests that the classroom setting and curriculum can support or hinder students' perceptions of themselves as learners based on the languages they speak and their cultural backgrounds. She found that although the homes of these four students provided rich environments for a variety of language uses and literacy, the school did little to capitalize on these strengths. In their classroom, for instance, these children rarely used Spanish, commenting that it was the language of the "dumb kids." As a result, Commins states: "Their reluctance to use Spanish in an academic context also limited their opportunities to practice talking about abstract ideas and to use higher level cognitive skills in Spanish" (p. 35). She also found that the content of the curriculum was almost completely divorced from the experiences of these youngsters, since the problems of poverty, racism, and discrimination, which were prominent in their lives, were not addressed in the curriculum.

In spite of teachers' reluctance to address such concerns, they are often compelling to students, particularly those who are otherwise invisible in the curriculum. Vinh, an 18-year-old Vietnamese student attending a high school in a culturally heterogeneous town, lived with his uncle and younger brothers and sisters. Although grateful for the education he was receiving, Vinh expressed concern about what he saw as insensitivity on the part of some of his teachers to the difficulties of adjusting to a new culture and learning English:

> [Teachers] have to know about our culture. . . . From the second language, it is very difficult for me and for other people.

Vinh's concern was echoed by Manuel, a nineteen-year-old Cape Verdean senior who, at the time of the interviews, was just getting ready to graduate, the first in his family of eleven children to do so:

> I was kind of afraid of school, you know, 'cause it's different when you're learning the language. . . . It's kind of scary at first, especially if you don't know the language and like if you don't have friends here.

In Manuel's case, the Cape Verdean Crioulo bilingual program served as a linguistic and cultural mediator, negotiating difficult experiences that he faced in school so that, by the time he reached high school, he had learned enough English to "speak up." Another positive curricular experience was the theater workshop he took as a sophomore. There, students created and acted in skits focusing on their lived experiences. He recalled with great enthusiasm, for example, a monologue he did about a student going to a new school, because it was based on his personal experience.

Sometimes a school's curriculum is unconsciously disrespectful of students' cultures and experiences. James, a student who proudly identified himself as Lebanese American, found that he was invisible in the curriculum, even in supposedly multicultural curricular and extracurricular activities. He mentioned a language fair, a multicultural festival, and a school cookbook, all of which omitted references to the Arabic language and to Lebanese people. About the cook-book, he said:

> They made this cookbook of all these different recipes from all over the world. And I would've brought in some Lebanese recipes if somebody'd let me know. And I didn't hear about it until the week before they started selling them. . . . I asked one of the teachers to look at it and there was nothing Lebanese in there.

James made an effort to dismiss this oversight, and although he said that it didn't matter, he seemed to be struggling with the growing realization that it mattered very much indeed:

> I don't know, I guess there's not that many Lebanese people in . . . I don't know; you don't hear really that much . . . Well, you hear it in the news a lot, but I mean, I don't know, there's not a lot of Lebanese kids in our school. . . . I don't mind, 'cause I mean, I don't know, just I don't mind it. . . . It's not really important. It *is* important for me. It would be important for me to see a Lebanese flag.

Lebanese people were mentioned in the media, although usually in negative ways, and these were the only images of James's ethnic group that made their way into the school. He spoke, for example, about how the Lebanese were characterized by his peers:

> Some people call me, you know, 'cause I'm Lebanese, so people say, "Look out for the terrorist! Don't mess with him or he'll blow up your house!" or some stuff like that. . . . But they're just joking around, though. . . . I don't think anybody's serious 'cause I wouldn't blow up anybody's house—and they know that. . . . I don't care. It doesn't matter what people say. . . . I just want everybody to know that, you know, it's not true.

Cultural ambivalence, both pride and shame, were evident in the responses of many of the students. Although almost all of them were quite clear that their culture was important to them, they were also confronted with debilitating messages about it from society in general. How to make sense of these contradictions was a dilemma for many of these young people.

Fern, who identified herself as Native American, was, at thirteen, one of the youngest students interviewed. She reflected on the constant challenges she faced in the history curriculum in her junior high school. Her father was active in their school and community and he gave her a great deal of support for defending her position, but she was the only Native American student in her entire school in this mid-size city in Iowa. She said:

> If there's something in the history book that's wrong, my dad always taught me that if it's wrong, I should tell them that it is wrong. And the only time I ever do is if I know it's *exactly* wrong. Like we were reading about Native Americans and scalping. Well, the French are really the ones that made them do it so they could get money. And my teacher would not believe me. I finally just shut up because he just would not believe me.

Fern also mentioned that her sister had come home angry one day because somebody in school had said "Geronimo was a stupid chief riding that stupid horse." The connection between an unresponsive curriculum and dropping out of school was not lost on Fern, and she talked about this incident as she wondered aloud why other Native Americans had dropped out of the town's schools. Similar sentiments were reported by students in Virginia Vogel Zanger's (1994) study of twenty Latinos from a Boston high school who took part in a panel discussion in which they reflected on their experiences in school. Some of the students who decided to stay in school claimed that dropping out among their peers was a direct consequence of the school's attempts to, in their words, "monoculture" them.

Fern was self-confident and strong in expressing her views, despite her young age. Yet she too was silenced by the way the curriculum was presented in class. This is because schools often avoid bringing up difficult, contentious, or conflicting issues in the curriculum, especially when these contradict the sanctioned views of the standard curriculum, resulting in what Michelle Fine has called "silencing." According to Fine: "Silencing is about who can speak, what can and cannot be spoken, and whose discourse must be controlled" (1991, p. 33). Two topics in particular that appear to have great saliency for many students, regardless of their backgrounds, are bias and discrimination, yet these are among the issues most avoided in classrooms. Perhaps this is because the majority of teachers are European Americans who are unaccustomed, afraid, or uncomfortable in discussing these issues (Sleeter, 1994); perhaps it is due to the pressure teachers feel to "cover the material"; maybe it has to do with the tradition of presenting information in schools as if it were free of conflict and controversy (Kohl, 1993); or, most likely, it is a combination of all these things. In any event, both students and teachers soon pick up the message that racism, discrimination, and other dangerous topics are not supposed to be discussed in school. We also need to keep in mind that these issues have disparate meanings for people of different backgrounds, and are often perceived as particularly threatening to those from dominant cultural and racial groups. Deidre, one of the young African American women in Fine's 1991 study of an urban high school, explained it this way: "White people might feel like everything's over and OK, but we remember" (p. 33).

Another reason that teachers may avoid bringing up potentially contentious issues in the curriculum is their feeling that doing so may create or exacerbate animosity and hostility among students. They may even believe, as did the reading teacher in Jonathan Kozol's 1967 classic book on the Boston Public Schools, *Death at an Early Age*, that discussing slavery in the context of U.S. history was just too complicated for children to understand, not to mention uncomfortable for teachers to explain. Kozol writes of the reading teacher:

> She said, with the very opposite of malice but only with an expression of the most intense and honest affection for the children in the class: "I don't want these children to have to think back on this year later on and to have to remember that we were the ones who told them they were Negro.
>
> (p. 68)

More than a quarter of a century later, the same kinds of disclaimers are being made for the failure to include in the curriculum the very issues that would engage students in learning. Fine (1991) found that although over half of the students in the urban high school she interviewed described experiences with racism, teachers were reluctant to discuss it in class, explaining, in the words of one teacher, "It would demoralize the students, they need to feel positive and optimistic—like they have a chance. Racism is just an excuse they use to not try harder" (p. 37). Some of these concerns may be sincere expressions of protectiveness towards students, but others are merely self-serving and manifest teachers' discomfort with discussing racism.

The few relevant studies I have found concerning the inclusion of issues of racism and discrimination in the curriculum suggest that discussions about these topics can be immensely constructive if they are approached with sensitivity and understanding. This was the case in Melinda Fine's description of the "Facing History and Ourselves" (FHAO) curriculum, a project that started in the Brookline (Massachusetts) Public Schools almost two decades ago (Fine, 1993). FHAO provides a model for teaching history that encourages students to reflect critically on a variety of contemporary social, moral, and political issues. Using the Holocaust as a case study, students learn to think critically about such issues as scapegoating, racism, and personal and collective responsibility. Fine suggests that moral dilemmas do not disappear simply because teachers refuse to bring them into the schools. On the contrary, when these realities are separated from the curriculum, young people learn that school knowledge is unrelated to their lives, and once again, they are poorly prepared to face the challenges that society has in store for them.

A good case in point is Vanessa, a young European American woman in my study who was intrigued by "difference" yet was uncomfortable and reluctant to discuss it; although she was active in a peer education group that focused on such concerns as peer pressure, discrimination, and exclusion, these were rarely discussed in the formal curriculum. Vanessa, therefore, had no language with which to talk about these issues. In thinking about U.S. history, she mused about some of the contradictions that were rarely addressed in school:

> It seems weird . . . because people came from Europe and they wanted to get away from all the stuff that was over there. And then they came here

and set up all the stuff like slavery, and I don't know, it seems the opposite of what they would have done.

The curriculum, then, can act to either enable or handicap students in their learning. Given the kind of curriculum that draws on their experiences and energizes them because it focuses precisely on those things that are most important in their lives, students can either soar or sink in our schools. Curriculum can provide what María Torres-Guzmán (1992) refers to as "cognitive empowerment," encouraging students to become confident, active critical thinkers who learn that their background experiences are important tools for further learning. The connection of the curriculum to real life and their future was mentioned by several of the students interviewed in my study. Avi, a Jewish boy of sixteen who often felt a schism between his school and home lives, for instance, spoke about the importance of school: "If you don't go to school, then you can't learn about life, or you can't learn about things that you need to progress [in] your life." And Vanessa, who seemed to yearn for a more socially conscious curriculum in her school, summed up why education was important to her: "A good education is like when you personally learn something . . . like growing, expanding your mind and your views."

Pedagogy

If curriculum is primarily the *what* of education, then pedagogy concerns the *why* and *how*. No matter how interesting and relevant the curriculum may be, the way in which it is presented is what will make it engaging or dull to students. Students' views echo those of educational researchers who have found that teaching methods in most classrooms, and particularly those in secondary schools, vary little from traditional "chalk and talk" methods; that textbooks are the dominant teaching materials used; that routine and rote learning are generally favored over creativity and critical thinking; and that teacher-centered transmission models prevail (Cummins, 1994; Goodlad, 1984; McNeil, 1986). Martin Haberman is especially critical of what he calls "the pedagogy of poverty," that is, a basic urban pedagogy used with children who live in poverty and which consists primarily of giving instructions, asking questions, giving directions, making assignments, and monitoring seat work. Such pedagogy is based on the assumption that before students can be engaged in creative or critical work, they must first master "the basics." Nevertheless, Haberman asserts that this pedagogy does not work and, furthermore, that it actually gets in the way of real teaching and learning. He suggests instead that we look at exemplary pedagogy in urban schools that actively involves students in real-life situations, which allows them to reflect on their own lives. He finds that good teaching is taking place when teachers welcome difficult issues and events and use human difference as the basis for the curriculum; design collaborative activities for heterogeneous groups; and help students apply ideals of fairness, equity, and justice to their world (Haberman, 1991).

Students in my study had more to say about pedagogy than about anything else, and they were especially critical of the lack of imagination that led to boring classes. Linda, who was just graduating as the valedictorian of her class in an urban high school, is a case in point. Her academic experiences had not always been smooth sailing. For example, she had failed both seventh and eighth grade twice, for a combination of reasons, including academic and medical problems. Consequently, she had experienced both exhilarating and devastating educational experiences. Linda had this to say about pedagogy:

> I think you have to be creative to be a teacher; you have to make it interesting. You can't just go in and say, "Yeah, I'm going to teach the kids just that; I'm gonna teach them right out of the book and that's the way it is, and don't ask questions." Because I know there were plenty of classes where I lost complete interest. But those were all because the teachers just, "Open the books to this page." They never made up problems out of their head. Everything came out of the book. You didn't ask questions. If you asked them questions, then the answer was "in the book." And if you asked the question and the answer *wasn't* in the book, then you shouldn't have asked that question!

Rich, a young Black man, planned to attend pharmacy school after graduation, primarily because of the interest he had developed in chemistry. He too talked about the importance of making classes "interesting":

> I believe a teacher, by the way he introduces different things to you, can make a class interesting. Not like a normal teacher that gets up, gives you a lecture, or there's teachers that just pass out the work, you do the work, pass it in, get a grade, good-bye!

Students were especially critical of teachers' reliance on textbooks and blackboards, a sad indictment of much of the teaching that encourages student passivity. Avi, for instance, felt that some teachers get along better when they teach from the point of view of the students: "They don't just come out and say, 'All right, do this, blah, blah, blah.' . . . They're not so *one-tone voice*." Yolanda said that her English teacher didn't get along with the students. In her words, "She just does the things and sits down." James mentioned that some teachers just don't seem to care: "They just teach the stuff. 'Here,' write a couple of things on the board, 'see, that's how you do it. Go ahead, page 25.' " And Vinh added his voice to those of the students who clearly saw the connection between pedagogy and caring: "Some teachers, they just go inside and go to the blackboard. . . . They don't care."

Students did more than criticize teachers' pedagogy, however; they also praised teachers who were interesting, creative, and caring. Linda, in a particularly moving testimony to her first-grade teacher, whom she called her mentor, mentioned that she would be "following in her footsteps" and studying elementary education. She added:

> She's always been there for me. After the first or second grade, if I had a

problem, I could always go back to her. Through the whole rest of my life, I've been able to go back and talk to her. . . . She's a Golden Apple Award winner, which is a very high award for elementary school teachers. . . . She keeps me on my toes. . . . When I start getting down . . . she peps me back up and I get on my feet.

Vinh talked with feeling about teachers who allowed him to speak Vietnamese with other students in class. Vinh loved working in groups. He particularly remembered a teacher who always asked students to discuss important issues, rather than focusing only on learning what he called "the word's meaning" by writing and memorizing lists of words. The important issues concerned U.S. history, the students' histories and cultures, and other engaging topics that were central to their lives. Students' preference for group work has been mentioned by other educators as well. Phelan et al. (1992), in their research on students' perspectives concerning school, found that both high- and low-achieving students of all backgrounds expressed a strong preference for working in groups because it helped them generate ideas and participate actively in class.

James also appreciated teachers who explained things and let everybody ask questions because, as he said, "There could be someone sitting in the back of the class that has the same question you have. Might as well bring it out." Fern contrasted classes where she felt like falling asleep because they're just "blah," to chorus, where the teacher used a "rap song" to teach history and involve all the students. And Avi, who liked most of his teachers, singled out a particular math teacher he had had in ninth grade for praise:

'Cause I never really did good in math until I had him. And he showed me that it wasn't so bad, and after that I've been doing pretty good in math and I enjoy it.

Yolanda had been particularly fortunate to have many teachers she felt understood and supported her, whether they commented on her bilingual ability, or referred to her membership in a folkloric Mexican dance group, or simply talked with her and the other students about their lives. She added:

I really got along with the teachers a lot. . . . Actually, 'cause I had some teachers, and they were always calling my mom, like I did a great job. Or they would start talking to me, or they kinda like pulled me up some grades, or moved me to other classes, or took me somewhere. And they were always congratulating me.

Such support, however, rarely represented only individual effort on the part of some teachers, but rather was often manifested by the school as a whole; that is, it was integral to the school's practices and policies. For instance, Yolanda had recently been selected "Student of the Month" and her picture had been prominently displayed in her school's main hall. In addition, she received a certificate and was taken out to dinner by the principal. Although Linda's first-grade teacher was her special favorite, she had others who also created an educational context in which all students felt welcomed and connected. The entire Tremont Elementary School had been special for Linda, and thus the context of the school, including its leadership and commitment, were the major ingredients that made it successful:

> All of my teachers were wonderful. I don't think there's a teacher at the whole Tremont School that I didn't like. . . . It's just a feeling you have. You know that they really care for you. You just know it; you can tell. Teachers who don't have you in any of their classes or haven't ever had you, they still know who you are. . . . The Tremont School in itself is a community. . . . I love that school! I want to teach there.

Vanessa talked about how teachers used their students' lives and experiences in their teaching. For her, this made them especially good teachers:

> [Most teachers] are really caring and supportive and are willing to share their lives and are willing to listen to mine. They don't just want to talk about what they're teaching you; they also want to know you.

Aside from criticism and praise, students in this study also offered their teachers many thoughtful suggestions for making their classrooms more engaging places. Rich, for instance, said that he would "put more activities into the day that can make it interesting." Fern recommended that teachers involve students more actively in learning: "More like making the whole class be involved, not making only the two smartest people up here do the whole work for the whole class." Vanessa added, "You could have games that could teach anything that they're trying to teach through notes or lectures." She suggested that in learning Spanish, for instance, students could act out the words, making them easier to remember. She also thought that other books should be required "just to show some points of view," a response no doubt to the bland quality of so many of the textbooks and other teaching materials available in schools. Avi thought that teachers who make themselves available to students ("You know, I'm here after school. Come and get help.") were most helpful.

Vinh was very specific in his suggestions, and he touched on important cultural issues. Because he came from Vietnam when he was fifteen, learning English was a difficult challenge for Vinh, and he tended to be very hard on himself, saying such things as "I'm not really good, but I'm trying" when asked to describe himself as a student. Although he had considered himself smart in Vietnam, he felt that because his English was not perfect, he wasn't smart anymore. His teachers often showered him with praise for his efforts, but Vinh criticized this approach:

> Sometimes, the English teachers, they don't understand about us. Because something we not do good, like my English is not good. And she say, "Oh, your English is great!" But that's the way the American culture is. But my culture is not like that. . . . If my English is not good, she has

to say, "Your English is not good. So you have to go home and study." And she tell me what to study and how to study and get better. But some Americans, you know, they don't understand about myself. So they just say, "Oh! You're doing a good job! You're doing great! Everything is great!" Teachers talk like that, but my culture is different. . . . They say, "You have to do better."

This is an important lesson not only because it challenges the overuse of praise, a practice among those that María de la Luz Reyes (1992) has called "venerable assumptions," but also because it cautions teachers to take into account both cultural and individual differences. In this case, the practice of praising was perceived by Vinh as hollow, and therefore insincere. Linda referred to the lesson she learned when she failed seventh and eighth grade and "blew two years":

I learned a lot from it. As a matter of fact, one of my college essays was on the fact that from that experience, I learned that I don't need to hear other people's praise to get by. . . . All I need to know is in here [pointing to her heart] whether I tried or not.

Students have important messages for teachers about what works and what doesn't. It is important, however, not to fall back on what Lilia Bartolomé (1994) has aptly termed the "methods fetish," that is, a simplistic belief that particular methods will automatically resolve complex problems of underachievement. According to Bartolomé, such a myopic approach results in teachers avoiding the central issue of why some students succeed and others fail in school and how political inequality is at the heart of this dilemma. Rather than using this or that method, Bartolomé suggests that teachers develop what she calls a "humanizing pedagogy" in which students' languages and cultures are central. There is also the problem that Reyes (1992) has called a "one-size-fits all" approach, where students' cultural and other differences may be denied even if teachers' methods are based on well-meaning and progressive pedagogy. The point here is that no method can become a sacred cow uncritically accepted and used simply because it is the latest fad. It is probably fair to say that teachers who use more traditional methods but care about their students and believe they deserve the chance to dream may have more of a positive effect than those who know the latest methods but do not share these beliefs. Students need more than such innovations as heterogeneous grouping, peer tutoring, or cooperative groups. Although these may in fact be excellent and effective teaching methods, they will do little by themselves unless accompanied by changes in teachers' attitudes and behaviors.

The students quoted above are not looking for one magic solution or method. In fact, they have many, sometimes contradictory, suggestions to make about pedagogy. While rarely speaking with one voice, they nevertheless have similar overriding concerns: too many classrooms are boring, alienating, and disempowering. There is a complex interplay of policies, practices, and attitudes that cause such pedagogy to continue. Tracking and testing are two powerful forces implicated in this interplay.

Tracking/Ability Grouping/Grades and Expectations of Student Achievement

> It is not low income that matters but low status. And status is always created and imposed by the ones on top.
>
> (Stein, 1971, p. 158)

In her 1971 article, Annie Stein cited a New York City study in which kindergarten teachers were asked to list in order of importance the things a child should learn in order to prepare for first grade. Their responses were coded according to whether they were primarily socialization or educational goals. In the schools with large Puerto Rican and African American student populations, the socialization goals were always predominant; in the mixed schools, the educational goals were first. Concluded Stein, "In fact, in a list of six or seven goals, several teachers in the minority-group kindergartens forgot to mention any educational goals at all" (p. 167). A kind of tracking, in which students' educational goals were being sacrificed for social aims, was taking place in these schools, and its effects were already evident in kindergarten.

Most recent research on tracking has found it to be problematic, especially among middle- and low-achieving students, and suggestions for detracking schools have gained growing support (Oakes, 1992; Wheelock, 1992). Nevertheless, although many tracking decisions are made on the most tenuous grounds, they are supported by ideological norms in our society about the nature of intelligence and the distribution of ability. The long-term effects of ability grouping can be devastating for the life chances of young people. John Goodlad (1984) found that first- or second-grade children tracked by teachers' judgments of their reading and math ability or by testing are likely to remain in their assigned track *for the rest of their schooling.* In addition, he found that poor children and children of color are more likely to face the negative effects of tracking than are other youngsters. For example, a recent research project by Hugh Mehan and Irene Villanueva (1993) found that when low-achieving high school students are detracked, they tend to benefit academically. The study focused on low-achieving students in the San Diego City Schools. When these students, mostly Latinos and African Americans, were removed from a low track and placed in college-bound courses with high-achieving students, they benefitted in a number of ways, including significantly higher college enrollment. The researchers concluded that a rigorous academic program serves the educational and social interests of such students more effectively than remedial and compensatory programs.

Most of the young people in my study did not mention tracking or ability grouping by name, but almost all referred to it circuitously, and usually in negative ways. Although by and large academically successful themselves, they were quick to point out that teachers' expectations often doomed their peers to failure. Yolanda, for instance, when asked what suggestions she would give teachers, said, "I'd say to teachers, 'Get along more with the kids that are not really into themselves. . . . Have more communication with them.' " When asked what she would like teachers to know about other Mexican American students, she quickly said, "They try real hard, that's one thing I know." She also criticized teachers for having low expectations of students, claiming that materials used in the classes were "too low." She added, "We are supposed to be doing higher things. And like they take us too slow, see, step by step. And that's why everybody takes it as a joke." Fern, although she enjoyed being at the "top of my class," did not like to be treated differently. She spoke about a school she attended previously where "you were all the same and you all got pushed the same and you were all helped the same. And one thing I've noticed in Springdale is they kind of teach 25 percent and they kinda leave 75 percent out." She added that, if students were receiving bad grades, teachers did not help them as much: "In Springdale, I've noticed if you're getting D's and F's, they don't look up to you; they look down. And you're always the last on the list for special activities, you know?"

These young people also referred to expectations teachers had of students based on cultural or class differences. Vanessa said that some teachers based their expectations of students on bad reputations, and found least helpful those teachers who "kind of just move really fast, just trying to get across to you what they're trying to teach you. Not willing to slow down because they need to get in what they want to get in." Rich, who attended a predominately Black school, felt that some teachers there did not expect as much as they should from the Black students: "Many of the White teachers there don't push. . . . Their expectations don't seem to be as high as they should be. . . . I know that some Black teachers, their expectations are higher than White teachers. . . . They just do it, because they know how it was for them. . . . Actually, I'd say, you have to be in Black shoes to know how it is." Little did Rich know that he was reaching the same conclusion as a major research study on fostering high achievement for African American students. In this study, Janine Bempechat determined that "across all schools, it seems that achievement is fostered by high expectations and standards" (Bempechat, 1992, p. 43).

Virginia Vogel Zanger's research with Latino and Latina students in a Boston high school focused on what can be called "social tracking." Although the students she interviewed were high-achieving and tracked in a college-bound course, they too felt the sting of alienation. In a linguistic analysis of their comments, she found that students conveyed a strong sense of marginalization, using terms such as "left out," "below," "under," and "not joined in" to reflect their feelings about school (Zanger, 1994). Although these were clearly academically successful students, they perceived tracking in the subordinate status they were assigned based on their cultural backgrounds and on the racist climate established in the school. Similarly, in a study on dropping out among Puerto Rican students, my colleague Manuel Frau-Ramos and I found some of the same kind of language. José, who had dropped out in eleventh grade, explained, "I was alone. . . . I was an outsider" (Frau-Ramos & Nieto, 1993, p. 156). Pedro, a young man who had actually graduated, nevertheless felt the same kind of alienation. When asked what the school could do to help Puerto Ricans stay in school, he said, "*Hacer algo para que los boricuas no se sientan aparte*" (Do something so that the Puerto Ricans wouldn't feel so separate) (p. 157).

Grading policies have also been mentioned in relation to tracking and expectations of achievement. One study, for example, found that when teachers de-emphasized grades and standardized testing, the status of their African American and White students became more equal, and White students made more cross-race friendship choices (Hallinan & Teixeira, 1987). In my own research, I found a somewhat surprising revelation: although the students were achieving successfully in school, most did not feel that grades were very helpful. Of course, for the most part they enjoyed receiving good grades, but it was not always for the expected reason. Fern, for instance, wanted good grades because they were one guarantee that teachers would pay attention to her. Marisol talked about the "nice report cards" that she and her siblings in this family of eight children received, and said, "and, usually, we do this for my mother. We like to see her the way she wants to be, you know, to see her happy."

But they were also quick to downplay the importance of grades. Linda, for instance, gave as an example her computer teacher, who she felt had been the least helpful in her high school:

> I have no idea about computer literacy. I got A's in that course. Just because he saw that I had A's, and that my name was all around the school for all the "wonderful things" I do, he just automatically assumed. He didn't really pay attention to who I was. The grade I think I deserved in that class was at least a C, but I got A just because everybody else gave me A's. . . . He didn't help me at all because he didn't challenge me.

She added,

> To me, they're just something on a piece of paper. . . . [My parents] feel just about the same way. If they ask me, "Honestly, did you try your best?" and I tell them yes, then they'll look at the grades and say okay.

Rich stated that, although grades were important to his mother, "I'm comfortable setting my own standards." James said, without arrogance, that he was "probably the smartest kid in my class." Learning was important to him and, unlike other students who also did the assignments, he liked to "really get into the work and stuff." He added,

> If you don't get involved with it, even if you do get, if you get perfect scores and stuff . . . it's not like really gonna sink in. . . . You can memorize the words, you know, on a test . . . but you know, if you memorize them, it's not going to do you any good. You have to *learn* them, you know?

Most of the students made similar comments, and their perceptions challenge schools to think more deeply about the real meaning of education. Linda was not alone when she said that the reason for going to school was to "make yourself a better person." She loved learning, and commented that "I just want to keep continuously learning, because when you stop learning, then you start dying." Yolanda used the metaphor of nutrition to talk about learning: "[Education] is good for you. . . . It's like when you eat. It's like if you don't eat in a whole day, you feel weird. That's the same thing for me." Vanessa, also an enthusiastic student, spoke pensively about success and happiness: "I'm happy. Success is being happy to me, it's not like having a job that gives you a zillion dollars. It's just having self-happiness."

Finally, Vinh spoke extensively about the meaning of education, contrasting the difference between what he felt it meant in the United States and what it meant in his home culture:

> In Vietnam, we go to school because we want to become educated people. But in the United States, most people, they say, "Oh, we go to school because we want to get a good job." But my idea, I don't think so. I say, if we go to school, we want a good job *also*, but we want to become a good person.
>
> [Grades] are not important to me. Important to me is education. . . . I not so concerned about [test scores] very much. . . . I just know I do my exam very good. But I don't need to know I got A or B. I have to learn more and more.
>
> Some people, they got a good education. They go to school, they got master's, they got doctorate, but they're just helping *themselves*. So that's not good. I don't care much about money. So, I just want to have a normal job that I can take care of myself and my family. So that's enough. I don't want to climb up compared to other people.

Racism and Discrimination

> The facts are clear to behold, but the BIG LIE of racism blinds all but its victims.
>
> (Stein, 1971, p. 179)

An increasing number of formal research studies, as well as informal accounts and anecdotes, attest to the lasting legacy of various forms of institutional discrimination in the schools based on race, ethnicity, religion, gender, social class, language, and sexual orientation. Yet, as Annie Stein wrote in 1971, these are rarely addressed directly. The major reason for this may be that institutional discrimination flies in the face of our stated ideals of justice and fair play and of the philosophy that individual hard work is the road to success. Beverly Daniel Tatum, in discussing the myth of meritocracy, explains why racism is so often denied, downplayed, or dismissed: "An understanding of racism as a system of advantage presents a serious challenge to the notion of the United States as a just society where rewards are based solely on one's merits" (Tatum, 1992, p. 6).

Recent studies point out numerous ways in which racism and other forms of discrimination affect students and their learning. For instance, Angela Taylor found that, to the extent that teachers harbor negative racial stereotypes, the African American child's race *alone* is probably sufficient to place him or her at risk for negative school outcomes (Taylor, 1991). Many teachers, of course, see it

differently, preferring to think instead that students' lack of academic achievement is due solely to conditions inside their homes or communities. But the
occurrence of discriminatory actions in schools, both by other students and by
teachers and other staff, has been widely documented. A 1990 study of Boston
high school students found that while 57 percent had witnessed a racial attack
and 47 percent would either join in or feel that the group being attacked deserved
it, only a quarter of those interviewed said they would report a racial incident to
school officials (Ribadeneira, 1990). It should not be surprising, then, that in a
report about immigrant students in California, most believed that Americans
felt negatively and unwelcoming toward them. In fact, almost every immigrant
student interviewed reported that they had at one time or another been spat
upon, and tricked, teased, and laughed at because of their race, accent, or the way
they dressed. More than half also indicated that they had been the victims of
teachers' prejudice, citing instances where they were punished, publicly embarrassed, or made fun of because of improper use of English. They also reported
that teachers had made derogatory comments about immigrant groups in front
of the class, or had avoided particular students because of the language difficulty
(Olsen, 1988). Most of the middle and high school students interviewed by Mary
Poplin and Joseph Weeres (1992) had also witnessed incidents of racism in
school. In Karen Donaldson's study in an urban high school where students used
the racism they experienced as the content of a peer education program, over
80 percent of students surveyed said that they had perceived racism to exist in
school (Donaldson, 1994).

Marietta Saravia-Shore and Herminio Martínez found similar results in their
ethnographic study of Puerto Rican young people who had dropped out of
school and were currently participating in an alternative high school program.
These adolescents felt that their former teachers were, in their words, "against
Puerto Ricans and Blacks" and had openly discriminated against them. One
reported that a teacher had said, "Do you want to be like the other Puerto Rican
women who never got an education? Do you want to be like the rest of your
family and never go to school?" (Saravia-Shore & Martínez, 1992, p. 242). In
Virginia Vogel Zanger's study of high-achieving Latino and Latina Boston high
school students, one young man described his shock when his teacher called him
"spic" right in class; although the teacher was later suspended, this incident had
left its mark on him (Zanger, 1994). Unfortunately, incidents such as these are
more frequent than schools care to admit or acknowledge. Students, however,
seem eager to address these issues, but are rarely given a forum in which such
discussions can take place.

How do students feel about the racism and other aspects of discrimination that
they see around them and experience? What effect does it have on them? In
interviews with students, Karen Donaldson found three major ways in which they
said they were affected: White students experienced guilt and embarrassment
when they were became aware of the racism to which their peers were subjected;
students of color sometimes felt they needed to overcompensate and overachieve
to prove they were equal to their White classmates; and students of color also
mentioned that discrimination had a negative impact on their self-esteem

(Donaldson, forthcoming). The issue of self-esteem is a complicated one and may include many variables. Children's self-esteem does not come fully formed out of the blue, but is *created* within particular contexts and responds to conditions that vary from situation to situation, and teachers' and schools' complicity in creating negative self-esteem certainly cannot be discounted. This was understood by Lillian, one of the young women in Nitza Hidalgo's study of an urban high school, who commented, "That's another problem I have, teachers, they are always talking about how we have no type of self-esteem or anything like that. . . . But they're the people that's putting us down. That's why our self-esteem is so low" (Hidalgo, 1991, p. 95).

The students in my research also mentioned examples of discrimination based on their race, ethnicity, culture, religion, and language. Some, like Manuel, felt it from fellow students. As an immigrant from Cape Verde who came to the United States at the age of eleven, he found the adjustment difficult:

> When American students see you, it's kinda hard [to] get along with them when you have a different culture, a different way of dressing and stuff like that. So kids really look at you and laugh, you know, at the beginning.

Avi spoke of anti-Semitism in his school. The majority of residents in his town were European American and Christian. The Jewish community had dwindled significantly over the years, and there were now very few Jewish students in his school. On one occasion, a student had walked by him saying, "Are you ready for the second Holocaust?" He described another incident in some detail:

> I was in a woods class, and there was another boy in there, my age, and he was in my grade. He's also Jewish and he used to come to the temple sometimes and went to Hebrew school. But then, of course, he started hanging around with the wrong people and some of these people were in my class, and I guess they were . . . making fun of him. And a few of them starting making swastikas out of wood. . . . So I saw one and I said to some kid, "What are you doing?" and the kid said to me, "Don't worry. It's not for you, it's for him." And I said to him, "What?!"

Other students talked about discrimination on the part of teachers. Both Marisol and Vinh specifically mentioned language discrimination as a problem. For Marisol, it had happened when a particular teacher did not allow Spanish to be spoken in her room. For Vinh, it concerned teachers' attitudes about his language: "Some teachers don't understand about the language. So sometimes, my language, they say it sounds funny." Rich spoke of the differences between the expectations of White and Black teachers, and concluded that all teachers should teach the curriculum *as if they were in an all-White school*, meaning that then expectations would be high for everybody. Other students were the object of teasing, but some, including James, even welcomed it, perhaps because it at least made his culture visible. He spoke of Mr. Miller, an elementary teacher he had been particularly fond of, who had called him "Gonzo" because he had a big nose and "Klinger" after the *M.A.S.H.* character who was Lebanese. James said, "And then everybody called me Klinger from then on. . . . I liked it, kind of . . . everybody laughing at me."

It was Linda who had the most to say about racism. As a young woman who identified herself as mixed because her mother was White and her father Black, Linda had faced discrimination or confusion on the part of both students and teachers. For example, she resented the fact that when teachers had to indicate her race, they came to their own conclusions without bothering to ask her. She explained what it was like:

> [Teachers should not] try to make us one or the other. And God forbid you should make us something we're totally not. . . . Don't write down that I'm Hispanic when I'm not. Some people actually think I'm Chinese when I smile. . . . Find out. Don't just make your judgments. . . . If you're filling out someone's report card and you need to know, then ask.

She went on to say:

> I've had people tell me, "Well, you're Black." I'm not Black; I'm Black and White. I'm Black and White American. "Well, you're Black!" No, I'm not! I'm both. . . . I mean, I'm not ashamed of being Black, but I'm not ashamed of being White either, and if I'm both, I want to be part of both. And I think teachers need to be sensitive to that.

Linda did not restrict her criticisms to White teachers, but also spoke of a Black teacher in her high school. Besides Mr. Benson, her favorite teacher of all, there was another Black teacher in the school:

> The other Black teacher, he was a racist, and I didn't like him. I belonged to the Black Students Association, and he was the advisor. And he just made it so obvious: he was all for Black supremacy. . . . A lot of times, whether they deserved it or not, his Black students passed, and his White students, if they deserved an A, they got a B. . . . He was insistent that only Hispanics and Blacks be allowed in the club. He had a very hard time letting me in because I'm not all Black. . . . I just really wasn't that welcome there. . . . He never found out what I was about. He just made his judgments from afar.

It was clear that racism was a particularly compelling issue for Linda, and she thought and talked about it a great deal. The weight of racism on her mind was evident when she said, "It's hard. I look at history and I feel really bad for what some of my ancestors did to some of my other ancestors. Unless you're mixed, you don't know what it's like to be mixed." She even wrote a poem about it, which ended like this:

But all that I wonder is who ever gave
them the right to tell me
What I can and can't do
Who I can and can't be
God made each one of us
Just like the other
the only difference is,
I'm darker in color.

Implications of Students' Views for Transformation of Schools

Numerous lessons are contained within the narratives above. But what are the implications of these lessons for the school's curriculum, pedagogy, and tracking? How can we use what students have taught us about racism and discrimination? How can schools' policies and practices be informed through dialogue with students about what works and doesn't work? Although the students in my study never mentioned multicultural education by name, they were deeply concerned with whether and in what ways they and their families and communities were respected and represented in their schools. Two implications that are inherently multicultural come to mind, and I would suggest that both can have a major impact on school policies and practices. It is important that I first make explicit my own view of multicultural education: It is my understanding that multicultural education should be *basic for all students, pervasive in the curriculum and pedagogy, grounded in social justice, and based on critical pedagogy* (Nieto, 1992). Given this interpretation of multicultural education, we can see that it goes beyond the "tolerance" called for in numerous proclamations about diversity. It is also a far cry from the "cultural sensitivity" that is the focus of many professional development workshops (Nieto, 1994). In fact, "cultural sensitivity" can become little more than a condescending "bandaid" response to diversity, because it often does little to solve deep-seated problems of inequity. Thus, a focus on cultural sensitivity in and of itself can be superficial if it fails to take into account the structural and institutional barriers that reflect and reproduce power differentials in society. Rather than promoting cultural sensitivity, I would suggest that multicultural education needs to be understood as "arrogance reduction"; that is, as encompassing *both* individual *and* structural changes that squarely confront the individual biases, attitudes, and behaviors of educators, as well as the policies and practices in schools that emanate from them.

Affirming Students' Languages, Cultures, and Experiences

Over twenty years ago, Annie Stein reported asking a kindergarten teacher to explain why she had ranked four of her students at the bottom of her list, noting that they were "mute." " 'Yes,' she said, 'they have not said one word for six months and they don't appear to hear anything I say.' 'Do they ever talk to the other children?' we asked. 'Sure,' was her reply. 'They cackle to each other in Spanish all day' " (Stein, 1971, p. 161). These young children, although quite vocal in their own language, were not heard by their teacher because the language they spoke was bereft of all significance in the school. The children were not, however, blank slates; on the contrary, they came to school with a language, culture, and experiences that could have been important in their learning. Thus, we need to look not only at the individual weaknesses or strengths of particular students, but also at the way in which schools assign status to entire groups of students based on the sociopolitical and linguistic context in which they live. Jim Cummins addressed this concern in relation to the kinds of superficial antidotes frequently proposed to solve the problem of functional illiteracy among students from culturally and economically dominated groups: "A remedial focus only on technical aspects of functional illiteracy is inadequate because the causes of educational underachievement and 'illiteracy' among subordinated groups are rooted in the systematic devaluation of culture and denial of access to power and resources by the dominant group" (1994, pp. 307–308). As we have seen in many of the examples cited throughout this article, when culture and language are acknowledged by the school, students are able to reclaim the voice they need to continue their education successfully.

Nevertheless, the situation is complicated by the competing messages that students pick up from their schools and society at large. The research that I have reviewed makes it clear that, although students' cultures are important to them personally and in their families, they are also problematic because they are rarely valued or acknowledged by schools. The decisions young people make about their identities are frequently contradictory and mired in the tensions and struggles concerning diversity that are reflected in our society. Schools are not immune to such debates. There are numerous ways in which students' languages and cultures are excluded in schools: they are invisible, as with James, denigrated, as in Marisol's case, or simply not known, as happened with Vinh. It is no wonder then that these young people had conflicted feelings about their backgrounds. In spite of this, all of them spoke about the strength they derived from family and culture, and the steps they took to maintain it. James and Marisol mentioned that they continued to speak their native languages at home; Fern discussed her father's many efforts to maintain their Native American heritage; Manuel made it clear that he would always consider himself first and foremost Cape Verdean. Vinh spoke movingly about what his culture meant to him, and said that only Vietnamese was allowed in the home and that his sisters and brothers wrote to their parents in Vietnamese weekly. Most of these young people also maintained solid ties with their religion and places of worship as an important link to their heritage.

Much of the recent literature on educating culturally diverse students is helping to provide a radically different paradigm that contests the equation *education = assimilation* (Trueba, 1989). This research challenges the old assumptions about the role of the school as primarily an assimilationist agent, and provides a foundation for policy recommendations that focus on using students' cultural background values to promote academic achievement. In the case of Asian Pacific American youth, Peter Kiang and Vivian Wai-Fun Lee state the following:

> It is ironic that strengths and cultural values of family support which are
> so often praised as explanations for the academic achievement of Asian

Pacific American students are severely undercut by the lack of program-matic and policy support for broad-based bilingual instruction and native language development, particularly in early childhood education.

(Kiang & Lee, 1993, p. 39)

A study by Jeannette Abi-Nader of a program for Hispanic youth provides an example of how this can work. In the large urban high school she studied, students' cultural values, especially those concerned with *familia*, were the basis of everyday classroom interactions. Unlike the dismal dropout statistics prevalent in so many other Hispanic communities, up to 65 percent of the high school graduates in this program went on to college. Furthermore, the youth attributed their academic success to the program, and made enthusiastic statements about it, including this one written on a survey: "The best thing I like about this class is that we all work together and we all participate and try to help each other. We're family!" (Abi-Nader, 1993, p. 213).

The students in my research also provided impassioned examples of the effect that affirming their languages and cultures had on them and, conversely, on how negating their languages and cultures negated a part of them as well. The attitudes and behaviors of the teachers in Yolanda's school, for example, were reflected in policies that seemed to be based on an appreciation for student diversity. Given the support of her teachers and their affirmation of her language and her culture, Yolanda concluded, "Actually, it's fun around here if you really get into learning. . . . I like learning. I like really getting my mind working." Manuel also commented on how crucial it was for teachers to become aware of students' cultural values and backgrounds. This was especially important for Manuel, since his parents were immigrants unfamiliar with U.S. schools and society, and although they gave him important moral support, they could do little to help him in school. He said of his teachers:

> If you don't know a student there's no way to influence him. If you don't know his background, there's no way you are going to get in touch with him. There's no way you're going to influence him if you don't know where he's been.

Fern, on the other hand, as the only Native American student in her school, spoke about how difficult it was to discuss values that were different from those of the majority. She specifically mentioned a discussion about abortion in which she was trying to express that for Native Americans, the fetus is alive: "And, so, when I try to tell them, they just, 'Oh, well, we're out of time.' They cut me off, and we've still got half an hour!" And Avi, although he felt that teachers tried to be under-standing of his religion, also longed for more cultural affirmation. He would have welcomed, for example, the support of the one Jewish teacher at school who Avi felt was trying to hide his Jewishness.

On the contrary, in Linda's case, Mr. Benson, her English teacher, who was also her favorite teacher, provided just that kind of affirmation. Because he was racially mixed like Linda, she felt that he could relate to the kinds of problems she confronted. He became, in the words of Esteban Díaz and his colleagues, a "socio-cultural mediator" for Linda by assigning her identity, language, and culture important roles in the learning environment (Díaz, Flores, Cousin, & Soo Hoo, 1992). Although Linda spoke English as her native language, she gave a wonderful example of how Mr. Benson encouraged her to be "bilingual," using what she referred to as her "street talk." Below is her description of Mr. Benson and the role he played in her education:

> I've enjoyed all my English teachers at Jefferson. But Mr. Benson, my English Honors teacher, he just threw me for a whirl! I wasn't going to college until I met this man. . . . He was one of the few teachers I could talk to . . . 'cause Mr. Benson, he says, I can go into Harvard and converse with those people, and I can go out in the street and "rap with y'all." It's that type of thing. I love it. I try and be like that myself. I have my street talk. I get out in the street and I say "ain't" this and "ain't" that and "your momma" or "wha's up?" But I get somewhere where I know the people aren't familiar with that language or aren't accepting that language, and I will talk properly. . . . I walk into a place and I listen to how people are talking and it just automatically comes to me.

Providing time in the curriculum for students and teachers to engage in discussions about how the language use of students from dominated groups is discriminated against would go a long way in affirming the legitimacy of the discourse of *all* students (Delpit, 1992). According to Margaret Gibson (1991), much recent research has confirmed that schooling may unintentionally contribute to the educational problems of students from culturally dominated groups by pressuring them to assimilate against their wishes. The conventional wisdom that assimilation is the answer to academic underachievement is thus severely challenged. One intriguing implication is that the more students are involved in resisting assimilation while maintaining their culture and language, the more successful they will be in school. That is, maintaining culture and language, although a conflicted decision, seems to have a positive impact on academic success. In any case, it seems to be a far healthier response than adopting an oppositional identity that effectively limits the possibility of academic success (Fordham & Ogbu, 1986; Skutnabb-Kangas, 1988). Although it is important not to overstate this conclusion, it is indeed a real possibility, one that tests the "melting pot" ideology that continues to dominate U.S. schools and society.

We know, of course, that cultural maintenance is not true in all cases of academic success, and everybody can come up with examples of students who felt they needed to assimilate to be successful in school. But the question remains whether this kind of assimilation is healthy or necessary. For instance, in one large-scale study, immigrant students clearly expressed a strong desire to maintain their native languages and cultures and to pass them on to their children (Olsen, 1988). Other research has found that bilingual students specifically appreciate hearing their native language in school, and want the opportunity to learn in that language (Poplin & Weeres, 1992). In addition, an intriguing study of Cambodian refugee children by the Metropolitan Indochinese Children and Adolescent Service found that the more successful they became at modeling their behavior to be like U.S. children, the more their emotional adjustment worsened (National Coalition, 1988). Furthermore, a study of Southeast Asian students found a significant connection between grades and culture: in this research, higher grade point averages correlated with the *maintenance* of traditional values, ethnic pride, and close social and cultural ties with members of the same ethnic group (Rumbaut & Ima, 1987).

All of the above suggests that it is time to look critically at policies and practices that encourage students to leave their cultures and languages at the school-house door. It also suggests that schools and teachers need to affirm, maintain, and value the differences that students bring to school as a foundation for their learning. It is still too common to hear teachers urging parents to "speak only English," as my parents were encouraged to do with my sister and me (luckily, our parents never paid attention). The ample literature cited throughout this article concerning diverse student populations is calling such practices into question. What we are learning is that teachers instead need to encourage parents to speak their *native* language, not English, at home with their children. We are also learning that they should emphasize the importance of family values, not in the rigid and limiting way that this term has been used in the past to create a sense of superiority for those who are culturally dominant, but rather by accepting the strong ethical values that all cultural groups and all kinds of families cherish. As an initial step, however, teachers and schools must first learn more about their students. Vinh expressed powerfully what he wanted teachers to know about him by reflecting on how superficial their knowledge was:

> They understand something, just not all Vietnamese culture. Like they just understand something *outside.* . . . But they cannot understand something inside our hearts.

Listen to Students

Although school is a place where a lot of talk goes on, it is not often student talk. Student voices sometimes reveal the great challenges and even the deep pain young people feel when schools are unresponsive, cold places. One of the students participating in a project focusing on those "inside the school," namely students, teachers, staff, and parents, said, "This place hurts my spirit" (Poplin & Weeres, 1992, p. 11). Ironically, those who spend the most time in schools and classrooms are often given the least opportunity to talk. Yet, as we saw in the many examples above, students have important lessons to teach educators and we need to begin to listen to them more carefully. Suzanne Soo Hoo captured the fact that educators are losing a compelling opportunity to learn from students while working on a project where students became coresearchers and worked on the question, "What are the obstacles to learning?" a question that, according to Soo Hoo, "electrified the group" (1993, p. 386). Including students in addressing such important issues places the focus where it rightfully belongs, said Soo Hoo:

"Somehow educators have forgotten the important connection between teachers and students. We listen to outside experts to inform us, and consequently, we overlook the treasure in our very own backyards: our students" (p. 390). As Mike, one of the coresearchers in her project, stated, "They think just because we're kids, we don't know anything" (p. 391).

When they are treated as if they do know something, students can become energized and motivated. For the ten young people in my study, the very act of speaking about their schooling experiences seemed to act as a catalyst for more critical thinking about them. For example, I was surprised when I met Marisol's mother and she told me that Marisol had done nothing but speak about our interviews. Most of the students in the study felt this enthusiasm and these feelings are typical of other young people in similar studies. As Laurie Olsen (1988) concluded in an extensive research project in California in which hundreds of immigrant students were interviewed, most of the students were gratified simply to have the opportunity to speak about their experiences. These findings have several implications for practice, including using oral histories, peer interviews, interactive journals, and other such strategies. Simply providing students with time to talk with one another, including group work, seems particularly helpful.

The feeling that adults do not listen to them has been echoed by many young people over the years. But listening alone is not sufficient if it is not accompanied by profound changes in what we expect our students to accomplish in school. Even more important than simply listening is assisting students to become agents of their own learning and to use what they learn in productive and critical ways. This is where social action comes in, and there have been a number of eloquent accounts of critical pedagogy in action (Peterson, 1991; Torres-Guzmán, 1992). I will quote at length from two such examples that provide inspiring stories of how listening to students can help us move beyond the written curriculum.

Iris Santos Rivera wrote a moving account of how a Freirian "problem-posing" approach was used with K-6 Chicano students in a summer educational program of the San Diego Public Schools in 1975 (Santos Rivera, 1983–1984). The program started by having the students play what she called the "Complain, Moan, and Groan Game." Using this exercise, in which students dialogued about and identified problems in the school and community, the young people were asked to identify problems to study. One group selected the school lunch program. This did not seem like a "real" problem to the teacher, who tried to steer the children toward another problem. Santos Rivera writes: "The teacher found it hard to believe in the problem's validity as an issue, as the basis for an action project, or as an integrating theme for education" (p. 5). She let the children talk about it for awhile, convinced that they would come to realize that this was not a serious issue. However, when she returned, they said to her, "Who is responsible for the lunches we get?" (p. 6). Thus began a summer-long odyssey in which the students wrote letters, made phone calls, traced their lunches from the catering truck through the school contracts office, figured out taxpayers' cost per lunch, made records of actual services received from the subcontractors, counted sandwiches and tested milk temperatures, and, finally, compared their findings with contract specifications, and found that there was a significant discrepancy. "We want to bring in the media," they told the teacher (p. 6). Both the local television station and the major networks responded to the press releases sent out by the students, who held a press conference to present the facts and answer reporters' questions. When a reporter asked who had told them all this, one nine-year old girl answered, "We found this stuff out. Nobody had to tell us anything. You know, you adults give yourselves too much credit" (p. 7). The postscript to this story is that state and federal laws had to be amended to change the kinds of lunches that students in California are served, and tapes from the students in this program were used in the state and federal hearings.

In a more recent example, Mary Ginley, a student in the doctoral program at the School of Education at the University of Massachusetts and a gifted teacher in the Longmeadow (Massachusetts) Public Schools, tries to help her second-graders develop critical skills by posing questions to them daily. Their responses are later discussed during class meeting time. Some of these questions are fairly straightforward ("Did you have a good weekend?"), while others encourage deeper thinking; the question posed on Columbus Day, "Was Columbus a hero?" was the culmination of much reading and dialogue that had previously taken place. Another activity she did with her students this year was to keep a daily record of sunrise and sunset. The students discovered to their surprise that December 21 was *not* the shortest day of the year. Using the daily almanac in the local newspaper, the students verified their finding and wrote letters to the editor. One, signed by Kaolin, read (spelling in original):

> Dear Editor,
>   Acorting to our chart December 21 was not the shotest day of the year. But acorting to your paper it is. Are teacher says it happens every year! What's going on?

As a result of this letter, the newspaper called in experts from the National Weather Service and a local planetarium. One of them said, "It's a fascinating question that [the pupils] have posed. . . . It's frustrating we don't have an adequate answer" (Kelly, 1994, p. 12). Katie, one of the students in Mary's class, compared her classmates to Galileo, who shook the scientific community by saying that the earth revolved around the sun rather than the other way around. Another, Ben, said, "You shouldn't always believe what you hear," and Lucy asserted, "Even if you're a grown-up, you can still learn from a second-grader!"

In the first part of this article, I posed the question, "Why listen to students?" I have attempted to answer this question using numerous comments that perceptive young people, both those from my study and others, have made concerning their education. In the final analysis, the question itself suggests that it is only by first listening *to* students that we will be able to learn to talk *with* them. If we believe that an important basis of education is dialogue and reflection about experience, then this is clearly the first step. Yolanda probably said it best when she commented, " 'Cause you learn a lot from the students. That's what a lot of teachers tell me. They learn more from their students than from where they go study."

Conclusion

I have often been struck by how little young people believe they deserve, especially those who do not come from economically privileged backgrounds. Although they may work hard at learning, they somehow believe that they do not deserve a chance to dream. This article is based on the notion that all of our students deserve to dream and that teachers and schools are in the best position for "creating a chance" to do so, as referred to in the title. This means developing conditions in schools that let students know that they have a right to envision other possibilities beyond those imposed by traditional barriers of race, gender, or social class. It means, even more importantly, that those traditional barriers can no longer be viewed as impediments to learning.

The students in my study also showed how crucial extracurricular activities were in providing needed outlets for their energy and for teaching them important leadership skills. For some, it was their place of worship (this was especially true for Avi, Manuel, and Rich); for others, it was hobbies (Linda loved to sing); and for others, sports were a primary support (Fern mentioned how she confronted new problems by comparing them to the sports in which she excelled: "I compare it to stuff, like, when I can't get science, or like in sewing, I'll look at that machine and I'll say, 'This is a basketball; I can overcome it' "). The schools' responsibility to provide some of these activities becomes paramount for students such as Marisol, whose involvement in the Teen Clinic acted almost like a buffer against negative peer pressure.

These students can all be characterized by an indomitable resilience and a steely determination to succeed. However, expecting all students, particularly those from subordinated communities, to be resilient in this way is an unfair burden, because privileged students might not need this quality, as the schools generally reflect their backgrounds, experiences, language, and culture. Privileged students learn that they are the "norm," and although they may believe this is inherently unfair (as is the case with Vanessa), they still benefit from it.

Nevertheless, the students in this research provide another important lesson about the strength of human nature in the face of adversity. Although they represented all kinds of families and economic and social situations, the students were almost uniformly upbeat about their future and their lives, sometimes in spite of what might seem overwhelming odds. The positive features that have contributed to their academic success, namely, caring teachers, affirming school climates, and loving families, have helped them face such odds. "I don't think there's anything stopping me," said Marisol, whose large family lived on public assistance because both parents were disabled. She added, "If I know I can do it, I should just keep on trying." The determination to keep trying was evident also in Fern, whose two teenage sisters were undergoing treatment for alcohol and drug abuse, but who nevertheless asserted, "I succeed in everything I do. If I don't get it right the first time, I always go back and try to do it again," adding, "I've always wanted to be president of the United States!" And it was evident as well in the case of Manuel, whose father cleaned downtown offices in Boston while his mother raised the remaining children at home, and who was the first of the eleven children to graduate from high school: "I can do whatever I want to do in life. Whatever I want to do, I know I could make it. I believe that strongly." And, finally, it was also clear in the case of Rich, whose mother, a single parent, was putting all three of her children through college at the same time. Rich had clearly learned a valuable lesson about self-reliance from her, as we can see in this striking image: "But let's not look at life as a piece of cake, because eventually it'll dry up, it'll deteriorate, it'll fall, it'll crumble, or somebody will come gnawing at it." Later he added, "As they say, self-respect is one gift that you give yourself."

Our students have a lot to teach us about how pedagogy, curriculum, ability grouping, and expectations of ability need to change so that greater numbers of young people can be reached. In 1971, Annie Stein expressed the wishes and hopes of students she talked with, and they differ little from those we have heard through the voices of students today: "The demands of high school youth are painfully reasonable. They want a better education, a more 'relevant' curriculum, some voice in the subject matter to be taught and in the running of the school, and some respect for their constitutional and human rights" (1971, p. 177). Although the stories and voices I have used in this article are primarily those of individual students, they can help us to imagine what it might take to transform entire schools. The responsibility to do so cannot be placed only on the shoulders of individual teachers who, in spite of the profound impact they can have on the lives of particular students, are part of a system that continues to be unresponsive to too many young people. In the final analysis, students are asking us to look critically not only at structural conditions, but also at individual attitudes and behaviors. This implies that we need to undertake a total transformation not only of our schools, but also of our hearts and minds.

Notes

1 I recognize that overarching terms, such as "European American," "African American," "Latino," etc., are problematic. Nevertheless, "European American" is more explicit than "White" with regard to culture and ethnicity, and thus challenges Whites also to think of themselves in ethnic terms, something they usually reserve for those from more clearly identifiable groups (generally, people of color). I have a more in-depth discussion of this issue in chapter two of my book, *Affirming Diversity* (1992).

2 The early arguments for cultural deprivation are well expressed by Carl Bereiter and Siegfried Englemann (1966) and by Frank Reissman (1962). A thorough review of a range of deficit theories can be found in Herbert Ginsburg (1986).

3 "Critical thinking," as used here, is not meant in the sense that it has come to be used conventionally to imply, for example, higher order thinking skills in math and science as disconnected from a political awareness. Rather, it means developing, in the Freirian (1970) sense, a consciousness of oneself as a critical agent in learning and transforming one's reality.

4 I was assisted in doing the interviews by a wonderful group of colleagues, most of whom contacted the students, interviewed them, and gave me much of the background information that helped me craft the case studies. I am grateful for the insights and help the following colleagues provided: Carlie Collins Tartakov, Paula Elliott, Haydée Font, Maya Gillingham, Mac Lee Morante, Diane Sweet, and Carol Shea.

5   "Holidays and Heroes" refers to an approach in which multicultural education is understood as consisting primarily of ethnic celebrations and the acknowledgment of "great men" in the history of particular cultures. Deeper structures of cultures, including values and lifestyle differences, and an explicit emphasis on power differentials as they affect particular cultural groups, are not addressed in this approach. Thus, this approach is correctly perceived as one that tends to romanticize culture and treat it in an artificial way. In contrast, multicultural education as empowering and liberating pedagogy confronts such structural issues and power differentials quite directly.

References

Abi-Nader, J. (1993). Meeting the needs of multicultural classrooms: Family values and the motivation of minority students. In M. J. O'Hair & S. Odell (Eds.), *Diversity and teaching: Teacher education yearbook 1* (pp. 212–236). Fort Worth, TX: Harcourt Brace Jovanovich.

Banks, J. A. (1991). *Teaching strategies for ethnic studies* (6th ed.). Boston: Allyn & Bacon.

Bartolomé, L. (1994). Beyond the methods fetish: Toward a humanizing pedagogy. *Harvard Educational Review, 64*, 173–194.

Bempechat, J. (1992). *Fostering high achievement in African American children: Home, school, and public policy influences.* New York: ERIC Clearinghouse on Urban Education, Teachers College, Columbia University.

Bereiter, C., & Englemann, S. (1966). *Teaching disadvantaged children in the preschool.* Englewood Cliffs, NJ: Prentice Hall.

Clark, R. M. (1983). *Family life and school achievement: Why poor Black children succeed or fail.* Chicago: University of Chicago Press.

Commins, N. L. (1989). Language and affect: Bilingual students at home and at school. *Language Arts, 66*, 29–43.

Cummins, J. (1994). From coercive to collaborative relations of power in the teaching of literacy. In B. M. Ferdman, R-M. Weber, & A. G. Ramírez (Eds.), *Literacy across languages and cultures* (pp. 295–331). Albany: State University of New York Press.

Delpit, L. (1992). The politics of teaching literate discourse. *Theory into Practice, 31*, 285–295.

Díaz, E., Flores, B., Cousin, P. T., & Soo Hoo, S. (1992, April). Teacher as sociocultural mediator. Paper presented at the Annual Meeting of the AERA, San Francisco.

Donaldson, K. (1994). Through students' eyes. *Multicultural Education, 2*(2), 26–28.

Fine, M. (1991). *Framing dropouts: Notes on the politics of an urban public high school.* Albany: State University of New York Press.

Fine, M. (1993). "You can't just say that the only ones who can speak are those who agree with your position": Political discourse in the classroom. *Harvard Educational Review, 63*, 412–433.

Fordham, S., & Ogbu, J. (1986) Black students' school success: Coping with the "burden of acting White." *Urban Review, 18*, 176–206.

Frau-Ramos, M., & Nieto, S. (1993). "I was an outsider": Dropping out among Puerto Rican youths in Holyoke, Massachusetts. In R. Rivera & S. Nieto (Eds.), *The education of Latino students in Massachusetts: Research and policy considerations* (pp. 143–166). Boston: Gastón Institute.

Freire, P. (1970). *Pedagogy of the oppressed.* New York: Seabury Press.

Gibson, M. (1991). Minorities and schooling: Some implications. In M. A. Gibson & J. U. Ogbu (Eds.), *Minority status and schooling: A comparative study of immigrant and involuntary minorities* (pp. 357–381). New York: Garland.

Ginsburg, H. (1986). The myth of the deprived child: New thoughts on poor children. In U. Neisser (Ed.), *The school achievement of minority children: New perspectives*. Hillsdale, NJ: Lawrence Erlbaum.

Goodlad, J. I. (1984). *A place called school*. New York: McGraw-Hill.

Haberman, M. (1991). The pedagogy of poverty versus good teaching. *Phi Delta Kappan, 73*, 290–294.

Hallinan, M., & Teixeira, R. (1987). Opportunities and constraints: Black-White differences in the formation of interracial friendships. *Child Development, 58*, 1358–1371.

Hidalgo, N. M. (1991). *"Free time, school is like a free time": Social relations in City High School classes*. Unpublished doctoral dissertation, Harvard University.

Hollins, E. R., King, J. E., & Hayman, W. C. (Eds.). (1994). *Teaching diverse populations: Formulating a knowledge base*. Albany: State University of New York Press.

Kelly, R. (1994, January 11). Class searches for solstice. *Union News*, p. 12.

Kiang, P. N., & Lee, V. W-F. (1993). Exclusion or contribution? Education K-12 policy. In *The State of Asian Pacific America: Policy Issues to the Year 2020* (pp. 25–48). Los Angeles: LEAP Asian Pacific American Public Policy Institute and UCLA Asian American Studies Center.

Kohl, H. (1993). The myth of "Rosa Parks, the tired." *Multicultural Education, 1*(2), 6–10.

Kozol, J. (1967). *Death at an early age: The destruction of the hearts and minds of Negro children in the Boston Public Schools*. New York: Houghton Mifflin.

Lee, V. E., Winfield, L. F., & Wilson, T. C. (1991). Academic behaviors among high-achieving African-American students. *Education and Urban Society, 24*(1), 65–86.

Lucas, T., Henze, R., & Donato, R. (1990). Promoting the success of Latino language-minority students: An exploratory study of six high schools. *Harvard Educational Review, 60*, 315–340.

McNeil, L. M. (1986). *Contradictions of control: School structure and school knowledge*. New York: Routledge & Kegan Paul.

Mehan, H., & Villanueva, I. (1993). Untracking low achieving students: Academic and social consequences. In *Focus on Diversity* (Newsletter available from the National Center for Research on Cultural Diversity and Second Language Learning, University of California, Santa Cruz, CA).

Moll, L. (1992). Bilingual classroom studies and community analysis: Some recent trends. *Educational Researcher, 21*(2), 20–24.

Moll, L., & Díaz, S. (1993). Change as the goal of educational research. In E. Jacob & C. Jordan (Eds.), *Minority education: Anthropological perspectives* (pp. 67–79). Norwood, NJ: Ablex.

National Coalition of Advocates for Students. (1988). *New voices: Immigrant students in U.S. public schools*. Boston: Author.

Newmann, F. M. (1993). Beyond common sense in educational restructuring: The issues of content and linkage. *Educational Researcher, 22*(2), 4–13, 22.

Nieto, S. (1992). *Affirming diversity: The sociopolitical context of multicultural education*. White Plains, NY: Longman.

Nieto, S. (1994). Affirmation, solidarity, and critique: Moving beyond tolerance in multicultural education. *Multicultural Education, 1*(4), 9–12, 35–38.

Oakes, J. (1992). Can tracking research inform practice? *Educational Researcher, 21*(4), 12–21.

Olsen, L. (1988). *Crossing the schoolhouse border: Immigrant students and the California public schools*. San Francisco: California Tomorrow.

Peterson, R. E. (1991). Teaching how to read the world and change it: Critical pedagogy in the intermediate grades. In C. E. Walsh (Ed.), *Literacy as praxis: Culture, language, and pedagogy* (pp. 156–182). New Jersey: Ablex.

Phelan, P., Davidson, A. L., & Cao, H. T. (1992). Speaking up: Students' perspectives on school. *Phi Delta Kappan, 73*, 695–704.

Poplin, M., & Weeres, J. (1992). *Voices from the inside: A report on schooling from inside the classroom.* Claremont, CA: Claremont Graduate School, Institute for Education in Transformation.

Reissman, F. (1962). *The culturally deprived child.* New York: Harper & Row.

Reyes, M. de la Luz (1992). Challenging venerable assumptions: Literacy instruction for linguistically different students. *Harvard Educational Review, 62*, 427–446.

Ribadeneira, D. (1990, October 18). Study says teenagers' racism rampant. *Boston Globe,* p. 31.

Rumbaut, R. G., & Ima, K. (1987). *The adaptation of Southeast Asian refugee youth: A comparative study.* San Diego: Office of Refugee Resettlement.

Santos Rivera, I. (1983–1984, October–January). Liberating education for little children. In *Alternativas* (Freirian newsletter from Río Piedras, Puerto Rico, no longer published).

Saravia-Shore, M., & Martínez, H. (1992). An ethnographic study of home/school role conflicts of second generation Puerto Rican adolescents. In M. Saravia-Shore & S. F. Arvizu (Eds.), *Cross-cultural literacy: Ethnographies of communication in multiethnic classrooms* (pp. 227–251). New York: Garland.

Shor, I. (1992). *Empowering education: Critical teaching for social change.* Chicago: University of Chicago Press.

Skutnabb-Kangas, T. (1988). Resource power and autonomy through discourse in conflict: A Finnish migrant school strike in Sweden. In T. Skutnabb-Kangas & J. Cummins (Eds.), *Minority education: From shame to struggle* (pp. 251–277). Clevedon, England: Multilingual Matters.

Sleeter, C. E. (1991). *Empowerment through multicultural education.* Albany: State University of New York Press.

Sleeter, C. E. (1994). White racism. *Multicultural Education, 1*(4), 5–8, 39.

Sleeter, C. E., & Grant, C. A. (1991). Mapping terrains of power: Student cultural knowledge vs. classroom knowledge. In C. E. Sleeter (Ed.), *Empowerment through multicultural education* (pp. 49–67). Albany: State University of New York Press.

Soo Hoo, S. (1993). Students as partners in research and restructuring schools. *Educational Forum, 57*, 386–393.

Stein, A. (1971). Strategies for failure. *Harvard Educational Review, 41*, 133–179.

Tatum, B. D. (1992). Talking about race, learning about racism: The application of racial identity development theory in the classroom. *Harvard Educational Review, 62*, 1–24.

Taylor, A. R. (1991). Social competence and the early school transition: Risk and protective factors for African-American children. *Education and Urban Society, 24*(1), 15–26.

Taylor, D., & Dorsey-Gaines, C. (1988). *Growing up literate: Learning from inner-city families.* Portsmouth, NH: Heinemann.

Torres-Guzmán, M. (1992). Stories of hope in the midst of despair: Culturally responsive education for Latino students in an alternative high school in New York City. In M. Saravia-Shore & S. F. Arvizu (Eds.), *Cross-cultural literacy: Ethnographies of communication in multiethnic classrooms* (pp. 477–490). New York: Garland.

Trueba, H. T. (1989). *Raising silent voices: Educating the linguistic minorities for the twenty-first century.* Cambridge, MA: Newbury House.

Wheelock, A. (1992). *Crossing the tracks: How "untracking" can save America's schools.* New York: New Press.

Zanger, V. V. (1994). Academic costs of social marginalization: An analysis of Latino students' perceptions at a Boston high school. In R. Rivera & S. Nieto (Eds.), *The education of Latino students in Massachusetts: Research and policy considerations* (pp. 167–187). Boston: Gastón Institute.

Critical Questions

1 Think about a particular student whose case is discussed in this article. How would a teacher build on his or her experiences and background? Be specific.

2 Why do you think that Vanessa, the only European American student interviewed, had a hard time defining herself in ethnic or racial terms? Can you think of other examples where this might be the case?

3 If it is true that pride in culture and language is crucial for academic success, what does it mean for school policies and practices? Discuss some of the policies and practices you think schools should change to promote educational equity for all students.

4 Given what students had to say about curriculum, pedagogy, and their experiences with discrimination, what are the implications for schools? What are the implications for your classroom? How might you change your practice?

Community-Based Activity and Advocacy

Develop a case study of a young person to help you think more deeply about the issues in this chapter. Some specific guidelines to help you create the case study follow:

- Select a young person of the approximate age that you will be (or are currently) teaching. It would probably be best not to select a student who you know well or teach.
- Choose a young person from a background with which you are not very familiar. The activity should be a rich learning experience for you, and this is most likely to occur when you interact with and do additional research about a person from a different background.
- As a class, develop and agree on a list of questions. What most interests you about young people? What do you most want to know? Think about identity, culture, school success, and the role of teachers and family in their lives.
- Decide how many times you will meet to interview the young people. It is generally better to meet for several short sessions of one hour or less than for one long session of one and a half or more hours. Dividing the questions by topic also makes sense.
- Make certain to meet the parents or guardians of the young people you plan to interview. Speak to them about the purpose and scope of the interviews and assure them of their child's confidentiality. Secure written permission and oral permission (on an audiotape), and let them know that they have the right to pull out at any time. Also tell them how you will be using the interview and that you will share it with the family when it is completed.

- Get as much information from the family as you will need to develop the case study, but be sensitive to their privacy and feelings. Do not impose yourself on them, and be discreet.
- Select a comfortable, quiet, stress-free environment for the interviews. I would suggest meeting away from school; consider a community center, their home, the park, or a place where you can have a soda and relax.
- Try to make the interviews as comfortable as possible. Ask the young person for permission to audiotape, as that will give you the most accurate record of the interviews. Do not ask questions in a rushed way, as if you are trying to get through an assignment; give your interviewee time to respond completely and then follow up with additional relevant questions. Ask the interviewee if he/she has any questions or concerns.
- Transcribe parts of the tapes. Transcribing all the tapes is very time-consuming and labor-intensive, so it may not be realistic to expect complete transcriptions for a one-semester course. However, you can still develop effective case studies. Listen to the tapes several times, then try to determine the conspicuous themes that keep coming up. Once you have done this, you can transcribe the parts that seem to be the most intriguing or relevant for the student you interviewed.
- Do some research on the context in which the student lives: find out about his or her ethnic, racial, and linguistic background and the history of their people in this country; look for information concerning the city or town in which they live; try to get some data on the school system they go to (e.g. number of students, types of programs, and so on). Also ask interviewees if they would like to share writing samples such as poems, letters, or essays with you.
- Write the case study. Begin with an introduction to the young person, including pertinent information about them, their family, community, cultural group, and schooling experience. Then let the young people speak for themselves by creating a narrative based on the themes you heard them address. Include any other information such as their writings or other material they may have given you.

Each case study is different, and there is no ideal model to follow, but these guidelines can help get you started on creating a convincing case study of a young person. The process may also help you develop useful insights about the lives of young people.

Supplementary Resources for Further Reflection and Study

Cammarota, J. & Fine, M. (Eds.). (2008). *Revolutionizing education: Youth participatory action research in motion*. New York: Routledge.

   This book provides a broad framework for understanding a groundbreaking critical research methodology known as Youth-led Participatory Action Research (YPAR). YPAR is a way to involve young people in defining the research questions and problems most relevant in their lives and, more importantly, a way of acting upon them. This collection offers the first, definitive statement of YPAR as it relates to sites of education in particular, drawing on a unique combination of theory and practice. It brings together student writings alongside those of major scholars in the field.

Igoa, C. (1995). *The inner world of the immigrant child.* New York: St. Martin's Press.

In this moving book about her experiences as a teacher of immigrant students, Igoa chronicles how she developed her teaching methodology to focus on literacy and the need for children to feel a sense of empowerment. Featuring the voices and artwork of many immigrant children, this text portrays the immigrant experience of uprooting, culture shock, and adjustment to a new world. It also describes cultural, academic, and psychological interventions that facilitate learning as immigrant students make the transition to a new language and culture.

Hoose, P. M. (1993). *It's our world too! Stories of young people who are making a difference.* New York: Little, Brown & Co.

This inspiring, action-oriented book geared for children from late elementary through high school features 14 teens who take a stand against racism, sexism, or crime, reach out to help those in need, fight to save the environment and, in general, attempt to create a world of peace.

9   Beyond Categories

The Complex Identities of Adolescents

(with John Raible)

As you have seen throughout Part II, everyone has multiple and hybrid identities. That is, race, ethnicity, gender, social class, ability, national origin, religion, sexual orientation, and other differences combine to influence who we are and how we identify. For young people, negotiating their identities while growing up and learning to live in a complex time and society is especially challenging.

In order to be effective, teachers and others who work with young people need to be aware of how they identify, and why. In turn, students need to know that there will be adults in their schools and communities who understand and support them. In the chapter that follows, John Raible and I present concrete case studies of three students, one each in middle school, high school, and college. They are eloquent in describing their identities, which, while complicated, are also quintessentially "American."

What does it mean to be an adolescent in the United States today? In this chapter we attempt to provide insights into this question, based on our varied experiences with young people of different backgrounds. We are both teachers and researchers with a special interest in how race and ethnicity, social class, language, gender, sexual orientation, and other differences manifest themselves in students' identities, and in how these identities are influenced by schooling. Both of us have taught for many years at levels ranging from elementary school through university. Our research—Sonia's previous work with students of diverse cultural backgrounds and John's ongoing research in "communities of adoption"—has rendered questions of identity enormously significant for both of us.[1] Our own backgrounds and developing identities are, of course, major reasons for this interest. Both John (biracial African American, adoptee and adoptive father, gay male teacher and professor, and grandfather) and Sonia (Puerto Rican, Spanish-speaking female, teacher and teacher educator, mother, and grandmother) recognize how our own identities have shifted over the years. Hence, we share a keen curiosity about young people and the identities they create and re-create, and how their identities change based on their experiences and the contexts in which they live and study at any given time.

Human beings are constantly evolving and redefining themselves over the course of a lifetime. Adolescence is a particularly significant phase of life, during which young people try to figure out who they are. The great task of adolescence is learning to express one's multiple identities in personally meaningful and socially acceptable ways. As educators, we need to understand the implications of adolescent identity formation for schooling. How are race and gender, for instance, affirmed or dismissed in school settings? What does it mean to be a lesbian in a school setting hostile to that identity? How can an adoptee explore his identity in a school environment where biological family ties are accorded higher status than ties of adoption? And how are students' quests for meaningful identities linked to learning?

The changes one undergoes in one's identifications are due not just to individual preferences and experiences; that is, they are not simply psychological transformations that take place in one's own head. Identities also change in response to the sociopolitical contexts in which people live. Our identities have been shaped and continue to be influenced by the people with whom we interact and the material and social conditions of our lives. In this chapter, we focus on two young people who several years ago allowed us into their worlds through a series of interviews. These students come from different cities and towns, and they hail from various kinds of families and different social classes. They identify in multiple ways, based on such factors as family structure, race, sexual orientation, and national origin. In spite of these differences, they share a need to belong and to feel free to explore who they are. Finally, to explore how a sense of self can reach a comfortable—although always changing—status as one leaves adolescence, we conclude with the thoughts of a young man in the early years of adulthood.

Creating Identities: Cases of Two Young People in Transition

Whether we are seasoned adults or young children, our identities are always in flux. The human impulse to categorize, however, has resulted in labeling people in ways that restrict the expression of complex identities. This tendency has been especially evident in the past several decades, given the resurgent interest in race and ethnicity in education. However, although significant in and of themselves, race, ethnicity, gender, and other traditional markers of identity do not tell the whole story.

Culture is a great deal messier than these static terms might imply. Researcher Steven Arvizu's description of culture as a verb rather than a noun begins to capture the dynamic nature of identity, particularly as defined by youth in an increasingly globalized world.[2] For instance, in their research focusing on adolescents, Shirley Brice Heath and Milbrey McLaughlin found that ethnic labels provided only partial descriptions of the young people they studied. Their research suggests that, rather than serving as a primary identifier, ethnicity gives adolescents an "additional layer of identity" they can adopt as a matter of pride.[3]

In her later work, Heath found that young people, particularly those who live in urban areas, are involved in the creation of new cultural categories based on shared experiences, not just shared identities. According to Heath, these young people "think of themselves as a *who* and not a *what*" (emphasis in original).[4]

Daniel Yon is another researcher who has found that conventional, static conceptions of culture are unsatisfactory for describing the multiple and hybrid realities of identities today. Yon conducted a study of high school students of various racial and ethnic backgrounds in Toronto, Ontario. In this research, he coined the term "elusive culture" to suggest the new and creative ways students made sometimes surprising and unpredictable identifications; for instance, a Serbian student identified as "Spanish" and a white male identified most closely with his Guyanese classmates. Yon concluded:

> Youth demonstrate tremendous flexibility in their capacity to make iden-tifications, to experiment, take risks, discard and create ideas, and in these processes they resist an understanding of culture as something to simply embody, apply, or force others to have.[5]

Raquel Romberg describes a similar phenomenon among Puerto Ricans on the U.S. mainland. "Cultural chameleons" is Romberg's term for those who "manage their lives through the combination, merging, or shifting of different cultural strategies."[6] In this way, Puerto Ricans and other young people with hybrid identities provide a far healthier model of cultural adaptation than is commonplace.

Given the pressures to assimilate to both peer culture and, in some cases, a new national culture and society, it should come as no surprise that students develop unpredictable identifications. In her ethnographic study of immigrant youth at Madison High (her pseudonym for a racially and ethnically diverse school in California), Laurie Olsen found that adapting to a new culture often meant that young people needed "to abandon the fullness of their human iden-tities as part of the process of becoming and being American."[7] In addition, Olsen found that many newcomers were surprised that coming to the United States did not automatically make them American. For some students, especially those whose backgrounds and physical characteristics differed most from the European American mainstream culture, factors such as skin color, religion, and language prevented a facile assimilation. Students at Madison High were often forced to construct narrow boundaries for themselves, limiting possibilities of multi-cultural interaction. This situation was especially painful for students of biracial and multiracial backgrounds, who were often forced to "choose sides," and for many immigrants who did not fit neatly into any of the already constructed categories.

Clearly, we live in a time of transition, one in which static labels can no longer contain the rich complexity of contemporary identities. We turn now to a closer look into the lived realities of two young people who shared with us their reflec-tions on their own unique identifications. (In what follows, the names of the young people, as well as the towns or cities where they live and the schools they attend, are pseudonyms.)

Nick Greenberg: The Identities of a Transracial Adoptee

Nick Greenberg is a 14-year-old middle school student. He is tall and tan, with wavy black hair and a ready smile. In physical appearance, Nick might be taken for any number of ethnicities, races, or nationalities. That is, he epitomizes a racially ambiguous individual. Nick was adopted when he was a few months old, but he maintains contact with his birth mother and his older brother, who lives with her. During his interview, Nick spoke honestly about his feelings regarding his multiracial heritage and other people's expectations for how he "should" act:

> I look more like my birth mother than my birth father because he was African American and my birth mother is white. . . . My adoptive father is Jewish, and my adoptive mother is Christian. I usually check off "African American" and "Native American" because I know I'm at least part Native American. Sometimes when I say I'm Jewish, this one kid says, "No, you're not Jewish. You have to act more Jewish." To me, I have no idea what it means to "act more Jewish." Maybe it means to wear a yarmulke or go to synagogue.
>
> I've been told that I talk white, but that was in a joking way. Certain black kids will say I shouldn't listen to a certain kind of music since I'm black. It kind of gets annoying to be told what music I'm supposed to listen to. They continue to press on and say I'm supposed to "act black." When I ask them how that's supposed to be, they can't really answer that because there's no way you're supposed to act if you're black, Chinese, white—you're just supposed to act the way you feel.

Nick identifies tastes in music and clothes, along with language styles, as important markers of identity that are frequently used to define him. Being raised by his white adoptive parents in a predominantly white environment, it is understandable why Nick "sounds white" to some. Yet partly because he listens to some rap artists, and partly because he regularly visits his birth family in a predominantly African American neighborhood of another city, Nick is able to "code-switch" and adopt an urban (some might say "black") manner of speech. Nevertheless, it has not always been easy for him to do so.

Talking about his interactions with African American students in his middle school, Nick related a few incidents that occurred in the halls during which he was forced to navigate tricky racial boundaries as a multiracial, racially ambiguous student. The names others hurl his way hint at their confusion about how to place Nick in the social circles at school:

> Most of the black people act kind of racist towards me because I don't act like them. They usually say "nigger," which I find pretty offensive. Like, "Out of my way, you nigger"—stuff like that. "Nigger" is probably

the worst thing I've ever been called. Some people have called me "gay." "Gay" and "nigger" are the things they call me the most. One black person was picking on me because I didn't "act black." And two other people, they kept on telling him to stop, and they said, "He doesn't have to act black, he can act however he wants to. He can act Chinese for all I care." The first guy wasn't too happy, but he left. I thought it was pretty good.

I think it's starting to sink in that people don't have to act like their race. They can act any way they want. Kids don't really have to tell anybody how they're supposed to act according to their race, or gender for that matter.

While on the surface Nick resists attempts by other students to get him to "act like his race," he nevertheless usually includes himself when he talks about black people; that is, he identifies as African American. At other times, Nick speaks about African Americans as others. This "now I'm one thing, now I'm something else, but I'm all of me simultaneously" approach reflects a hybridized, "both/and" approach to racial identification, especially characteristic of how identifications are made by individuals who are multiracial. Such an approach is a refreshing change from the outdated "either/or" model from an earlier era, which forced people to identify with only one or the other parent's racial designation.

When asked explicitly to describe where he feels he fits, Nick answered:

I don't really choose friends by color; I choose them by who they are on the inside. I watch what they do. If they do a lot of laughing and smiling and are not acting like jerks, then I consider them nice people, and I'll see if I can make friends with them. I have a variety of friends from different races, not just a single race. I have white people, black people, Asian people, German, Russian, Canadian, et cetera, as friends.

I don't feel I fit in with totally black people. I feel like if it's more mixed, I have a better chance of fitting in. I would actually have to say I fit in best in the water. I know it sounds kind of weird, but that's something that I'm really good at. I can just swim around and forget about everything that's happened to me.

Nick's comment about "forgetting about everything" when he's swimming serves as a poignant reminder of the strife he experiences as a result of rigid racial categories. For him, how people act is more important than how they identify. Nick explains that he "has a better chance of fitting in" in mixed settings. Although schools sometimes respond to diversity by offering cultural clubs (such as black student unions or Hispanic student associations), which are mod-eled after groups popularized on college campuses in the 1960s and 1970s, culture-specific clubs may not meet the identity needs of students like Nick. One hopeful sign is that there are more and more organizations for mixed-race students on college campuses around the country. Perhaps soon they will become established at secondary schools as well. Nick's situation further suggests that schools can do more to promote interracial activities for those who actively seek involvement in pluralistic, rather than ethnocentric, extracurricular experiences.

Elsewhere in the interview, Nick talked about visiting his birth mother and brother in the large northeastern city where they reside. Because he maintains contact with his birth family, Nick's adoption is considered an open adoption. Growing up in an open adoption has provided Nick with access to people who can answer many of the identity questions with which adoptees often grapple: Why was I adopted? Where did I come from? What does my biological family look like? Nick talked about how he handles being adopted and other people's curiosity about his unique family:

> When people find out I'm adopted, they usually say, "You're adopted?" They are kind of shocked, because they thought that I was just—that they were my "real" parents and I just had a little bit darker skin.
>
> I go to this group where everybody there is adopted. It meets maybe once or twice a month, maybe a little more. We do social activities, but we always talk about adoption and what our lives are like and how we feel about it. It kind of feels useful to be able to get it out and tell other adoptees what it's like, like children your age. We like the stuff we do, but we also like being able to talk to each other really well.

Nick's reference to people who wonder about his "real" parents indicates a common mistake made by well-intentioned individuals when discussing adoption. Some adoptees insist that the parents who raised them are their real parents, while others reject the term altogether. It is more appropriate to be specific and to talk about "birth" (or "biological") and "adoptive" parents, since all of them, whether they are known or not by the adoptee, are real people with real identities. Moreover, all have a real influence in the life of the adopted adolescent.

As an adoptee, Nick is fortunate to be able to integrate two powerful influences that shape his identity: namely, his birth family and his adoptive family. While open adoptions are becoming more commonplace, most adoptees are faced with knowing little, if anything, about their biological family origins. Discriminatory laws remain on the books and continue to deny teenagers knowledge about their birth parents, medical histories, possible siblings, and so on, until they reach the age of eighteen. At this age of majority, state laws usually allow adoptees to request access to their records, but even then information may be withheld, if it is available at all.

Nick's case is remarkably different. Because Nick's is a transracial adoption, when people see him with his adoptive parents it usually becomes obvious that he is adopted. Furthermore, since he knows his birth mother and brother, should he ever decide he wants to meet his birth father, he can always ask them for his name and whereabouts. The open nature of Nick's adoption circumvents the problem of access to identity information; it is not restricted by outdated laws that privilege the rights of parents over those of adopted young people.

Whether adoptions are done in the innovative open manner or follow the traditional closed approach, the presence of adoptees in school raises questions for teachers who may inadvertently send biased messages to students and families.

Schools help to maintain the higher status of families connected biologically by reproducing mainstream definitions of family. For instance, a school form that asks simply for "mother's name" and "father's name" dishonors the reality of the multiple parents in a complex family configuration like Nick's. Similarly, students and parents should be able to check or write in more than one category if authorities insist on asking students to identify themselves by racial group.

In addition, assignments to chart family trees in social studies or biology classes typically privilege biological ancestors and descendants, making it difficult for adoptees to participate fully. For adoptees who do have relevant information, fitting it all into the traditional linear family tree model poses a challenge. Quite simply, their huge family tree diagrams would look more like forests. For adoptees who don't have access to their birth families' histories, having to fill in the tree chart as if they were not adopted can feel dishonest at best and like a betrayal of family ties at worst. Moreover, adopted young people are often keenly aware of the contingent nature of their identities, as reflected in various family ties, family names, legal documents such as birth certificates (which in their case have already been falsified or "amended"), and other identity markers most people take for granted. Simply to appear more inclusive, if not to become more affirming of the array of student identities, schools can change to accommodate the reality of complex families that have been formed through adoption or otherwise.

Rebecca Florentia: Coming Out Safely in High School

Rebecca Florentina is seventeen years old and attends public school in the small New England city of West Blueridge, which has a visible and active lesbian, gay, bisexual, and transgender (LGBT) community. Shortly before the time of her interview, Rebecca "came out"; that is, she began acknowledging her homosexuality openly. Rebecca wears her hair boyishly short and dyed green, and a string of multicolored pride rings hangs around her neck. During the interview she wore a T-shirt that read, "I'm not a dyke, but my girlfriend is." Rebecca belongs to the school's gay-straight alliance (GSA), one of a growing number of school-sanctioned clubs that provide a sense of safety and support to LGBT students and their allies. She describes the level of tolerance of homosexuality in her community and school:

> When I came out, my friends were awesome. I didn't lose a single one. So it was pretty cool. I think, in West Blueridge, if you don't approve of the lifestyle, you don't say it, because you're going to be offending a heck of a lot of people. There are so many lesbians around. I think if people do mind, they keep their mouths shut. I just think that because we're in West Blueridge we get treated so much better than people in other schools. I mean, people have gotten killed. You know the school is accepting because the school has a gay-straight alliance. I'm in the school's GSA. We've gone around and asked teachers to put Safe Zone stickers on their door. The majority of them actually have them on their doors. Most of the teachers don't mind. There's a couple that are kind of iffy.

> There are probably three of us who are "out" at school. I walk around wearing this shirt: "I'm not a dyke, but my girlfriend is." I'm lesbian, butch lesbian, whatever you want to call it. I just want people to know that I'm not a little femmie. That's basically how I define myself.

Rebecca identifies herself not simply as a lesbian student. It is important to her that people recognize her as a particular kind of lesbian, an out, butch lesbian (or, in her words, "not a little femmie").

As an openly gay student, Rebecca has taken advantage of the GSA offered at her school. There she has found allies who share her interest in increasing the visibility of LGBT issues and in promoting a more tolerant atmosphere. But other comments Rebecca makes suggest that not all spaces in the school make her feel equally safe to express aspects of her identity:

> I'm in music, and everybody there knows about me and my girlfriend, because we're both in music. They're all cool with it. And if they're not, they don't say anything. But I'll be reluctant—like I wear my sweatshirt [over the T-shirt] all the time, but I'll be reluctant to wear this in the halls, or in the bathroom or something. I don't wear this T-shirt when I'm alone in school. I don't think teachers could do anything. You're not going to stop the kids from doing something they want to do. If I'm in the hall and some other kid is in the hall, and there's no teachers around, he can hit me if he wants. Or she.

Clothing arises as an important marker of identity in Rebecca's story. She talks about her desire to increase lesbian visibility within the school by wearing her "dyke" T-shirt. At the same time, she worries about other people's reactions and threats to her physical safety. In some schools, dress codes prohibit students from wearing T-shirts that might be considered offensive, or that contain a message that might distract students from learning. Rebecca's T-shirt, no doubt, would present a challenge for teachers and administrators in charge of enforcing dress codes in such schools. It is worth bearing in mind the important role that freedom of expression plays in adolescent identity, particularly for students like Rebecca. Being able to decide where and when to display her T-shirt serves a significant function in Rebecca's exploration of her newfound identity as an out lesbian.

Rebecca's fears for her safety came up at numerous times in the interview, as well as her belief that teachers play an important role in the extent to which she feels free to express who she is:

> This girl said, "Oh, you faggot" in one of my classes, but I don't know if the teacher heard or not. Students just say "faggot" all the time. It makes me angry. I mean, there's nothing you can do, really. It made me feel so much safer when I had a teacher say, in his class the first day, "There will be no swearing, there will be no slurs like 'faggot' or whatever in my class." I have had only two teachers in four years of high school that have

ever said something like that. I think if you had to hold your tongue in class without saying that stuff, it would help a little bit.

When you get out in the halls, it's a totally different atmosphere. People act basically the opposite of how they act in class. The climate is like, if you're generally like everybody else, you're fine. But if you're totally opposite of what everybody else looks like and acts like, you'll get shoved into a locker or something, or told to shut up. All we can do is hope to educate teachers, because there's kids in middle school getting beat up in the hallways because of homophobia, and the teachers don't do anything about it.

Even when teachers make it a point to set standards for respectful interaction in their individual classrooms, there is often a discrepancy, as Rebecca points out, between students' behavior in class and their actions in common areas, such as the school hallways, cafeteria, library, or restrooms. This discrepancy may reflect the need for some students to gain a sense of control over the ways their identities are being constructed by their schooling experience. For example, one common way adolescent identities get expressed is through resistance to adult norms. If teachers simply impose what may seem like superficial "political correctness" about the use of slurs and put-downs, then students may well reject these values when teachers are out of sight and out of earshot.

Similarly, Rebecca's remarks about the messages students receive from school curricula are particularly insightful:

The health class in the high school looks at same-sex whatever, or queer whatever, in a derogatory way. The curriculum says, "Here's these lesbian people, and we should accept them," something like that. It's not like, "Here's the great things about being gay." It's like, "Here's all the things that happen, and things that people think of them." And I don't even think it's that accepting. It's just like, "There are people who are gay." And that's the whole curriculum. And, "Here's a dental dam," and that's it. And the whole class would laugh, and they'd move on. So I think if you want to educate people better, get the health teachers to put better curriculum for teaching about same-sex, transgender, anything. Because it's looked at in a negative way instead of in a positive way.

Rebecca articulates the limits of supposedly inclusive health lessons, which do make mention of lesbians, but then don't provide students with accurate, possibly controversial information about real lesbian lives and gay-related health issues. Merely mentioning a dental dam in the context of a lesson on safer sex, for instance, only gives students something to snicker about, rather than increasing their understanding of lifesaving health concerns. Clearly, teachers need assistance not only with gathering appropriate resources but also with fashioning their own personal approaches to presenting issues that may make themselves or their students—not to mention parents or administrators—uncomfortable. By glossing over and oversimplifying LGBT issues in the way Rebecca describes, teachers reinforce simplistic labeling that can restrict the lives of LGBT students.

Rebecca sums up her assessment of how much teachers at her school support her lesbian identity as follows:

> We have an English teacher who has a lesbian daughter. That's the only reason he brings stuff up like that. Now he's talking about gay issues, like every other day in class. He doesn't talk about his daughter, but he's letting the kids read books that are very liberal and very queer-friendly. I think the teachers who are like that are the teachers who have a lesbian daughter, or are gay themselves, or who have the kids in class saying, "I'm a lesbian. You're offending me in class, like me and my other friends." That's the only reason they do it.
>
> Lesbians are just like everybody else. I mean, everybody sees it as somebody who's different and not normal. But it's just your sexuality. I don't identify myself as like, "Hi, I'm Rebecca and I'm a lesbian." It's like, "This is me, and this is my sexuality." That's as far as I'm going to go with it. I mean, I'll wear a T-shirt or something—I'm proud of who I am. But by wearing this T-shirt, all I'm saying is that here's a happy kid, I'm fine, whatever.
>
> Teachers should value open-mindedness, I think, and being inclusive of everybody. It's hard to be politically correct in everything, every second in every word you say. But I don't know. There are some teachers you just don't want to approach sometimes, because they are very closed.

We cannot overstate the significant role played by the teacher in establishing the climate in the classroom. Even when teachers attempt to share power and run their classes in a democratic fashion, students may still see the classroom as belonging to the adult authority figure. Rebecca placed as much responsibility on her teachers as she took herself. For example, she expresses appreciation for the teachers who make an effort to use inclusive language, who set class expectations for tolerance, and who bring gay content into their lessons. At the same time, she doesn't wait for the world to change before she herself takes action. In the way she negotiates the expression of her unfolding lesbian identity, Rebecca is an inspiring example of the power of one individual to make a difference, simply by insisting on being true to herself.

Implications of Complex Identities for Educational Practice

While identity construction might appear to be a profoundly personal matter, it is also a social and political matter, precisely because it is deeply implicated in the struggle to develop a sense of self within a social sphere. Thus, these are not just individual issues; rather, they have implications for educational practice, as well as for the social and cultural climate created in schools. These implications relate to teachers' professional development as well as school policy and practices. For educators who choose to provide a safe space for the free exploration of adolescent identities in schools, a number of important lessons can be drawn from the students' experiences presented in this chapter.

The themes of choice and flexibility are crucial for youth. Because their identities are in flux and more complicated than static labels can hope to convey, neither of the young people featured here would appreciate being labeled permanently with any one descriptor. For example, Rebecca is not simply a lesbian; she wants to be known as a butch lesbian, and not a "femmie." Furthermore, at the same time she makes visible her lesbian identity and advocates for its equality with other identities, she insists that she is more than her sexuality. She also identifies as Italian and as a musician, for example. Similarly, Nick is African American, European American, Native American, Jewish, and Christian simultaneously. He is also part of and loved by the members of both his birth family and his adoptive family, all of whom are "real" family to him. Schools need to catch up to the fast-changing identifications being created and re-created as today's students make their way through complicated social contexts.

Opportunities for peer association are valuable to students, in class and out. In their own ways, Nick and Rebecca articulate the benefits they gain from speaking with other young people who share similar situations. For example, Nick discussed the importance of his adoptees' group, and Rebecca mentioned the meaning she finds as an active member of the GSA. Although none existed at her school, Rebecca mentioned that she would join an Italian American cultural club, were one available; similarly, Nick might benefit from participating in a multicultural interest group, particularly one organized specifically for multiracial students.

While both students expressed the opinion that "teachers can't really do anything" about harassment in school, it is nonetheless incumbent upon educators to create school environments that are free from bullying. Teachers can do more to share power with students in order to develop school climates that genuinely respect diversity. Specifically, teachers can work with students in ways that go further than forcing them to pay lip service to politically correct verbiage only when adults are around.

How do teachers invite students to co-create respectful school climates? Rebecca's case suggests that modeling behavior that takes LGBT concerns seriously is one place to start. Elsewhere in her interview, Rebecca talked about a teacher who commented casually at the end of class that he had seen an article in the newspaper about a gay issue. Rebecca described feeling accepted and affirmed when he unexpectedly brought up a topic of concern to her as a lesbian. Having such conversations publicly, within earshot of other students, sends a clear message that LGBT topics are not taboo. Moreover, students learn that gay issues can be discussed seriously by gays and straights alike.

Teachers need more time to focus on issues of identity and diversity, both through their preservice education and through inservice professional development. Although schools and colleges of education are devoting more attention to concerns of diversity and identity, there is still much work to be done. Teachers who are planning curricula around themes of family heritage, genetics, or genealogy, for example, might benefit from professional time set aside to think through the implications of their lesson plans for marginalized groups, such as adopted, bicultural, or LGBT youth. Using curricula to reflect the realities of nontraditional families, such as those headed by two lesbian moms as well as families formed through adoption, invites all students to feel freer to express their unique identities in a climate of openness, safety, and mutual respect. Finally, providing teachers with time to reflect on and reconsider their own ideas about race and ethnicity, sexual orientation, and changing definitions of family can help schools become more affirming of the complex identities of today's students.

Joaquín Rosario: Beginning Adulthood with a Strong Sense of Self

We conclude our exploration of adolescent identity with the words of a man in the next stage of his life, young adulthood. Joaquín Rosario is twenty-two years old, and he currently attends one of the most prestigious liberal arts colleges in the nation. He grew up in poverty in a large urban area where he attended public schools, excelling so much that he received a full scholarship to the college. Joaquín confessed that in high school he had the "freedom" to excel academically because, besides being a strong student, he was an accomplished athlete. This identity gave him tremendous credibility in the eyes of his peers. But claiming his identity as both an urban Puerto Rican and a good student was not always easy. How could he be both in a context that only valued one or the other?

Joaquín noticed at the college's orientation that he was one of only two Latinos in the entering class. In spite of this context, it took going to a college steeped in privilege for Joaquín to be given the opportunity to study his heritage. It was after this experience that he began the process of claiming both identities of Puerto Rican and scholar, and along the way he picked up even more ways to define himself. Thus, Joaquín has emerged with a strong sense of self, comfortable with the complexity of his identity. And although he is "only" Puerto Rican, Joaquín recognizes that even what may seem to be a fairly straightforward identity is more complicated than it may appear. He says he can neither "limit his identity" nor define it solely in terms of his ancestral homeland. While he feels connected to the island of Puerto Rico through family stories and through cultural traits such as language, music, food, and clothing, to name a few, Joaquín remarks that his identity is always more complex than "just one thing." Here are his thoughts about who he is and how he arrived at this point:

> Physically, I can only trace my roots as far back as my great-grandparents. One of my great-grandmothers is still alive. She's ninety-eight years old and can still remember how she had to fetch water from the well, and how her house was made of wooden planks and sheets of aluminum with a dirt floor. Historically, however, I am aware that as a Puerto Rican I come from a long history of merging and mixing of bloods and cultures. The indigenous inhabitants of the island now called Puerto Rico; the

European traders, conquistadors, and slave owners; the African slaves (who were a diverse group to begin with) that were brought to the island both to work and be traded, are all ingredients of who I am.

But I cannot limit my identity to the history of the island where all four of my grandparents were born. Being born and raised in the urban center of a Northeast city, many more things have been factors in molding my life and my identity. I am an urban, bilingual, heterosexual, Roman Catholic, Puerto Rican male that enjoys listening to salsa as much as hip-hop, who can savor the taste of *tostones* [fried plantains] as much as a side of collard greens. I can wear baggy jeans, a "hoodie," and "Timbs," put on a three-piece suit with high polished shoes, or a *guayabera* and Dockers, and fit in anywhere I go.

My multiple cultures allow me to move seamlessly across borders. I can speak proper English with an almost undetectable accent, I can talk as much trash about "yo momma" as anyone else in my neighborhood, or I can drop some knowledge while spitting/speaking my Spanish/Spanglish slang. My identity cannot be classified or contained into one or two categories. I am always much more than just one thing.

It is clear that border-crossing for Joaquín is not simply a metaphor, but an expression of his lived reality. Joaquín can and does move literally across boundaries marking different neighborhoods and even nations, as well as different social contexts and linguistic communities. This mobility leads to the hybridity, adaptability, and freedom of choice he enjoys.

Learning from Young People with Complex Identities

Unfortunately, not all young people have the privileges that Joaquín enjoys. As elementary and high schools move to affirm students in their identity explorations, students will have fewer reasons to struggle through adolescence in silence and confusion before claiming their selfhood. It is imperative that all educators understand how race, gender, and other differences matter in school. Many teachers, particularly those at the secondary level, would rather focus on the content they teach than on the emotional and social concerns of their students. But it is becoming more obvious that these cannot be separated.

In her research at Madison High, Laurie Olsen found that the great majority of teachers did not believe that they needed additional preparation to serve the new diversity at the school. Most reported that being "color blind" was enough. Yet Olsen's research revealed tremendous discordance and rage among the students in the school, as well as a silence concerning racism and other forms of exclusion.[8] This underscores the need for teachers to come to grips with what impact identity has on students' learning and their sense of belonging at school.

For students who do not fit into tidy identity boxes, raising teachers' awareness of changing identifications among adolescents can enhance this sense of belonging. In our interviews with students who negotiate complex identities on a daily basis, they expressed a need for teachers to take notice of intolerance based on identities rendered invisible by the school. Both Nick and Rebecca spoke poignantly of the impact of harassment in the hallways, and even in classrooms, about which teachers apparently knew and did nothing.

The task of supporting the complex identities of students like Nick and Rebecca is as complex as these students are themselves. Yet as researcher Frederick Erickson has written, "When we think of culture and social identity in more fluid terms . . . we can find a foundation for educational practice that is transformative."[9] How can teachers and other educators engage in the kind of transformative practices that Erickson suggests? One way might be to envision multicultural school communities as "cultures of commitment" (to borrow a term from anthropologist Gerd Baumann).[10] These are associations of diverse individuals that cut across national, religious, ethnic, and other identifications but are united by a common purpose, a shared project and vision.

If educators, for example, united their school communities around a vision of high expectations and democratic participation for all students, schools might more effectively foster inclusive, respectful, accepting, and empowering school climates. In such environments, perhaps more students would find the freedom to explore their unfolding identities and form new identifications based not on outmoded, confining labels, but on their real needs.

Notes

1 Sonia Nieto and Patty Bode, *Affirming diversity: The sociopolitical context of multicultural education*, 5th ed. (Boston: Pearson/Allyn & Bacon, 2008); Sonia Nieto, "Lessons from Students on Creating a Chance to Dream," *Harvard Educational Review* 64, no. 4 (Winter 1994): 392–426; John Raible, "Re/Constructing Race: An Ethnography of Transracial Adoption," paper presented at the conference of Ethnography and Qualitative Research in Education, Pittsburgh, June 2002.

2 Steven F. Arvizu, "Building Bridges for the Future: Anthropological Contributions to Diversity and Classroom Practice," in Robert A. DeVillar, Christian J. Faltis, and James Cummins (Eds.), *Cultural diversity in schools: From rhetoric to reality* (Albany: State University of New York Press, 1994), 75.

3 Shirley Brice Heath and Milbrey McLaughlin (Eds.), *Identity and inner-city youth: Beyond ethnicity and gender* (New York: Teachers College Press, 1993), 222.

4 Shirley Brice Heath, "Race, Ethnicity, and the Defiance of Categories," in Willis D. Hawley and Anthony W. Jackson (Eds.), *Toward a common destiny: Improving race and ethnic relations in America* (San Francisco: Jossey-Bass, 1995), 45.

5 Daniel A. Yon, "Urban Portraits of Identity: On the Problem of Knowing Culture and Identity in Intercultural Studies," *Journal of Intercultural Studies* 21, no. 2 (2000): 143.

6 Raquel Romberg, "Saints in the Barrio: Shifting, Hybrid, and Bicultural Practices in a Puerto Rican Community," *MultiCultural Review* 5, no. 2 (1996): 16–25.

7 Laurie Olsen, *Made in America: Immigrant students in our public schools* (New York: New Press, 1997), 239.

8 Olsen, *Made in America*.

9 Frederick Erickson, "Culture, Politics, and Educational Practice," *Educational Foundations* 4, no. 2 (1990): 22.

10 Gerd Baumann, *The multicultural riddle: Rethinking national, ethnic, and religious identities* (New York: Routledge, 1999), 153.

Critical Questions

1 What do Raible and Nieto mean when they say that adolescents "create" their identities? Why is adolescence a particularly meaningful time to create an identity?

2 Why are identities "always in flux?" Give some examples from your own life.

3 Nick Greenberg and Rebecca Florentina both described their lives in complex ways. Did anything about their identities surprise you? If so, what?

4 Joaquín Rosario wrote "My identity cannot be classified or contained into one or two categories. I am always much more than just one thing." What does he mean by this, and what implications do these statements have for teaching students today?

5 As a teacher, what do you need to learn in order to be effective with students such as Joaquín, Rebecca, and Nick?

Activity for Your Classroom

Develop an "alternative family tree" lesson for your classroom, adapting it for the grade level you teach. How can you honor family roots without falling back on stereotypical notions of family? How can you involve your students' families so that everyone, regardless of family structure, feels included?

Community-Based Activity and Advocacy

For Rebecca Florentina, the GSA provided a safe haven in her school. Does your school offer all students such a safe haven? In addition, what is available for them in your city or town? What clubs, sports, religious, cultural, and other activities can they engage in after school and on weekends? Are all students represented? Do some research and develop a school and community resource list for adolescents in your town or city and share it with your school council.

Supplementary Resources for Further Reflection and Study

Howard, G. R. (2006). *We can't teach what we don't know: White teachers, multi-racial schools*, 2nd ed. New York: Teachers College Press.

With our nation's student population becoming more diverse than ever and teachers remaining largely White, this book makes an important contribution to the discussion on identity, race, and privilege. Gary Howard outlines what good teachers know and do, and how they embrace culturally responsive teaching by, first, acknowledging their own identities, and second, learning about and affirming the identities of their students.

Morrell, E. (2008). *Critical literacy and urban youth: Pedagogies of access, dissent, and liberation.* New York: Routledge.

Based on the author's extensive work with young people in urban classrooms, urban neighborhoods and institutions of higher education, this book explores the meaning of critical literacy for students, teachers, and researchers, while also examining implications for practice in secondary and postsecondary schools.

Sadowski, M. (Ed.). (2008). *Adolescents at school: Perspectives on youth, identity, and education*, 2nd ed. Cambridge, MA: Harvard Education Press.

This book, which contains the chapter you just read, examines the complex, changing identities that young people manage while they confront the challenges of school. It also points to ways to promote the success of every student in our schools.

Tatum, B. D. (2003). *"Why are all the Black kids sitting together in the cafeteria?" A psychologist explains the development of racial identity*, rev. ed. New York: Basic Books.

An insightful exploration of racial and cultural identity development among adolescents, this groundbreaking book also tackles the question of White privilege. It suggests what teachers, counselors, and other adults can do to help young people navigate the difficult terrain of identity formation, particularly as related to race and ethnicity.

Part III

Becoming Critical Teachers

It should be clear by now that teachers' relationships with students are central to student learning. Becoming competent and caring mentors for a broad range of students, therefore, means developing specific skills and competencies for teaching students who speak languages other than English and whose cultural and racial backgrounds differ from their own. But these competencies are not acquired out of the blue; they need to be developed and nurtured. Teachers and prospective teachers, especially those who have not had extensive experience with students of diverse backgrounds, need to learn to understand human differences in order to tap into the intelligence and capacity of all students. This is a life-long journey, and professional development is a central component of the journey.

In the two chapters that follow, the question of how to become effective with students of diverse backgrounds is addressed. These chapters bring up weighty issues for teachers concerning the questions they should be asking themselves about human differences and the political realities of our society. In Chapter 10, I challenge the notion that either "celebrating diversity" or "sensitivity training"—both of which are traditional responses to diversity—is sufficient to address the serious problems of inequality faced by students of diverse backgrounds in our schools. Instead, I propose that teachers learn to ask what I have called "profoundly multicultural questions," that is, questions that get at the heart of access and equity and that are, in the end, far more significant in terms of student learning and achievement. Chapter 11 includes vignettes that describe the experiences of teachers who epitomize "solidarity, courage, and heart," and I suggest what all teachers can learn from them.

10 Profoundly Multicultural Questions

What are "profoundly multicultural questions?" This is a term that I coined a number of years ago when it became evident that many people thought of multicultural education as simply lessons in getting along with people of diverse backgrounds, or as celebrations of "heroes and holidays" of particular ethnic groups. Yet to me it has always been clear that if multicultural education is to make a difference, it needs to go beyond celebrations and ethnic boosting. Although culturally responsive pedagogy and a more complete and honest curriculum are certainly needed, these things alone will not change the life chances of students living in poverty, nor will they help level the playing field.

In the following chapter, I pose some profoundly multicultural questions that get at the heart of multicultural education when it is conceptualized in broader and more meaningful ways.

I still recall the question that my friend Maddie, also an educator, asked me a number of years ago when I was describing an initiative to bring a multicultural program to a particular urban school district. A supporter of multicultural education, she was nonetheless becoming frustrated by the ways in which many districts were implementing it. She was especially concerned that many students from that particular district were doing poorly in school, and she asked impatiently, "But can they do math?"

Her question stayed with me for a long time—and prompted me to think about what it means to provide an education that is both multicultural and equitable (Nieto, 1999). Sadly, issues of equity and access are not always linked with multicultural education. Sometimes, multicultural education is seen as little more than a way to promote self-esteem, or simply as a curriculum that substitutes one set of heroes for another. When that happens, we may end up with young people who feel good about themselves and their heritage but who have few skills that prepare them for life; or alternatively, who know how to do math and science and read, but who know little about their cultural backgrounds and are even ashamed and embarrassed by them.

Let me make clear that I strongly believe in multicultural education. That first exhilarating course that I took on the subject nearly 30 years ago put into words many of the ideas I had wanted to express since becoming a teacher. More recently, the term culturally responsive pedagogy has come into use and been advocated persuasively (Gay, 2000; Ladson-Billings, 1994). An outgrowth of multicultural education, culturally responsive pedagogy is founded on the notion that—rather than deficits—students' backgrounds are assets that students can and should use in the service of their learning and that teachers of all backgrounds should develop the skills to teach diverse students effectively.

Despite my great support for these philosophies, however, I am also concerned that they can be used in simplistic ways that fail to address the tremendous inequities that exist in our schools. For example, to adopt a multicultural basal reader is far easier than to guarantee that all children will learn to read; to plan an assembly program of ethnic music is easier than to provide music instruction for all students; and to train teachers in a few behaviors in cultural awareness or curriculum inclusion is easier than to address widespread student disengagement in learning. Although these may be valuable activities, they fail to confront directly the deep-seated inequalities that exist in schools. Because they are sometimes taken out of context—isolated as prepackaged programs or "best practices"—multicultural education and culturally responsive pedagogy can become band-aid approaches to serious problems that require nothing short of major surgery.

I define multicultural education as an anti-racist education that is firmly related to student learning and permeates all areas of schooling (Nieto, 1994). It is a hopeful way to confront the widespread and entrenched inequality in U.S. schools because its premise is that students of all backgrounds and circumstances can learn and achieve to high levels, and—even more essential—that they deserve to do so. Multicultural education needs to be accompanied by a deep commitment to social justice and equal access to resources. Multicultural education needs, in short, to be about much more than ethnic tidbits and cultural sensitivity.

For instance, although educators may call attention to the fact that the curriculum in U.S. schools is becoming more multicultural (an overblown claim in any event), they may neglect to note that the achievement gap between white students and students of color is growing. Although the gap was reduced by about half between 1970 and 1988, it has been widening since then. The reversal is evident in grades, test scores, dropout rates, and other indicators, and it has taken place in every type of school district and in all socioeconomic groups (D'Amico, 2001). Just one example: The average 12th grade low-income student of color reads at the same level as the average 8th grade middle-class white student (Kahlenberg, 2000). In terms of high school completion, 88 percent of white students have graduated from high school, but the rate for Hispanics is just 56 percent (U.S. Census Bureau, 2000a). Given these alarming statistics, the claim that education is equally available to all is more of a fiction than ever. Multicultural education and culturally responsive pedagogy by themselves cannot solve these problems.

It makes sense, then, to look carefully at two factors besides cultural differences that influence student learning: the sociopolitical context of education, and school policies and practices. The former includes societal ideologies, governmental policies and mandates, and school financing. School policies and practices—specifically, curriculum, pedagogy, tracking, testing, discipline, and hiring—can also either promote or hinder learning among students of different backgrounds.

Besides focusing on matters of culture and identity, educators also need to ask profoundly multicultural questions—that is, troubling questions that often go unanswered or even unasked. The answers tell us a great deal about what we value because the questions are about equity, access, and social justice in education. Here are a few of the questions that we must address if we are serious about giving all students of all backgrounds an equal chance to learn.

Who's Taking Calculus?

I use "calculus" as a place marker for any number of other high-status and academically challenging courses that may open doors for students to attend college and receive advanced training. For instance, we find that although slightly more than 12 percent of white students are enrolled in calculus, only 6.6 percent of African Americans and 6.2 percent of Latinos and Native Americans are enrolled. In the case of physics, the numbers are 30.7 percent for whites, 21.4 percent for African Americans, 18.9 percent for Hispanics, and 16.2 percent for Native Americans (National Center for Education Statistics [NCES], 2002). This situation has serious implications for reforming such policies as rigid tracking, scheduling, and counseling services. Access to high-level and demanding academic courses has a long-term and dramatic effect in terms of college attendance and subsequent quality of life. For instance, the 2000 U.S. Census reported that annual average earnings for those with a bachelor's degree were nearly double the amount for those with just a high school diploma: $45,678 compared with $24,572 (U.S. Census Bureau, 2000b).

Which Classes Meet in the Basement?

The continuing segregation of students on the basis of race and ethnicity is a trend that has been escalating for the past 20 years. According to Gary Orfield (2001), most of the progress made toward desegregating schools in the two decades prior to 1988 has been lost in the past 15 years. For African Americans, the 1990s witnessed the largest backward movement toward segregation since the Brown v. Board of Education decision. Latinos are now the most segregated of all ethnic groups—not just in race and ethnicity, but also poverty. U.S. schools are becoming more separate and unequal than ever.

Language-minority students and students with special needs are too often hidden away in the basement—or in the hall closet, or the room with the leaky ceiling on the fourth floor, or the modular unit separated from the rest of the school. Administrators offer seemingly logical reasons for placing these students in these areas: There's no other available space in the building; these students were the last to arrive and therefore need to be placed where there's room; now they're closer to the English as a Second Language teacher. But placing programs for marginalized students in less desirable places is a powerful metaphor for the low status and little attention that they receive. It also serves in many cases to segregate these students from the so-called "regular" (English-speaking) or so-called "normal" (non-special needs) students, in this way creating an even greater gulf between them and the rest of the school.

Who's Teaching the Children?

The question of who is teaching the children is inextricably linked to matters of social justice in education. Teachers working in poor urban schools tend to have less experience and less preparation than do those in schools that serve primarily white and middle-class students (Editorial Projects in Education, 1998). In addition, poor urban districts are more likely to hire teachers out of field than are suburban and middle-class school districts (David & Shields, 2001). These situations would be deemed unacceptable in more affluent districts.

Related to teachers' experience and training is the issue of teachers' race and ethnicity. Although all educators—teachers, administrators, curriculum coordinators, and others—need to develop the attitudes and skills to be effective with our increasingly diverse student population, we need a concerted effort to recruit a more diverse faculty. At present, the number of students of color in U.S. classrooms is growing dramatically at the same time that the number of teachers of color is declining. In 1972, just 22 percent of students in public schools were considered "minority"; by 1998, it was 37 percent (NCES, 2000a). The teaching force, on the other hand, is about 87 percent white. These trends show little sign of changing (U.S. Census Bureau, 2001).

The growing gap is problematic because mounting evidence indicates that a higher number of teachers of color in a school—particularly African American and Hispanic—can promote the achievement of African American and Hispanic students (Clewell, Puma, & McKay, 2001; Dee, 2000). In fact, one study found that a higher number of teachers of color can have an even greater impact on the achievement of white students (Meier, Wrinkle, & Polinard, 1999). Another study found that having same race and gender role models was "significantly and consistently predictive of a greater investment in achievement concerns" on the part of young people (Zirkel, 2002, p. 371).

Associated with teacher quality is the question of teachers' influence on their students. The proof is growing that all teachers—regardless of race, ethnicity, or gender—who care about, mentor, and guide their students can have a dramatic impact on their futures, even when these students face tremendous barriers related to poverty, racism, and other social ills (Flores-González, 2002; Noddings, 1992; Valenzuela, 1999). Stanton-Salazar, for instance, suggests that mentoring and support from teachers can provide students with the social capital they need to succeed, thus creating networks that "function as pathways of privilege and power"—pathways not generally available to poor students of color (1997, p. 4).

How Much Are Children Worth?

What do we pay for education, and how does the answer differ according to students' race, ethnicity, social class, and above all, home address? The well-known facts are that school financing is vastly unequal and that students with wealthier parents are fortunate to live in towns that spend more on their education, whereas young people who live in financially strapped urban or rural areas are much less fortunate (Kozol, 1991). Regrettably, the children who need the most get the fewest funds and resources (NCES, 2000b).

We also need to ask what our most vulnerable students are worth in terms of attention and care. A recent court case is a good example of the low value placed on students who attend poor urban schools. In June 2002, an appeals court in New York State ruled that youngsters who drop out of the New York City schools by 8th grade nevertheless receive "a sound basic education" (cited in González, 2002). The result of this astonishing ruling was to overturn a 2001 landmark decision that had found the state's formula for funding public schools unfair because it favored schools in suburban areas. The majority opinion in the appeals ruling, written by Judge Alfred Lerner, said in part, the skills required to enable a person to obtain employment, vote, and serve on a jury are imparted between grades 8 and 9 (cited in González, 2002).Although Judge Lerner conceded that such a meager education might qualify young people for only the lowest-paying jobs, he added, "Society needs workers at all levels of jobs, the majority of which may very well be low-level" (cited in González, 2002). I am left wondering whether Judge Lerner would want this level of education for his own children or would think it fair and equitable.

These, then, are some of the profoundly multicultural questions that I suggest we ask ourselves. Certainly they are not the only questions that we can ask, but they give us an inkling of the vast inequities that continue to exist in U.S. public schools. My questions are not meant to diminish the noble efforts of educators who struggle daily to reach students through culturally responsive education or through an accurate representation in the curriculum of students' histories and cultures. But as we focus on these approaches—approaches that I wholeheartedly support—we also need to ask troubling questions about equity, access, and fair play. Until we do something about these broader issues, we will be only partially successful in educating all our young people for the challenges of the future.

References

Clewell, B. C., Puma, M., & McKay, S. A. (2001). *Does it matter if my teacher looks like me? The impact of teacher race and ethnicity on student academic achievement.* Report to the Ford Foundation. New York: Ford Foundation.

D'Amico, J. J. (2001). A closer look at the minority achievement gap. *ERS Spectrum, 19* (2), 4–10.

David, J. L., & Shields, P. M. (2001). *When theory hits reality: Standards-based reform in urban districts, final narrative report.* Menlo Park, CA: SRI International.

Dee, T. S. (2000). *Teachers, race, and student achievement in a randomized experiment.* Cambridge, MA: National Bureau of Economic Research.

Editorial Projects in Education. (1998). *Education Week: Quality counts 1998.* Bethesda, MD: Author.

Flores-González, N. (2002). *School kids, street kids: Identity and high school completion among Latinos.* New York: Teachers College Press.

Gay, G. (2000). *Culturally responsive teaching: Theory, research, and practice.* New York: Teachers College Press.

González, J. (2002, June 27). Schools ruling defies logic. *New York Daily News,* p. 24.

Kahlenberg, R. D. (2000). *Economic school integration* (Idea Brief no. 2). Washington, DC: The Century Foundation.

Kozol, J. (1991). *Savage inequalities: Children in America's schools.* New York: Crown.

Ladson-Billings, G. (1994). *The dreamkeepers: Successful teachers of African American children.* San Francisco: Jossey-Bass.

Meier, K. J., Wrinkle, R. D., & Polinard, J. L. (1999). Representative bureaucracy and distributional equity: Addressing the hard question. *Journal of Politics, 61,* 1025–1039.

National Center for Education Statistics. (2000a). *Editorial projects in education, 1998.* Washington, DC: U.S. Department of Education, Office of Educational Research and Improvement.

National Center for Education Statistics. (2000b). *Trends in disparities in school district level expenditures per pupil.* Washington, DC: U.S. Department of Education, Office of Educational Research and Improvement.

National Center for Education Statistics. (2002). *Digest of education statistics, 2001.* Washington, DC: U.S. Department of Education, Office of Educational Research and Improvement.

Nieto, S. (1994). Affirmation, solidarity, and critique: Moving beyond tolerance in multicultural education. *Multicultural Education, 1*(4), 9–12, 35–38.

Nieto, S. (1999). *The light in their eyes: Creating multicultural learning communities.* New York: Teachers College Press.

Noddings, N. (1992). *The challenge to care in schools: An alternative approach to education.* New York: Teachers College Press

Orfield, G. (2001). *Schools more separate: Consequences of a decade of resegregation.* Cambridge, MA: The Civil Rights Project, Harvard University.

Stanton-Salazar, R. D. (1997). A social capital framework for understanding the socialization of racial minority children and youth. *Harvard Educational Review, 67*(1), 1–40.

U.S. Census Bureau. (2000a). *Educational attainment in the United States: March 1999* (P20-528). Washington, DC: U.S. Department of Commerce.

U.S. Census Bureau. (2000b). *Educational attainment in the United States (Update): March 2000.* Washington, DC: U.S. Department of Commerce.

U.S. Census Bureau. (2001). *Statistical abstract of the United States: Education* [Online]. Available: www.census.gov/prod/2001pubs/statab/sec04.pdf

Valenzuela, A. (1999). *Subtractive schooling: U.S.-Mexican youth and the politics of caring.* Albany, NY: SUNY Press.

Zirkel, S. (2002). "Is there a place for me?": Role models and academic identity among white students and students of color. *Teachers College Record, 104*(2), 357–376.

Critical Questions

1   Develop some "profoundly multicultural questions" for your teaching context. How would they differ from the questions posed in this chapter?

2   Consider what the following statement means to you: "Multicultural education needs to be accompanied by a deep commitment to social justice and equal access to resources." Does this statement challenge some of your previously held ideas about multicultural education?

3   Think about one or two policies in your schools that, if changed, might positively affect student learning outcomes. Describe the nature of the change you think is needed.

Activity for Your Classroom

With your students, investigate some of the school policies and practices that they feel are unfair. Why do they think this? What can they do to change things? If they are high school students, read the Duncan-Andrade and Morrell book on the list of Suggested Resources at the end of this chapter to get some ideas. If they are elementary school students, tell them about what students did in the Gebhard et al. chapter on the list. Come up with a list of suggestions for advocacy and action.

Community-Based Activity and Advocacy

Present the results of the previous activity to your school council, administrative or leadership team, or local school committee.

Supplementary Resources for Further Reflection and Study

Anyon, J. (2005). *Radical possibilities: Public policy, urban education, and a new social movement*. New York: Routledge.

The author makes the case that urban education can only be reformed when a new social movement presses for drastic changes in public policy. Health care, housing, employment, and other policies would need radical restructuring in order to reform education and create a more socially just society.

Duncan-Andrade, J. & Morrell, E. (2008). *The art of critical pedagogy: Possibilities for moving from theory to practice in urban contexts*. New York: Peter Lang.

Duncan-Andrade and Morrell investigate the core tenets of critical pedagogy, and describe what it looks like in work with urban youths. In so doing, they challenge conventional school policies and practices traditionally used with youths of diverse backgrounds in urban schools.

Gebhard, M., Harman, R., & Seger, W. (2007). Reclaiming recess in urban schools: The potential of systemic functional linguistics for ELLs and their teachers. *Language Arts 84* (5), 419–430.

In this article, university researchers Meg Gebhard and Ruth Harman and classroom teacher Wendy Seger document how elementary ELL students whose school had eliminated recess "reclaimed" it by learning academic literacy skills through systemic functional linguistics.

Oakes, J. & Lipton, M. (2006). *Teaching to change the world*, 3rd ed. New York: McGraw Hill.

A highly readable and engaging, multicultural, critical overview of the teaching profession, this book considers the values and politics that pervade education. It asks critical questions about how conventional thinking and practice came to be, and who benefits from them. The book takes the position that a hopeful, democratic future depends on whether all students learn. It pays particular attention to inequalities associated with race, social class, language, gender, and other social categories, and looks for alternatives to the inequalities.

11 Solidarity, Courage, and Heart

Learning From a New Generation of Teachers

Learning to become effective teachers of students of diverse backgrounds—whether those differences are racial, ethnic, gender, linguistic, social class, ability, or others—takes time, attention, and hard work. It means becoming learners of one's students and stepping into, as much as is possible, their realities and their worlds. In the words of Paulo Freire (1998):

> Educators need to know what happens in the world of the children with whom they work. They need to know the universe of their dreams, the language with which they skillfully defend themselves from the aggressiveness of their world, what they know independently of school, and how they know it.
>
> (pp. 72–73)

It is clear, then, that becoming a learner of one's students means rejecting conventional wisdom about learning, teaching, and intelligence. For example, rather than believe that intelligence is only inherent and inherited, effective teachers of students of diverse backgrounds believe that intelligence is learned and nurtured. Such beliefs form the core of a set of values, beliefs, and dispositions of effective teachers. In the following chapter, I describe a group of teachers who embody these values, beliefs, and dispositions, and suggest some of the changes needed to recruit and retain such teachers.

Freire, P. (1998). *Teachers as cultural workers: Letters to those who dare teach.* Boulder, CO: Westview Press.

In this chapter, I take up the challenge of how teachers should be prepared for diverse classrooms by exploring some essential questions for teacher preparation in our current sociopolitical global context. These questions include:

- How can teachers and future teachers be adequately prepared for classrooms that are diverse in terms of race/ethnicity, nationality, social class, language and other differences?

- What kinds of dispositions and abilities do teachers need to teach in today's diverse schools, and how can they develop these?
- What does it mean to teach with solidarity, courage and heart, and how can current practices in teacher education programs be changed to reflect these ideals?
- And most importantly, why should these questions matter to *all* of us—teacher educators, teachers, students and the public at large—not only in our own nations but around the world?

I want to suggest that, in the end, the answers to these questions say a great deal about who we are, what we value and believe in, and how we educate our young people. I also believe that the questions I pose here take on greater urgency than ever because of the sociopolitical context in which teachers and students teach and learn every day. Although most of my examples are based on the US context and on my research within that context, much of what I have to say is similar to other contexts around the world, because globalization is making our world smaller and more connected than ever. As a result, whether we are in a large urban school in Boston, Massachusetts, a *colegio* in Cádiz, Spain, a rural school outside Beijing, a sprawling high-rise community on the outskirts of Paris, or in numerous other places around the world, we face many of the same challenges and problems brought on by immigration and global economic issues. As I discuss particular components of this sociopolitical context, I hope you will consider how these components may also be evident in your particular contexts, and how they may differ.

The sociopolitical context in the US to which I refer includes the rapid turnover of new teachers. In the US, about 20% of new teachers leave during the first three years of teaching, and the rate is increasing (National Center for Education Statistics, 1999; Boser, 2000). This situation has the greatest impact on students who are the most vulnerable because nearly half of all new teachers in urban public schools leave within five years. To complicate matters further, a 40% turnover of new teachers is expected within this decade, the highest rate since at least 1990 (Haycock, 1998).

The context also includes dramatically changing demographics in both society in general and in classrooms in particular. Whether we live in small hamlets or large urban centers, whether we are from Europe, the Americas, Asia, or Africa, our world is changing. What were once fairly homogeneous populations are now characterized by a tremendous diversity of race, ethnicity and language, among other differences. In some cases, such as the US, diversity has always been a fact of life—although it has not always been accepted or adequately dealt with. In other nations, the demographic changes have proven to be cataclysmic, challenging the sense of nationhood and community that once seemed fairly straightforward and secure. In all these contexts, children living in poverty, children of backgrounds that differ from the majority, and those who speak native languages other than the common language are now becoming the majority in urban centers and urbanized suburbs, and even in rural areas.

In the US, we also have what is generally referred to as an "achievement gap" between White students and students of color, between middle-class and poor children, and between native English-speaking children and those who speak languages other than English as their native languages. This so-called "achievement gap" refers to the fact that Latino, African American and Native American, as well as some Asian American, students achieve substantially less than their White, English-speaking peers.

Yet I want to suggest that the so-called "achievement gap" could just as legitimately be called the resource gap, because the gap is often a result of widely varying resources provided to students based on where they live and who they are. According to a recent report from the US-based organization Education Trust (2005),

> we organize our systems of public education in ways that make things worse. One way we do this is by simply spending less in schools serving high concentrations of low-income and minority children than we do on schools serving more affluent and White children.
>
> (p. 1)

They found, for instance, that across the US, $907 less is spent per student in the highest-poverty districts than in the most affluent districts. Yet we persist in calling attention to the so-called "achievement gap, "once again laying the blame squarely on the children rather than on the system that creates the gap in the first place.

A growing standardization, bureaucratization and privatization in education are also part of the international sociopolitical context. In the US, this has meant, among other things, a growing pressures to "teach to the test", influenced by the No Child Left Behind federal legislation that is, in fact, leaving many children behind, particularly those that this legislation was supposed to help. For example, evidence is mounting that the testing frenzy, which is a direct result of the call for "high standards", is limiting the kinds of pedagogical approaches that teachers use, as well as constricting the curriculum, especially in classrooms serving the most educationally disadvantaged students. Recent research has found that high-stakes testing, rather than increasing student learning, is actually raising dropout rates and leading to less engagement with schooling: Amrein and Berliner (2002) reported findings from research in 18 states that student learning was unchanged or actually went down when high-stakes testing policies were instituted.

Another component of the sociopolitical context includes the physical and emotional condition of public schools, especially those in deteriorating and devastated communities. In the US, many of the schools that the most vulnerable children attend, especially those in economically strapped urban and rural areas, are rundown and abandoned, and they receive little financial and moral support. A recent article in a US weekly newspaper dedicated to education issues presented disturbing statistics about the physical condition of schools: one in four US schools is overcrowded and 3.5 million children attend public schools that are in very poor or even non-operative condition, this in the richest country in the world. The author concluded:

> Even as policymakers seek to improve equity and close gaps in educational outcomes, disparities in facilities send disadvantaged students a visible and unmistakable message that we care less about their education than that of their more affluent peers.
>
> (Mead, 2005)

Paradoxically, as schools in our various nations become more diverse, they are also becoming more racially, ethnically and economically segregated, and this too is part of the sociopolitical context of education. As Orfield (2001) has exhaustively documented in the US, poor students attend schools that are today more segregated than at any time since the historic 1954 *Brown v. Board of Education* Supreme Court decision that was supposed to lead to desegregated schools. In contrast, however, today poor children of all backgrounds, but particularly poor Latino and African American children and children for whom English is a second language, go to the most segregated and least well-resourced schools. Morever, today Latino (Mexican American, Puerto Rican, Dominican, Cuban and other Latin American) students are the most segregated of all students in terms of both ethnicity and social class.

The final piece of the sociopolitical context I shall mention is the long-standing and growing structural and social inequality throughout the world that results in related negative effects of poverty, joblessness, poor access to health care, and the attendant racism and hopelessness experienced by many people on a daily basis. In the US, Anyon (2005), Berliner (2005) and Rothstein (2004) have all argued that macroeconomic policies that have severe consequences for those living in poverty—that is, policies that regulate such things as the minimum wage, job availability, tax rates, health care and affordable housing, among others—are chiefly responsible for creating school failure, because educational policies by themselves cannot transcend these larger policies. While Rothstein, Anyon and Berliner do not deny the importance and necessity of school reform, they make it clear that what schools can accomplish will be limited if these larger macroeconomic policies do not change.

In summary, then, it is clear that dramatic inequalities exist in the access that students around the globe have to an excellent, high quality education, inequalities that are lamentably too frequently based on race, social class, language, and other differences.

The Role of Good Teaching

In spite of the dismal picture I have sketched, we know that good teaching can help to alleviate—although it certainly cannot completely overcome—the situation in which many children attend school. There is growing research, for instance, that good teachers make the single greatest difference in promoting or deterring student achievement. In the US, for example, the landmark 1996 report of the National Commission on Teaching and America's Future (1996) found that "what teachers know and do is one of the most important influences on what students learn". One widely cited study found that students who are assigned to several highly effective teachers in a row have significantly greater gains in achievement than those assigned to less effective teachers, and that the influence of each teacher has effects that spill over into later years (Sanders & Rivers, 1996). Consequently, in a review of dozens of studies in the late 1990s, researchers Linda Darling-Hammond and Beverly Falk (1997) suggested that, until schools address the enormous inequalities in students' access to qualified teachers, other reforms would have little effect on student achievement.

Because of the potential they have for changing the course of students' lives, good teachers who care about students and make a difference in their lives should be viewed as national treasures. But in this difficult time for public education around the world, they're often thought of in demeaning ways that question their professionalism, stifle their creativity and dampen their joy. Yet it is only by understanding the motivations of teachers that we can hope to understand what sustains them and, in the process, attempt to accomplish the as yet unrealized goals of equality and justice through public education. This is the context that led me to the project that I shall focus on in the remainder of this article.

The "Why We Teach" Project

In 2004, I undertook a project that I called "Why We Teach". My goal was to ask a group of teachers in the US who are caring, committed and passionate about their work to write essays about why they teach. I especially wanted to engage those who teach students of diverse backgrounds because it occurred to me that their thoughts would be beneficial for teacher educators struggling with the question of how best to prepare teachers for diverse classrooms. I offer their insights and my analysis of their writing, in the hope that they may be helpful for those in countries other than the US as they think about transforming teaching preparation for diversity.

The result of the "Why We Teach" project is a book (Nieto, 2005) that includes reflections by 21 teachers who work in US public elementary, middle and high schools. Some of the teachers are new to teaching, others have been in the profession for a decade or more, and still others are veteran teachers with more than 30 years' experience. Most teach students of diverse ethnic, racial, linguistic and social class backgrounds, and their own backgrounds are also diverse in terms of ethnicity, race, social class backgrounds, sexual orientation and other differences. I have known and worked with some of them for many years; others I had not met face to face until after I contacted them to write their essays. Friends and colleagues recommended some of them to me as teachers who would have interesting stories to tell. I read about one of them in a local newspaper; I met another one by chance at a meeting. While I was not looking for "stars", that is, well-known and award-winning teachers (although some turned out to be both), my major criterion was that all of them share a passion for teaching, whether it was acknowledged publicly or not. But having worked with thousands of teachers in many schools in the US over the years, I am convinced that teachers such as these can be found in all schools throughout the world. These are teachers who care about students, who love what they do, and who would choose to do it over again. Some are also frustrated, angry, and concerned about the state of public education today and, in this way also, they reflect the sentiments of many teachers not only in the US, but in many other countries as well.

A Word of Caution

In education, we have the tendency to jump on the bandwagon of the latest "quick fix." As a result, new ideas, especially those that come attractively packaged, are spoon-fed to teachers and administrators through articles, programs, kits, checklists, university courses or in-service workshops as if they were the answer we had all been waiting for. Some of these ideas may have merit; they often do. But quick fixes never work. I should especially hate to see the ideas I suggest in my paper turn up on a list of "dispositions of excellent teachers", as if a checklist could determine what it means to be an excellent, caring and committed teacher. The values I propose, such as having solidarity with students or thinking of teaching as a mission, do not lend themselves to facile measurement.

In addition, given the current conservative political climate in the US and elsewhere that I described at the beginning of this paper, we also need to be mindful of the fact that ideas that seem "soft" and "unscientific" are likely to be attacked as romantic and unrealistic. In a recent newspaper editorial titled "Schools of Reeducation?" (Hess, 2006), for instance, Frederick Hess, the Director of Education Policy Studies at the American Enterprise Institute, a decidedly right-wing think tank, wrote about what he considers a troubling tendency among schools of education in the US to "regulate the dispositions and beliefs of those who would teach in our nation's classrooms" (p. B07) Hess has a point if he is suggesting that it is impossible to capture something as dynamic and intangible as teaching in a pre-packaged program or sterile list. However, such criticisms, posed as objective arguments, are frequently used to hide what is fundamentally a political argument against anything that smells of liberal or progressive ideas. Hence, cloaking himself in the garb of political neutrality, Hess argues, "screening on 'dispositions' serves primarily to cloak academia's biases in the garb of professional necessity" (p. B07).

I begin with the recognition that no set of teacher qualities is comprehensive enough or true for all teachers in all contexts and all time. But if we were to look for teachers with the characteristics and dispositions I shall be describing in this paper, I know we shall have come a long way in fulfilling the promises of public education for all students. In spite of the misgivings I have about describing these qualities, I believe a discussion of the common dispositions shared by the teachers in the "Why We Teach" project can benefit others. Before describing them, I begin with some of the widely acknowledged qualities of effective teachers gleaned from the research.

A review of the research (García, 1999; Haberman, 1988; Gordon, 1999; Irvine,

2003; Knapp *et al.*, 1995; Ladson-Billings, 1994; Lucas *et al.*, 1990; Rose, 1995; Villegas & Lucas, 2002) reveals that effective teachers share:

- a solid general education background
- a deep knowledge of their subject matter
- familiarity with numerous pedagogical approaches
- strong communication skills, and
- effective organizational skills.

We can all agree that these skills are absolutely essential in good teaching. But I want to propose an additional set of qualities, dispositions, values and sensibilities based on my analysis of the "Why We Teach" teachers' essays that can expand this list of skills. The qualities I am proposing are:

- a sense of mission
- solidarity with, and empathy for, their students
- the courage to challenge mainstream knowledge
- improvisation, and
- a passion for social justice.

I shall describe each of these by providing examples from the teachers' essays.

A Sense of Mission

In every case, the teachers wrote about their sense of mission as a major reason for teaching. It is this sense of mission, this "elusive something" that brought Bob Amses to teaching after he had been a filmmaker for 17 years. Using humor to capture both the joys and the financial hardships of teaching, Bob wrote: "With teaching, I'd found that elusive *something* that challenged me intellectually, philosophically, emotionally, physically, and as I'd find out too late, financially!"

Although the teachers describe their work as a *mission*, they shy away from seeing teaching as *missionary* work. They see themselves as serving the common good, but they do not describe themselves as saviors, and they lack the self-righteousness that inevitably dooms good intentions. Nina Tepper, a 25-year veteran teacher, wrote

> I teach for the youth and the future. No more do I believe as I did when I first entered the teaching profession that I can "change the world" or the public schools for that matter . . . What I do believe is that, as a teacher, I can affect the future, one child at a time.

The Massachusetts Teacher of the Year in 2004, Melinda Pellerin-Duck wrote "I teach because I see extraordinary possibilities in students."

Nevertheless, having a sense of mission does not mean that teachers are completely selfless: they realize that they too benefit from teaching because they know they make a difference—for some children, a life-saving difference—and they feel good about that.

Kerri Warfield, a middle school art teacher, described teachers as "life-touchers", and she writes, "In what other job can we help improve the future, share our knowledge, and learn every day?" Another young teacher, Yahaira Marquez, echoes these sentiments:

> As a teacher I'm able to help others better themselves, share one of the subjects I'm passionate about, interact with and learn more about others, establish different kinds of relationships, and learn more about myself while making myself stronger. All that with one job and at the age of 23!

Having a sense of mission also means that teachers believe in public education. Jennifer Welborn, a middle school science teacher writes:

> I teach in public school because I still believe in public education. I believe that the purpose of public school, whether it delivers or not, is to give a quality education to all kids who come through the doors. I want to be part of that lofty mission . . . I may be naïve, but I believe that what I do day in and day out *does* makes a difference. Teachers *do* change lives forever.

For 32 years, Mary Ginley was a kindergarten, 1st and 2nd grade teacher, first in Holyoke and later in Longmeadow, Massachusetts, the former a poor town with a crumbling infrastructure and a school population that is 75% Puerto Rican, and the latter a wealthy suburb that is overwhelmingly White. For the past four years, she has been a 5th grade teacher, first in Longmeadow and currently in Tampa, where she teaches in a working-class community. When she taught in Holyoke, she had a student named Steven [the children's names are pseud-onyms] who was hard to forget. She describes how Steven wrote her a letter telling her how she had saved his life. Here is the letter he wrote to her several years ago, almost ten years after he was in her first-grade classroom, and her response to it:

> Dear Mrs. Ginley,
>   I don't know if you remember me. I was in your kindergarten and first grade class at the Early Childhood Center in Holyoke. I don't remember a lot about kindergarten but I remember I was scared and you were nice to me.
>   Recently, I was accepted to a specialized high school in Tampa and my mom and I were celebrating. Remember my mom? She's a recovered alcoholic and she wasn't in good shape back then. Anyway, my mom told me that I owed everything to you, that you were the one who got me headed in the right direction. So she told me I should try to find you and thank you and I did find you and want to thank you for all you did.

I am enclosing a picture of me in my kindergarten class. I put an arrow in case you didn't recognize me. I'm sending you one of me at the eighth grade dance we had a few weeks ago too.

I hope you are well. Thank you very much for all you did.

Your former student,

Steven Jackson

Mary continues:

I looked at the pictures, at the frightened little boy in the front row (with an arrow pointing to him in case I really forgot him) and at the young man dressed up for the eighth grade formal. Oh, Steven, I thought, how on earth could you ever think I'd forget you?

Steven arrived one day in mid-October. I was teaching twenty-something kindergarten kids in Holyoke in a tiny classroom on the second floor of a renovated junior college. Steven had a rough start that day. While his mom was filling out the paperwork and chatting with the principal, Steve escaped and ran out the front door. He hid behind the bushes and only came out when our secretary coaxed him out with the promise of a cherry lollipop. So, it was a tear-streaked, sticky fingered little kid that appeared at my door around 9:30 that morning with the principal and his mom.

I knelt down to talk to him (he spit at me) and then looked at my principal with a question in my eyes. "Why me"? I wanted to say but couldn't because Steven's mom was right there. "I have the most kids already. It's someone else's turn." Instead, I smiled at his mom, asked if she'd like to stay for a few minutes and coaxed Steven onto the rug to listen to the story. Slowly, very slowly, Steven unwrapped himself and moved to the rug. When the story and singing were over and we were moving to centers, I told his mom it was probably time for her to leave. She hesitated, kissed Steven good-bye and headed for the door.

"No!", he shrieked and started after her. I blocked the door and sent her on her way. He kicked me and threw his lollipop in my hair, screaming and sobbing and wailing. I scooped him and rocked him for the next hour, watching the other five year olds from the rocking chair in the front of the room and silently cursing my principal who later told me the reason she put Steven in my room was that he needed me.

Steven had a rough year. He flew into a rage without warning, turning into a miniature tornado, throwing blocks and ripping papers off the wall as he catapulted around the room. He'd sit and sulk if he didn't get his way, describe in minute detail what AA meetings were like and why his mom went to them, refuse to join the circle, refuse to write his name, refuse to share a toy. The only time he seemed calm was when I was rocking him or he was off in a corner with a picture book. He taught himself to read that year but he never learned how to make a friend.

I kept those kids for a second year. I remember when I was discussing this with my principal. She knew how Steven wore me out. She knew that I walked in the room every day saying "Dear God, help me love Steven a little more today."

"I could move him to another class" she offered. "You can't. He needs the stability more than anyone does and I can't let him think I don't want him." So first grade rolled around and Steven arrived the first day, grinning and glad to be back.

Steven still had his days that year but he had mellowed and as he began to feel safe, at school and even at home, we saw a very different little boy. Toward the end of that year, he and his mom moved and I never heard from him again . . . Until now.

Foolish child, to think I wouldn't remember him.

I suppose the reason I still teach, after thirty-five years, is because there are some Stevens every year who might need me. Most likely, they won't write me letters (a few do) and they may not even remember me, but I need to be there for them. School is supposed to be the great equalizer. That may be the American dream but I have never been in a school (other than the one I was in when I had Steven) where there was an active policy to make sure that every child had equal access to quality education, where every child was made to feel welcome, respected, valued, safe. From the minute a child walks through the school doors in kindergarten, the rich get richer and the poor get poorer and the smart get smarter too. It seems schools say that everyone is valued, but when you look closely, you'll find it isn't so.

Solidarity with, and Empathy for, Students

Another quality that the "Why We Teach" teachers share is solidarity with, and empathy for, their students. By now, it is a taken-for-granted truth that relationships are at the heart of teaching (Noddings, 1992; Valenzuela, 1999). While it is problematic to place the entire responsibility for student achievement on teachers—as if issues of inequality, structural barriers due to racism and other biases, lack of resources, poor infrastructure, unfair bureaucratic policies, and so on, did not matter—it is nevertheless important to point out that caring relationships *can* make a difference in spite of these conditions.

Solidarity with and empathy for students are not simply sentimental emotions. For teachers who think deeply about their work, solidarity and empathy mean having genuine respect for their students' identities—including their language and culture—as well as high expectations and great admiration for them. Elementary school teacher Elaine Stinson writes about solidarity and empathy by describing the necessity of close relationships: "I've found that meaningful learning happens through meaningful interaction, whether it's with peers, teachers, music, authors, or poets, or though nature." Sandra Jenoure, a science teacher for over 30 years in Harlem, New York City, describes how teachers must avoid paying attention to negative discourse that targets those students who most need empathy and solidarity: "I know it's easy to sit back and listen to the gossip in schools. 'These kids can't learn', is what you hear. The truth is they can and do. We have to see and believe."

Seth Peterson is a young teacher of English in a public high school in Boston. He shows his solidarity with students by trusting them. He writes:

> I begin to see returns on my trust when a student marked absent appears in the doorway at 10:23 with a sheepish grin. In her hand, she carries a note from the hospital where she spent the night. She hands me the note and says, "I didn't want to miss my group's presentation." Sometimes trust means listening with extreme bias and positive partiality, as in the case of Jolene, who let my voice pull her off another girl, breaking up a fierce, crowded hallway fight: "Hey, it's me . . . Mr. P. Look at me. It's just me. Let's take a walk."
>
> I feel trusted, and therefore validated, when, after two years of silence, Raoul writes me from prison asking for a character witness. He is still confident I will write about his charisma and concern for others, qualities we both know he possesses regardless of one bad decision made in anger one ill-fated night. When Ashanti whines rhetorically, "Mister, how come I feel so guilty when I don't do the homework for this class?" I know some level of trust, some connection between what we do and what she could become has been formed. Some days, these signposts of trust, these affirmations are nowhere to be found. Those days are filled with deafening silences between bells, heavy eyelids, and endless train rides home, but they dissolve into others that hold another chance to earn trust and actually teach.

The Courage to Question Mainstream Knowledge

Why do teachers need to question mainstream knowledge and conventional wisdom? Greene (2001) has addressed this question by writing, "The curriculum has to leave so many questions open so that children will explore and wonder and not believe there is a final answer, because they can only be devastated when they find out there isn't."

According to Elaine Stinson, to question conventional wisdom means "to teach outside the lines". The challenge for teachers is to develop the courage to confront, and to teach their students to confront, what Foucault (2002) calls the "regimes of truth", that is, the kind of discourses promoted by each society as truth, and produced, transmitted and kept in place by systems of power such as universities, the military and the media. The result of these "regimes of truth" is that perspectives and realities different from those that are officially sanctioned tend to remain invisible. This means that, as teacher educators, we need to create learning environments for pre-service teachers in which they can develop more nuanced understandings of complex issues, in order to learn to confront and learn from different perspectives.

A good example comes from Mary Cowhey, a first and second grade teacher who has made it her job to learn as much as she can, and from as many different perspectives as she can, in order to be a more effective teacher to her students. One day a few years ago, I ran into Mary and her family at Old Deerfield, a reconstructed colonial town in Western Massachusetts. She had been on a tour, and she was particularly interested in the Native American experience and how it is depicted in the museum. After fielding many of her questions, the guide said to her, "You sure ask a lot of questions!", and she said, "I have to! I'm a first-grade teacher." The point, as Mary knows, is not simply knowing how to ask questions, but more importantly, knowing how to read answers and keep questioning them.

In her essay, Beth Wohlleb Adel, a middle school social studies teacher currently on leave to raise her two small children, wrote about the day that one of her students saw her at the movies with her partner, another woman. The student who saw her assumed it was Beth's boyfriend, so Beth had no recourse but to tell him that it was her girlfriend. She never intended to "come out" to her students in this way, but she could not lie to them. In the long run, it turned out to be a positive outcome because the incident forced her to be honest with her students and herself. Both her teaching and her relationships with her students benefited as a result. She writes, "I teach because it requires that I become my most courageous self, and I am constantly inspired by students who learn the power of being whole people along with me."

Jennifer Welborn, a middle school science teacher, provides a vivid example of questioning mainstream knowledge and conventional wisdom. It was the book *The Mismeasure of Man* by Stephen Jay Gould (1981) that helped change how she looked at science. The book became the impetus for a unit on scientific racism and the social construction of race that she has taught every year for the past 10 years. Jennifer wrote the following in her essay:

> I want my students to realize that science is not the objective pursuit of knowledge that it is professed to be. I want them to understand that data may support a hypothesis that is not valid to begin with. I want them to know that correlation does not imply causality. I want them to know there are hidden variables that may affect an experiment. I want them to know about researcher bias. I want them to know all this so that when they read in the newspaper that "minority SAT scores are down", they know that these data must be due to social, economic, and political inequities in our society. They are not due to genetic inferiority.

Jennifer also wrote that she wants her students to "learn to be skeptics", to "differentiate between good science, bad science, and pseudoscience". She wants students to think about the advantages and disadvantages that race automatically confers to individuals and groups because according to Jennifer, "it is through this knowledge and dialogue that students can understand the complexity of racism in our country".

Improvisation

For educator, artist and performer Theresa Jenoure (2000), jazz improvisation is a system of composing but beyond music, according to Jenoure, it is "a way of thinking and behaving". In teaching, she sees jazz improvisation as a metaphor for creativity within structure. Improvisation means being prepared for uncertainty, both the joy and the frustration of it. This requires a great deal of elasticity.

In the same way, excellent teachers use improvisation to see beyond frameworks, rubrics, models and templates, all of which increasingly characterize education today. In fact, according to veteran teacher Judith Baker, many schools are in "template heaven", viewing templates as the end rather than the means to effective instruction. In contrast, education is never static. For Ayla Gavins, an elementary school teacher when she wrote her essay, and now a resource teacher, teaching means "being on a moving train" because "on any given day, teachers make hundreds, even thousands of decisions to keep a balance of fairness and equity". She continues, "I am a part of something—globally, nationally, and locally. That is an empowering thought and it gives me a choice of contexts where I can make changes." Not all teachers view their profession in this way; being fearful of change, some continue to do the same thing year after year. Nina Tepper, who has taught in urban schools for over 25 years, writes that when she first started teaching, she was astonished to hear another teacher boast about being on *exactly the same page* as the previous year in her plan book!

Melinda Pellerin-Duck speaks of teaching as the "colors and strands of teaching", comparing teaching to a kente cloth, a treasured cultural symbol for her and her family. Improvisation also means taking advantage of the moment, even putting aside the planned lesson for the time being. As these teachers demonstrate, using improvisation means learning to go beyond the template, or even to *question* the template.

A Passion for Social Justice

For the "Why We Teach" teachers, social justice is very much a part of why they teach. As Mary Ginley, who has taught children who live in extreme poverty as well as very privileged children, writes, "If I just teach them how to survive in this inequitable society, how to get along, I am doing them a tremendous disservice." Ambrizeth Lima, a Cape Verdean teacher of primarily Cape Verdean students, says this: "Teaching is always about power. That is why it must also be about social justice . . . I teach because I believe that young people have rights, including the right to their identities and their languages." Therefore, she asks: "Is it morally right for me, as a teacher, to witness injustice toward students and remain quiet?"

Melinda Pellerin-Duck, a high school teacher in Springfield, Massachusetts, an urban school district, described a community action project in which her students took a leadership role:

> While teaching at Duggan Middle School in Springfield, students enrolled in my Law Related Education class became actively involved in a campaign

to re-open our local public library branches. Budget cuts had prompted the city to close the libraries in some neighborhoods, and my students believed this would deny them a powerful learning tool while denying the community a central gathering place and resource. Working with a voluntary social activist organization, my students and I campaigned before, during, and after school as well as on weekends to share our message about the importance of neighborhood libraries to community leaders. Students produced a multimedia display on the role libraries play in their lives. They learned civil rights strategies for non-violent confrontation and participated in demonstrations, speaking at rallies and labor meetings. They wrote to the mayor and city council, and addressed parent groups and the Superintendent. Our commitment to this effort, and the students' hard work, have resulted in a new library system and longer branch hours. Even more importantly, this collaboration has forged life-long relationships and a sense of activism in my students.

A veteran high school teacher of English and Social Studies at an urban vocational high school, Bill Dunn teaches mostly students who live in poverty, including a large percentage of Puerto Rican students. Bill writes about the unfairness of the MCAS, the high-stakes test in Massachusetts, and the unrecognized rich resources his students have, including their bilingualism and biculturalism. He calls his essay, "Confessions of an Underperforming Teacher", and he begins it this way:

> The stresses which students and teachers encounter in schools today should evoke compassion and admiration from the public; unfortunately, quite the opposite occurs, and this troubles me . . . Test results are released and inner-city students and their teachers are ridiculed in bold headlines. My favorite label is "underperforming." I sincerely couldn't have come up with a word with nastier connotations to attach to schools and the human beings who inhabit them.

Bill ends his compelling essay in this way:

> So why do I teach? I teach because someone has to tell my students that they are not the ones who are dumb. They need to know that only the blissfully ignorant and profoundly evil make up tests to prove that they and people like them are smart. I teach because my students need to know that poverty does not equal stupidity, and that surviving a bleak, dismal childhood makes you strong and tough and beautiful in ways that only survivors of similar environments can appreciate and understand. I teach because my students need to know that in their struggle to acquire a second language, they participate in one of the most difficult of human feats. My students also need to know that four days of reading in a second language under "high-stakes" testing conditions would shut down even Einstein's brain. I teach because my students need to know that right and

wrong are relative to one's culture, and that even these definitions become laughable over time. I teach because the people who make up these tests don't know these things, or worse, they do.

Bill Dunn's sentiments describe a policy climate that is characterized by a profound disrespect for poor students, students of color, and students for whom English is a second language, and for the teachers who work with them.

Lessons from the "Why We Teach" Teachers

There are many lessons to be learned from these teachers for professional development. One is that we need to go beyond current reforms that focus only on certification tests, on increasing teachers' subject matter knowledge, or on giving them a few more "tricks of the trade" for their classrooms. While some of these may be important and necessary, they are simply not enough.

Subject matter knowledge is important, of course, but if teachers do not learn how to question it, they end up reproducing conventional wisdom and encouraging students to do the same. Knowing pedagogy is also necessary, but if teachers do not develop meaningful relationships with their students of all backgrounds— no matter what their own backgrounds are—the students simply will not succeed. If teachers do not understand the life-and-death implications of the work they do, no amount of certification requirements or tricks of the trade will help.

Rather than rely on bureaucratic responses for complex problems, we should instead transform teacher education programs to be more responsive to our nations' educational needs. We can, for instance, develop teacher education programs that encourage prospective teachers to learn more about the students they will teach and the contexts in which they live, and to respect their families and communities. We can provide experiences—through courses, field experiences and extracurricular activities—that will help prospective and practicing teachers learn to speak other languages and learn about cultures other than their own. We can create a climate through innovative courses and assignments, for example, in which prospective and practicing teachers can become critical thinkers. We can help practicing and prospective teachers understand—through dialogue in courses and seminars, through interactions with excellent teachers, through critical readings, and through reflection in journals and essays—that teaching is more than a job but different from missionary work.

Change is also possible if we reform the climate in universities and schools of education. This is a tall order, but it is absolutely necessary if we are to make a difference. Here are some of the changes that universities and schools of education need to make:

- We need to provide course work both in arts and sciences *and* in pedagogy that expands students' minds and enriches their experiences.
- We must actively search for prospective teachers who have the enthusiasm and dispositions to teach students of diverse backgrounds in neglected areas, and who demonstrate excellence in actual teaching.

- We need to set up field placements that more closely match the schools in which most students will end up teaching. Many pre-service teachers, at both the undergraduate and graduate levels, are woefully unprepared to teach students of diverse backgrounds in urban schools. Unless we make sure to place students for at least some of their field placement in urban schools with excellent teachers as their mentors, most pre-service teachers will continue to do their student teaching in suburban and majority White schools and will therefore have little experience in or knowledge of urban schools with a diverse student body.

- There is a dire need to hire a more diverse teacher education faculty. As Howard (1999), borrowing from the words of Malcolm X, writes in his book on White teachers and multiracial schools, "you can't teach what you don't know", and that goes for teacher education faculty as well as for teachers. I am not suggesting that White faculty cannot teach courses in multicultural education or courses that focus on diversity; of course, they can, as long as they have the training, experience, and heart to do so. This also means that hiring faculty of color does not necessarily mean that they are trained, experienced or have the heart to teach courses in diversity, a mistake that many schools of education make. But the fact is that, when you have a more diverse teacher education faculty, you also have a diversity of experiences, viewpoints and expertise, and this enriches the climate for everybody.

- There is also a great need to recruit a more diverse student body. We need to think creatively about how to diversify the teaching pool, and this means looking beyond traditional criteria. Many schools of education have student bodies that are overwhelmingly White, even if they are located in urban centers. We need academically strong students as pre-service teachers, as well as students who have had different experiences that can improve both the learning experience for their peers, and educational outcomes for their future students. This means providing incentives such as scholarships to prospective students, developing relationships with community-based groups as sources of prospective students, looking beyond the 18–22-year-old cohort, and finding other innovative ways to diversify the student body.

- Change is also possible at the societal level by advocating for teachers to be well paid for their work, and given the respect they deserve for doing one of the most difficult jobs there is. This means committing the nation's full economic and moral resources to the problem. It also means demonstrating a fierce determination to improving education for all students, and especially for those who are most poorly served. Above all, the "Why We Teach" essays tell us that teaching is not just about reading, or math or art. It is also about *who* is heard, listened to and read about, *who* gets to count, and *who* can paint the picture. To use the current discourse of the "No Child Left Behind" legislation, it is about who moves ahead and who gets left behind. Many of the policies and practices that are needed to turn things around require no additional resources. Others *do* require resources, not only at the school level, but also at the societal level. This means not only supporting equitable funding for all schools, but also working for affordable housing, decent jobs for everybody and a health system that restores dignity to all people.

In the US, we need to decide, as a nation, whether public education is worth the price. Surely there are implications of this work for Europe, Asia, Africa and Latin America as well. The question to be addressed is this: is it worth the trouble to commit both moral and material resources to the task of providing all young people—especially those who have been left out—with the best teachers? Whether we are teachers, teacher educators, parents and guardians, or concerned citizens, our answer to this question may well determine the future of public education in our world.

References

Amrein, A. I. & Berliner, D. C. (2002) High-stakes testing, uncertainty, and student learning. *Educational Policy Analysis Archives*, 10(18). Available online at: http://epaa.asu.edu/epaa/v1On18/

Anyon, J. (2005) *Radical possibilities: Public policy, urban education, and a new social movement* (New York, Routledge).

Berliner, D. C. (2005, August 2) Our impoverished view of educational reform. *Teachers College Record*. Available online at http://tcrecord.org/content.asp?contentID+12106

Boser, U. (2000) A picture of the teacher pipeline: Baccalaureate and beyond. *Education Week: Quality Counts*, 13 January.

Cochran-Smith, M. & Zeichner, K. M. (2005) *Studying teacher education: The report of the AERA panel on research and teacher education* (Washington, DC, American Educational Research Association, and Mahwah, NJ, Lawrence Erlbaum Associates).

Darling-Hammond, L. & Falk, B. (1997) Using standards and assessments to support student learning. *Phi Delta Kappan*, 79(3), 190–199.

Education Trust (2005) *The funding gap 2005: Low-income and minority students shortchanged by most states* (Washington, DC, Education Trust).

Foucault, M. (1980) Truth and power, in: C. Gordon (Ed.) *Power/knowledge: Selected interviews and other writings, 1972–1977* (Brighton, UK, Harvester Press), 107–133.

García, E. E. (1999) *Student cultural diversity: Understanding and meeting the challenge* (Boston, Houghton Mifflin).

Gordon, G. (1999) Teacher talent and urban schools, *Phi Delta Kappan*, 81(5), 304–306.

Gould, S. J. (1981) *The mismeasure of man* (New York, Norton).

Greene, M. (2001) Reflections: Implications of September 11th for curriculum, *Division B: Curriculum Studies Newsletter* (Washington, DC, American Educational Research Association.)

Haberman, M. (1988) *Preparing teachers for urban schools* (Bloomington, IN, Phi Delta Kappa Educational Foundation).

Haycock, K. (1998) No more settling for less, *Thinking 6–16*, 4(1), 3–12.

Hess, F. M. (2006) Schools of re-education? *Washington Post*, 5 February, p. B07.

Howard, G. R. (1999) *"We can't teach what we don't know": White teachers, multiracial schools* (New York, Teachers College Press).

Irvine, J. J. (2003) *Educating teachers for diversity: Seeing with a cultural eye* (New York, Teachers College Press).

Jenoure, T. (2000) *Navigators: African American musicians, dancers, and visual artists in academe* (Albany, State University of New York Press).

Knapp, M. S., Shields, P. M. & Turnbull, B. J. (1995) Academic challenge in high-poverty classrooms, *Phi Delta Kappan*, 76(10), 770–776.

Ladson-Billings, G. (1994) *The dreamkeepers: successful teachers of African American children* (San Francisco, Jossey-Bass).

Lucas, T., Henze, R. & Donato, R. (1990) Promoting the success of Latino language-minority students: An exploratory study of six high schools, *Harvard Educational Review*, 60(3), 315–340.

Mead, S. (2005) Schooling's crumbling infrastructure: Addressing a serious and unappreciated problem. Available online at http://www.edweek.org/ew/articles/2005/06/15/a40mead.h24.html

National Center for Education Statistics (1999) *Digest of education statistics, 1999* (Washington, DC, National Center for Education Statistics).

National Commission on Teaching and America's Future (1996) *What matters most: Teaching for America's future* (New York, National Commission on Teaching and America's Future).

Nieto, S. (Ed.). (2005) *Why we teach* (New York, Teachers College Press).

Noddings, N. (1992) *The challenge to care in schools: An alternative approach to education* (New York, Teachers College Press).

Orfield, G. (2001) *Schools more separate: Consequences of a decade of resegregation* (Cambridge, MA, The Civil Rights Project at Harvard University).

Rose, M. (1995) *Possible lives: The promise of public education in America* (New York, Penguin Books).

Rothstein, R. (2004) *Class and schools: Using social, economic, and educational reform to close the black/white achievement gap* (Washington, DC, Economic Policy Institute, and New York, Teachers College Press).

Sanders, W. L. & Rivers, J. C. (1996) *Cumulative and residual effects of teachers on future student academic achievement* (Knoxville, TN, University of Tennessee Value-Added Research and Assessment Center).

Valenzuela, A. (1999) *Subtractive schooling: US–Mexican youth and the politics of caring* (Albany, State University of New York Press).

Villegas, A. M. & Lucas, T. (2002) Preparing culturally responsive teachers: Rethinking the curriculum, *Journal of Teacher Education*, 53(1), 20–32.

Critical Questions

1   Is there an "achievement gap" in your school? If so, describe it. What, if anything, is being done to address it? Is it being addressed in an effective manner?

2   Have you met teachers who are successful with their students of diverse backgrounds in spite of the conditions in which the students live or the conditions of the school and community? How would you define "success"? What does this teacher (or these teachers) do that is different from others? What can you learn from this in your own context?

3   Besides the five values and qualities described in the chapter, what others would you add? Why? Give examples.

4   Write an essay about why you teach.

Activity for Your Classroom

How can you develop solidarity with, and empathy for, your students? Develop an action plan for doing so, and share it with a colleague or classmate.

Community-Based Activity and Advocacy

Reread the passage from Melinda Pellerin-Duck about how she and her students tackled the problem of library closings. With your students, think about a problem in your community that could use some advocacy. Develop a game plan, using the skills of advocacy and engagement that Pellerin-Duck described, to address the issue.

Supplementary Resources for Further Reflection and Study

Ayers, W., Ladson-Billings, G., Michie, G. & Noguera, P. A. (Eds.). (2008). *City kids, city schools: More reports from the front row.* New York: The New Press.

   With writings from youths and some of the nation's leading educators, this book provides a context for understanding the challenges and possibilities of education in the nation's cities. With stories, poems, essays, and articles, this collection provides hope about our urban schools and the children and teachers who inhabit them.

Christensen, L. (2000). *Reading, writing, and rising up: Teaching about social justice and the power of the written word.* Milwaukee, WI: Rethinking Schools.

   Written by an inspiring teacher and one of the editors of Rethinking Schools, this practical and engaging book offers essays, lesson plans, and a remarkable collection of student writing, all rooted in an unwavering focus on language arts teaching for justice.

Cowhey, M. (2006). *Black ants and Buddhists: Thinking critically and teaching differently in the primary grades.* Portland, ME: Stenhouse.

   Through engaging anecdotes based on her own experiences in her first- and second-grade classroom, teacher Mary Cowhey describes how she uses critical pedagogy with even the youngest students. Not a cookie-cutter approach with specific lesson plans, this moving and heartfelt book nevertheless includes many suggestions for becoming critical teachers.

Nieto, S. (2003). *What keeps teachers going?* New York: Teachers College Press.

   Documenting a year-long inquiry group project in which Boston high school teachers explored the question of what sustains them, this book provides compelling examples of teachers who have been in the classroom—sometimes for as long as 35 years—and why they remain.

Part IV

Praxis in the Classroom

This final section includes three chapters that provide concrete applications of a sociocultural and sociopolitical lens to teaching and learning. Using specific scenarios of five schools, Chapter 12 defines what it means to move beyond tolerance in multicultural education in terms of school policies and practices related to culture and language. Chapter 13 is a brief piece that gives suggestions for actual classroom practice when teaching students of color. Chapter 14 answers the question "What does it mean to affirm diversity in our nation's schools?" by proposing a number of recommendations for thinking critically about pedagogy, instruction, and other classroom- and school-based policies and practices.

12 Affirmation, Solidarity, and Critique

Moving Beyond Tolerance in Multicultural Education

"Tolerance" is a word commonly used when speaking about appropriate responses to difference. In fact, practicing "tolerance" is what many educators see as the best indication of a civil and respectful society. In the chapter that follows, I challenge this belief and suggest that tolerance actually represents a low level of support for differences. I submit that tolerance does little to encourage true diversity or help schools develop a multicultural perspective. If all we expect of our students is tolerance, can we ever hope that they will reach the point where they understand, respect, and affirm differences? That is the question this article seeks to answer.

By describing scenarios of various levels of support for diversity in a number of school settings, I propose an answer to this question by discussing both the conceptualization and the concrete implementation of a multicultural education that moves beyond tolerance. The chapter also suggests that implementation needs to take place not only inside the classroom but also in the school as a whole and, as such, that teachers and other educators have a significant role to play in supporting whole school reform.

Tolerance: the capacity for or the practice of recognizing and respecting the beliefs or practices of others.
—The American Heritage Dictionary, *as quoted in* Teaching Tolerance, *Spring, 1993.*

"We want our students to develop tolerance of others," says a teacher when asked what multicultural education means to her. "The greatest gift we can give our students is a tolerance for differences," is how a principal explains it. A school's mission statement might be more explicit: "Students at the Jefferson School will develop critical habits of the mind, a capacity for creativity and risk-taking, and tolerance for those different from themselves." In fact, if we were to listen to pronouncements at school board meetings, or conversations in teachers' rooms, or if we perused school handbooks, we would probably discover that when mentioned at all, multicultural education is associated more often with the term tolerance than with any other.

My purpose in this article is to challenge readers, and indeed the very way that multicultural education is practiced in schools in general, to move beyond tolerance in both conceptualization and implementation. It is my belief that a movement beyond tolerance is absolutely necessary if multicultural education is to become more than a superficial "bandaid" or a "feel-good" additive to our school curricula. I will argue that tolerance is actually a low level of multicultural support, reflecting as it does an acceptance of the status quo with but slight accommodations to difference. I will review and expand upon a model of multicultural education that I have developed elsewhere (See Sonia Nieto, *Affirming Diversity: The Sociopolitical Context of Multicultural Education*, Longman, 1992) in order to explore what multicultural education might actually look like in a school's policies and practices.

Levels of Multicultural Education Support

Multicultural education is not a unitary concept. On the contrary, it can be thought of as a range of options across a wide spectrum that includes such diverse strategies as bilingual/bicultural programs, ethnic studies courses, Afrocentric curricula, or simply the addition of a few "Holidays and Heroes" to the standard curriculum (See James A. Banks, *Teaching Strategies for Ethnic Studies*, Allyn & Bacon, 1991), just to name a few. Although all of these may be important parts of multicultural education, they represent incomplete conceptualizations and operationalizations of this complex educational reform movement. Unfortunately, however, multicultural education is often approached as if there were a prescribed script.

The most common understanding of multicultural education is that it consists largely of additive content rather than of structural changes in content and process. It is not unusual, then, to hear teachers say that they are "doing" multicultural education this year, or, as in one case that I heard, that they could not "do it" in the Spring because they had too many other things to "do." In spite of the fact that scholars and writers in multicultural education have been remarkably consistent over the years about the complexity of approaches in the field (see, especially, the analysis by Christine E. Sleeter & Carl A.Grant, "An Analysis of Multicultural Education in the United States, *Harvard Educational Review*, November, 1987), it has often been interpreted in either a simplistic or a monolithic way. It is because of this situation that I have attempted to develop a model that clarifies how various levels of multicultural education support may actually be apparent in schools.

Developing categories or models is always an inherently problematic venture, and I therefore present the following model with some hesitancy. Whenever we classify and categorize reality, we run the risk that it will be viewed as static and arbitrary, rather than as messy, complex, and contradictory, which we know it to be. Notwithstanding the value that theoretical models may have, they tend to represent information as if it were fixed and absolute. Yet we know too well that nothing happens exactly as portrayed in models and charts, much less social interactions among real people in settings such as schools. In spite of this, models or categories can be useful because they help make concrete situations more understandable and manageable. I therefore present the following model with both reluctance and hope: reluctance because it may improperly be viewed as set in stone, but hope because it may challenge teachers, administrators, and educators in general to rethink what it means to develop a multicultural perspective in their schools.

The levels in this model should be viewed as necessarily dynamic, with penetrable borders. They should be understood as "interactive," in the words of Peggy McIntosh (see her *Interactive Phases of Curricular Re-vision: A Feminist Perspective*, Wellesley College Center for Research on Women, 1983). Thus, although these levels represent "ideal" categories that are internally consistent and therefore set, the model is not meant to suggest that schools are really like this. Probably no school would be a purely "monocultural" or "tolerant" school, given the stated characteristics under each of these categories. However, these categories are used in an effort to illustrate how support for diversity is manifested in schools in a variety of ways. Because multicultural education is primarily a set of beliefs and a philosophy, rather than a set program or fixed content, this model can assist us in determining how particular school policies and practices need to change in order to embrace the diversity of our students and their communities.

The four levels to be considered are: tolerance; acceptance; respect; and, finally, affirmation, solidarity, and critique. Before going on to consider how multicultural education is manifested in schools that profess these philosophical orientations, it is first helpful to explore the antithesis of multicultural education, namely, monocultural education, because without this analysis we have nothing with which to compare it.

In the scenarios that follow, we go into five schools that epitomize different levels of multicultural education. All are schools with growing cultural diversity in their student populations; differences include staff backgrounds, attitudes, and preparation, as well as curriculum and pedagogy. In our visits, we see how the curriculum, interactions among students, teachers, and parents, and other examples of attention to diversity are either apparent or lacking. We see how students of different backgrounds might respond to the policies and practices around them. (In another paper entitled "Creating Possibilities: Educating Latino Students in Massachusetts, in *The Education of Latino Students in Massachusetts: Policy and Research Implications*, published by the Gaston Institute for Latino Policy and Development in Boston, which I co-edited with R. Rivera, I developed scenarios of schools that would provide different levels of support specifically for Latino students.)

Monocultural Education

Monocultural education describes a situation in which school structures, policies, curricula, instructional materials, and even pedagogical strategies are primarily representative of only the dominant culture. In most United States schools, it can be defined as "the way things are."

We will begin our tour in a "monocultural school" that we'll call the George Washington Middle School. When we walk in, we see a sign that says "NO UNAUTHORIZED PERSONS ARE ALLOWED IN THE SCHOOL. ALL VISITORS MUST REPORT DIRECTLY TO THE PRINCIPAL'S OFFICE." The principal, assistant principal, and counselor are all European American males, although the school's population is quite diverse, with large numbers of African American, Puerto Rican, Arab American, Central American, Korean, and Vietnamese students. As we walk down the hall, we see a number of bulletin boards. On one, the coming Christmas holiday is commemorated; on another, the P.T.O.'s bake sale is announced; and on a third, the four basic food groups are listed, with reference to only those foods generally considered to be "American."

The school is organized into 45-minutes periods of such courses as U.S. history, English, math, science, music appreciation, art, and physical education. In the U. S. history class, students learn of the proud exploits, usually through wars and conquest, of primarily European American males. They learn virtually nothing about the contributions, perspectives, or talents of women or those outside the cultural mainstream. U.S. slavery is mentioned briefly in relation to the Civil War, but African Americans are missing thereafter. In English class, the students have begun their immersion in the "canon," reading works almost entirely written by European and European American males, although a smattering of women and African American (but no Asian, Latino, or American Indian) authors are included in the newest anthology. In music appreciation class, students are exposed to what is called "classical music," that is, European classical music, but the "classical" music of societies in Asia, Africa, and Latin America is nowhere to be found. In art classes, students may learn about the art work of famous European and European American artists, and occasionally about the "crafts" and "artifacts" of other cultures and societies mostly from the Third World.

Teachers at the George Washington Middle School are primarily European American women who have had little formal training in multicultural approaches or perspectives. They are proud of the fact that they are "color-blind," that is, that they see no differences among their students, treating them all the same. Of course, this does not extend to tracking, which they generally perceive to be in the interest of teaching all students to the best of their abilities. Ability grouping is a standard practice at the George Washington Middle School. There are four distinct levels of ability, from "talented and gifted" to "remedial." I.Q. tests are used to detemmine student placement and intellectually superior students are placed in "Talented and Gifted" programs, and in advanced levels of math, science, English, and social studies. Only these top students have the option of taking a foreign language. The top levels consist of overwhelmingly European American and Asian American students, but the school rationalizes that this is due to either the native intelligence of these students, or to the fact that they have a great deal more intellectual stimulation and encouragement in their homes. Thus, teachers have learned to expect excellent work from their top students, but little of students in their low-level classes, who they often see as lazy and disruptive.

Students who speak a language other than English as their native language are either placed in regular classrooms where they will learn to "sink or swim" or in "NE" (non-English) classes, where they are drilled in English all day and where they will remain until they learn English sufficiently well to perform in the regular classroom. In addition, parents are urged to speak to their children only in English at home. Their native language, whether Spanish, Vietnamese, or Korean, is perceived as a handicap to their learning, and as soon as they forget it, they can get on with the real job of learning.

Although incidents of racism have occurred in the George Washington Middle School, they have been taken care of quietly and privately. For example, when racial slurs have been used, students have been admonished not to say them. When fights between children of different ethnic groups take place, the assistant principal has insisted that race or ethnicity has nothing to do with them; "kids will be kids" is the way he describes these incidents.

What exists in the George Washington Middle School is a monocultural environment with scant reference to the experiences of others from largely subordinated cultural groups. Little attention is paid to student diversity, and the school curriculum is generally presented as separate from the community in which it is located. In addition, "dangerous" topics such as racism, sexism, and homophobia are seldom discussed, and reality is represented as finished and static. In summary, the George Washington School is a depressingly familiar scenario because it reflects what goes on in most schools in American society.

Tolerance

How might a school characterized by "tolerance" be different from a monocultural school? It is important here to mention the difference between the denotation and the connotation of words. According to the dictionary definition given at the beginning of this article, tolerance is hardly a value that one could argue with. After all, what is wrong with "recognizing and respecting the beliefs or practices of others"? On the contrary, this is a quintessential part of developing a multicultural perspective. (*Teaching Tolerance*, a journal developed by the Southern Anti-Poverty Law Project, has no doubt been developed with this perspective in mind, and my critique here of tolerance is in no way meant to criticize this wonderful classroom and teacher resource.)

Nevertheless, the connotation of words is something else entirely. When we think of what tolerance means in practice, we have images of a grudging but somewhat distasteful acceptance. To tolerate differences means that they are endured, not necessarily embraced. In fact, this level of support for multicultural education stands on shaky ground because what is tolerated today can too easily be rejected tomorrow. A few examples will help illustrate this point.

Our "tolerant" school is the Brotherhood Middle School. Here, differences are understood to be the inevitable burden of a culturally pluralistic society. A level up from a "color-blind" monocultural school, the "tolerant" school accepts differences but only if they can be modified. Thus, they are accepted, but because the ultimate goal is assimilation, differences in language and culture are replaced as quickly as possible. This ideology is reflected in the physical environment, the attitudes of staff, and the curriculum to which students are exposed.

When we enter the Brotherhood School, there are large signs in English welcoming visitors, although there are no staff on hand who can communicate with the families of the growing Cambodian student population. One prominently-placed bulletin board proudly portrays the winning essays of this year's writing contest with the theme of "Why I am proud to be an American." The winners, a European American sixth grader and a Vietnamese seventh grader, write in their essays about the many opportunities given to all people in our country, no matter what their race, ethnicity, or gender. Another bulletin board boasts the story of Rosa Parks, portrayed as a woman who was too tired to give up her seat on the bus, thus serving as a catalyst for the modern civil rights movement. (The Fall 1993 issue of *Multicultural Education* includes a powerful example of how people such as Rosa Parks have been de-contextualized to better fit in with the U.S. mainstream conception of individual rather than collective struggle, thus adding little to children's understanding of institutionalized discrimination on our society; see "The Myth of 'Rosa Parks the Tired;'" by Herbert Kohl, pages 6–10, in which Kohl reports that based on his research, most stories used in American schools present Rosa Parks simply as "Rosa Parks the Tired.")

Nevertheless, a number of important structural changes are taking place at the Brotherhood School. An experiment has recently begun in which the sixth and seventh graders are in "family" groupings, and these are labeled by family names such as the Jones family, the Smith family, and the Porter family. Students remain together as a family in their major subjects (English, social studies, math, and science) and there is no ability tracking in these classes. Because their teachers have a chance to meet and plan together daily, they are more readily able to develop integrated curricula. In fact, once in a while, they even combine classes so that they can team-teach and their students remain at a task for an hour and a half rather than the usual three quarters of an hour. The students seem to like this arrangement, and have done some interesting work in their study of Washington, D.C. For instance, they used geometry to learn how the city was designed, and have written to their congressional representatives to ask how bills become laws. Parents are involved in fund-raising for an upcoming trip to the capital, where students plan to interview a number of their local legislators.

The curriculum at the Brotherhood School has begun to reflect some of the changes that a multicultural society demands. Students are encouraged to study a foreign language (except, of course, for those who already speak one; they are expected to learn English and in the process, they usually forget their native language). In addition, a number of classes have added activities on women, African Americans, and American Indians. Last year, for instance, Martin Luther King Day was celebrated by having all students watch a video of the "I Have a Dream" speech.

The majority of changes in the curriculum have occurred in the social studies and English departments, but the music teacher has also begun to add a more international flavor to her repertoire, and the art classes recently went to an exhibit of the work of Romare Bearden. This year, a "multicultural teacher" has been added to the staff. She meets with all students in the school, seeing each group once a week for one period. Thus far, she has taught students about Chinese New Year, *Kwanzaa*, *Ramadan*, and *Dia de los Reyes*. She is getting ready for the big multicultural event of the year, Black History Month. She hopes to work with other teachers to bring in guest speakers, show films about the civil rights movement, and have an art contest in which students draw what the world would be like if Dr. King's dream of equality became a reality.

Students who speak a language other than English at the Brotherhood School are placed in special E.S.L. classes, where they are taught English as quickly, but sensitively, as possible. For instance, while they are encouraged to speak to one another in English, they are allowed to use their native language, but only as a last resort. The feeling is that if they use it more often, it will become a "crutch." In any event, the E.S.L. teachers are not required to speak a language other than English; in fact, being bilingual is even considered a handicap because students might expect them to use their other language.

The principal of the Brotherhood School has made it clear that racism will not be tolerated here. Name-calling and the use of overtly racist and sexist textbooks and other materials are discouraged. Recently, some teachers attended a workshop on strategies for dealing with discrimination in the classroom. Some of those who attended expect to make some changes in how they treat students from different backgrounds.

Most teachers at the Brotherhood School have had little professional preparation to deal with the growing diversity of the student body. They like and genuinely want to help their students, but have made few changes in their curricular or instructional practices. For them, "being sensitive" to their students is what multicultural education should be about, not overhauling the curriculum. Thus, they acknowledge student differences in language, race, gender, and social class, but still cannot quite figure out why some students are more successful than others. Although they would like to think not, they wonder if genetics or poor parental attitudes about education have something to do with it. If not, what can explain these great discrepancies?

Acceptance

Acceptance is the next level of supporting diversity. It implies that differences are acknowledged and their importance is neither denied nor belittled. It is at this level that we see substantial movement toward multicultural education. A look at how some of the school's policies and practices might change is indicative of this movement.

The name of our school is the Rainbow Middle School. As we enter, we see signs in English, Spanish, and Haitian Creole, the major languages besides English spoken by students and their families. The principal of the Rainbow School is Dr. Belinda Clayton, the first African-American principal ever appointed. She has designated her school as a "multicultural building," and has promoted a number of professional development opportunities for teachers that focus on diversity. These include seminars on diverse learning styles, bias-free assessment, and bilingual education. In addition, she has hired not only Spanish- and Haitian Creole-speaking teachers for the bilingual classrooms, but has also diversified the staff in the "regular" program.

Bulletin boards outside the principal's office display the pictures of the "Students of the Month." This month's winners are Rodney Thomas, a sixth-grader who has excelled in art, Neleida Cortes, a seventh-grade student in the bilingual program, and Melissa Newton, an eighth-grader in the special education program. All three were given a special luncheon by the principal and their homeroom teachers. Another bulletin board focuses on "Festivals of Light" and features information about Chanukah, Kwanzaa, and Christmas, with examples of Las Posadas in Mexico and Saint Lucia's Day in Sweden.

The curriculum at the Rainbow Middle School has undergone some changes to reflect the growing diversity of the student body. English classes include more choices of African-American, Irish, Jewish, and Latino literature written in English. Some science and math teachers have begun to make reference to famous scientists and mathematicians from a variety of backgrounds. In one career-studies class, a number of parents have been invited to speak about their job and the training they had to receive in order to get those positions. All students are encouraged to study a foreign language, and choices have been expanded to include Spanish, French, German, and Mandarin Chinese.

Tracking has been eliminated in all but the very top levels at the Rainbow School. All students have the opportunity to learn algebra, although some are still counseled out of this option because their teachers believe it will be too difficult for them. The untracked classes seem to be a hit with the students, and preliminary results have shown a slight improvement among all students. Some attempts have been made to provide flexible scheduling, with one day a week devoted to entire "learning blocks" where students work on a special project. One group recently engaged in an in-depth study of the elderly in their community. They learned about services available to them, and they touched on poverty and lack of health care for many older Americans. As a result of this study, the group has added a community service component to the class; this involves going to the local Senior Center during their weekly learning block to read with the elderly residents.

Haitian and Spanish-speaking students are tested and, if found to be more proficient in their native language, are placed in transitional bilingual education programs. Because of lack of space in the school, the bilingual programs are located in the basement, near the boiler room. Here, students are taught the basic curriculum in their native language while learning English as a second language during one period of the day with an ESL specialist. Most ESL teachers are also fluent in a language other than English, helping them understand the process of acquiring a second language. The bilingual program calls for students to be "mainstreamed" (placed in what is called a "regular classroom") as quickly as possible, with a limit of three years on the outside. In the meantime, they are segregated from their peers for most of the day, but have some classes with English-speaking students, including physical education, art, and music. As they proceed through the program and become more fluent in English, they are "exited" out for some classes, beginning with math and social studies. While in the bilingual program, students' native cultures are sometimes used as the basis of the curriculum, and they learn about the history of their people. There is, for instance, a history course on the Caribbean that is offered to both groups in their native languages. Nevertheless, neither Haitian nor Latino students who are not in the bilingual program, nor students of other backgrounds, have access to these courses.

Incidents of racism and other forms of discrimination are beginning to be faced at the Rainbow Middle School. Principal Clayton deals with these carefully, calling in the offending students as well as their parents, and she makes certain that students understand the severe consequences for name-calling or scapegoating others. Last year, one entire day was devoted to "diversity" and regular classes were canceled while students attended workshops focusing on discrimination, the importance of being sensitive to others, and the influence on U.S. history of many different immigrants. They have also hosted a "Multicultural Fair" and published a cookbook with recipes donated by many different parents.

The Rainbow Middle School is making steady progress in accepting the great diversity of its students. They have decided that perhaps assimilation should not be the goal, and have eschewed the old idea of the "melting pot." In its place, they have the "salad bowl" metaphor, in which all students bring something special that need not be reconstituted or done away with.

Respect

Respect is the next level of multicultural education support. It implies admiration and high esteem for diversity. When differences are respected, they are used as the basis for much of what goes on in schools. Our next scenario describes what this might look like.

The Sojourner Truth Middle School is located in a mid-size town with a changing population. There is a fairly large African-American population with a growing number of students of Cape Verdean and Vietnamese background, and the school staff reflects these changes, including teachers, counselors, and special educators of diverse backgrounds. There is, for example, a Vietnamese speech pathologist, and his presence has helped to alleviate the concerns of some teachers that the special needs of the Vietnamese children were not being addressed. He has found that while some students do indeed have speech problems, others do not, but teachers' unfamiliarity with the Vietnamese language made it difficult for them to know this.

When we enter the Sojourner Truth Middle School, we are greeted by a parent volunteer. She gives us printed material in all the languages represented in the school, and invites us to the parents' lounge for coffee, tea, and danish. We are then encouraged to walk-around and explore the school. Bulletin boards boast of students' accomplishments in the Spanish Spelling Bee, the local *Jeopardy*

Championship, and the W.E.B. DuBois Club of African-American history. It is clear from the children's pictures that there is wide participation of many students in all of these activities. The halls are abuzz with activity as students go from one class to another, and most seem eager and excited by school.

Professional development is an important principle at the Sojourner Truth Middle School. Teachers, counselors, and other staff are encouraged to take courses at the local university and to keep up with the literature in their field. To make this more feasible, the staff gets released time weekly to get together. As a consequence, the curriculum has been through tremendous changes. Teachers have formed committees to develop their curriculum. The English department decided to use its time to have reading and discussion groups with some of the newly available multicultural literature with which they were unfamiliar. As a result, they have revamped the curriculum into such overarching themes as coming of age, immigration, change and continuity, and individual and collective responsibility. They have found that it is easier to select literature to reflect themes such as these, and the literature is by its very nature multicultural. For instance, for the theme of individual and collective responsibility they have chosen stories of varying difficulty, including *The Diary of Anne Frank, Bridge to Terabithia* (by Katherine Paterson), *Morning Girl* (by Michael Dorris), and *Let the Circle be Unbroken* (by Mildred D. Taylor), among others. The English teachers have in turn invited the history, art, and science departments to join them in developing some integrated units with these themes. Teachers from the art and music departments have agreed to work with them, and have included lessons on Vietnamese dance, Guatemalan weaving, Jewish Klezmer music, and American Indian storytelling as examples of individual and collective responsibility in different communities.

Other changes are apparent in the curriculum as well, for it has become more antiracist and honest. When studying World War II, students learn about the heroic role played by the United States, and also about the Holocaust, in which not only six million Jews, but millions of others, including Gypsies, gays and lesbians, and many dissenters of diverse backgrounds, were exterminated. They also learn, for the first time, about the internment of over a hundred thousand Japanese and Japanese Americans on our own soil.

It has become "safe" to talk about such issues as the crucial role of labor in U.S. history and the part played by African Americans in freeing themselves from bondage, both subjects thought too "sensitive" to be included previously. This is one reason why the school was renamed for a woman known for her integrity and courage.

The Sojourner Truth Middle School has done away with all ability grouping. When one goes into a classroom, it is hard to believe that students of all abilities are learning together because the instruction level seems to be so high. Upon closer inspection, it becomes apparent that there are high expectations for all students. Different abilities are accommodated by having some students take more time than others, providing cooperative groups in which students change roles and responsibilities, and through ongoing dialogue among all students.

Students who speak a language other than English are given the option of being in a "maintenance bilingual program," that is, a program based on using their native language throughout their schooling, not just for three years. Changing the policy that only students who could not function in English were eligible for bilingual programs, this school has made the program available to those who speak English in addition to their native language. Parents and other community members who speak these languages are invited in to classes routinely to talk about their lives, jobs, or families, or to tell stories or share experiences. Students in the bilingual program are not, however, segregated from their peers all day, but join them for a number of academic classes.

Teachers and other staff members at this middle school have noticed that incidents of name-calling and interethnic hostility have diminished greatly since the revised curriculum was put into place. Perhaps more students see themselves in the curriculum and feel less angry about their invisibility; perhaps more teachers have developed an awareness and appreciation for their students' diversity while learning about it; perhaps the more diverse staff is the answer; or maybe it's because the community feels more welcome in the school. Whatever it is, the Sojourner Truth Middle School has developed an environment in which staff and students are both expanding their ways of looking at the world.

Affirmation, Solidarity, and Critique

Affirmation, solidarity, and critique is based on the premise that the most powerful learning results when students work and struggle with one another, even if it is sometimes difficult and challenging. It begins with the assumption that the many differences that students and their families represent are embraced and accepted as legitimate vehicles for learning, and that these are then extended. What makes this level different from the others is that conflict is not avoided, but rather accepted as an inevitable part of learning. Because multicultural education at this level is concerned with equity and social justice, and because the basic values of different groups are often diametrically opposed, conflict is bound to occur.

Affirmation, solidarity, and critique is also based on understanding that culture is not a fixed or unchangeable artifact, and is therefore subject to critique. Passively accepting the status quo of any culture is thus inconsistent with this level of multicultural education; simply substituting one myth for another contradicts its basic assumptions because no group is inherently superior or more heroic than any other. As eloquently expressed by Mary Kalantzis and Bill Cope in their 1990 work *The Experience of Multicultural Education in Australia: Six Case Studies*, "Multicultural education, to be effective, needs to be more active. It needs to consider not just the pleasure of diversity but more fundamental issues that arise as different groups negotiate community and the basic issues of material life in the same space—a process that equally might generate conflict and pain."

Multicultural education without critique may result in cultures remaining at the romantic or exotic stage. If students are to transcend their own cultural experience in order to understand the differences of others, they need to go through a process of reflection and critique of their cultures and those of others. This process of critique, however, begins with a solid core of solidarity with others who are different from themselves. When based on true respect, critique is not only necessary but in fact healthy.

The Arturo Schomburg Middle School is located in a mid-size city with a very mixed population of Puerto Ricans, Salvadoreans, American Indians, Polish Americans, Irish Americans, Chinese Americans, Philippinos, and African Americans. The school was named for a Black Puerto Rican scholar who devoted his life to exploring the role of Africans in the Americas, in the process challenging the myth he had been told as a child in Puerto Rico that Africans had "no culture."

The school's logo, visible above the front door, is a huge tapestry made by the students, and it symbolizes a different model of multicultural education from that of either the "melting pot" or the "salad bowl." According to a publication of the National Association of State Boards of Education (*The American Tapestry: Educating a Nation*), "A tapestry is a handwoven textile. When examined from the back, it may simply appear to be a motley group of threads. But when reversed, the threads work together to depict a picture of structure and beauty" (p. 1). According to Adelaide Sanford, one of the study group members who wrote this publication, a tapestry also symbolizes, through its knots, broken threads, and seeming jumble of colors and patterns on the back, the tensions, conflicts, and dilemmas that a society needs to work out. This spirit of both collaboration and struggle is evident in the school.

When we enter the Schomburg Middle School, the first thing we notice is a banner proclaiming the school's motto: LEARN, REFLECT, QUESTION, AND WORK TO MAKE THE WORLD A BETTER PLACE. This is the message that reverberates throughout the school. Participation is another theme that is evident, and the main hall contains numerous pictures of students in classrooms, community service settings, and extracurricular activities. Although housed in a traditional school building, the school has been transformed into a place where all children feel safe and are encouraged to learn to the highest levels of learning. While there are typical classrooms of the kind that are immediately recognizable to us, the school also houses centers that focus on specific areas of learning. There is, for instance, a studio where students can be found practicing traditional Philippino dance and music, as well as European ballet, and modern American dance, among others. Outside, there is a large garden that is planted, cared for, and harvested by the students and faculty. The vegetables are used by the cafeteria staff in preparing meals and they have noticed a marked improvement in the eating habits of the children since the menu was changed to reflect a healthier and more ethnically diverse menu.

We are welcomed into the school by staff people who invite us to explore the many different classrooms and other learning centers. Those parents who are available during the day can be found assisting in classrooms, in the Parent's Room working on art projects or computer classes, or attending workshops by other parents or teachers on topics ranging from cross-cultural child-rearing to ESL. The bulletin boards are ablaze with color and include a variety of languages, displaying student work from critical essays on what it means to be an American to art projects that celebrate the talents of many of the students. Learning is going on everywhere, whether in classrooms or in small-group collaborative projects in halls.

What might the classrooms look like in this school? For one, they are character-ized by tremendous diversity. Tracking and special education, as we know them, have been eliminated at the Schomburg Middle School. Students with special needs are taught along with all others, although they are sometimes separated for small-group instruction with students not classified as having special needs. All children are considered "talented" and special classes are occasionally organized for those who excel in dance, mathematics, poetry, or science. No interested students are excluded from any of these offerings. Furthermore, all students take algebra and geometry, and special coaching sessions are available before, after, and during school hours for these and other subjects.

Classes are flexible, with an interdisciplinary curriculum and team-teaching, resulting in sessions that sometimes last as long as three hours. The physical environment in classrooms is varied: some are organized with round work tables, others have traditional desks, and still others have scant furniture to allow for more movement. Class size also varies from small groups to large, depending on the topic at hand. Needless to say, scheduling at this school is a tremendous and continuing challenge, but faculty and students are committed to this more flexible arrangement and willing to allow for the daily problems that it may cause.

There are no "foreign languages" at the Schomburg Middle school, nor is there, strictly speaking, a bilingual program. Rather, the entire school is multilingual, and all students learn at least a second language in addition to their native language. This means that students are not segregated by language, but instead work in bilingual settings where two languages are used for instruction. At pre-sent, the major languages used are English, Spanish, and Tagalog, representing the most common languages spoken by this school's community. It is not unusual to see students speaking these languages in classrooms, the hallways, or the playgrounds, even among those for whom English is a native language.

Students at the Schomburg Middle School seem engaged, engrossed, and excited about learning. They have been involved in a number of innovative long-range projects that have resulted from the interdisciplinary curriculum. For instance, working with a Chinese-American artist in residence, they wrote, directed, and produced a play focusing on the "Know-Nothing" Movement in U.S. history that resulted in, among other things, the Chinese Exclusion Act of 1882. In preparation for the play, they read a great deal and did extensive research. For example, they contacted the Library of Congress for information on primary sources and reviewed newspapers and magazines from the period to get a sense of the climate that led to Nativism. They also designed and sewed all the costumes and sets. In addition, they interviewed recent immigrants of many backgrounds, and found that they had a range of experiences from positive to negative in their new country. On the day of the play, hundreds of parents and other community members attended. Students also held a debate on the pros and cons of continued immigration, and received up-to-date information concerning immigration laws from their congressional representative.

The curriculum at the Schomburg Middle School is dramatically different from the George Washington School, the first school we visited. Teachers take very seriously their responsibility of teaching complexity. Thus, students have learned that there are many sides to every story, and that in order to make informed decisions, they need as much information as they can get. Whether in English, science, art, or any other class, students have been encouraged to be critical of every book, newspaper, curriculum, or piece of information by asking questions such as: Who wrote the book? Who's missing in this story? Why? Using questions such as these as a basis, they are learning that every story has a point of view and that every point of view is at best partial and at worst distorted. They are also learning that their own backgrounds, rich and important as they may be, have limitations that can lead to parochial perceptions. Most of all, even at this age, students are learning that every topic is fraught with difficulties and they are wrestling with issues as diverse as homelessness, global warming, and how the gender expectations of different cultures might limit opportunities for girls. Here, nothing is taboo as a topic of discussion as long as it is approached with respect and in a climate of caring.

What this means for teachers is that they have had to become learners along with their students. They approach each subject with curiosity and an open mind, and during the school day they have time to study, meet with colleagues, and plan their curriculum accordingly. Professional development here means not only attending courses at a nearby university, but collaborating with colleagues in study groups that last anywhere from half a day to several months. These provide a forum in which teachers can carefully study relevant topics or vexing problems. Some of these study groups have focused on topics such as Reconstruction and the history of the Philippines, to educational issues such as cooperative learning and diverse cognitive styles.

Especially noteworthy at this school is that multicultural education is not separated from education; that is, all education is by its very nature multicultural. English classes use literature written by a wide variety of people from countries where English is spoken. This has resulted in these classes becoming not only multicultural, but international as well. Science classes do not focus on contributions made by members of specific ethnic groups, but have in fact been transformed to consider how science itself is conceptualized, valued, and practiced by those who have traditionally been outside the scientific mainstream. Issues such as AIDS education, healing in different cultures, and scientific racism have all been the subject of study.

One of the major differences between this school and the others we visited has to do with its governance structure. There is a Schomburg School Congress consisting of students, faculty, parents, and other community members, and it has wide decision-making powers, from selecting the principal to determining reasonable and equitable disciplinary policies and practices. Students are elected by their classmates and, although at the beginning these were little more than popularity contests, in recent months it has been clear that students are beginning to take this responsibility seriously. This is probably because they are being taken seriously by the adults in the group. For instance, when students in one class decided that they wanted to plan a class trip to a neighboring city to coincide with their study of toxic wastes and the environment, they were advised to do some preliminary planning: what would be the educational objectives of such a trip? how long would it take? how much would it cost? After some research and planning, they presented their ideas to the Congress and a fund-raising plan that included students, parents, and community agencies was started.

The Schomburg School is a learning center that is undergoing important changes every day. As teachers discover the rich talents that all students bring to school, they develop high expectation for them all. The climate that exists in this school is one of possibility, because students' experiences are used to build on their learning and expand their horizons. Students in turn are realizing that while their experiences are important and unique, they are only one experience of many. A new definition of "American" is being forged at this school, one that includes everybody. Above all, learning here is exciting, engrossing, inclusive, and evolving.

Conclusion

One might well ask how realistic these scenarios are, particularly the last one. Could a school such as this really exist? Isn't this just wishful thinking? What about the reality of bond issues rejected by voters?, of teachers woefully unprepared to deal with the diversity in their classrooms?, of universities that do little more than offer stale "Mickey Mouse" courses?, of schools with no pencils, paper, and chalk, much less computers and video cameras?, of rampant violence in streets, homes, and schools?, of drugs and crime?, of parents who are barely struggling to keep their families together and can spare precious little time to devote to volunteering at school?

These are all legitimate concerns that our society needs to face, and they remind us that schools need to be understood within their sociopolitical contexts. That is, our schools exist in a society in which social and economic stratification are facts of life, where competition is taught over caring, and where the early sorting that takes place in educational settings often lasts a lifetime. Developing schools with a multicultural perspective is not easy; if it were, they would be everywhere. But schools with a true commitment to diversity, equity, and high levels of learning are difficult to achieve precisely because the problems they face are pervasive and seemingly impossible to solve. Although the many problems raised above are certainly daunting, the schools as currently organized are simply not up to the challenge. In the final analysis, if we believe that all students deserve to learn at the very highest levels, then we need a vision of education that will help achieve this end.

The scenarios above, however, are not simply figments of my imagination. As you read through the scenarios, you probably noticed bits and pieces of your own school here and there. However, because the "monocultural school" is the one with which we are most familiar, and unfortunately even comfortable, the other scenarios might seem far-fetched or unrealistic. Although they are ideal in the sense that they are not true pictures of specific schools, these scenarios never-theless describe possibilities because they all exist to some degree in our schools today. These are not pie-in-the-sky visions, but composites of what goes on in schools every day. As such, they provide building blocks for how we might go about transforming schools. In fact, were we to design schools based on the ideals that our society has always espoused, they would no doubt come close to the last scenario.

It is not, however, a monolithic model or one that can develop overnight. The participants in each school need to develop their own vision so that step by step, with incremental changes, schools become more multicultural, and thus more inclusive and more exciting places for learning. If we believe that young people deserve to be prepared with skills for living ethical and productive lives in an increasingly diverse and complex world, then we need to transform schools so that they not only teach what have been called "the basics," but also provide an apprenticeship in democracy and social justice. It is unfair to expect our young people to develop an awareness and respect for democracy if they have not experienced it, and it is equally unrealistic to expect them to be able to function in a pluralistic society if all we give them are skills for a monocultural future. This is our challenge in the years ahead: to conquer the fear of change and imagine how we might create exciting possibilities for all students in all schools.

Critical Questions

1   Do you agree with the assertion that "tolerance" is a low level of support for multicultural education? Why or why not? Explain.
2   Using the levels described in the scenarios in this article, where would you place your school? Does it fit neatly into any of the levels? Why or why not? Give examples.
3   If you were to design a school that promoted diversity as you believe it should be promoted, what would it look like? Write a description of it.
4   Do you think the scenarios described above are realistic? If not, what would make them more so?

Activities for Your Classroom

1   Think about your classroom and what you can do within your own four walls to make it more responsive to higher levels of multicultural education. Make a list of changes you can begin to implement. Next to each, describe what resources you need, how you can get them, and a reasonable timeline for implementation. Begin implementing one of the ideas you have and report back to the other participants in the course about your progress.
2   Review some of your other ideas, and follow the same process as above. At the end of the semester, figure out how many of these ideas you have put into practice. Have they had an impact on the climate of your classroom? on student enthusiasm and learning? on family involvement? on your own thoughts on diversity?

Community-Based Activity and Advocacy

If there is a site-based management team in your school, consider becoming a member of it. Develop alliances with other teachers or parents who have expressed support for diversity. Bring up with the group some of the changes you considered for your own classroom and suggest how they might be implemented at the school level. Think about starting small, with incremental changes. Document your success with these changes, and reflect on why things have or have not worked. How might you change your approach in the future?

Supplementary Resources for Further Reflection and Study

Darling-Hammond, L. (2001). *The right to learn: A blueprint for creating schools that work*. San Francisco: Jossey-Bass.

In this book, Darling-Hammond emphasizes the process of learning rather than the pervasiveness of testing. She believes that what is wrong with public schools today can, in great measure, be attributed to bureaucratization that leaves teachers with little time for teaching. American children do worse than students from other industrialized nations, Darling-Hammond suggests, because the American educational system is predicated on a "factory model" that processes students instead of teaching them.

Delpit, Lisa (1988). The silenced dialogue: Power and pedagogy in educating other people's children. *Harvard Educational Review, 58* (3), 280–298.

In this classic article, Delpit argues that as a first step toward a more just society, teachers need to teach all students, particularly Black and poor children, the explicit and implicit rules of power.

Entin, J. Rosen, R. C., & Vogt, L. (Eds.). (2008). *Controversies in the classroom: A Radical Teacher reader*. New York: Teachers College Press.

A compilation of some of the most thoughtful and inspiring articles published in the journal *Radical Teacher* during the past 15 years, this book includes pieces by well-known education reformers, researchers, classroom teachers, and others interested in promoting a democratic vision of public education.

Ladson-Billings, G. (1994). *The dreamkeepers: Successful teachers of African American children*. San Francisco, CA: Jossey-Bass.

This highly readable book documents the characteristics and teaching practices of teachers who are especially effective with African American students. The last chapter, "Making Dreams into Reality," describes the Paul Robeson Elementary School, the author's vision of a culturally responsive learning environment.

13 Nice is Not Enough

Defining Caring for Students of Color

As the following brief article suggests, caring for students of color must go beyond being "nice" to them. It is not enough to be kind and sympathetic when kindness and sympathy are located within systems of inequality and oppression. Sometimes going beyond being nice means just the opposite of what one might define as "nice." That is, it means having high expectations and rigorous standards, pushing students further than they might believe they can go, and supporting them as they try to accomplish their goals. Going beyond niceness also means creating classroom and school environments that are defined by deep confidence in students, acknowledgment that they have talents and strengths, and respect for their identities and their communities.

Nice is Not Enough: Defining Caring for Students of Color

"But I'm a nice guy," the young man sitting across from me said plaintively, attempting to explain why all the talk about racism in education in our class was so unsettling to him. He would soon begin his teaching career, no doubt in an urban school, and he believed that being "nice" would see him through the challenges of teaching young people with whom he had had very little experience or connection until then.

This scene took place fifteen years ago, but it was not the first time, and it certainly would not be the last, that a student had come into my office to try to shed the guilt he was feeling about being white and to reaffirm his sense of being a nice person who was trying to help students of color. In my thirty years of teaching teachers and prospective teachers, this scene has been repeated countless times, sometimes accompanied by hand-wringing, sometimes by tears, often by frustration or remorse. Usually the feelings students describe are brought on by readings and discussions in my classes in multicultural education, which convey a message that is hard for some of them to hear: that, regardless of our individual personalities, we are all situated within a racially unequal structure that we often unwittingly perpetuate. When confronting stark realities they have never thought about, or have chosen not to see, many white students experience palpable pain and disconcerting disequilibrium. My greatest challenge as a teacher educator has been to help white students and students of color understand that racism is not simply a personal attitude or individual disposition and that feeling guilty or "being nice" are not enough to combat racism. Racism involves the systemic failure of people and institutions to care for students of color on an ongoing basis. Although most of my students who experience guilt and frustration about their role in an unequally caring structure are white, I include student teachers of color in my analysis. Being a person of color does not insulate us from biased perceptions and actions toward those whose backgrounds are unlike our own. Latinos may harbor biased views of African Americans, African Americans may have prejudiced views of Cambodians, and so on. People can even harbor biased views about their own group.

Caring within a structure plagued by inequality takes multiple forms, and at some moments when we think we are caring for students of color we actually are harming them because we are failing to counter a social structure that treats them unequally. Mary Ginley, a gifted white teacher, articulated this idea beautifully in a journal entry for one of my classes:

> School is a foreign land to most kids (where else in the world would you spend time circling answers and filling in the blanks?), but the more distant a child's culture and language are from the culture and language of school, the more at risk that child is. A warm, friendly, helpful teacher is nice but it isn't enough. We have plenty of warm friendly teachers who tell the kids nicely to forget their Spanish and ask mommy and daddy to speak to them in English at home; who give them easier tasks so they won't feel badly when the work becomes difficult; who never learn about what life is like at home or what they eat or what music they like or what stories they have been told or what their history is. Instead, we smile and give them a hug and tell them to eat our food and listen to our stories and dance to our music. We teach them to read with our words and wonder why it's so hard for them. We ask them to sit quietly and we tell them what's important and what they must know to "get ready for the next grade." And we never ask them who they are and where they want to go.[1]

As this reflection makes clear, teachers can participate in practices of racism— that is, practices that deny students of color equal opportunities along racial lines—even when they think they are individually being "nice." In the examples Ginley provides, "nice" educators sometimes convey, even unwittingly, a deep disdain and disrespect for families by suggesting that home cultural values have no place in school. I have seen numerous cases in which "nice" teachers expected less of their students of color, believing that by refusing to place the same rigorous demands on their students of color as they do on white students, they were making accommodations for the students' difficult home life, poverty, or lack of English-language proficiency. Such "accommodations" may unintentionally give students the message that teachers believe these students are incapable of learning.

Even as we purport to care about all students equally, we also often tolerate policies in our districts and schools that harm students of color, especially those who are poor and those for whom English is a second language: unequal resources, punitive high-stakes testing, and rigid ability-group tracking are some key examples.[2] Racism in these forms involves failing to ensure that institutions care for students. The late Meyer Weinberg (1982), a historian who studied school desegregation, defined racism as a system of privilege and penalty. According to this definition, a student is rewarded or punished in education (as in housing, employment, health, and so on) by the simple fact of belonging to a particular racialized group, regardless of his or her individual merits or faults. Within such an unequal system, even "nice" people can accept and even distribute these unfair rewards and punishments. This idea is difficult, even wrenching, for many people to accept.

I have utilized several strategies to get pre-service teachers to consider and debate how, despite their best intentions, they might actually participate in various institutional practices of not caring for students. To ensure that their institutions *are* caring for students, educators can begin to ask one another, in so many words, what it *means* to "care" for their student body. Participants should make this discussion of caring safe, but not necessarily personally comfortable; participants will need to struggle with hard ideas about themselves and about institutions.

To help teachers explore particularly critically what sort of caring assists students of color struggling within unequal systems, I ask them to do an in-depth case study of a student (for guidelines, see Nieto & Bode, 2008, Resource list). Looking carefully at an individual member of a group dispels stereotypes about the needs of all people from particular backgrounds, while at the same time giving teachers a more complete understanding of how group membership affects the contexts in which students live. I also have them read "coming of age" stories of young people from various backgrounds (see Nieto & Bode, 2008) so that they understand the specific challenges of encountering racism and start thinking about what students of color might need from their teachers. These activities are followed by dialogue, reflection, and analysis designed to get teachers discussing how they and their students are members of structurally positioned groups. Teachers come to see that caring for students within unequal structures requires going beyond "niceness" to challenge institutional inequality.

I then ask teachers to think deeply about and debate what it means to demonstrate care in a classroom. Teachers may think of caring as unconditional praise, or as quickly incorporating cultural components into the curriculum, or even as lowering standards. On the contrary, others have argued, an "ethic of care"[3] means a combination of respect, admiration, and rigorous standards. What is needed, as described by researcher Rosalie Rolón-Dow,[4] is *critical care* that responds to students' actual personal lives and to the institutional barriers they encounter as members of racialized groups. Teachers must understand individual students within their concrete sociopolitical contexts and devise specific pedagogical and curricular strategies to help them navigate those contexts successfully. This work begins when we ask what it means to "care."

Notes

1   Ginley, M. (1999), "Being nice is not enough." In S. Nieto, *The light in their eyes* (pp. 85–86). New York: Teachers College Press.
2   For a review of the research, see Nieto, S. (2004). *Affirming diversity: The sociopolitical context of multicultural education*. Boston: Allyn & Bacon.
3   Noddings, N. (1992). *The challenge to care in schools: An alternative approach to education*. New York: Teachers College Press; Valenzuela, A. (1998). *Subtractive schooling; U.S.-Mexican youth and the politics of caring*. Albany: State University of New York Press.
4   Rolón-Dow, R. (2005). Critical care: A color(full) analysis of care narratives in the schooling experiences of Puerto Rican girls. *American Educational Research Journal, 42* (1), 77–111.

Critical Questions

1   Why do you think that it is so difficult for some people to discuss race, inequality, and privilege? How can this difficulty be addressed?
2   Reread Mary Ginley's piece and think about what suggestions you would give for "going beyond niceness" to the kinds of teachers she is describing.
3   Describe some uncomfortable situations you have had with discussions of race, inequality, and privilege.
4   What might help educators with difficult conversations about inequality?

Activity for Your Classroom

Create a lesson plan for your classroom context—keeping in mind the subject area you teach and the developmental level of your students—on addressing race and inequality in a forthright and honest way. See the below Supplementary Resources for Further Reflection and Study for ideas.

Community-Based Activity and Advocacy

Initiate a reading group on discussions of race and inequality in schools. Begin with the Mica Pollock book listed below. Given its size (over 50 brief essays), you may want to tackle a few at each meeting. You might also ask each teacher to write an essay about their own (successful or unsuccessful) experiences of addressing issues of race and inequality.

Supplementary Resources for Further Reflection and Study

Cushman, K. (2005). *Fires in the bathroom: Advice to teachers from high school students*. New York: The New Press.
   This book offers compelling reflections on teaching teenagers in urban schools from the point of view of the students themselves. The text provides both novice and veteran teachers with insights into who their students are and what they need to succeed.

Nieto, S. (1999). *The light in their eyes: Creating multicultural learning communities.* New York: Teachers College Press.

Going beyond curriculum integration, this book reviews the social context of education, the manifestations of educational inequity in classrooms, and the influence of culture on learning. Centering on multicultural education as a transformative and critical pedagogy, the text also includes reflections of teachers who have undergone this process and whose experiences may serve as models for other teachers.

Pollock, M. (2008). *Everyday antiracism: Concrete ways to successfully navigate the relevance of race in school.* New York: The New Press.

This compilation, which includes the chapter you have just read, includes brief reflections by researchers and teachers about specific ways to confront the issues of race and racism in classrooms and schools. The more than 50 authors describe concrete ways to deal with racial inequality and teach to high standards across racial lines.

Rethinking Schools, v. 23, n. 1 (2008). Special section on Language, Race, and Power.

Issues of race and language are often on the front burner in classrooms, yet they get little attention in the media. The six essays in this section, led off by a powerful article, "Putting Out the Linguistic Welcome Mat," by *Rethinking Schools* editor, Linda Christensen, argue for critique and inclusion—with race at the center.

14 What Does it Mean to Affirm Diversity in Our Nation's Schools?

Affirming diversity, as you know from the readings in this book, is not simply a question of having a special assembly about Chinese New Year or making a few curricular changes. It is, instead, a transformative project that concerns our *society*'s commitment to social justice, our *schools*' responsibility to fulfill its pledge of equal opportunity for all students, and our *teachers*' knowledge, attitudes, values, and beliefs concerning their students' identities and abilities. If this is the case, then the question posed in the title of the article below needs to be answered in a more broad-based way than might be evident at first glance. That is, affirming diversity needs to be approached as *personal, collective,* and *institutional* change.

In this chapter, I propose five realities that educators need to understand in order to create schools that are effective for all students. As you read, think about the journey you have taken until now in your effort to affirm diversity.

About 15 years ago, I was interviewing a young woman for admission to our multicultural teacher education program and I asked her why she had chosen to apply for this particular program. (At the time, we had a number of undergraduate teacher preparation programs from which students could choose).

The young woman, let's call her Nancy, mentioned that she was doing a prepracticum at Marks Meadow School, the laboratory school of our School of Education at the University of Massachusetts. Marks Meadow is an extraordinarily diverse place with children from every corner of the globe representing multiple languages and various social and economic backgrounds.

When the children in her 1st-grade classroom were doing self-portraits, one of them asked Nancy for a brown crayon. She was momentarily confounded by his request, thinking Why brown? It never before had occurred to her that children would make their faces anything other than the color of the white paper they used. "I decided then and there that I needed this program," she confessed.

As naive as her reaction was, it was the beginning of Nancy's awakening to diversity. It was also a courageous disclosure of her own ignorance.

Ill-Prepared for Diversity

It is by now a truism that our country's public schools are undergoing a dramatic shift that reflects the growing diversity of our population. Yet many educators and the schools in which they work seem no better prepared for this change than was Nancy a decade and a half ago. Most educators nationwide are very much like Nancy: white, middle-class, monolingual English-speaking women and men who have had little direct experience with cultural, ethnic, linguistic or other kinds of diversity, but they are teaching students who are phenomenally diverse in every way.

Given this scenario, what do educators—teachers, aides, curriculum developers, principals, superintendents and school board members—need to know to create effective schools for students of all backgrounds, and how can they learn it? Let me suggest five realities that educators need to appreciate and understand if this is to happen:

Affirming Diversity is Above All About Social Justice

Contrary to what the pundits who oppose multicultural education might say, multicultural education is not about political correctness, sensitivity training or ethnic cheerleading. It is primarily about social justice. Given the vastly unequal educational outcomes among students of different backgrounds, equalizing conditions for student learning needs to be at the core of a concern for diversity.

If this is the case, "celebrating diversity" through special assembly programs, multicultural dinners or ethnic celebrations are hollow activities if they do not also confront the structural inequalities that exist in schools.

A concern for social justice means looking critically at why and how our schools are unjust for some students. It means that we need to analyze school policies and practices that devalue the identities of some students while overvaluing others: the curriculum, testing, textbooks and materials, instructional strategies, tracking, the recruitment and hiring of staff and parent involvement strategies. All of these need to be viewed with an eye toward making them more equitable for all students, not just those students who happen to be white, middle class and English speaking.

Students of Color and Poor Students Bear the Brunt of Structural Inequality

Schools inevitably reflect society, and the evidence that our society is becoming more unequal is growing every day. We have all read the headlines: The United States has one of the highest income disparities in the world, and the combined wealth of the top 1 percent of U.S. families is about the same as the entire bottom 80 percent.

Growing societal inequities are mirrored in numerous ways in schools, from highly disparate financing of schools in rich and poor communities, to academic tracking that favors white above black and brown students, to SAT scores that correlate perfectly with income rather than with intelligence or ability. Although it is a worthy goal, equality is far from a reality in most of our schools, and those who bear the burden of inequality are our children, particularly poor children of all backgrounds and many children of Latino, Native American, Asian American and African American backgrounds. The result is schools that are racist and classist, if not by intention, at least by result.

Inequality is a fact of life, but many educators refuse to believe or accept it, and they persist in blaming children, their families, their cultural and linguistic backgrounds, laziness or genetic inferiority as the culprits. Once educators accept the fact that inequality is alive and thriving in our schools, they can proceed to do something about it. Until they do, little will change. Below are examples of how educators can learn to address diversity in a more positive way.

Positive Acculturation

Diversity is a Valuable Resource

I went to elementary school in Brooklyn, N.Y., during the 1950s. My classmates were enormously diverse in ethnicity, race, language, social class and family structure. But even then, we were taught as if we were all cut from the same cloth. Our mothers were urged to speak to us in English at home (fortunately, my mother never paid attention, and it is because of this that I am fluent in Spanish today), and we were given the clear message that anything having to do with our home cultures was not welcome in school. To succeed in school, we needed to learn English, forget our native language and behave like the kids we read about in our basal readers.

Of course, learning English and learning it well is absolutely essential for academic and future life success, but the assumption that one must discard one's identity along the way needs to be challenged. There is nothing shameful in knowing a language other than English. In fact, becoming bilingual can benefit individuals and our country in general.

As educators, we no longer can afford to behave as if diversity were a dirty word. Every day, more research underscores the positive influence that cultural and linguistic diversity has on student learning. Immigrant students who maintain a positive ethnic identity as they acculturate and who become fluent bilinguals are more likely to have better mental health, do well academically and graduate from high school than those who completely assimilate. Yet we insist on erasing cultural and linguistic differences as if they were a burden rather than an asset.

Effectively Teaching Students of All Backgrounds Means Respecting and Affirming Who They Are

To become effective teachers of all students, educators must undergo a profound shift in their beliefs, attitudes and values about difference.

In many U.S. classrooms, cultural, linguistic and other differences are commonly viewed as temporary, if troublesome, barriers to learning. Consequently, students of diverse backgrounds are treated as walking sets of deficiencies, as if they had nothing to bring to the educational enterprise.

Anybody who has walked into a classroom knows that teaching and learning are above all about relationships, and these relationships can have a profound impact on students' futures. But significant relationships with students are difficult to develop when teachers have little understanding of the students' families and communities. The identities of non–mainstream students frequently are dismissed by schools and teachers as immaterial to academic achievement.

When this is the case, it is unlikely that students will form positive relationships with their teachers or, as a result, with learning. It is only when educators and schools accept and respect who their students are and what they know that they can begin to build positive connections with them.

Affirming Diversity Means Becoming a Multicultural Person

Over the years, I have found that educators believe they are affirming diversity simply because they say they are. But mouthing the words is not enough. Children sense instantly when support for diversity is superficial.

Because most educators in the United States have not had the benefit of firsthand experiences with diversity, it is a frightening concept for many of them. If we think of teaching as a lifelong journey of personal transformation, becoming a multicultural person is part of the journey. It is different for each person.

For Nancy, it began with recognition of her own ignorance. For others, it means learning a second language or working collaboratively with colleagues to design more effective strategies of reaching all students. However we begin the journey, until we take those tentative first steps, what we say about diversity is severely limited by our actions.

Comfort with Differences

Taking these realities to heart means we no longer can think of some students as void of any dignity and worth simply because they do not confirm to our conventional image. All students of all backgrounds bring talents and strengths to their learning and as educators we need to find ways to build on these.

Acknowledging and affirming diversity is in everyone's interest, including middle-class white students. Understanding people of other backgrounds, speaking languages other than English and learning to respect and appreciate differences are skills that benefit all students and our nation as a whole. We do all our students a disservice when we prepare them to live in a society that no longer exists.

Given the tremendous diversity in our society, it makes eminent good sense to educate all our students to be comfortable with differences.

Critical Questions

1   Do you agree with the five realities I have suggested that educators need to know in order to be effective with their students? Why or why not?

2   Develop your own list of essential understandings that educators need in order to affirm diversity.

3   How might your school be different if the principal, other administrators, teachers, and all school staff knew and believed the five realities that are proposed? Give concrete examples.

Activity for Your Classroom

How far have you progressed in learning to affirm diversity? Do a fishbowl exercise in which you and several other course participants discuss some of the changes in attitudes and beliefs you have experienced in the past few months. Describe some of the changes you have made in your classroom, and evaluate how effective those changes have been. Discuss as well some of the projects you have in mind for the future.

Community-Based Activities and Advocacy

1   Join the PTO or PTA of your school and present some ideas that you think can lead to a more effective school climate for more students. Suggest some of the changes that you believe are needed and present them to your school committee or local board of education.

2   Think about some of the ways that your school, school system, or state discredits or disadvantages some students. Is there an "English-Only" policy in your school? Are the Special Education classrooms in the basement? Who is on the hiring committees at the district level? Are textbooks representative of the U.S. population? Has there been a recent effort to do away with state-mandated bilingual education? Consider how you can be involved in making change at each of these levels. Take on one of these issues and write about the results of your involvement.

Supplementary Resources for Further Reflection and Study

Bigelow, B., Christensen, L., Karp, S., Miner, B., & Peterson, B. (Eds.). (1994). *Rethinking our classrooms: Teaching for equity and justice.* Milwaukee: Rethinking Schools; and Bigelow, B., Harvey, B., Karp, S., and Miller, L. (Eds.). (2001). *Rethinking our classrooms: Teaching for equity and justice,* vol. 2. Milwaukee: Rethinking Schools.

   These two books are a treasure trove of classroom-tested ideas written by classroom teachers and based on a social justice conception of multicultural education. Also, visit www.rethinkingschools.org for their many other publications.

Landsman, J., & Lewis, C. W. (Eds.). (2006). *White teachers, diverse classrooms: A guide to building inclusive schools, promoting high expectations, and eliminating racism.* New York: Stylus Publishing.

   With numerous examples of practical strategies and sage advice for teachers and administrators on ways to improve the education of students of color, the book addresses such issues as White privilege, multicultural education, institutional racism, and the challenges of educating minority students in predominantly White schools.

Lee, E., Menkart, D., & Okazawa-Rey, M. (2006). *Beyond heroes and holidays: A practical guide to K-12 anti-racist, multicultural education and staff development,* updated edition. Washington, DC: Teaching for Change.

After developing a conceptual basis for anti-racist multicultural education, this book tackles the difficult job of actual implementation in classrooms. It is written for and by teachers of classrooms and professional development activities.

Index